SKETCHES OF THE HISTORY OF MAN

BOOK I

NATURAL LAW AND
ENLIGHTENMENT CLASSICS

Knud Haakonssen
General Editor

Henry Home, Lord Kames

NATURAL LAW AND
ENLIGHTENMENT CLASSICS

Sketches of the History of Man

*Considerably Enlarged by
the Last Additions and
Corrections of the Author*

BOOK I

Progress of Men Independent of Society

Henry Home, Lord Kames

Edited and with an Introduction by
James A. Harris

Major Works of Henry Home, Lord Kames

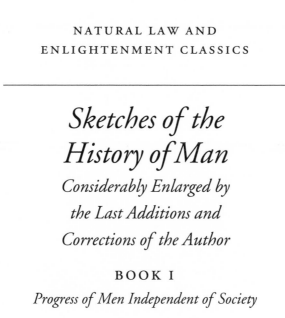

LIBERTY FUND

Indianapolis

This book is published by Liberty Fund, Inc., a foundation established
to encourage study of the ideal of a society of free and responsible individuals.

𒂼𒄄

The cuneiform inscription that serves as our logo and as the design motif for
our endpapers is the earliest-known written appearance of the word
"freedom" (*amagi*), or "liberty." It is taken from a clay document written
about 2300 B.C. in the Sumerian city-state of Lagash.

Frontispiece and cover (detail): Portrait of Henry Home, Lord Kames, by David Martin.
Reproduced with permission of the National Galleries of Scotland.

Introduction, annotations © 2007 by Liberty Fund, Inc.

Printed in the United States of America

11 10 09 08 07 C 5 4 3 2 1
11 10 09 08 07 P 5 4 3 2 1

Library of Congress Cataloging-in-Publication Data
Kames, Henry Home, Lord, 1696–1782.
Sketches of the history of man/Henry Home, Lord Kames;
edited and with an introduction by James A. Harris.
v. cm.—(Natural law and enlightenment classics)
"Considerably enlarged by the last additions and corrections of the author."
Originally published in 4 v.: Edinburgh: A. Strahan and T. Cadell. 1788.
Includes bibliographical references and index.
Contents: bk. 1. Progress of men independent of society—
bk. 2. Progress of men in society—bk. 3. Progress of sciences.
ISBN 978-0-86597-500-2 (hardcover: set)   ISBN 978-0-86597-505-7 (pbk: set)
1. Civilization—History.   2. Human beings—History.
I. Harris, James A., 1968–   II. Title.
CB25.K3 2007
901—dc22   2006028369
ISBN 978-0-86597-501-9 (v. 1: hc)   ISBN 978-0-86597-506-4 (v. 1: sc)

LIBERTY FUND, INC.
8335 Allison Pointe Trail, Suite 300
Indianapolis, Indiana 46250-1684

CONTENTS

INTRODUCTION

Henry Home was born at Kames in Berwickshire, not far from the English border, in 1696. The family was not wealthy, and Henry did not attend a university. Around 1712 he went to Edinburgh to train as a solicitor, but he soon directed his considerable energies instead toward being called to the Scottish bar and was admitted to the Faculty of Advocates in 1723. His legal career seems to have begun slowly. However, by the mid-1730s his practice was flourishing, and political connections enabled him to rise in the profession to the rank of advocate deputy around 1738 and to the Court of Session, Scotland's highest civil court, in 1752. Henry had inherited his father's estate at Kames in 1741, and with his seat on the Court of Session came the title Lord Kames. When his wife's estate at Blair Drummond in Stirlingshire came to him in 1766, Kames became a rich man. A year earlier, he had been elevated to the High Court of Justiciary, Scotland's supreme criminal court, and appointed to the court's Western Circuit. He remained active as a judge until shortly before his death on December 27, 1782. Kames played a central role in the efflorescence of work in letters and science that we now call the Scottish Enlightenment. He was a member of several of Edinburgh's literary and philosophical clubs. He corresponded with David Hume about the publication of *A Treatise of Human Nature* in the late 1730s, and fifty years later he had a prolonged exchange with Thomas Reid on the metaphysics of causation. He was instrumental in the commissioning of Adam Smith to give a famous series of lectures in Edinburgh from 1748 to 1751, John Millar tutored his son in the late 1750s, and James Boswell entertained the idea of writing his life. Kames wrote a great deal, principally on subjects related to his profession, but also on philosophy, criticism, and education. In addition he did much to encourage the modernization and improvement of Scottish agriculture and industry. In 1755 he was appointed to the Board of Trustees for the Encouragement of Fisheries, Arts, and Manufactures of Scotland. He published a pamphlet on flax husbandry in 1766 and, at the age of eighty,[1] produced *The Gentleman Farmer,* the result of years of research into soils and their improvement.

Sketches of the History of Man was published in two folio volumes in 1774. Kames says he had been at work on the book for "above thirty years" (Book I, p. 11).[2] The *Sketches* can be regarded as its author's magnum opus, as well as the culmination of his literary career and the definitive statement of his views concerning the history of human manners, morals, and institutions. As the bibliography constructed for the present edition suggests, the *Sketches* was the fruit of a lifetime's reading in an extraordinarily diverse range of subjects, from ancient history to modern economics, from a Scandinavian epic to the tales of the explorers of the South Seas. Kames had high hopes for the book and negotiated with his publishers, William Creech in Edinburgh and Thomas Cadell and William Strahan in London, a payment of one thousand pounds sterling. Several of the reviews were positive, flattering even, but privately skepticism was expressed by those whose opinion probably mattered most to Kames. "Lord Kames has published two very dear Volumes of *Sketches of the History of Man,*" Boswell wrote to Bennet Langton: "At least I think them very dear, from what I have read of them. He has a prodigious quantity of Quotation, and there seems to be little of

1. The best modern biography of Kames is Ian Simpson Ross, *Lord Kames and the Scotland of His Day* (Oxford: Clarendon Press, 1972). See also William C. Lehmann, *Henry Home, Lord Kames and the Scottish Enlightenment: A Study in National Character and in the History of Ideas* (The Hague: Martinus Nijhoff, 1971), and Roger L. Emerson, "Henry Home, Lord Kames," in *Dictionary of Literary Biography,* vol. 104, *British Prose Writers, 1660–1800,* ed. D. T. Siebert (Detroit: Gale Research International). For contemporary accounts of Kames's life, works, and character, see William Smellie, *Literary and Characteristical Lives of John Gregory, M.D., Henry Home, Lord Kames, David Hume, Esq., and Adam Smith, L.L.D.* (Edinburgh, 1800); Alexander Fraser Tytler of Woodhouselee, *Memoirs of the Life and Writings of the Honourable Henry Home of Kames,* 2 vols. (Edinburgh, 1807); John Ramsay of Ochtertyre, *Scotland and Scotsmen in the Eighteenth Century,* ed. Alexander Allardyce, 2 vols. (Edinburgh and London, 1888); James Boswell, "Materials for Writing the Life of Lord Kames, 1778–82," in *Private Papers of James Boswell from Malahide Castle,* ed. Geoffrey Scott and Frederick A. Pottle (privately printed, 1932), 15:259–316.

2. Cross-references in the introduction refer to page numbers in the Liberty Fund edition.

what he gives as his own that is just, or that has not been better said by others."[3] "A man who reads thirty years, with a view to collect facts in support of two or three whimsical theories," remarked James Beattie, "may no doubt collect a great number of facts, and make a very large book."[4] Beattie regretted that in the *Sketches* (as in several other places in his writings) Kames denies the existence of a principle of universal benevolence. Samuel Johnson, by contrast, complained to Boswell that Kames "maintained that virtue is natural to man . . . a thing which all mankind know not to be true."[5] "Lord Kaims's Sketches have here been published some weeks," Hume wrote to Strahan, "and by the Reception it has met with, is not likely to be very popular, according to the prodigiously sanguine Expectations of the Author."[6] Despite Hume's prediction, a second edition of the *Sketches* was called for and appeared in 1778, this time in four volumes of octavo; a third edition "considerably enlarged by the last additions and corrections of the author" came out ten years later. The *Sketches* was translated into German in 1787 and was also published in Philadelphia and Basel. Several further editions appeared in the 1790s and in the first decades of the nineteenth century.[7]

"The Human Species is in every view an interesting subject, and has been in every age the chief inquiry of philosophers. The faculties of the mind have been explored, and the affections of the heart; but there is still wanting a history of the species, in its progress from the savage state to its highest civilization and improvement" (Book I, p. 11): so Kames begins his *Sketches*. His subject, then, is the history of humankind as a whole, rather than the history of a particular nation or city. The wealth of new information about primitive or "savage" peoples made available by the literature of travel and exploration had opened up the possibility of such a history. If it was ac-

3. Charles N. Fifer, ed., *The Correspondence of James Boswell with Certain Members of the Club* (London: Heinemann, 1976; Yale Edition of *The Private Papers of James Boswell*, vol. 3), 43.

4. Quoted in Ross, *Lord Kames,* 344.

5. Ibid., 345.

6. *The Letters of David Hume,* ed. J. Y. T. Greig, 2 vols. (Oxford: Clarendon Press, 1932), 2:289.

7. For the reception of the *Sketches,* see Ross, *Lord Kames,* 344–48; and John Valdimir Price, introduction to a facsimile copy of the second edition (Bristol: Thoemmes, 1994).

ceptable to conjecture that the story of every people began with a state of savagery and moved through the same stages of development toward civilization, then accounts given of Siberia, Japan, China, Guinea, and the Americas could be combined with the Bible, Homer, and other more familiar sources to yield hints toward a "history of the species." To the modern reader this might appear a rather large "if," but the project of the *Sketches* is of a piece with a widespread commitment on the part of eighteenth-century Scots to what Dugald Stewart called "Theoretical or Conjectural History." "In examining the history of mankind, as well as in examining the phenomena of the natural world," Stewart wrote in his life of Adam Smith, "when we cannot trace the process by which an event *has been* produced, it is often of importance to be able to show how it *may have been* produced by natural causes."[8] Kames had been one of the earliest among the Scots to deploy this method of reasoning, most particularly in the history of criminal law presented in the *Historical Law-Tracts* of 1758. In prefaces to the first and second editions of the *Sketches,* Kames describes his project as "a natural history of man." The kind of natural history he means is not that of taxonomists such as Ray and Linnaeus. Rather, it can be defined as an attempt to understand human nature in what we now call "evolutionary" terms, an attempt to explain the present condition of humankind in terms of a long process of interaction between humans and their physical environment.[9]

Progress and Pessimism

In 1769 Kames wrote to his friend Elizabeth Montagu, "My present work is a general history of the human race in its gradual progress toward maturity; distributed into many articles, Religion, morality, manners, arts, commerce with many others."[10] While the *Sketches* is a multifarious and

8. Dugald Stewart, *Biographical Memoirs of Adam Smith, LL.D., of William Robertson, D.D., and of Thomas Reid, D.D.* (Edinburgh: G. Ramsay, 1811), 48.

9. For a contemporary discussion of Kames as conjectural historian, and of the *Sketches* considered more generally, see Woodhouselee, *Memoirs,* 2:108–65.

10. Quoted in Helen Whitcomb Randall, *The Critical Theory of Lord Kames* (Northampton, Mass.: Department of Modern Languages of Smith College, 1944), 110.

miscellaneous work, the notion of "progress" provides a means of lending it a degree of coherence and order. Each of its three books, and many of the individual sketches, have "progress" in their title. Here "progress" means not just movement from one place or stage to another (as in the progress of a monarch around his kingdom) but also improvement, transition from savagery to civilization, from rudeness to refinement. This was to reverse the perspective of many earlier historians who, up to and including the great French naturalist Buffon, had conceived of human history as a narrative of declension and degeneration. The Scottish practitioners of "conjectural" history shared an understanding of the key moments or stages of the human race's journey from infancy toward maturity: in the beginning men and women subsisted by hunting and fishing; then came the shepherd state; then the cultivation of land; and, finally, there arrived the world of mercantilism and commerce. Among thinkers such as Hume, Smith, Adam Ferguson, Kames, and Millar there was, in the main, little of Rousseau's pessimism about the capacity of human nature to adapt to the move away from the savage state. They all regarded men as having been social beings from the first and as being naturally fitted to a life of coexistence and cooperation with others. Progress was a realization of capacities and proclivities deeply rooted in the human constitution. That said, none of the Scots had an unequivocally positive and optimistic understanding of the transition from savagery to civilization. With the development of commerce, especially, came a variety of risks and costs. The particular ambivalences and hesitancies about progress that Kames reveals in the *Sketches* provide a means of locating the book a little more precisely in its contemporary context.[11]

11. A very useful overview of the complexities of Kames's conception of human history is provided by George W. Stocking Jr., "Scotland as the Model of Mankind: Lord Kames' Philosophical View of Civilization," in *Towards a Science of Man: Essays in the History of Anthropology,* ed. Timothy H. H. Thoresen (The Hague: Mouton, 1975). For a detailed study of the four-stage theory of progress, see Ronald L. Meek, *Social Science and the Ignoble Savage* (Cambridge: Cambridge University Press, 1976). See also Gladys Bryson, *Man and Society: The Scottish Inquiry of the Eighteenth Century* (Princeton: Princeton University Press, 1945). One prominent Scottish writer who stuck with the traditional picture of human history as a story of decline was James Burnet, Lord Monboddo: a comparison between the anthropological thought of Kames and Mon-

As we have seen, Kames conceives of the *Sketches* as a contribution to a history of the human species. One of the things that distinguishes the human species is, precisely, its natural tendency toward development, change, and refinement. No other species of animal shows signs of such a propensity. It quickly appears, though, that in Kames's view there is not one single, ubiquitous race of human beings. In the "Preliminary Discourse Concerning the Origin of Men and Languages," he argues, principally against Buffon, that the empirical evidence—meaning the physical and moral differences between the various peoples of the earth—speaks in favor of there being a number of different races. Kames rejects the claim, made by writers from Vitruvius to Montesquieu, that differences of climate are sufficient to explain differences in appearance and national character. Two peoples— for example, the Laplanders and the Finns—can share the same climate but be very different in stature and beauty. The same climate does not even always produce similarity of complexion. Moreover, in the Americas the native peoples live in very different climates and yet share the same complexion. Some parts of the world have proved quite impossible for Europeans to adapt to. Again, inhabitants of neighboring islands have sometimes been observed to have very different moral dispositions. Kames concludes that "were all men of one species, there never could have existed, without a miracle, different kinds, such as exist at present" (Book I, p. 46). The existence of a variety of separate human races opens up the possibility that, in fact, not all peoples are destined to follow the path from infancy to maturity. As the nineteenth century was to show, racialist thought very easily becomes racist thought. It is true that Kames wonders whether the "inferiority" of Negroes "may not be occasioned by their condition," but a comparison between the industry of "Hindows" (i.e., the peoples of India) and the "indolence" of Africans makes him hesitate: "after all, there seems to be some original difference between the Negroes and the Hindows" (Book I, pp. 41–42).[12]

---

boddo is given in Robert Wokler, "Apes and Races in the Scottish Enlightenment: Monboddo and Kames on the Nature of Man," in *Philosophy and Science in the Scottish Enlightenment,* ed. Peter Jones (Edinburgh: John Donald, 1988).

12. My attention was drawn to the conflicting tendencies of Kames's thought on race

military service should be rotated among the male population so that everyone would serve for seven years.[16]

This suggestion is made in a spirit of optimism: such a system would serve the competing concerns of both commerce and liberty. When in this mood, Kames appears to share Adam Ferguson's belief that, while there is much in modern society for the lover of liberty to fear, it is not inconceivable that important elements of, at least, civic virtue and liberty might yet be preserved and nurtured. In many other places in the *Sketches,* however, Kames manifests a rather extreme pessimism about the ability of commercial society to maintain itself in equilibrium and about the future of Britain in particular. (He remarked to Elizabeth Montagu that the disease of selfishness and luxury that Ferguson sought to cure in his *Essay on the History of Civil Society* "is too far advanced to be cured by any characters that can be formed with ink.")[17] Pessimism is perhaps especially obvious in Book III's account of the progress of morality "from birth to burial" (Book III, p. 761). The development of society does not come to a halt when maturity is arrived at. On the contrary, maturity, in the form of peace, contains the seeds of decline, in the form of ever-increasing general concern for luxury at the expense of patriotism. Maturity is followed by degeneracy, in the case of societies just as surely as in the case of individual living creatures. "In all times luxury has been the ruin of every state where it prevailed," Kames writes in the sketch on luxury. "Nations originally are poor and virtuous. They advance to industry, commerce, and perhaps to conquest and empire. But this state is never permanent: great opulence opens a wide door to indolence, sensuality, corruption, prostitution, perdition" (Book II, p. 333). Wise legislation might slow the process of decay for a short time but is powerless to prevent it altogether.[18]

16. By far the best discussion of the militia question in eighteenth-century Scotland is John Robertson, *The Scottish Enlightenment and the Militia Issue* (Edinburgh: John Donald, 1985); for a brief account of Kames's contribution, see pp. 210–11.

17. Woodhouselee, *Memoirs,* 2:48–49.

18. In this connection, Kames's viewpoint might be usefully compared and contrasted with what Duncan Forbes called "scientific Whiggism": see "'Scientific' Whiggism: Adam Smith and John Millar," *Cambridge Journal* 7 (1954): 643–70.

Because of the difficulty of reconciling a plurality of races with the biblical story of the derivation of mankind from a single human couple, Kames looks for a miracle to explain human diversity and finds one in the confusion of peoples and languages that followed the building of the Tower of Babel. However, in the sketch "Origin and Progress of American Nations," Kames is less circumspect and argues directly for the need of a "local creation" to explain the peopling of America (Book II, p. 560). The native American peoples, like the Africans, are something of a problem for Kames's belief in the inevitable progress of humankind: on the whole, they had simply failed to move on from hunting to the shepherd state. A problem of a different kind was posed by the poems of Ossian, a supposedly ancient poet of the Scottish Highlands whose works were "discovered" and "translated" by James Macpherson in 1760. As the sketch on manners amply demonstrates, Kames, like many of his Scottish (and German) contemporaries, was an enthusiastic believer in the authenticity of Ossian. But the ancient Caledonians depicted in the poems had manners remarkably pure for men in the original state of society—their sentiments are always elevated and tender, and women are always treated with respect and delicacy. "In Homer's time," Kames notes, "heroes were greedy of plunder; and like robbers, were much disposed to insult a vanquished foe. According to Ossian, the ancient Caledonians had no idea of plunder: and as they fought for fame only, their humanity overflowed to the vanquished" (Book I, p. 224). Kames describes going to great lengths to prove, by finding other examples of noble savagery in Scandinavian epics, that Ossian's Caledonians were not suspiciously unique. His faith in Ossian reveals a tendency toward nostalgic primitivism at odds with the "official" view of history as the development out of infancy and into maturity.[13]

by Aaron Garrett, "Human Nature," in *The Cambridge History of Eighteenth-Century Philosophy,* ed. Knud Haakonssen (Cambridge: Cambridge University Press, 2006), 199–200. Garrett's article provides much detail regarding the eighteenth-century debate about race.

13. For more on Kames and Ossian, see Stocking, "Scotland as the Model," 76; Wokler, "Apes and Races," 153–54; and Arthur E. McGuinness, *Henry Home, Lord Kames* (New York: Twayne, 1970), chap. 6.

A certain fondness on Kames's part for the simplicity and austerity of earlier ages is made manifest also in the sketch on luxury. Condemnation of luxury, needless to say, is not unusual in the eighteenth century. Indeed, in his view that general obsession with superfluity and consumption for consumption's sake was debilitating to both the state and the individual human being, Kames is at one with a long tradition of thought that stretches from Roman moralists through Machiavelli to Rousseau in France and the "Country Party" of eighteenth-century England. In this tradition commerce is set against property, and where property is associated with freedom and virtuous citizenship, commerce is associated with dependency and selfishness. What is peculiar is that one should find such extreme condemnations of luxury as are expressed in the *Sketches* coming from the pen of one who, at other times, appears to regard the commercial state as the culmination of the human journey toward maturity and refinement.[14] It is to be admitted that even the most ardent advocates of the material, moral, and political benefits of commerce—Hume and Smith, for example—were sensitive to its shortcomings and dangers. However, Kames's attitude toward luxury is incomparably more negative than Hume's or Smith's. Natural benevolence and regard for the dictates of justice are being corroded away by the free expression of love of avarice and selfishness made possible in a commercial society. He warns that "the epidemic distempers of luxury and selfishness are spreading wide in Britain" (Book II, p. 426). It is difficult to know how to reconcile this aspect of Kames's thought with, for example, the opposition to entails expressed in the "Sketches Concerning Scotland," contained in the appendix to the *Sketches*. An entail allowed a property owner to fix the inheritance of his land for several generations to come and prevented an heir from selling or mortgaging. Kames regarded entails as obstructive of commerce in so far as they prevented capital from being released and invested in new enterprises. It has been argued that much of Kames's writing on law was intended as an attempt to help Scottish law escape its feudal origins in order to better serve the interests of commercial

14. A commercial state needs to be able to feed itself, Kames believes, and so agriculture remains essential even while commerce develops. Hence Kames's lifelong interest in means of maximizing agricultural production.

society. Judging by what is said about luxury in the *Sketches,* Kames appears not to have a settled and consistent view as to whether the corrupting effects of commerce are outweighed by the possibilities it opens up of refinement and improvement.[15]

A similar ambivalence is evident in Kames's treatment of another stock topic of eighteenth-century moralizing, the advantage of a militia over the maintenance of a standing army (see especially the sketch "Military Branch of Government"). One of the reasons why luxury was condemned in the eighteenth century, as in previous ages, was that it made men weak and effeminate and therefore unsuited them for the task of defending their country's liberty. Defense had then to be assigned to hirelings who fought for money only, and the result was a weakness of the state that complemented the weakness of individual citizens. When Kames says at the opening of Book II of the *Sketches* that "patriotism is the corner-stone of civil society" (Book II, p. 337), what he means is not simply a warm feeling for one's country but a willingness to devote oneself to its defense. The problem, as Kames well knew, was that it was impossible for commerce to flourish if the adult male population was permanently liable, for extended periods, to be drafted into military or naval service. This would inevitably seriously obstruct sustained attention to the improvement of agriculture, industry, and trade. Kames fails to engage with the arguments of Hume and (especially) Smith that a country is better defended by professionals than by amateurs, that it is impossible in modern conditions for an army to maintain itself at its own expense, and that there is in any case no contradiction between political liberty and the existence of a standing army. His solution to the problem he perceives to be posed by the rise of commerce is a typically idiosyncratic compromise: he suggests that compulsory

15. An account of the eighteenth-century debate about luxury, with particular reference to Mandeville, Hume, and Smith, but with reference also to Kames, is given in Christopher Berry, *The Idea of Luxury: A Conceptual and Historical Investigation* (Cambridge: Cambridge University Press, 1994), chap. 6. On the ambitions of Kames's jurisprudence, see David Lieberman, *The Province of Legislation Determined: Legal Theory in Eighteenth-Century Britain* (Cambridge: Cambridge University Press, 1989), chaps. 7 and 8.

Providence

Despite the pessimism that complicates his conception of history as progress from savagery to refinement, Kames is able to regard both the general
scheme of the history of humankind and a great many of the incidental
details as evidence of divine providence. As Ramsey of Ochtertyre noted,
"no speculations pleased [Kames] more than the unfolding of final
causes."[19] Illustrations of the wisdom and benevolence of the divine plan
are everywhere in the *Sketches*. Even where providence cannot be perceived,
Kames insists, it can be assumed to be at work. Even where a nation declines
and falls under the weight of selfishness and corruption, the hand of God
is visible, working to turn evil to advantage. This is surely the lesson that
Kames was most concerned to communicate to his reader. According to
William Smellie, Kames "never wrote a sentence, notwithstanding his numerous publications, without a direct and a manifest intention to benefit
his fellow creatures."[20] At one level the *Sketches* is meant to benefit its reader
simply in virtue of the huge amount of information it contains about the
history of humankind; at another and deeper level it seeks to add to the
stock of reasons to believe that, despite appearances, whatever is, is right.
Some among Kames's readers, however, disagreed with his understanding
of providence. According to David Doig, a master at the grammar school
in Stirling, the hypothesis that human beings were all originally savage, as
well as being incredible as history, is inconsistent with divine beneficence.
Kames would have it that "the Father of the universe unnaturally abandoned his new-found infants, turning them into an uncultivated world,
naked, untutored, unsheltered orphans."[21] Samuel Stanhope Smith, professor of moral philosophy at Princeton, also rejected the basic elements of
Kames's history of the human race and mounted an influential defense of
the view that all men and women are descended from a single pair. Human
diversity could be explained, he argued, in terms of the influence of climate
and "the state of society." The goodness of the Creator reveals itself pre-

19. Ramsey, *Scotland and Scotsmen*, 1:194.
20. Smellie, *Literary and Characteristical Lives*, 146.
21. David Doig, *Two Letters on the Savage State Addressed to the Late Lord Kaims* (London: G.G.J. and J. Robinson, 1792), 8–9.

cisely in our native adaptability. Stanhope Smith exposes Kames's lack of firsthand experience of the places and peoples so confidently discussed and assessed in the *Sketches*. "Like many other philosophers," he complains, "Kames judges and reasons only from what he has seen in a state of society highly improved; and is led to form many wrong conclusions from his own habits and prepossessions."[22]

22. Samuel Stanhope Smith, *An Essay on the Causes of the Variety of Complexion and Figure in the Human Species. To which are added, Strictures on Lord Kames's Discourse on the Original Diversity of Mankind,* 2nd ed. (Philadelphia and London: John Ormrod, 1788; first published 1787), 212.

A NOTE ON THE TEXT

The text of this edition of *Sketches of the History of Man* is based on the posthumous third edition of 1788. The third edition was published in four volumes. *Sketches,* however, comprises three "Books": *Progress of Men Independent of Society, Progress of Men in Society,* and *Progress of Sciences.* The three-volume format of the present edition is meant to reflect the work's fundamental principle of structuring. Page breaks in the third edition are indicated in the body of the text by the use of angle brackets. (For example, page 112 begins after <112>.) Substantive differences between the first, second, and third editions are noted in order to give the reader a sense of how energetically Kames continued to work on the book right up until the end of his life. In places where the first edition differs significantly from subsequent editions, the relevant passage from the first edition, with its volume and page number, is supplied in a note. A fully annotated text of *Sketches* would be the work of many years. Kames was a conspicuous consumer of references and allusions, even by the standards of his day, and *Sketches* is a particular showpiece in this regard. Accordingly, an exhaustive annotation would seriously clutter the text, and I have settled for much less.

Supplementary notes to Kames's own footnotes are enclosed in double square brackets. For fuller information, a bibliography is provided, indicating the complete title, author, place of publication, and date of as many of the works cited by Kames (or Thomas Reid) as it has been possible to identify. The reader should bear in mind that in cases where it is unclear which of an author's works is being cited, the bibliography is necessarily somewhat speculative. Very familiar and easily identified works (such as those by Euripides, Sophocles, Herodotus, Thucydides, Plato, Aristotle, and Shakespeare) have not been included. Where a modern translation has been quoted in a supplementary footnote, the translation used is indicated in parentheses after the entry in the bibliography. Where an original text was in a modern language other than English or French, a contemporary translation is given as well. Obvious typographical errors in the text have been corrected without comment.

ACKNOWLEDGMENTS

For various kinds of help with the preparation of this edition, I should like to thank Rebecca Armstrong, Alexander Broadie, Aaron Garrett, Ian Simpson Ross, Åsa Söderman, Agnieszka Steczowicz, and Astrid Wind. I am especially grateful to Knud Haakonssen for inviting me to edit Kames's *Sketches* for this Liberty Fund series and for being remarkably patient while being bombarded with what must have seemed an endless series of questions and appeals for advice. The work on this edition was completed while I was a Postdoctoral Fellow of the British Academy.

James A. Harris

BOOK I

PROGRESS OF MEN INDEPENDENT OF SOCIETY

SKETCHES

OF THE

HISTORY OF MAN.

CONSIDERABLY ENLARGED
BY THE LAST ADDITIONS
AND CORRECTIONS
OF THE AUTHOR.

IN FOUR VOLUMES.

VOLUME I.

EDINBURGH:

PRINTED FOR A. STRAHAN AND T. CADELL, LONDON;
AND FOR WILLIAM CREECH, EDINBURGH.

M,DCC,LXXXVIII.

PREFACE

The following Work is the substance of various speculations, which occasionally occupied the author, and enlivened his leisure hours. It is not intended for the learned; they are above it: nor for the vulgar; they are below it. It is intended for those who, free from the corruption of opulence and depression of bodily labour, are fond of useful knowledge; who, even in the delirium of youth, feel the dawn of patriotism, and who, in riper years, enjoy its meridian warmth. To such men this Work is dedicated; and that they may profit by it, is the author's ardent wish; and probably will be while he retains life sufficient to form a wish. <vi>

May not he hope, that this Work, child of his gray hairs, will survive, and bear testimony for him to good men, that even a laborious calling, which left him not many leisure hours, never banished from his mind, that he would little deserve to be of the human species, were he indifferent about his fellow-creatures:

Homo sum: humani nihil a me alienum puto.[1]

Most of the subjects handled in the following sheets, admit but of probable reasoning; and, with respect to such reasonings, it is often difficult to say, what degree of conviction they ought to produce. It is easy to form plausible arguments; but to form such as can stand the test of time, is not always easy. I could amuse the reader with numerous examples of conjectural arguments, which, fair at a distant view, vanish like a cloud on a near approach. Several examples, not to go farther, are mentioned in the prelim-

---

1. "I am a man: I count nothing that is human foreign to me": Terence, *Heauton Timoroumenos* (*The Self-Tormentor*), l.77.

inary <vii> discourse. The hazard of being misled by such arguments, gave the author much anxiety; and, after his utmost attention, he can but faintly hope, that he has not often wandered far from truth.[2] <viii>

2. In the 1st and 2nd editions, Kames continues: "Above thirty years ago, he began to collect materials for a natural history of man; and in the vigour of youth, did not think the undertaking too bold, not even for a single hand. He has discovered of late, that his utmost abilities are scarce sufficient for executing a few imperfect sketches." In the 1st and 2nd editions a date is given for the completion of the work: "Edinburgh, Feb. 23. 1774."

APPENDIX.

Sketches concerning Scotland.

SKETCHES

OF THE

HISTORY OF MAN.

The Human Species is in every view an interesting subject, and has been in every age the chief inquiry of philosophers. The faculties of the mind have been explored, and the affections of the heart; but there is still wanting a history of the species, in its progress from the savage state to its highest civilization and improvement. Above thirty years ago, the author began to collect materials for that history; and, in the vigour of youth, did not think the undertaking too bold even for a single hand: but, in the progress of the work, he found <2> his abilities no more than sufficient for executing a few imperfect Sketches. These are brought under the following heads. 1. Progress of Men independent of Society. 2. Progress of Men in Society. 3. Progress of the Sciences. To explain these heads a preliminary discourse is necessary; which is, to examine, Whether all men be of one lineage, descended from a single pair, or whether there be different races originally distinct.[1] <3>

1. Paragraph added in 2nd edition.

Preliminary Discourse,
concerning the Origin of Men
and of Languages.[1]

Whether there are different races of men, or whether all men are of one race without any difference but what proceeds from climate or other external cause, is a question which philosophers differ widely about. As the question is of moment in tracing the history of man, I purpose to contribute my mite. And, in order to admit all the light possible, a view of brute animals as divided into different races or kinds, will make a proper introduction.

As many animals contribute to our well-being, and as many are noxious, man would be a being not a little imperfect, were he provided with no means but experience for distinguishing the one sort from the other. Did every animal make a species by itself (indulging the expression) differing from all others, a man would finish his course without acquiring <4> as much knowledge of animals as is necessary even for self-preservation: he would be absolutely at a loss with respect to unknown individuals. The Deity has left none of his works imperfect. Animals are formed of different kinds; resemblance prevailing among animals of the same kind, dissimilitude among animals of different kinds. And, to prevent confusion, kinds are distinguished externally by figure, air, manner, so clearly as not to escape even a child.* Nor does Divine Wisdom stop here: to complete the system,

---

* "And out of the ground the Lord God formed every beast of the field, and every fowl of the air, and brought them unto Adam to see what he would call them. And Adam gave names to all cattle, and to the fowl of the air, and to every beast of the field." *Gen.* ii. 19.

1. In the 1st edition the following "Preliminary Discourse" is the first sketch and is entitled "Diversity of Men and Languages."

we are endued with an innate conviction, that each kind has properties peculiar to itself; and that these properties belong to every individual of the kind (*a*). Our road to the knowledge of animals is thus wonderfully short-ened: the experi-<5>ence we have of the disposition and properties of any animal, is applied without hesitation to every one of the kind. By that con-viction, a child, familiar with one dog, is fond of others that resemble it: An European, upon the first sight of a cow in Africa, strokes it as gentle and innocent: and an African avoids a tiger in Hindostan as at home.

If the foregoing theory be well founded, neither experience nor argu-ment is required to prove, that a horse is not an ass, or that a monkey is not a man (*b*). In some individuals indeed, there is such a mixture of resem-blance and dissimilitude, as to render it uncertain to what species they be-long. But such instances are rare, and impinge not on the general law.[2] Such questions may be curious, but they are of little use.

Whether man be provided by nature with a faculty to distinguish in-nocent animals from what are noxious, seems not a clear point: such a fac-ulty may be thought unnecessary to man, being supplied by reason and experience. But as reason and <6> experience have little influence on brute animals, they undoubtedly possess that faculty.*[3] A beast of prey would be

---

* Brute animals have many instincts that are denied to man; because the want of them can be supplied by education. An infant must be taught to walk; and it is long before it acquires the art in perfection. Brutes have no teacher but nature. A foal, the moment it sees the light, walks no less perfectly than its parents. And so does a partridge, lapwing, &c.

> Dente lupus, cornu taurus petit; unde nisi intus Monstratum?
> HORACE.

[[Horace, *Satires*, II.i, ll. 52–53: "The wolf attacks with fangs, the bull with horns—how was each taught, if not by instinct?" Note added in 2nd edition.]]

(*a*) See Elements of Criticism, vol. 2. p. 490. edit. 5.

(*b*) See M. Buffon's natural history.

2. "But such instances . . . the general law": added in 3rd edition. In 1st and 2nd editions: "But in every such instance there is little need to be solicitous; for I venture to affirm, that both will be found gentle or fierce, wholesome food or unwholesome."

3. "Whether man be . . . possess that faculty": added in 2nd edition. In 1st edition: "The division of brute animals into different kinds, is not more useful to man than to the animals themselves."

ill fitted for its station, if nature did not teach it what creatures to attack, what to avoid. A rabbit is the prey of the ferret. Present a rabbit, even dead, to a young ferret that never had seen a rabbit: it throws itself upon the body, and bites it with fury. A hound has the same faculty with respect to a hare; and most dogs have it. Unless directed by nature, innocent animals would not know their enemy till they were in its clutches. A hare flies with pre- cipitation from the first dog it ever saw; and a chicken, upon the sight of a kite, cowers under its dam. Social animals, without scruple, connect with their <7> own kind, and as readily avoid others.* Birds are not afraid of quadrupeds; not even of a cat, till they are taught by experience that a cat is their enemy. They appear to be as little afraid of a man naturally; and upon that account are far from being shy when left unmolested. In the uninhabited island of Visia Grandé, one of the Philippines, Kempfer says, that birds may be taken with the hand. Hawks, in some of the South-sea islands, are equally tame. At Port Egmont in the Falkland islands, geese, far from being shy, may be knocked down with a stick. The birds that in- habit certain rocks hanging over the sea, in the island of Annabon, take food readily out of a man's hand. In Arabia Felix, foxes and apes show no fear of man; the inhabitants of hot countries having no notion of hunting. In the uninhabited island Bering, adjacent to <8> Kamskatka, foxes are so little shy that they scarce go out of a man's way. Doth not this observation suggest a final cause? A partridge, a plover, a pheasant, would be lost to man for food, were they naturally as much afraid of him as of a hawk or a kite.

The division of animals into different kinds, serves another purpose, no less important than those mentioned; which is, to fit them for different climates. We learn from experience, that no animal nor vegetable is equally fitted for every climate; and from experience we also learn, that there is no animal nor vegetable but what is fitted for some climate, where it grows to perfection. Even in the torrid zone, plants of a cold climate are found upon mountains where plants of a hot climate will not grow; and the height of a mountain may be determined with tolerable precision from the plants it

---

* The populace about Smyrna have a cruel amusement. They lay the eggs of a hen in a stork's nest. Upon seeing the chickens, the male in amazement calls his neighbouring storks together; who, to revenge the affront put upon them, destroy the poor innocent female; while he bewails his misfortune in heavy lamentation.

produces. Wheat is not an indigenous plant in Britain: no farmer is ignorant that foreign seed is requisite to preserve the plant in vigour. To prevent flax from degenerating in Scotland and Ireland, great quantities of foreign seed are annually imported. A ca-<9>mel is peculiarly fitted for the burning sands of Arabia; and Lapland would be uninhabitable but for rain-deer, an animal so entirely fitted for piercing cold, that it cannot subsist even in a temperate climate. Arabian and Barbary horses degenerate in Britain; and, to preserve the breed in some degree of perfection, frequent supplies from their original climate are requisite. Spanish horses degenerate in Mexico; but improve in Chili, having more vigour and swiftness there, than even the Andalusian race, whose off-spring they are. Our dunghill fowl, imported originally from a warm country in Asia, are not hardened, even after many centuries, to bear the cold of this country like birds originally native: the hen lays few or no eggs in winter, unless in a house warmed with fire. The deserts of Zaara and Biledulgerid in Africa, may be properly termed the native country of lions: there they are nine feet long and five feet high. Lions in the south of Africa toward the Cape of Good Hope, are but five feet and a half long, and three and a half high. A breed of lions transplanted from the latter to the former, would rise to the full size; and <10> sink to the smaller size, if transplanted from the former to the latter.*

To preserve the different kinds or species of animals entire, as far as necessary, Providence is careful to prevent a mixed breed. Few animals of different species copulate together. Some may be brought to copulate, but without effect; and some produce a mongrel, a mule for example, which

---

* That every species of plants has a proper climate where it grows to perfection, is a fact uncontroverted. The same holds in brute animals. Biledulgerid, the kindly climate for lions, would be mortal to the bear, the wolf, the deer, and other inhabitants of a cold region. Providence has not only fitted the productions of nature for different climates, but has guarded these productions against the extremities of the weather in the same climate. Many plants close their leaves during night; and some close them at mid-day against the burning rays of the sun. In cold climates, plants during winter are protected against cold by snow. In these climates, the hair of some animals grows long in winter: several animals are covered with much fat, which protects them against cold; and many birds are fatter in winter than in summer, though probably their nourishment is less plentiful. Several animals sleep during winter in sheltered places; and birds of passage are taught by nature to change the climate, when too hot or too cold. [[Note added in 2nd edition.]]

seldom procreates, if at all. In <11> some few instances, where a mixture of species is harmless, procreation goes on without limitation. All the different species of the dog-kind copulate together; and the mongrels produced generate others without end.[4]

M. Buffon, in his natural history, borrows from Ray (*a*) a very artificial rule for ascertaining the different species of animals: "Any two animals that can procreate together, and whose issue can also procreate, are of the same species" (*b*). A horse and an ass can procreate together; but they are not, says he, of the same species, because their issue, a mule, cannot procreate. He applies that rule to man; holding all men to be of the same species, because a man and a woman, however different in size, in shape, in complexion, can procreate together without end. And by the same rule he holds all dogs to be of the same species. With respect to other animals, the author should peaceably be indulged in his fancy; but as it com-<12>prehends also man, I cannot pass it without examination. Providence, to prevent confusion, hath in many instances withheld from animals of different species a power of procreating together: but as our author has not attempted to prove that such restraint is universal without a single exception, his rule is evidently a *petitio principii*. Why may not two animals different in species produce a mixed breed? M. Buffon must say, that it is contrary to a law of nature. But has he given any evidence of this supposed law of nature? On the contrary, he proves it by various instances not to be a law of nature. He admits the sheep and the goat to be of different species; and yet we have his authority for affirming, that a he-goat and a ewe produce a mixed breed which generate for ever (*c*). The camel and the dromedary, though nearly related, are however no less distinct than the horse and the ass. The dromedary is less than the camel, more slender, and remarkably more swift of foot: it has but one bunch on its back, the camel has two: the race is more nu-<13>merous than that of the camel, and more widely spread. One

(*a*) Wisdom of God in the works of creation.
(*b*) Octavo edit. vol. 8. p. 104. and in many other parts.
(*c*) Vol. 10. p. 138.
4. The 1st edition adds: "But dogs are by their nature companions to men; and Providence probably has permitted a mixture, in order that every man may have a dog to his liking" [1:5].

would not desire distinguishing marks more satisfying; and yet these two species propagate together, no less freely than the different races of men and of dogs. M. Buffon indeed, with respect to the camel and dromedary, endeavours to save his credit by a distinction without a difference. "They are," says he, "one species; but their races are different, and have been so past all memory" (a). Is not this the same with saying that the camel and the dromedary are different species of the same genus? which also holds true of the different species of men and of dogs. If our author will permit me to carry back to the creation the camel and the dromedary as two distinct races, I desire no other concession. He admits no fewer than ten kinds of goats, visibly distinguishable, which also propagate together; but says, that these are varieties only, though permanent and unchangeable. No difficulty is unsurmountable, if words be allowed to pass without meaning. Nor does he even adhere to the same opi-<14>nion: though in distinguishing a horse from an ass, he affirms the mule they generate to be barren; yet afterward, entirely forgetting his rule, he admits the direct contrary (b). At that rate, a horse and an ass are of the same species. Did it never once enter into the mind of this author, that the human race would be strangely imperfect, if they were unable to distinguish a man from a monkey, or a hare from a hedge-hog, till it were known whether they can procreate together?

But it seems unnecessary after all to urge any argument against the foregoing rule, which M. Buffon himself inadvertently abandons as to all animals, men and dogs excepted. We are indebted to him for a remark, That not a single animal of the torrid zone is common to the old world and to the new. But how does he verify his remark? Does he ever think of trying whether such animals can procreate together? "They are," says he, "of different kinds, having no such resemblance as to make us pronounce them to be of the same kind. Linnaeus and Brisson," <15> he adds, "have very improperly given the name of the camel to the lama and the pacos of Peru. So apparent is the difference, that other writers class these animals with sheep. Wool however is the only circumstance in which a pacos resembles a sheep: nor doth the lama resemble a camel except in length of neck." He

(a) Vol. 10. p. 1.
(b) Vol. 12. p. 223.

distinguisheth, in the same manner, the true Asiatic tiger from several American animals that bear the same name. He mentions its size, its force, its ferocity, the colour of its hair, the stripes black and white that like rings surround alternately its trunk, and are continued to the tip of its tail; "characters," says he, "that clearly distinguish the true tiger from all animals of prey in the new world; the largest of which scarce equals one of our mastives." And he reasons in the same manner upon the other animals of the torrid zone (*a*). Here truth obliges our author to acknowledge, that we are taught by nature to distinguish animals into different kinds by visible <16> marks, without regard to his artificial rule. And if so, there must be different kinds of men; for certain tribes differ visibly from each other, no less than the lama and pacos from the camel or from the sheep, nor less than the true tiger from the American animals of that name.*[5] For proving that dogs were created of different kinds, what better evidence can be expected than that the kinds continue distinct to this day? Our author pretends to derive the mastiff, the bull-dog, the hound, the greyhound, the terrier, the water-dog, &c. all of them from the prick-eared shepherd's cur. Now, admitting the progeny of the original male and female cur to have suffered every possible alteration from climate, food, domestication; the result would be endless varieties, so that no one individual should resemble another. Whence then are derived the different species of dogs above mentioned, or the different races or varieties, as M. Buffon is pleased to name <17> them? Uniformity invariable must be a law in their nature, for it never can be ascribed to chance. There are mongrels, it is true, among dogs, from want of choice, or from a depraved appetite: but as all animals prefer their own kind, mongrels are few compared with animals of a true breed. There are mongrels also among men: the several kinds however continue distinct; and probably will so continue for ever.

There remains an argument against the system of M. Buffon with respect

---

* No person thinks that all trees can be traced back to one kind. Yet the figure, leaves, fruit, &c. of different kinds, are not more distinct, than the difference of figure, colour, &c. in the different races of men. [[Note added in 2nd edition.]]

(*a*) See vol. 8. sect. Of animals common to the two continents.

5. The 1st edition adds: "Which of his rules are we to follow? Must we apply different rules to different animals? and to what animals are we to apply the different rules?" [1:8].

to dogs, still more conclusive. Allowing to climate its utmost influence, it may possibly have an effect upon the size and figure; but surely M. Buffon cannot seriously think, that the different instincts of dogs are owing to climate. A terrier, whose prey burrows under ground, is continually scraping the earth, and thrusting its nose into it. A hound has always its nose on the surface, in order to trace a hare by smell. The same instinct is remarkable in spaniels. It is by nature that these creatures are directed to be continually going about, to catch the smell, and trace their prey. A greyhound, which has not <18> the smelling-faculty, is constantly looking about for its prey. A shepherd's dog may be improved by education, but nature prompts it to guard the flock. A house-dog makes its round every night to protect its master against strangers, without ever being trained to it. Such dogs have a notion of property, and are trusty guardians of their master's goods: in his absence, no person dares lay hold of his hat or his great coat. Waggoners employ dogs of that kind to watch during night the goods they carry. Is it conceivable, that such different instincts, constantly the same in the same species, can proceed from climate, from mixture of breed, or from other accidental cause?[6]

The celebrated Linnaeus, instead of describing every animal according to its kind, as Adam our first parent did, has wandered far from nature in classing animals. He distributes them into six classes, viz. *Mammalia, Aves, Amphibia, Pisces, Insecta, Vermes.*[7] The *Mammalia* are distributed into seven orders, chiefly from their teeth, viz. *Primates, Bruta, Ferae, Glires, Pecora, Belluae, Cetae.*[8] And the *Primates* <19> are, *Homo, Simia, Lemur, Vespertilio.*[9] What may have been his purpose in classing animals so contrary to nature, I cannot guess, if it be not to enable us, from the nipples and teeth of any particular animal, to know where it is to be found in his book. It resembles the classing books in a library by size, or by binding, without regard to the contents: it may serve as a sort of dictionary; but to no other purpose. How whimsical is it to class together animals that nature hath widely separated, a man for example and a bat? What will a plain man

6. This paragraph added in 2nd edition.
7. That is, mammals, birds, amphibians, fish, insects, worms.
8. For Linnaeus's explications of these terms, see *The Animal Kingdom*, pp. 38–39.
9. That is, man, apes, macauco, bat: see *The Animal Kingdom*, p. 40.

think of a manner of classing, that denies a whale to be a fish? In classing animals, why does he confine himself to the nipples and the teeth, when there are many other distinguishing marks? Animals are no less distinguishable with respect to tails; long tails, short tails, no tails: nor less distinguishable with respect to hands; some having four, some two, some none, &c. &c. Yet, after all, if any solid instruction can be acquired from such classing, I shall listen, not only with attention, but with satisfaction. <20>

Now more particularly of man, after discussing other animals. If the only rule afforded by nature for classing animals can be depended upon, there are different species of men as well as of dogs: a mastiff differs not more from a spaniel, than a white man from a negro, or a Laplander from a Dane. And if we have any belief in Providence, it ought to be so. Plants were created of different kinds to fit them for different climates, and so were brute animals. Certain it is, that all men are not fitted equally for every climate. Is there not then reason to conclude, that as there are different climates, so there are different species of men fitted for these different climates? The inhabitants of the frozen regions of the north, men, birds, beasts, fish, are all provided with a quantity of fat which guards them against cold. Even the trees are full of rosin.[10] The island St. Thomas, under the line, is extremely foggy; and the natives are fitted for that sort of weather, by the rigidity of their fibres. The fog is dispelled in July and August by dry winds; which give vigour to Europeans, whose fibres are relaxed by a moist atmosphere as by a warm bath. <21> The natives, on the contrary, who are not fitted for a dry air, have more diseases in July and August than during the other ten months. On the other hand, instances are without number of men degenerating in a climate to which they are not fitted by nature; and I know not of a single instance where in such a climate people have retained their original vigour. Several European colonies have subsisted in the torrid zone of America more than two centuries; and yet even that length of time has not familiarised them to the climate: they cannot bear heat like the original inhabitants, nor like negroes transplanted from a country equally hot: they are far from equalling in vigour of mind or body

10. The 1st edition adds: "The Esquimaux inhabit a bitter cold country; and their blood and their breath are remarkably warm" [1:10].

the nations from which they sprung. The Spanish inhabitants of Cartha-
gena in South America lose their vigour and colour in a few months. Their
motions are languid; and their words are pronounced in a low voice, and
with long and frequent intervals. The offspring of Europeans born in Ba-
tavia, soon degenerate. Scarce one of them has talents sufficient to bear a
part in the administration. There is not an office of trust but must be filled
with na-<22>tive Europeans. Some Portuguese, who have been for ages
settled on the sea-coast of Congo, retain scarce the appearance of men.
South Carolina, especially about Charlestown, is extremely hot, having no
sea-breeze to cool the air: Europeans there die so fast, that they have not
time to degenerate. Even in Jamaica, though more temperate by a regular
succession of land and sea-breezes, recruits from Britain are necessary to
keep up the numbers.* The climate of the northern provinces resembles
our own, and population goes on rapidly.

What means are employed by Providence to qualify different races of
men for different climates, is a subject to which little attention has been
given. It lies too far out of sight to expect a complete discovery; but facts
carefully collected might afford some glimmering of light. In that view, I
mention the following fact. The inhabitants of the kingdom of Senaar in
<23> Africa are true negroes, a jet black complexion, thick lips, flat nose,
curled woolly hair. The country itself is the hottest in the world. From the
report of a late traveller, they are admirably protected by nature against the
violence of the heat. Their skin is to the touch remarkably cooler than that
of an European; and is so in reality, no less than two degrees on Fahrenheit's
thermometer. The young women there are highly prized by the Turks for
that quality.[11]

Thus it appears, that there are different races of men fitted by nature for
different climates. Upon examination, another fact will perhaps also appear,
that the natural productions of each climate make the most wholesome
food for the people who are fitted to live in it. Between the tropics, the

---

* As the Europeans lose vigour by the heat of the climate, the free negroes, especially
those in the mountains, are the safeguard of the island; and it was by their means chiefly
that a number of rebellious negro slaves were subdued in the year 1760. [[Note added
in 2nd edition.]]

11. This paragraph added in 2nd edition.

natives live chiefly on fruits, seeds, and roots; and it is the opinion of the most knowing naturalists, that such food is of all the most wholesome for the torrid zone; comprehending the hot plants, which grow there to perfection, and tend greatly to fortify the stomach. In a temperate climate, a mixture of animal and vegetable food is held to be the most wholesome; <24> and there both animals and vegetables abound. In a cold climate, animals are in plenty, but few vegetables that can serve for food to man. What physicians pronounce upon that head, I know not; but, if we dare venture a conjecture from analogy, animal food will be found the most wholesome for such as are fitted by nature to live in a cold climate.

M. Buffon, from the rule, That animals which can procreate together, and whose progeny can also procreate, are of one species, concludes, that all men are of one race or species; and endeavours to support that favourite opinion, by ascribing to the climate, to food, or to other accidental causes, all the varieties that are found among men. But is he seriously of opinion, that any operation of climate, or of other accidental cause, can account for the copper colour and smooth chin universal among the Americans, the prominence of the *pudenda* universal among Hottentot women, or the black nipple no less universal among female Samoides? The thick fogs of the island St. Thomas may relax the fibres of the natives, but cannot make them more <25> rigid than they are naturally. Whence, then, the difference with respect to rigidity of fibres between them and Europeans, but from original nature? Can one hope for belief in ascribing to climate the low stature of the Esquimaux, the smallness of their feet, or the overgrown size of their head; or in ascribing to climate the low stature of the Laplanders,* and their ugly visage. Lapland is indeed piercingly cold; but so is Finland, and the northern parts of Norway, the inhabitants of which are tall, comely, and well proportioned. The black colour of negroes, thick lips, flat nose, crisped woolly hair, and rank smell, distinguish them from every other race of men. The Abyssinians, on the contrary, are tall and well made, their complexion a brown olive, features well proportioned, eyes large, and of a

---

* By late accounts, it appears that the Laplanders are originally Huns. Pere Hel, an Hungarian, made lately this discovery, when sent to Lapland for making astronomical observations.

sparkling black, lips thin, a nose rather high than flat. There is no such difference of climate between Abyssinia and Negroland as to produce these striking differences. At <26> any rate, there must be a considerable mixture both of soil and climate in these extensive regions; and yet not the least mixture is perceived in the people.

If the climate have any commanding influence, it must be displayed upon the complexion chiefly; and in that article, accordingly, our author exults. "Man," says he, "white in Europe, black in Africa, yellow in Asia, and red in America, is still the same animal, tinged only with the colour of the climate. Where the heat is excessive, as in Guinea and Senegal, the people are perfectly black; where less excessive, as in Abyssinia, the people are less black; where it is more temperate, as in Barbary and in Arabia, they are brown; and where mild, as in Europe and Lesser Asia, they are fair" (a). But here he triumphs without a victory: he is forced to acknowledge, that the Samoides, Laplanders, and Greenlanders, are of a sallow complexion; for which he has the following salvo, that the extremities of heat and of cold produce nearly the same effects on the skin. <27> But he is totally silent upon a fact that alone overturns his whole system of colour, viz. that all Americans, without exception, are of a copper colour, though in that vast continent there is every variety of climate. The southern Chinese are white, though in the neighbourhood of the torrid zone; and women of fashion in the island Otaheite, who cover themselves from the sun, have the European complexion.[12] Neither doth the black colour of some Africans, nor the brown colour of others, correspond to the climate. The people of the desert of Zaara, commonly termed Lower Ethiopia, though exposed to the vertical rays of the sun in a burning sand yielding not in heat even to Guinea, are of a tawny colour, far from being jet-black like negroes. The natives of Monomotapa are perfectly black, with crisped wooly hair, though the southern parts of that extensive kingdom are in a temperate climate. And the Caffres, even those who live near the Cape of Good Hope, are the same sort of people. The heat of Abyssinia approacheth nearer to

(a) Book 5.
12. "The southern Chinese . . . the European complexion": added in 2nd edition.

that of Guinea; and yet, as mentioned above, the inhabitants are not black. Nor will our author's ingenious observation <28> concerning the extremities of heat and cold account for the sallow complexion of the Samoides, Laplanders, and Greenlanders. The Finlanders and northern Norwegians live in a climate no less cold that that of the people mentioned, and yet are fair beyond other Europeans. I say more, there are many instances of races of people preserving their original colour in climates very different from their own; and not a single instance of the contrary, as far as I can learn. There have been four complete generations of negroes in Pennsylvania, without any visible change of colour: they continue jet-black as originally. The Moors in Hindostan retain their natural colour, though transplanted there more than three centuries ago. And the Mogul family continue white, like their ancestors the Tartars, though they have reigned in Hindostan above four centuries. Shaw, in his travels through Barbary, mentions a people inhabiting the mountains of Auress, bordering upon Algiers on the south, who appeared to be of a different race from the Moors. Their complexion, far from swarthy, is fair and ruddy; and their hair a deep yellow, in-<29>stead of being dark, as among the neighbouring Moors. He conjectures them to be a remnant of the Vandals, perhaps the tribe mentioned by Procopius in his first book of the Vandalic war. If the European complexion be proof against a hot climate for a thousand years, I pronounce that it will never yield to climate. In the suburbs of Cochin, a town in Malabar, there is a colony of industrious Jews of the same complexion they have in Europe. They pretend that they were established there during the captivity of Babylon: it is certain that they have been many ages in that country. Those who ascribe all to the sun, ought to consider how little probable it is, that the colour it impresses on the parents should be communicated to their infant children, who never saw the sun: I should be as soon induced to believe, with a German naturalist whose name has escaped me, that the negro colour is owing to an ancient custom in Africa of dying the skin black. Let a European for years expose himself to the sun in a hot climate, till he be quite brown, his children will nevertheless have the same complexion with those in Europe. <30> The Hottentots are continually at work, and have been for ages, to darken their complexion; but that operation has no effect on their children. From the action of the sun, is it possible to explain why a negro, like a European, is born with a ruddy skin, which turns jet-black the eighth or ninth day?*

Different tribes are distinguishable no less by internal disposition than by external figure. Nations are for the most part so blended by war, by commerce, or by other means, that vain would be the attempt to trace out an original character in any cultivated nation. But there are savage tribes, which, as far as can be discovered, continue to this day pure without mixture, which act by instinct not art, which have not learned to disguise their passions: to such I confine the inquiry. There is no propensity in human nature more general than aversion from strangers, as will be made evident after-<31>ward (a). And yet some nations must be excepted, not indeed many in number, who are remarkably kind to strangers; by which circumstance they appear to be of a singular race. In order to set the exceptions in a clear light, a few instances shall be premised of the general propensity. The nations that may be the most relied on for an original character, are islanders at a distance from the continent and from each other. Among such, great variety of character is found. Some islands adjacent to New Guinea are inhabited by negroes, a bold, mischievous, untractable race; always ready to attack strangers when they approach the shore. The people of New Zealand are of a large size and of a hoarse voice. They appeared shy according to Tasman's account. Some of them, however, ventured on board in order to trade; but finding opportunity, they surprised seven of his men in a shallop, and without the slightest provocation killed three of them, the rest having escaped by swimming. The island called *Recreation,* 16th degree southern latitude, and 148th of longitude west from London, was discovered <32> in Roggewein's voyage. Upon sight of the ships, the natives flocked to the shore with long pikes. The crew made good their landing, having by fire-arms beat back the natives; who, returning after a short interval, accepted presents of beads, small looking-glasses, and other trinkets, without shewing the least fear: they even assisted the crew in gath-

---

* Different flowers derive their colour from nature, and preserve the same colour in every climate. What reason is there to believe, that climate should have greater influence upon the colour of men than of flowers? [[Note added in 2nd edition.]]
(a) Book 2, sketch 1.

ering herbs for those who were afflicted with the scurvy. Some of the crew traversing the island in great security, and trusting to some natives who led the way, were carried into a deep valley surrounded with rocks; where they were instantly attacked on every side with large stones: with difficulty they made their escape, but not without leaving several dead upon the field. In Commodore Byron's voyage to the South Sea, an island was discovered, which he named *Disappointment*. The shore was covered with natives in arms to prevent landing. They were black; and without clothing except what covered the parts that nature teaches to hide. But a specimen is sufficient here, as the subject will be fully illustrated in the sketch referred to above. <33>

The kindness of some tribes to strangers deserves more attention, being not a little singular. Gonneville, commander of a French ship in a voyage to the East Indies in the year 1503, was driven by a tempest into an unknown country, and continued there six months, while his vessel was refitting. The manners he describes were in all appearance original. The natives had not made a greater progress in the arts of life, than the savage Canadians have done; ill clothed; and worse lodged, having no light in their cabins but what came in through a hole in the roof. They were divided into small tribes, governed each by a king; who, though neither better clothed nor lodged than others, had power of life and death over his subjects. They were a simple and peaceable people, and in a manner worshipped the French, providing them with necessaries, and in return thankfully receiving knives, hatchets, small looking-glasses, and other such baubles. In a part of California the men go naked, and are fond of feathers and shells. They are governed by a king with great mildness; and of all savages are the most humane, even to strangers. An island <34> discovered in the South Sea by Tasman, 21st degree of southern latitude, and 177th of longitude west from London, was called by him *Amsterdam*. The natives, who had no arms offensive or defensive, treated the Dutch with great civility, except in being given to pilfering. At no great distance, another island was discovered, named *Annamocha* by the natives, and *Rotterdam* by Tasman; possessed by a people resembling those last mentioned, particularly in having no arms. The Dutch, sailing round the island, saw abundance of cocoa-trees planted in rows, with many other fruit-bearing trees, kept in excellent order. Commodore Roggewein, commander of a Dutch fleet, discovered, *anno* 1721, a new island in the South Sea; inhabited by a people lively, active, and swift of foot; of a sweet and modest deportment: but timorous and faint-hearted; for having on their knees presented some refreshments to the Dutch, they retired with precipitation. Numbers of idols cut in stone were placed along the coast, in the figure of men with large ears, and the head covered with a crown; the whole nicely proportioned and highly fi-<35>nished. They fled for refuge to these idols: and they could do no better; for they had no weapons either offensive or defensive. Neither was there any appearance of government or subordination; for they all spoke and acted with equal freedom. This island, situated 28 degrees 30 minutes southern latitude, and about 115 degrees of longitude west from London, is by the Dutch called *Easter* or *Pasch Island.** The Commodore directing his course north-west, discovered in the southern latitude of 12 degrees, and in the longitude of 190, a cluster of islands, planted with variety of fruit-trees, and bearing herbs, corn, and roots, in plenty. When the ships approached the shore, the inhabitants came in their canoes with fish, cocoa-nuts, Indian figs, and other refreshments; for which they received small looking-glasses, strings of beads, and other toys. These islands were well peopled: many thousands thronged to the shore to see the ships, the men being armed with bows and arrows, and appearing <36> to be governed by a chieftain: they had the complexion of Europeans, only a little more sun-burnt. They were brisk and lively, treating one another with civility; and in their behaviour expressing nothing wild nor savage. Their bodies were not painted; but handsomely clothed, from the middle downward, with silk fringes in neat folds. Large hats screened the face from the sun, and collars of odoriferous flowers surrounded the neck. The view of the country is charming, finely diversified with hills and vallies. Some of the islands are ten miles in circumference, some fifteen, some twenty. The historian adds, that these islanders are in all respects the most civilized and the best tempered people he discovered in the South Sea. Far from being afraid, they treated the Dutch with great kindness; and expressed much regret at their departure. These

* The women were very loving, enticing the Dutchmen by every female art to the most intimate familiarity.

islands got the name of *Bowman's islands,* from the captain of the Tien-hoven, who discovered them. In Commodore Byron's voyage to the South Sea, while he was passing through the streights of Magellan, some natives approached in their canoes; and upon invitation came <37> on board, without fear, or even shyness. They at the same time appeared grossly stupid; and particularly, could not comprehend the use of knives, offered to them in a present. In another part of the streights, the natives were highly delighted with presents of the same kind. M. Bougainville, in his voyage round the world, describes a people in the streights of Magellan, probably those last mentioned, as of small stature, tame and peaceable, having scarce any clothing in a climate bitterly cold. Commodore Byron discovered another island in the South Sea covered with trees, which was named *Byron island.* The inhabitants were neither savage nor shy, trafficking freely with the crew, though they seemed addicted to thieving. One of them ventured into the ship. After leaving Otaheite, Mr. Banks and Dr. Solander, sailing westward, discovered a cluster of islands, termed by them *Society islands:* the natives were extremely civil, and appeared to have no aversion to strangers. The island of Oahena, north-west from that of Otaheite, is a delightful spot; the soil fertile, and the shores adorned with fruit-trees of various kinds. The in-<38>habitants are well proportioned, with regular engaging features; the women uncommonly beautiful and delicate. The inhabitants behaved with great hospitality and probity to the crew of the ship in which these gentlemen lately made a voyage round the world.

To find the inhabitants of these remote islands differing so widely from the rest of the world, as to have no aversion to strangers, but on the contrary showing great kindness to the first they probably ever saw, is a singular phenomenon. It is vain here to talk of climate; because in all climates we find an aversion to strangers. From the instances given above, let us select two islands, or two clusters of islands, suppose for example Bowman's islands inhabited by Whites, and those adjacent to New Guinea inhabited by Blacks. Kindness to strangers is the national character of the former, and hatred to strangers is the national character of the latter. Virtues and vices of individuals depend on causes so various, and so variable, as to give an impression of chance more than of design. We are not always certain of uniformity in the conduct even of the same <39> person; far less of different persons, however intimately related: how small is the chance, that sons will inherit their father's virtues or vices? In most countries, a savage who has no aversion to strangers, nor to neighbouring clans, would be noted as singular: to find the same quality in every one of his children, would be surprising: and would be still more so, were it diffused widely through a multitude of his descendents. Yet a family is as nothing compared with a whole nation; and when we find kindness to strangers a national character in certain tribes, we reject with disdain the notion of chance, and perceive intuitively that effects so regular and permanent must be owing to a constant and invariable cause. Such effects cannot be accidental, more than the uniformity of male and female births in all countries and at all times. They cannot be accounted for from education nor from example; which indeed may contribute to spread a certain fashion or certain manners, but cannot be their fundamental cause. Where the greater part of a nation is of one character, education and example may extend it over the whole; but the character of <40> that greater part can have no foundation but nature. What resource then have we for explaining the opposite manners of the islanders above mentioned, but that they are of different races?

The same doctrine is strongly confirmed upon finding courage or cowardice to be a national character. Individuals differ widely as to these; but a national character of courage or cowardice must depend on a permanent and invariable cause. I therefore proceed to instances of national courage and cowardice, that the reader may judge for himself, whether he can discover any other cause for such steady uniformity but diversity of race.

The northern nations of Europe and Asia have at all times been remarkable for courage. Lucan endeavours to account for the courage of the Scandinavians from a firm belief, universal among them, that they will be happy in another world.

> *Vobis auctoribus, umbrae,*
> *Non tacitas Erebi sedes, Ditisque profundi*
> *Pallida regna petunt; regit idem spiritus artus*
> *Orbe alio: longae (canitis si cognita) vitae*
> *Mors media est. Certe populi, quos despicit Arctos,*
> *Felices errore suo; quos ille, timorum* <41>
> *Maximus, haud urget leti metus. Inde ruendi*

In ferrum mens prona viris, animaeque capaces
Mortis (*a*).*

Pretty well reasoned for a poet! but among all nations the soul is believed to be immortal, though all nations have not the courage of the Scandinavians. The Caledonians were eminent for that virtue; and yet had no such opinion of happiness after death, as to make them fond of dying. Souls after death were believed to have but a gloomy sort of existence, like what is de-<42>scribed by Homer (*b*). Their courage therefore was a gift of nature, not of faith. The people of Malacca and of the neighbouring islands, who are all of the same race, and speak the same language, are fierce, turbulent, and bold above any other of the human species, though they inhabit the torrid zone, held commonly to be the land of cowardice. They never observe a treaty of peace when they have any temptation to break it; and are perpetually at war with their neighbours, or with one another. Instances there are of twenty-five or thirty of them in a boat, with no other weapons but poniards, venturing to attack a European ship of war. These men inhabit a fertile country, which should naturally render them indolent and effeminate; a country abounding with variety of exquisite fruits and odor-

---

*   If dying mortals dooms they sing aright,
    No ghosts descend to dwell in endless night;
    No parting souls to grisly Pluto go,
    Nor seek the dreary silent shades below;
    But forth they fly, immortal in their kind,
    And other bodies in new worlds they find.
    Thus life for ever runs its endless race,
    And, like a line, Death but divides the space;
    A stop which can but for a moment last,
    A point between the future and the past.
    Thrice happy they beneath the northern skies,
    Who that worst fear, the fear of death, despise;
    Hence they no cares for this frail being feel,
    But rush undaunted on the pointed steel;
    Provoke approaching fate, and bravely scorn
    To spare that life which must so soon return.
                              Rowe.

(*a*) Lib. 1.
(*b*) Odyssey, b. 11.

iferous flowers in endless succession, sufficient to sink any other people into voluptuousness. They are a remarkable exception from the observation of Herodotus, "That it is not given by the gods to any country, to produce rich crops and warlike men." <43> This instance, with what are to follow, show past contradiction, that a hot climate is no enemy to courage. The inhabitants of New Zealand are the most intrepid, and the least apt to be alarmed at danger. The Giagas are a fierce and bold people in the midst of the torrid zone of Africa: and so are the Ansieki, bordering on Loango. The wild Arabs, who live mostly within the torrid zone, are bold and resolute, holding war to be intended for them by Providence. The African negroes, though living in the hottest known country, are yet stout and vigorous, and the most healthy people in the universe. I need scarcely mention again the negroes adjacent to New Guinea, who have an uncommon degree of boldness and ferocity. But I mention with pleasure the island Otaheite, discovered in the South Sea by Wallis, because the inhabitants are not exceeded by any other people in firmness of mind. Though the Dolphin was probably the first ship they had ever seen, yet they resolutely marched to the shore, and attacked her with a shower of stones. Some volleys of small shot made them give way: but returning with redoubled ardour, they <44> did not totally lose heart till the great guns thundered in their ears. Nor even then did they run away in terror; but advising together, they assumed looks of peace, and signified a willingness to forbear hostilities. Peace being settled, they were singularly kind to our people, supplying their wants, and mixing with them in friendly intercourse.* When Mr. Banks and Dr. Solander were on the coast of New Holland, the natives, seeing some of our men fishing near the shore, singled out a number of their own equal to those in the boat, who marching down to the water-edge, challenged the strangers to fight them; an instance of true heroic courage. The people in that part of New Holland must be of a race very different from those whom Dampier saw.

---

* It is remarkable, that these people roast their meat with hot stones, as the Caledonians did in the days of Ossian.

A noted author (*a*) holds all savages to be bold, impetuous, and proud; assigning for a cause, their equality and independence. As in that observation he seems to lay no weight on climate, and as little <45> on original disposition, it is with regret that my subject leads me in this public manner to differ from him with respect to the latter. The character he gives in general to all savages, is indeed applicable to many savage tribes, our European forefathers in particular; but not to all. It but faintly suits even the North-American savages, whom our author seems to have had in his eye; for in war they carefully avoid open force, relying chiefly on stratagem and surprise. They value themselves, it is said, upon saving men; but as that motive was no less weighty in Europe, and indeed every where, the proneness of our forefathers to open violence, demonstrates their superiority in active courage. The following incidents reported by Charlevoix give no favourable idea of North-American boldness. The fort de Vercheres in Canada, belonging to the French, was in the year 1690 attacked by some Iroquois. They approached silently, preparing to scale the palisade, when a musket-shot or two made them retire. Advancing a second time, they were again repulsed, wondering that they could discover none but a woman, who was seen <46> every where. This was Madame de Vercheres, who appeared as resolute as if supported by a numerous garrison. The hopes of storming a place without men to defend it, occasioned reiterated attacks. After two days siege, they retired, fearing to be intercepted in their retreat. Two years after, a party of the same nation appeared before the fort so unexpectedly, that a girl of fourteen, daughter of the proprietor, had but time to shut the gate. With the young woman there was not a soul but one raw soldier. She showed herself with her assistant, sometimes in one place, sometimes in another; changing her dress frequently, in order to give some appearance of a garrison, and always firing opportunely. The faint-hearted Iroquois decamped without success.

But if the Americans abound not with active courage, their passive courage is beyond conception. Every writer expatiates on the torments they endure, not only patiently, but with singular fortitude; deriding their tor-

(*a*) Mr. Ferguson.

mentors, and braving their utmost cruelty. North-American savages differ indeed so widely from those formerly in Europe, as to render it highly im-<47>probable that they are of the same race. Passive courage they have even to a wonder; but abound not in active courage: our European forefathers, on the contrary, were much more remarkable for the latter than for the former. The Kamskatkans in every article resemble the North-Americans. In war they are full of stratagem, but never attack openly if they can avoid it. When victorious, they murder without mercy, burn their prisoners alive, or tear out their bowels. If they be surrounded and cannot escape, they turn desperate, cut the throats of their wives and children, and throw themselves into the midst of their enemies. And yet these people are abundantly free. Their want of active courage is the more surprising, because they make no difficulty of suicide when they fall into any distress. But their passive courage is equal to that of the Americans: when tortured in order to extort a confession, they show the utmost firmness; and seldom discover more than what they freely confess at their first examination.

The savages of Guiana are indolent, good-natured, submissive, and a little cow-<48>ardly; though they are on a footing with the North-Americans in equality and independence. The inhabitants of the Marian or Ladrone islands live in a state of perfect equality: every man avenges the injury done to himself; and even children are regardless of their parents. Yet these people are great cowards: in battle indeed they utter loud shouts; but it is more to animate themselves than to terrify the enemy. The negroes on the slave-coast of Guinea are good-natured and obliging; but not remarkable for courage.* The Laplanders are of all men the most timid: upon the slightest surprise they fall down in a swoon, like the feeblest female in England: thunder deprives them of their five senses. The face of their country is nothing but rocks covered with moss: it would be scarce habitable but for rain-deer, on which the Laplanders chiefly depend for food. <49>

* The Cormantees, a tribe of negroes on the Gold coast, are indeed brave and intrepid. When kindly treated in the West Indies, they make excellent servants. The negroes of Senegal are remarkable in the West Indies for fidelity and good understanding. [[Note added in 2nd edition.]]

The Macassars, inhabitants of the island Celebes in the torrid zone, differ from all other people. They have active courage above even the fiercest
European savages; and they equal the North-American savages in passive
courage. During the reign of Cha Naraya King of Siam, a small party of
Macassars who were in the King's pay having revolted, it required a whole
army of Siamites to subdue them. Four Macassars, taken alive, were cruelly
tortured. They were beaten to mummy with cudgels, iron pins were thrust
under their nails, all their fingers broken, the flesh burnt off their arms,
and their temples squeezed between boards; yet they bore all with unparalleled firmness. They even refused to be converted to Christianity, though
the Jesuits offered to intercede for them. A tiger, let loose, having fastened
on the foot of one of them, the man never once offered to draw it away.
Another, without uttering a word, bore the tiger breaking the bones of his
back. A third suffered the animal to lick the blood from his face, without
shrinking, or turning away his eyes. During the whole of that horrid spectacle, they never once bewailed <50> themselves, nor were heard to utter
a groan.

The frigidity of the North-Americans, men and women, differing in that
particular from all other savages, is to me evidence of a separate race. And
I am the more confirmed in that opinion, when I find a celebrated writer,
whose abilities no person calls in question, endeavouring in vain to ascribe
that circumstance to moral and physical causes. *Si Pergama dextra defendi
posset.* [13]

In concluding from the foregoing facts that there are different races of
men, I reckon upon strenuous opposition; not only from men biassed
against what is new or uncommon, but from numberless sedate writers,
who hold every distinguishing mark, internal as well as external, to be the
effect of soil and climate. Against the former, patience is my only shield;
but I cannot hope for any converts to a new opinion, without removing
the arguments urged by the latter.

Among the endless number of writers who ascribe supreme efficacy to

---

13. "If Troy's towers could be saved by strength of hand": Virgil, *Aeneid,* bk. II, l.
291. The passage continues, "etiam hac defensa fuissent" ("by mine, too, had they been
saved"). Paragraph added in 2nd edition.

the climate, Vitruvius shall take the lead. The first chapter of his sixth book is entirely <51> employed in describing the influence of climate on the constitution and temper. The following is the substance. "For the sun, where he draws out a moderate degree of moisture, preserves the body in a temperate state; but where his rays are more fierce, he drains the body of moisture. In very cold regions, where the moisture is not suck'd up by the heat, the body sucking in the dewy air, rises to a great size, and has a deep tone of voice. Northern nations accordingly, from cold and moisture, have large bodies, a white skin, red hair, gray eyes, and much blood. Nations, on the contrary, near the equator, are of small stature, tawny complexion, curled hair, black eyes, slender legs, and little blood. From want of blood they are cowardly: but they bear fevers well, their constitution being formed by heat. Northern nations, on the contrary, sink under a fever; but, from the abundance of blood, they are bold in war." In another part of the chapter he adds, "From the thinness of the air and enlivening heat, southern nations are quick in thought, and acute in reasoning. <52> Those in the north, on the contrary, who breathe a thick and cold air, are dull and stupid." And this he illustrates from serpents, which in summer-heat are active and vigorous; but in winter, become torpid and immoveable. He then proceeds as follows. "It is then not at all surprising, that heat should sharpen the understanding, and cold blunt it. Thus the southern nations are ready in counsel, and acute in thought; but make no figure in war, their courage being exhausted by the heat of the sun. The inhabitants of cold climates, prone to war, rush on with vehemence without the least fear; but are slow of understanding." Then he proceeds to account, upon the same principle, for the superiority of the Romans in arms, and for the extent of their empire. "For as the planet Jupiter lies between the fervid heat of Mars and the bitter cold of Saturn; so Italy, in the middle of the temperate zone possesses all that is favourable in either climate. Thus by conduct in war, the Romans overcome the impetuous force of northern barbarians; and by vigour of arms <53> confound the politic schemes of her southern neighbours. Divine Providence appears to have placed the Romans in that happy situation, in order that they might become masters of the world."—Vegetius accounts for the different characters of men from the same principle: "Omnes nationes quae vicinae sunt soli, nimio calore siccatas, amplius quidem sapere, sed minus habere sanguinis dicunt: ac propterea constantiam ac fiduciam cominus non habere pugnandi, quia metuunt vulnera, qui se exiguum sanguinem habere noverunt. Contra, septentrionales populi, remoti a solis ardoribus, inconsultiores quidem, sed tamen largo sanguine redundantes, sunt ad bella promptissimi" (a).*—<54>Servius, in his commentary on the Aeneid of Virgil (b), says, "Afri versipelles, Graeci leves, Galli pigrioris ingenii, quod natura climatum facit."†—Mallet, in the introduction to his history of Denmark, copying Vitruvius and Vegetius, strains hard to derive ferocity and courage in the Scandinavians from the climate:

> A great abundance of blood, fibres strong and rigid, vigour inexhaustible, formed the temperament of the Germans, the Scandinavians, and of all other people who live under the same climate. Robust by the climate, and hardened with exercise; confidence in bodily strength formed their character. A man who relies on his own force, cannot bear restraint, nor submission to the arbitrary will of another. As he has no occasion for artifice, he is altogether a stranger to fraud or dissimulation. As he is always ready to repel force by force, he is not suspicious nor <55> distrustful. His courage prompts him to be faithful in friendship, generous, and even magnanimous. He is averse to occupations that require more assiduity than action; because moderate exercise affords not to his blood and fibres that degree of agitation which suits them. Hence his disgust at arts and manufactures; and as passion labours to justify itself, hence his opinion, that war only and hunting are honourable professions.

Before subscribing to this doctrine, I wish to be satisfied of a few particulars. Is our author certain, that inhabitants of cold countries have the greatest quantity of blood? And is he certain, that courage is in every man

---

* "Nations near the sun, being exsiccated by excessive heat, are said to have a greater acuteness of understanding, but less blood: on which account, in fighting they are deficient in firmness and resolution; and dread the being wounded, as conscious of their want of blood. The northern people, on the contrary, removed from the ardor of the sun, are less remarkable for the powers of the mind; but abounding in blood, they are prone to war."

† "The Africans are subtle and full of stratagem, the Greeks are fickle, the Gauls slow of parts, all which diversities are occasioned by the climate."

(a) Lib. 1. cap. 2. De re militari.

(b) Lib. 6. ver. 724.

proportioned to the quantity of his blood?* Is he also certain, that ferocity and love of war did universally obtain a-<56>mong the northern Europeans? Tacitus gives a very different character of the Chauci, who inhabited the north of Germany: "Tam immensum terrarum spatium non tenent tantum Chauci, sed et implent: populus inter Germanos nobilissimus, quique magnitudinem suam malit justitia tueri. Sine cupiditate, sine impotentia, quieti, secretique, nulla provocant bella, nullis raptibus aut latrociniis populantur. Idque praecipuum virtutis ac virium argumentum est, quod ut superiores agunt, non per injurias assequuntur. Prompta tamen omnibus arma, ac, si res poscat, exercitus" (a).† Again, with respect to <57> the Arii, he bears witness, that beside ferocity, and strength of body, they were full of fraud and artifice. Neither do the Laplanders nor Samoides correspond to his description, being remarkable for pusillanimity, though inhabitants of a bitter-cold country.‡ Lastly, a cold climate doth not always make the inhabitants averse to occupations that require more assiduity than action: the people of Iceland formerly were much addicted to study and literature; and for many centuries were the chief historians of the north. They <58> are to this day fond of chess, and spend much of their time in

---

* At that rate, the loss of an ounce of blood may turn the balance. Courage makes an essential ingredient in magnanimity and heroism: are such elevated virtues corporeal merely? is the mind admitted for no share? This indeed would be a mortifying circumstance in the human race. But even supposing courage to be corporeal merely, it is however far from being proportioned to the quantity of blood: a greater quantity than can be circulated freely and easily by the force of the heart and arteries, becomes a disease, termed a *plethora*. Bodily courage is chiefly founded on the solids. When by the vigour and elasticity of the heart and arteries a brisk circulation of blood is produced, a man is in good spirits, lively, and bold; a greater quantity of blood, instead of raising courage to a higher pitch, never fails to produce sluggishness, and depression of mind.

† "So immense an extent of country is not possessed only, but filled by the Chauci; a race of people the noblest among the Germans, and who chuse to maintain their grandeur by justice rather than by violence. Confident of their strength, without the thirst of increasing their possessions, they live in quietness and security: they kindle no wars; they are strangers to plunder and to rapine; and what is the chief evidence both of their power and of their virtue, without oppressing any, they have attained a superiority over all. Yet, when occasion requires, they are prompt to take the field; and their troops are speedily raised."

‡ Scheffer, in his history of Lapland, differs widely from the authors mentioned; for he ascribes the pusillanimity of the Laplanders to the coldness of their climate.

(a) De moribus Germanorum, cap. 35.

that amusement: there is scarce a peasant but who has a chess-board and men. Mr. Banks and Dr. Solander report, that the peasants of Iceland are addicted to history, not only of their own country, but of that of Europe.*
<59>

The most formidable antagonist remains still on hand, the celebrated Montesquieu, who is a great champion for the climate; observing, that in hot climates people are timid like old men, and in cold climates bold like young men. This in effect is to maintain, that the torrid zone is an unfit habitation for men; that they degenerate in it, lose their natural vigour, and even in youth become like old men. That au-<60>thor certainly intended not any imputation on Providence; and yet, doth it not look like an imputation, to maintain, that so large a portion of the globe is fit for beasts only, not for men? Some men are naturally fitted for a temperate or for a

---

* A French author (*a*) upon this subject observes, that like plants we are formed by the climate; and that as fruits derive their taste from the soil, men derive their character and disposition from the air they breathe. "The English," says he, "owe to the foggyness of their air, not only their rich pasture, but the gloominess of their disposition; which makes them violent in their passions, because they pursue with ardor every object that relieves them from melancholy. By that gloominess, they are exhausted, and rendered insensible to the pleasures of life. Depressed in mind, they are unable to endure pain; as it requires strength of mind to suffer without extreme impatience. They are never content with their lot, hating tranquillity as much as they love liberty." Where a fact is known to be true, any thing will pass for a cause; and shallow writers deal in such causes. I need no better instance than the present: for, if I mistake not, effects directly opposite may be drawn from the cause assigned by this writer; as plausible at least, I do not say better founded on truth. I will make an attempt: it may amuse the reader. And to avoid disputing about facts, I shall suppose the foggyness of the fens of Lincoln and Essex to be general, which he erroneously seems to believe. From that supposition I reason thus: "The foggyness of the English air makes the people dull and languid. They suffer under a constant depression of spirits; and scarce know what it is to joke, or even to laugh at a joke. They loiter away their time without feeling either pleasure or pain; and yet have not resolution to put an end to an insipid existence. It cannot be said that they are content with their lot, because there is pleasure in content; but they never think of a change. Being reduced to a passive nature from the influence of climate, they are fitted for being slaves: nor would they have courage to rebel, were they even inclined." Were the character here delineated that of the English nation, instead of the opposite, the argument would at least be plausible. But superficial reasoners will plunge into the depth of philosophy, without ever thinking it necessary to serve an apprenticeship. [[Note added in 2nd edition.]]

(*a*) [[Jean-Bernard Le Blanc,]] Lettres d'un François.

*

cold climate: he ought to have explained, why other men may not be fitted for a hot climate. There does not appear any opposition between heat and courage, more than between cold and courage: on the contrary, courage seems more connected with the former than with the latter. The fiercest and boldest animals, the lion, for example, the tiger, the panther, thrive best in the hottest climates. The great condor of Peru, in the torrid zone, is a bird not a little fierce and rapacious. A lion visibly degenerates in a temperate climate. The lions of Mount Atlas, which is sometimes crowned with snow, have not the boldness, nor the force, nor the ferocity of such as tread the burning sands of Zaara and Biledulgerid. This respectable author, it is true, endeavours to support his opinion from natural causes. These are ingenious and plausible; but unluckily they are contradicted by stubborn facts; which will ap-<61>pear upon a very slight survey of this globe. The Samoides and Laplanders are living instances of uncommon pusillanimity in the inhabitants of a cold climate; and instances, not few in number, have been mentioned of warlike people in a hot climate. To these I add the Hindows, whom our author will not admit to have any degree of courage; though he acknowledges, that, prompted by religion, the men voluntarily submit to dreadful tortures, and that even women are ambitious to burn themselves alive with their deceased husbands. In vain does he endeavour to account for such extraordinary exertions of fortitude, active as well as passive, from the power of imagination; as if imagination could operate more forcibly in a woman to burn herself alive, than on a man to meet his enemy in battle. The Malayans and Scandinavians live in opposite climates, and yet are equally courageous. Providence has placed these nations, each of them, in its proper climate: cold would benumb a Malayan in Sweden, heat would enervate a Swede in Malacca; and both would be rendered cowards. I stop here; for to enter the lists against an antagonist of so <62> great fame, gives me a feeling as if I were treading on forbidden ground.

It is my firm opinion, that neither temper nor talents have much dependence on climate. I cannot discover any probable exception, if it be not a taste for the fine arts. Where the influence of the sun is great, people are enervated with heat: where little, they are benumbed with cold. A clear sky, with moderate heat, exhibit a very different scene: the chearfulness they produce disposes men to enjoyment of every kind. Greece, Italy, and the

Lesser Asia, are delicious countries, affording variety of natural beauties to feast every sense: and men accustomed to enjoyment, search for it in art as well as in nature; the passage from the one to the other being easy and inviting. Hence the origin and progress of statuary and of painting, in the countries mentioned. It has not escaped observation, that the rude manners of savages are partly owing to the roughness and barrenness of uncultivated land. England has few natural beauties to boast of: even high mountains, deep valleys, impetuous torrents, and such other wild and awful beauties, are rare. But of late years, <63> that country has received manifold embellishments from its industrious inhabitants; and in many of its scenes may now compare with countries that are more favoured by the sun or by nature. Its soil has become fertile, its verdure enlivening, and its gardens the finest in the world. The consequence is what might have been foreseen: the fine arts are gaining ground daily. May it not be expected, that the genius and sensibility of the inhabitants, will in time produce other works of art, to rival their gardens? How delightful to a true-hearted Briton is the prospect, that London, instead of Rome, may become the centre of the fine arts!

Sir William Temple is of opinion, that courage depends much on animal food. He remarks, that the horse and the cock are the only animals of courage that live on vegetables. Provided the body be kept in good plight, I am apt to think, that the difference of food can have little influence on the mind. Nor is Sir William's remark supported by experience. Several small birds, whose only food is grain, have no less courage than the cock. The wolf, the fox, the vulture, on the other hand, are <64> not remarkable for courage, though their only food is the flesh of animals.[14]

The colour of the Negroes, as above observed, affords a strong presumption of their being a different species from the Whites; and I once thought, that the presumption was supported by inferiority of understanding in the former. But it appears to me doubtful, upon second thoughts, whether that inferiority may not be occasioned by their condition. A man never ripens in judgment nor in prudence but by exercising these powers. At home, the negroes have little occasion to exercise either: they live upon

14. This and the previous paragraph added in 2nd edition.

fruits and roots, which grow without culture: they need little clothing: and they erect houses without trouble or art.* Abroad, they are miserable slaves, having no encouragement either to think or to act. Who can say how far they might improve in a state of freedom, were they obliged, like Europeans, to procure bread with the sweat of <65> their brows? Some nations in Negroland, particularly that of Whidah, have made great improvements in government, in police, and in manners. The negroes on the Gold coast are naturally gay: they apprehend readily what is said to them, have a good judgment, are equitable in their dealings, and accommodate themselves readily to the manners of strangers. And yet, after all, there seems to be some original difference between the Negroes and Hindows. In no country are food and raiment procured with less labour than in the southern parts of Hindostan, where the heat is great: and yet no people are more industrious than the Hindows.[15]

I shall close the survey with some instances that seem to differ widely from the common nature of man. The Giagas, a fierce and wandering nation in the heart of Africa, are in effect land-pirates, at war with all the world. They indulge in polygamy; but bury all their children the moment of birth, and choose in their stead the most promising children taken in war. There is no principle among animals more prevalent than affection to offspring: supposing the Giagas to be born without <66> hands or without feet, would they be more distinguishable from the rest of mankind?† To

---

* The negro slaves in Jamaica, who have Sunday only at command for raising food to themselves, live as well, if not better, than the free negroes who command every day of the week. Such, in the latter, is the effect of indolence from want of occupation. [[Note added in 2nd edition.]]

† I have oftener than once doubted whether the authors deserve credit from whom this account is taken; and after all, I do not press it upon my readers. There is only one consideration that can bring it within the verge of probability, viz. the little affection that male savages have for their new-born children, which appears from the ancient practice of exposing them. The affection of the mother commences with the birth of the child; and, had she a vote, no infant would ever be destroyed. But as the affection of the father begins much later, the practice of destroying new-born infants may be thought not altogether incredible in a wandering nation, who live by rapine, and who can provide themselves with children more easily than by the tedious and precarious method of rearing them.

15. "And yet, after . . . than the Hindows": added in 2nd edition.

move the Giagas, at first, to murder their own children, and to adopt those of strangers, is a proof of some original principle peculiar to that people: and the continuance of the same practice among the persons adopted, is a strong instance of the force of custom prevailing over one of the most vigorous laws of nature.[16] The author of an account of Guiana, mentioning a deadly poison composed by the natives, says, "I do not find, that even in their wars, they ever use poisoned arrows. And yet it may be wondered, that a <67> people living under no laws, actuated with no religious principle, and unrestrained by the fear of present or future punishment, should not sometimes employ that fatal poison for gratifying hatred, jealousy, or revenge. But in a state of nature, though there are few restraints, there are also fewer temptations to vice; and the different tribes are doubtless sensible, that poisoned arrows in war would upon the whole do more mischief than good."[17] This writer, it would seem, has forgot that prospects of future good or evil never have influence upon savages. Is it his opinion, that fear of future mischief to themselves, would make the negroes of New Guinea abstain from employing poisoned arrows against their enemies? To account for manners so singular in the savages of Guiana, there is nothing left but original disposition. The Japanese resent injuries in a manner that has not a parallel in any other part of the world: it would be thought inconsistent with human nature, were it not well vouched. Others wreak their resentment on the person who affronts them; but an inhabitant of Japan wreaks it on himself: he rips up his own belly. <68> Kempfer reports the following instance. A gentleman going down the great stair of the Emperor's palace, passed another going up, and their swords happened to clash. The person descending took offence: the other excused himself, saying that it was accidental; adding, that the swords only were concerned, and that the one was as good as the other. I'll show you the difference, says the person who began the quarrel: he drew his sword, and ripped up his own belly. The other, piqued at being thus prevented in revenge, hastened up with a plate he had in his hand for the Emperor's table; and returning with equal speed,

---

16. "To move the . . . laws of nature": added in 3rd edition.

17. Kames quotes from Edward Bancroft's *Essay on the Natural History of Guiana, in South America.*

he in like manner ripped up his belly in sight of his antagonist, saying, "If I had not been serving my prince, you should not have got the start of me; but I shall die satisfied, having show'd you that my sword is as good as yours." The same author gives an instance of uncommon ferocity in the Japanese, blended with manners highly polished. In the midst of a large company at dinner, a young woman, straining to reach a plate, unwarily suffered wind to escape. Ashamed and confounded, she raised her breasts <69> to her mouth, tore them with her teeth, and expired on the spot. The Japanese are equally singular in some of their religious opinions. They never supplicate the gods in distress; holding, that as the gods enjoy uninterrupted bliss, such supplications would be offensive to them. Their holidays accordingly are dedicated to feasts, weddings, and all public and private rejoicings. It is delightful to the gods, say they, to see men happy. They are far from being singular in thinking that a benevolent Deity is pleased to see men happy; but nothing can be more inconsistent with the common feelings of men, than to hold, that in distress it is wrong to supplicate the Author of our being for relief, and that he will be displeased with such supplication. In deep affliction, there is certainly no balm equal to that of pouring out the heart to a benevolent Deity, and expressing entire resignation to his will.

In support of the foregoing doctrine, many particulars still more extraordinary might have been quoted from Greek and Roman writers: but truth has no occasion for artifice; and I would not take advan-<70>tage of celebrated names to vouch facts that appear incredible or doubtful. The Greeks and Romans made an illustrious figure in poetry, rhetoric, and all the fine arts; but they were little better than novices in natural history. More than half of the globe was to them the *Terra Australis incognita;* and imagination operates without controul, when it is not checked by knowledge: the ignorant at the same time are delighted with wonders; and the most wonderful story is always the most welcome. This may serve as an apology for ancient writers, even when they relate and believe facts to us incredible. Men at that period were ignorant in a great measure of nature, and of the limits of her operations. One concession will chearfully be made to me, that the writers mentioned, who report things at second-hand, are much more excusable than the earliest of our modern travellers, who pretend to vouch endless wonders from their own knowledge. Natural history, that of man especially, is of late years much ripened: no improbable tale is suffered to pass without a strict examination; and I have been careful to adopt no facts, but what <71> are vouched by late travellers and writers of credit. Were it true, what Diodorus Siculus reports, on the authority of Agatharchides of Cnidus, concerning the Ichthyophages on the east coast of Afric, it would be a more pregnant proof of a distinct race of men, than any I have discovered. They are described to be so stupid, that even when their wives and children are killed in their sight, they stand insensible, and give no signs either of anger or of compassion. This I cannot believe upon so slight testimony; especially as the Greeks and Romans were at that time extremely credulous, being less acquainted with neighbouring nations, than we are with the Antipodes. Varro, in his treatise *De re rustica,* reports it as an undoubted truth, that in Lusitania mares were impregnated by the west wind; and both Pliny and Columella are equally positive.[18] The Balearic islands, Majorca, Minorca, Yvica, are at no great distance from Sicily; and yet Diodorus the Sicilian reports of the inhabitants, that at the solemnization of marriage all the male friends, and even the household servants, enjoyed the bride before the bridegroom was admit-<72>ted. *Credat Judaeus appella.* It would not be much more difficult to make me believe what is said by Pliny of the Blemmyans, that they had no head, and that the mouth and eyes were in the breast; or of the Arimaspi, who had but one eye, placed in the middle of the forehead; or of the Astomi, who, having no mouth, could neither eat nor drink, but lived upon smelling; or of a thousand other absurdities which Pliny relates, with a grave face, in the 6th book of his natural history, cap. 30. and in the 7th book, cap. 2.

Thus, upon an extensive survey of the inhabited parts of our globe, many nations are found differing so widely from each other, not only in complexion, features, shape, and other external circumstances, but in temper and disposition, particularly in two capital articles, courage, and behaviour to strangers, that even the certainty of different races could not make one expect more striking varieties. Doth M. Buffon think it sufficient to say dryly, that such varieties may possibly be the effect of climate, or of

18. "Varro, in his . . . are equally positive": added in 2nd edition.

other accidental causes? The presumption is, that the varieties subsisting at present have always sub-<73>sisted; which ought to be held as true, till positive evidence be brought of the contrary: instead of which we are put off with mere suppositions and possibilities.

But not to rest entirely upon presumptive evidence, to me it appears clear from the very frame of the human body, that there must be different races of men fitted for different climates. Few animals are more affected than men generally are, not only with change of seasons in the same climate, but with change of weather in the same season. Can such a being be fitted for all climates equally? Impossible. A man must at least be hardened by nature against the slighter changes of seasons or weather: he ought to be altogether insensible of such changes. Yet from Sir John Pringle's observations on the diseases of the army, to go no further, it appears, that even military men, who ought of all to be the hardiest, are greatly affected by them. Horses and horned cattle sleep on the bare ground, wet or dry, without harm, and yet are not made for every climate: can a man be made for every climate, who is so much more delicate, that <74> he cannot sleep on wet ground without hazard of some mortal disease?

But the argument I chiefly rely on is, That were all men of one species, there never could have existed, without a miracle, different kinds, such as exist at present. Giving allowance for every supposable variation of climate or of other natural causes, what can follow, as observed about the dog-kind, but endless varieties among individuals, as among tulips in a garden, so as that no individual shall resemble another? Instead of which, we find men of different kinds, the individuals of each kind remarkably uniform, and differing no less remarkably from the individuals of every other kind. Uniformity without variation is the offspring of nature, never of chance.

There is another argument that appears also to have weight. Horses, with respect to size, shape, and spirit, differ widely in different climates. But let a male and a female of whatever climate be carried to a country where horses are in perfection, their progeny will improve gradually, and will acquire in time the perfection of their kind. Is not this a proof, that all <75> horses are of one kind? If so, men are not all of one kind; for if a White mix with a Black in whatever climate, or a Hottentot with a Samoide, the result will not be either an improvement of the kind, or the contrary, but a mongrel breed differing from both parents.

It is thus ascertained beyond any rational doubt, that there are different races or kinds of men, and that these races or kinds are naturally fitted for different climates: whence we have reason to conclude, that originally each kind was placed in its proper climate, whatever change may have happened in later times by war or commerce.

There is a remarkable fact that confirms the foregoing conjectures. As far back as history goes, or tradition kept alive by history, the earth was inhabited by savages divided into many small tribes, each tribe having a language peculiar to itself. Is it not natural to suppose, that these original tribes were different races of men, placed in proper climates, and left to form their own language?

Upon summing up the whole particulars mentioned above, would one hesitate <76> a moment to adopt the following opinion, were there no counterbalancing evidence, namely, "That God created many pairs of the human race, differing from each other both externally and internally; that he fitted these pairs for different climates, and placed each pair in its proper climate; that the peculiarities of the original pairs were preserved entire in their descendents; who, having no assistance but their natural talents, were left to gather knowledge from experience, and in particular were left (each tribe) to form a language for itself; that signs were sufficient for the original pairs, without any language but what nature suggests; and that a language was formed gradually, as a tribe increased in numbers and in different occupations, to make speech necessary"? But this opinion, however plausible, we are not permitted to adopt; being taught a different lesson by revelation, namely, That God created but a single pair of the human species. Though we cannot doubt of the authority of Moses, yet his account of the creation of man is not a little puzzling, as it seems to con-<77>tradict every one of the facts mentioned above. According to that account, different races of men were not created, nor were men framed originally for different climates. All men must have spoken the same language, that of our first parents. And what of all seems the most contradictory to that account, is the savage state: Adam, as Moses informs us, was endued by his Maker with an eminent degree of knowledge; and he certainly must have been an excellent preceptor to his children and their progeny, among whom he lived many generations. Whence then the degeneracy of all men into the savage state? To account for that dismal catastrophe, mankind must have suffered some terrible convulsion.

That terrible convulsion is revealed to us in the history of the tower of Babel, contained in the 11th chapter of Genesis, which is, "That for many centuries after the deluge, the whole earth was of one language, and of one speech; that they united to build a city on a plain in the land of Shinar, with a tower whose top might reach into heaven; that the Lord beholding the people to be one, and <78> to have all one language, and that nothing would be restrained from them which they imagined to do, confounded their language, that they might not understand one another; and scattered them abroad upon the face of all the earth." Here light breaks forth in the midst of darkness. By confounding the language of men, and scattering them abroad upon the face of all the earth, they were rendered savages. And to harden them for their new habitations, it was necessary that they should be divided into different kinds, fitted for different climates. Without an immediate change of bodily constitution, the builders of Babel could not possibly have subsisted in the burning region of Guinea, nor in the frozen region of Lapland; especially without houses, or any other convenience to protect them against a destructive climate. Against this history it has indeed been urged, "That the circumstances mentioned evince it to be purely an allegory; that men never were so frantic as to think of building a tower whose top might reach to heaven; and that it is grossly absurd, taking the matter lite-<79>rally, that the Almighty was afraid of men, and reduced to the necessity of saving himself by a miracle." But that this is a real history, must necessarily be admitted, as the confusion of Babel is the only known fact that can reconcile sacred and profane history.

And this leads us to consider the diversity of languages.* If the common

* As the social state is essential to man, and speech to the social state, the wisdom of Providence in fitting men for acquiring that necessary art, deserves more attention than is commonly bestowed on it. The Oran Outang has the external organs of speech in perfection; and many are puzzled to account why it never speaks. But the external organs

lan-<80>guage of men had not been confounded upon their undertaking the tower of Babel, I affirm, that there never could have been but one language. Antiquaries constantly suppose a migrating spirit in the original inhabitants of this earth; not only without evidence, but contrary to all probability. Men never desert their connections nor their country without necessity: fear of enemies and of wild beasts, as well as the attraction of society, are more than sufficient to restrain them from wandering; not to mention, that savages are peculiarly fond of their natal soil.* The <81> first migrations were probably occasioned by factions and civil wars; the next by commerce. Greece affords instances of the former, Phoenicia of the latter. Unless upon such occasions, members of a family or of a tribe will never retire farther from their fellows than is necessary for food; and by

---

of speech make but a small part of the necessary apparatus. The faculty of imitating sounds is an essential part; and wonderful would that faculty appear, were it not rendered familiar by daily practice: a child of two or three years is able, by nature alone, without the least instruction, to adapt its organs of speech to every articulate sound; and a child of four or five years can pitch its windpipe so as to emit a sound of any elevation, which enables it, with an ear, to imitate the songs it hears. But, above all the other parts, sense and understanding are essential to speech. A parrot can pronounce articulate sounds, and it has frequently an inclination to speak; but, for want of understanding, none of the kind can form a single sentence. Has an Oran Outang understanding to form a mental proposition? has he a faculty to express that proposition in sounds? and supposing him able to express what he sees and hears, what would he make of the connective and disjunctive particles?

* With respect to the supposed migrating spirit, even Bochart must yield to Kempfer in boldness of conjecture. After proving, from difference of language and from other circumstances, that Japan was not peopled by the Chinese, Kempfer, without the least hesitation, settles a colony there of those who thought of building the tower of Babel. Nay, he traces most minutely their route to Japan; and concludes, that they must have travelled with great expedition, because their language has no tincture of any other. He did not think it necessary to explain, what temptation they had to wander so far from home; nor why they settled in an island, not preferable either in soil or climate to many countries they must have traversed.

An ingenious French writer observes, that plausible reasons would lead one to conjecture, that men were more early polished in islands than in continents; as people crowded together soon find the necessity of laws to restrain them from mischief. And yet, says he, the manners of islanders and their laws are commonly the latest formed. A very simple reflection would have unfolded the mystery. Many many centuries did men exist without thinking of navigation. That art was not invented till men, straitened in their quarters upon the continent, thought of occupying adjacent islands.

retiring gradually, they lose neither their connections nor their manners, far less their language, which is in constant exercise. As far back as history carries us, tribes without number are discovered, each having a language peculiar to itself. Strabo (*a*) reports, that the <82> Albanians were divided into several tribes, differing in external appearance and in language. Caesar found in Gaul several such tribes; and Tacitus records the names of many tribes in Germany. There are a multitude of American tribes which to this day continue distinct from each other, and have each a different language. The mother-tongues at present, though numerous, bear no proportion to what formerly existed. We find original tribes gradually enlarging; by conquest frequently, and more frequently by the union of weak tribes for mutual defense. Such events lessen the number of languages. The Coptic is not a living language any where. The Celtic tongue, once extensive, is at present confined to the Highlands of Scotland, to Wales, to Britany, and to a part of Ireland. In a few centuries, it will share the fate of many other original tongues: it will totally be forgotten.

If men had not been scattered every where by the confusion of Babel, another particular must have occurred, differing no less from what has really happened than that now mentioned. As paradise is conjectured to have been situated in the <83> heart of Asia, the surrounding regions, for the reason above given, must have been first peopled; and the civilization and improvements of the mother-country were undoubtedly carried along to every new settlement. In particular, the colonies planted in America and the South Sea islands,[19] must have been highly polished; because, being at the greatest distance, they probably were the latest. And yet these and other remote people, the Mexicans and Peruvians excepted, remain to this day in the original savage state of hunting and fishing.

Thus, had not men wildly attempted to build a tower whose top might reach to heaven, all men would not only have had the same language, but would have made the same progress towards maturity of knowledge and civilization. That deplorable event reversed all nature: by scattering men over the face of all the earth, it deprived them of society, and rendered them

(*a*) Book 2.

19. In 1st edition: "in America, the South-sea islands, and the *Terra Australis incognita*" [1:43].

savages. From that state of degeneracy, they have been emerging gradually. Some nations, stimulated by their own nature, or by their climate, have made a ra-<84>pid progress; some have proceeded more slowly; and some continue savages. To trace out that progress toward maturity in different nations, is the subject of the present undertaking. <85>

BOOK I

Progress of Men Independent of Society

〇〇 S K E T C H I 〇〇

Progress respecting Food and Population[1]

In temperate climes, men fed originally on fruits that grow without culture, and on the flesh of land-animals. As such animals become shy when often hunted, there is a contrivance of nature, no less simple than effectual, which engages men to bear with chearfulness the fatigues of <86> hunting, and the uncertainty of capture; and that is, an appetite for hunting. Hunger alone is not sufficient: savages who act by sense, not by foresight, move not when the stomach is full; and it would be too late when the stomach is empty, to form a hunting-party. As that appetite is common to all savages whose food depends on hunting; it is an illustrious instance of providential care, the adapting the internal constitution of man to his external circumstances.* The ap-<87>petite for hunting, though among us little necessary

---

1. In 1st edition: "Progress of Men with respect to Food and Population"; in 2nd edition: "Progress of Food and Population."

* It would be an agreeable undertaking, to collect all the instances where the internal constitution of man is adapted to his external structure, and to other circumstances; but it would be a laborious work, as the instances are extremely numerous; and, in the course of the present undertaking, there will be occasion to mark several of them. "How finely are the external parts of animals adjusted to their internal dispositions! That strong and nervous leg armed with tearing fangs, how perfectly does it correspond to the fierceness

53

for food, is to this day remark-<88>able in young men, high and low, rich and poor. Natural propensities may be rendered faint or obscure, but never are totally eradicated.

Fish was not early the food of man. Water is not our element; and savages probably did not attempt to draw food from the sea or from rivers, till land-animals became scarce. Plutarch in his Symposiacs observes, that the Syrians and Greeks of old abstained from fish. Menelaus (*a*) complains, that his companions had been reduced by hunger to that food; and though the Grecian camp at the siege of Troy was on the sea-shore, there is not in Homer a single hint of their feeding on fish. We learn from Dion Cassius, that the Caledonians did not eat fish, though they had them in plenty;

---

of the lion! Had it been adorned like the human arm with fingers instead of fangs, the natural energies of a lion had been all of them defeated. That more delicate structure of an arm terminating in fingers so nicely diversified, how perfectly does it correspond to the pregnant invention of the human soul! Had these fingers been fangs, what had become of poor Art that procures us so many elegancies and utilities! 'Tis here we behold the harmony between the visible world and the invisible" (*b*). The following is another instance of the same kind, which I mention here because it falls not under common observation. How finely, in the human species, are the throat and the ear adjusted to each other, the one to emit musical sounds, the other to enjoy them! the one without the other would be an useless talent. May it not be justly thought, that to the power we have of emitting musical sounds by the throat, we owe the invention of musical instruments? A man would never think of inventing a musical instrument, but in order to imitate sounds that his ear had been delighted with. But there is a faculty in man still more remarkable, which serves to correct the organs of external sense, where they tend to mislead him. I give two curious instances. The image of every visible object is painted on the *retina tunica,* and by that means the object makes an impression on the mind. In what manner this is done, cannot be explained; because we have no conception how mind acts on body, or body on mind. But, as far as we can conceive or conjecture, a visible object ought to appear to us inverted, because the image painted on the *retina tunica* is inverted. But this is corrected by the faculty mentioned, which makes us perceive objects as they really exist. The other instance follows. As a man has two eyes, and sees with each of them, every object naturally ought to appear double; and yet with two eyes we see every object single, precisely as if we had but one. Many philosophers, Sir Isaac Newton in particular, have endeavoured to account for this phaenomenon by mechanical principles, but evidently without giving satisfaction. To explain this phaenomenon, it appears to me that we must have recourse to the faculty mentioned acting against mechanical principles. [[Note added in 2nd edition.]]

(*a*) Book 4. of the Odyssey.
(*b*) Harris [[*Philosophical Arrangements*]].

which is confirmed by Adamannus, a Scotch historian, in his <89> life of
St. Columba. The ancient Caledonians depended almost entirely on deer
for food; because in a cold country the fruits that grow spontaneously afford
little nourishment; and domestic animals, which at present so much
abound, were not early known in the north of Britain.

Antiquaries talk of acorns, nuts, and other shell-fruits, as the only vegetable food that men had originally, overlooking wheat, rice, barley, &c.
which must from the creation have grown spontaneously: for surely, when
agriculture first commenced, it did not require a miracle to procure the
seeds of these plants.* The <90> Laplanders, possessing a country where
corn will not grow, make bread of the inner bark of trees; and Linnaeus
reports, that swine there fatten on that food, as well as in Sweden upon
corn.

Plenty of food procured by hunting and fishing, promotes population:
but as consumption of food increases with population, wild animals, sorely
persecuted, become not only more rare, but more shy. Men, thus pinched
for food, are excited to try other means for supplying their wants. A fawn,
a kid, or a lamb, taken alive and tamed for amusement, suggested probably
flocks and herds, and introdu-<91>ced the shepherd-state. Changes are not
perfected but by slow degrees: hunting and fishing continue for a long time

---

* Writers upon natural history have been solicitous to discover the original climate
of these plants, but without much success. The original climate of plants left to nature,
cannot be a secret: but in countries well peopled, the plants mentioned are not left to
nature: the seeds are carefully gathered, and stored up for food. As this practice could
not fail to make these seeds scarce, agriculture was early thought of, which, by introducing plants into new soils and new climates, has rendered the original climate obscure.
If we can trace that climate, it must be in regions destitute of inhabitants, or but thinly
peopled. Anson found in the island Juan Fernandez many spots of ground covered with
oats [[sentence added in 2nd edition]]. The Sioux, a very small tribe in North America,
possess a vast country, where oats grow spontaneously in meadows and on the sides of
rivers, which make part of their food, without necessity of agriculture. While the French
possessed Port Dauphin, in the island of Madagascar, they raised excellent wheat. That
station was deserted many years ago; and wheat to this day grows naturally among the
grass in great vigour. In the country about Mount Tabor in Palestine, barley and oats
grow spontaneously. In the kingdom of Siam, there are many spots where rice grows
year after year, without any culture. Diodorus Siculus is our authority for saying, that in
the territory of Leontinum, and in other places of Sicily, wheat grew wild without any
culture. And it does so at present about Mount Etna.

favourite occupations; and the few animals that are domesticated, serve as
a common stock to be distributed among individuals, according to their
wants. But as the idle and indolent, though the least deserving, are thus the
greatest consumers of the common stock, an improvement crept in, that
every family should rear a stock for themselves. Men by that means being
taught to rely on their own industry, displayed the hoarding principle,
which multiplied flocks and herds exceedingly. And thus the shepherd-state
was perfected, plenty of food being supplied at home, without ranging the
woods or the waters. Hunting and fishing, being no longer necessary for
food, became an amusement merely, and a gratification of the original appetite for hunting.

The finger of God may be clearly traced in the provision made of animal
food for man. Gramenivorous animals, perhaps all, make palatable and
wholesome food. I except not the horse: some nations feed on it; others do
not, because <92> it is more profitable by its labour. Carnivorous animals,
generally speaking, make not wholesome food nor palatable. The first-
mentioned animals are gentle, and easily tamed: the latter are fierce, not
easily tamed, and uncertain in temper when tamed. Grass grows every
where in temperate regions; and men beside can multiply animal food without end, by training domestic animals to live on turnip, carrot, potatoe,
and other roots. Herodotus adds the following admirable reflection: "We
may rationally conjecture, that Divine Providence has rendered extremely
prolific such creatures as are naturally fearful, and serve for food, lest they
should be destroyed by constant consumption: whereas the rapacious and
cruel are almost barren. The hare, which is the prey of beasts, birds, and
men, is a great breeder: a lioness, on the contrary, the strongest and fiercest
of beasts, brings forth but once."

The shepherd-state is friendly to population. Men by plenty of food
multiply apace; and, in process of time, neighbouring tribes, straitened in
their pasture, go to war for extension of territory, or mi-<93>grate to land
not yet occupied. Necessity, the mother of invention, suggested agriculture.
When corn growing spontaneously was rendered scarce by consumption,
it was an obvious thought to propagate it by art: nature was the guide, which
carries on its work of propagation with seeds that drop from a plant in their
maturity, and spring up new plants. As the land was possessed in common,

the seed of course was sown in common; and the product was stored in a common repository, to be parcelled out among individuals in want, as the common stock of animals had been formerly. We have for our authority Diodorus Siculus, that the Celtiberians divided their land annually among individuals, to be laboured for the use of the public; and that the product was stored up, and distributed from time to time among the necessitous. A lasting division of the land among the members of the state, securing to each man the product of his own skill and labour, was a great spur to industry, and multiplied food exceedingly. Population made a rapid progress, and government became an art; <94> for agriculture and commerce cannot flourish without salutary laws.

Natural fruits ripen to greater perfection in a temperate than in a cold climate, and cultivation is more easy; which circumstances make it highly probable, that agriculture became first an art in temperate climes. The culture of corn was so early in Greece, as to make a branch of its fabulous history: in Egypt it must have been coeval with the inhabitants; for while the Nile overflows, they cannot subsist without corn (*a*). Nor without corn could the ancient monarchies of Assyria and Babylon have been so populous and powerful as they are said to have been. In the northern parts of Europe, wheat, barley, pease, and perhaps oats, are foreign plants: as the climate is not friendly to corn, agriculture must have crept northward by slow degrees; and, even at present, it requires no small portion both of skill and industry to bring corn to maturity in such a climate. Hence it may be inferred with certainty, that the shepherd-state continued longer in northern climates than in those nearer the sun. <95> Cold countries, however, are friendly to population; and the northern people, multiplying beyond the food that can be supplied by flocks and herds, were compelled to throw off many swarms in search of new habitations. Their frequent migrations were for many years a dreadful scourge to neighbouring nations. People, amazed at the multitude of the invaders, judged, that the countries from whence they issued must have been exceedingly populous; and hence the North was termed *officina gentium*. But scarcity of food in the shepherd-state was the true cause; the north of Europe, in all probability, is as well

(*a*) Historical Law-tracts, tract I.

peopled at present as ever it was, though its migrations have ceased, corn and commerce having put an end to that terrible scourge.* Denmark at present feeds <96> 2,000,000 inhabitants; Sweden, according to a list made up *anno* 1760, 2,383,113; and these countries must be much more populous than of old, when over-run with immense woods, and when agriculture was unknown. Had the Danes and Norwegians been acquainted with agriculture in the ninth and tenth centuries, when they poured out multitudes upon their neighbours, they would not have ventured their lives in frail vessels upon a tempestuous ocean, in order to distress nations who were not their enemies. But hunger is a cogent motive; and hunger gave to these pirates superiority in arms above every nation that enjoyed plenty at home. Luckily such depredations must have intervals; for as they necessarily occasion great havock even among the victors, the remainder finding sufficiency of <97> food at home, rest there till an increasing population forces them again to action.† Agriculture, which fixes people to a spot, is an invincible obstacle to migration; and happy it is for Europe, that this art, now universally diffused, has put an end for ever to that scourge, more destructive than a pestilence: people find now occupation and subsistence at home, without infesting others. Agriculture is a great blessing: it not only affords us food in plenty, but secures the fruits of our industry from hungry and rapacious invaders.‡

* *Aliquando bonus dormitat Homerus.* Montesquieu accounts as follows for the great swarms of Barbarians that overwhelmed the Roman empire. "Ces essaims de Barbares qui sortirent autrefois du nord, ne paroissent plus aujourd'hui. Les violences des Romains avoient fait retirer les peuple du midi au nord: tandis que la force qui les contenoit subsista, ils y resterent; quand elle fut affoiblie, ils se repandirent de toutes parts." *Grandeur des Romains,* c. 16.—[*In English thus:* "The swarms of Barbarians who poured formerly from the north, appear no more. The violence of the Roman arms had driven those nations from the south towards the north: there they remained during the subsistence of that force which retained them; but that being once weakened, they spread abroad to every quarter."]—It has quite escaped him, that men cannot, like water, be damm'd up without being fed.

† Joannes Magnus, in the 8th book of his history of the Goths, mentions, that a third part of the Swedes, being compelled by famine to leave their native country, founded the kingdom of the Longobards in Italy.

‡ Mahomet Bey, King of Tunis, was dethroned by his subjects; but having the reputation of the philosopher's stone, he was restored by the Dey of Algiers, upon promising

That the progress above traced must have proceeded from some vigorous impulse, will be admitted, considering the <98> prevailing influence of custom: once hunters, men will always be hunters, till they be forced out of that state by some overpowering cause. Hunger, the cause here assigned, is of all the most overpowering; and the same cause, overcoming indolence and idleness, has introduced manufactures, commerce, and variety of arts.*

<99>

The progress here delineated has, in all temperate climates of the Old World, been precisely uniform; but it has been different in the extremes of cold and hot climates. In very cold regions, which produce little vegetable food for man, the hunter-state was originally essential. In temperate regions, as observed above, men subsisted partly on vegetable food, which is more or less plentiful in proportion to the heat of the climate. In the torrid zone, natural fruits are produced in such plenty and perfection, as to be more than sufficient for a moderate population: and, in case of extraordinary population, the transition to husbandry is easy. There are found, accordingly, in every populous country of the torrid zone, crops of rice, maize, roots, and other vegetable food, raised by the hand of man. As hunting becomes thus less and less necessary in the progress from cold to hot countries, the appetite for hunting keeps pace with that progress: it is vig-

---

to communicate the secret to him. Mahomet, with pomp and solemnity, sent a plough; intimating, that agriculture is the strength of a kingdom, and that the only philosopher's stone is a good crop, which may be easily converted into gold.

* M. Buffon, discoursing of America, "Is it not singular," says he, "that in a world composed almost wholly of savages, there never should have been any society or commerce between them and the animals about them? There was not a domestic animal in America when discovered by Columbus, except among the polished people of Mexico and Peru. Is not this a proof, that man, in his savage state, is but a sort of brute animal; having no faculties but to provide for his subsistence, by attacking the weak, and avoiding the strong; and having no idea of his superiority over other animals, which he never once thinks of bringing under subjection? This is the more surprising, as most of the American animals are by nature docile and timid." Our author, without being sensible of it, lays a foundation for a satisfactory answer to these questions, by what he adds, That in the whole compass of America, when discovered by the Spaniards, there were not half the number of people that are in Europe; and that such scarcity of men favoured greatly the propagation of wild animals, which had few enemies, and much food. Was it not obvious to conclude from these premises, that while men, who by nature are fond of hunting, have game in plenty, they never think of turning shepherds?

orous in very cold countries, where men depend on hunting for <100> food: it is less vigorous in temperate countries, where they are partly fed with natural fruits; and there is scarce any vestige of it in hot countries, where vegetables are the food of men, and where meat is an article of luxury. The original occupation of savages, both in cold and temperate climates, is hunting, altogether essential in the former, as the only means of procuring food. The next step of the progress in both, is the occupation of a shepherd; and there the progress stops short in very cold regions, unfit for corn. Lapland, in particular, produces no vegetable but moss, which is the food of no animal but the rain-deer. This circumstance solely is what renders Lapland habitable by men. Without rain-deer, the sea-coasts within the reach of fish would admit some inhabitants; but the inland parts would be a desert. As the swiftness of that animal makes it not an easy prey, the taming it for food must have been early attempted; and its natural docility made the attempt succeed. It yields to no other animal in usefulness: it is equal to a horse for draught: its flesh is excellent food; and the female gives milk more <101> nourishing than that of a cow: its fur is fine; and the leather made of its skin is both soft and durable. In Tartary, though a great part of it lies in a temperate zone, there is little corn. As far back as tradition reaches, the Tartars have had flocks and herds; and yet, in a great measure, they not only continue hunters, but retain the ferocity of that state: they are not fond of being shepherds, and have no knowledge of husbandry. This, in appearance, is singular; but nothing happens without a cause. Tartary is one continued mountain from west to east, rising high above the countries to the south, and declining gradually to the northern ocean, without a single hill to intercept the bitter blasts of the north. A few spots excepted, a tree above the size of a shrub cannot live in it.* In Europe, the mountains of Norway and Lapland are a comfortable screen against the north wind: whence it is, that the land about Stockholm (*a*) pro-<102> duces both trees and corn; and even about Abo (*b*) the climate is tolerable. Great Tartary abounds with pasture; but extreme cold renders it very little

* May not a similar situation in some parts of North America be partly the occasion of the cold that is felt there, beyond what Europe feels in the same latitude?

(*a*) Latitude 59.

(*b*) Latitude 61.

capable of corn. Through all Chinese Tartary, even as low as the 43d degree of latitude, the frost continues seven or eight months yearly; and that country, though in the latitude of France, is as cold as Iceland. The causes are its nitrous soil, and its height, without any shelter from the west wind, that has passed through an immense continent extremely cold. A certain place near the source of the river Kavamhuran, and within 80 leagues of the great wall, was found by Father Verbeist to be 3000 geometrical paces above the level of the sea. Thus the Tartars, like the Laplanders, are chained to the shepherd-state, and can never advance to be husbandmen. If population among them ever become so considerable as to require more food than the shepherd-state can supply, migration will be their only resource.

In every step of the progress, the torrid zone differs. We have no evidence that either the hunter or shepherd state ever <103> existed there: the inhabitants, at present, subsist on vegetable food; and probably did so from the beginning. In Manila, one of the Philippine islands, the trees bud, blossom, and bear fruit all the year round. The natives, driven by Spanish invaders from the sea-coast to the inland parts, have no particular place of abode, but live under the shelter of trees, which afford them food as well as habitation; and, when the fruit is consumed in one spot, they remove to another. The orange, lemon, and other European trees, bear fruit twice a-year: a sprig planted bears fruit within the year. And this picture of Manila answers to numberless places in the torrid zone. The Marian or Ladrone islands are extremely populous, and yet the inhabitants live entirely on fish, fruits, and roots. The inhabitants of the new Philippine islands live on cocoa-nuts, salads, roots, and fish. The inland negroes make but one meal a-day, which is in the evening. Their diet is plain, consisting mostly of rice, fruits, and roots. The island of Otaheite is healthy, the people tall and well made; and by temperance, vegetables and fish being their chief nourishment, they live to <104> a good old age, almost without any ailment. There is no such thing known among them as rotten teeth: the very smell of wine or spirits is disagreeable; and they never deal in tobacco nor spiceries. In many places Indian corn is the chief nourishment, which every man plants for himself. The inhabitants of Biledulgerid and the desert of Zaara have but two meals a-day, one in the morning, and one in the evening. Being temperate, and strangers to diseases arising from luxury, they generally live to a great age. Sixty with them is the prime of life, as thirty is in Europe. An inhabitant of Madagascar will travel two or three days without any food but a sugar-cane. There is indeed little appetite for animal food in hot climates; though beef and fowl have in small quantities been introduced to the tables of the great, as articles of luxury. In America are observable some variations from the progress; but these are reserved for a separate sketch (*a*).

With respect to population, that plenty of food is its chief cause, may be illustrated by the following computation. The south-<105>ern provinces of China produce two crops of rice in a year, sometimes three; and an acre, well cultivated, gives food to ten persons. The peasants go almost naked; and the better sort wear but a single garment made of cotton, of which as much is produced upon an acre as may clothe four or five hundred. Hence the extreme populousness of China and other rice countries. The Cassave root, which serves the Americans for bread, is produced in such plenty, that an acre of it will feed more persons than six acres of wheat. It is not, then, for want of food that America is ill peopled. That Negroland is well peopled is past doubt, considering the great annual draughts from that country to America, without any apparent diminution of numbers. Instances are not extremely rare, of 200 children born to one man by his different wives. Food must be in great plenty, to enable a man to maintain so many children. It would require wonderful skill and labour to make Europe so populous: an acre and a half of wheat is barely sufficient to maintain a single family of peasants; and their clothing requires many acres more. A country <106> where the inhabitants live chiefly by hunting, must be very thin of inhabitants, as 10,000 acres, or double that number, are no more than sufficient for maintaining a single family. If the multiplication of animals depended chiefly on fecundity, wolves would be more numerous than sheep: a great proportion of the latter are deprived of the procreating power, and many more of them are killed than of the former: yet we see every where large flocks of sheep, seldom a wolf; for what reason, other than that the former have plenty of food, the latter very little? A wolf resembles a savage who lives by hunting, and consumes the game of five or six thousand acres.

(*a*) Book 2. sketch 12.

Waving the question, Whether the human race be the offspring of one pair or of many, it appears the intention of Providence, that the earth should be peopled, and population be kept up by the ordinary means of procreation. By these means a tribe soon becomes too populous for the primitive state of hunting and fishing: it may even become too populous for the shepherd-state; but it cannot easily become too populous for husbandry. In the <107> two former states, food must decrease in quantity as consumers increase in number: but agriculture has the signal property of producing, by industry, food in proportion to the number of consumers. In fact, the greatest quantities of corn and of cattle are commonly produced in the most populous districts, where each family has its proportion of land. An ancient Roman, sober and industrious, made a shift to maintain his family on the produce of a few acres.*

The bounty given in Britain for exporting corn is friendly to population in two respects; first, because husbandry requires many hands; and, next, because the bounty lowers the price of corn at home. To give a bounty for exporting cattle would obstruct population; because pasture requires few hands, and exportation raises the price of cattle at home. From the single port of Cork, *an.* 1735, were ex-<108>ported 107,161 barrels of beef, 7379 barrels of pork, 13,461 casks of butter, and 85,727 firkins of the same commodity. Thus a large portion of Ireland is set apart for feeding other nations. What addition of strength would it not be to Britain, if that large quantity of food were consumed at home by useful manufacturers!

No manufacture contributes more to population than that of silk. It employs as many hands as wool; and it withdraws no land from tillage or pasture.[2]

Lapland is but thinly inhabited even for the shepherd-state, the country being capable of maintaining a greater number of rain-deer, and conse-

---

* Scotland must have been very ill peopled in the days of its fifth James, when at one hunting in the high country of Roxburghshire, that prince killed three hundred and sixty red-deer; and in Athol, at another time, six hundred, beside roes, wolves, foxes, and wild cats.

2. Paragraph added in 2nd edition.

quently a greater number of the human species than are found in it. Yet
the Laplanders are well acquainted with private property: every family has
tame rain-deer of their own, to the extent sometimes of four or five hundred: they indeed appear to have more rain-deer than there is a demand
for. Why then is Lapland so thinly peopled? Either it must have been but
lately planted, or the inhabitants are not prolific. I incline to the latter, upon
the authority of Scheffer. Tartary is also but thinly <109> peopled; and as
I find not that the Tartars are less prolific than their neighbours, it is probable that Tartary, being the most barren country in Asia, has not been early
planted. At the same time, population has been much retarded by the restless and roaming spirit of that people: it is true, they have been forced into
the shepherd-state by want of food; but so averse are they to the sedentary
life of a shepherd, that they trust their cattle to slaves, and persevere in their
favourite occupation of hunting. This disposition has been a dreadful pest
to the human species, the Tartars having made more extensive conquests,
and destroyed more men, than any other nation known in history: more
cruel than tigers, they seemed to have no delight but in blood and massacre,
without any regard either to sex or age.* Luckily for the human species, rich
spoils dazzled their eyes, and roused an appetite for wealth. Avarice is sometimes productive of good: it moved these monsters <110> to sell the conquered people for slaves, which preserved the lives of millions. Conquests,
however successful, cannot go on for ever; they are not accomplished without great loss of men; and the conquests of the Tartars depopulated their
country.

But as some centuries have elapsed without any considerable eruption
of that fiery people, their numbers must at present be considerable by the
ordinary progress of population. Have we not reason to dread new erup-
tions, like what formerly happened? Our foreknowledge of future events
extends not far; but in all appearance we have nothing to fear from that
quarter. The Tartars subdued a great part of the world by ferocity and undaunted courage, supported by liberty and independence. They acknowl-

---

* When the Tartars under Genhizkan conquered China, it was seriously deliberated,
whether they should not kill all the inhabitants, and convert that vast country into
pasture-fields for their cattle.

edged Genhizkan as their leader in war, but were as far from being slaves, as the Franks were when they conquered Gaul. Tamerlane again enjoyed but a substituted power, and never had the boldness to assume the title of Chan or Emperor. But the Tartars have submitted to the same yoke of despotism that their ferocity imposed upon <111> others; and being now governed by a number of petty tyrants, their courage is broken by slavery, and they are no longer formidable to the rest of mankind.*

Depopulation enters into the present sketch as well as population. The latter follows not with greater certainty from equality of property, than the former from inequality. In every great state, where the people by prosperity and opulence are sunk into voluptuousness, we hear daily complaints of depopulation. Cookery depopulates like a pestilence; because, when it becomes an art, it brings within the compass of one stomach what is sufficient for ten in days of temperance; and is so far worse than a pestilence, that the people <112> never recruit again. The inhabitants of France devour at present more food than the same number did formerly. The like is observable in Britain, and in every country where luxury abounds. Remedies are proposed and put in practice, celibacy disgraced, marriage encouraged, and rewards given for a numerous offspring. All in vain! The only effectual remedies are to encourage husbandry, and to repress luxury. Olivares hoped to repeople Spain by encouraging matrimony. Abderam, a Mahometan king of Cordova, was a better politician. By encouraging industry, and procuring plenty of food, he repeopled his kingdom in less than thirty years.†

---

* "Gallos in bellis floruisse accepimus," says Tacitus in his life of Agricola; "mox segnities cum otio intravit, amissa virtute pariter ac libertate." [*In English thus:* "We have heard that the Gauls formerly made a figure in war; but becoming a prey to indolence, the consequence of peace, they lost at once their valour and their liberty."]—Spain, which defended itself with great bravery against the Romans, became an easy prey to the Vandals in the fifth century. When attacked by the Romans, it was divided into many free states: when attacked by the Vandals, it was enervated by slavery under Roman despotism.

† A foundling-hospital is a greater enemy to population, than liberty to expose infants, which is permitted to parents in China and in some other countries. Both of them, indeed, encourage matrimony: but in such hospitals, thousands perish yearly beyond the ordinary proportion; whereas few infants perish by the liberty of exposing them, parental affection prevailing commonly over the distress of poverty. And, upon the whole, population gains more by that liberty than it loses.

Luxury is a deadly enemy to population, not only by intercepting food from the industrious, but by weakening the power of <113> procreation. Indolence accompanies voluptuousness, or rather is a branch of it: women of rank employ others to move them, being too delicate to move themselves; and a woman enervated by indolence and intemperance, is ill qualified for the severe labour of child-bearing. Hence it is, that people of rank, where luxury prevails, are not prolific. This infirmity not only prevents population, but increases luxury, by accumulating wealth among a few blood-relations. A barren woman among the labouring poor, is a wonder. Could women of rank be persuaded to make a trial, they would find more self-enjoyment in temperance and exercise, than in the most refined luxury; nor would they have cause to envy others the blessing of a numerous and healthy offspring.

Luxury is not a greater enemy to population by enervating men and women, than despotism is by reducing them to slavery, and destroying industry. Despotism is a greater enemy to the human species than an Egyptian plague; for, by rendering men miserable, it weakens both the appetite for procreation and the power. <114> Free states, on the contrary, are always populous: a man who is happy, longs for children to make them also happy; and industry enables him to accomplish his longing. This observation is verified from the history of Greece, and of the Lesser Asia: the inhabitants anciently were free and numerous: the present inhabitants are reduced by slavery to a small number. A pestilence destroys those only who exist, and the loss is soon repaired; but despotism, as above observed, strikes at the very root of population.

An overflowing quantity of money in circulation, is another cause of depopulation. In a nation that grows rich by commerce, the price of labour increases with the quantity of circulating coin, which of course raises the price of manufactures; and manufacturers, who cannot find a vent for their high-rated goods in foreign markets, must give over business and commence beggars, or retire to another country where they may have a prospect of success. But luckily, there is a remedy, in that case, to prevent depopulation: land is cultivated to greater perfection by the spade than by the plough; and the more <115> plentiful crops produced by the former, are fully sufficient to defray the additional expence. This is a resource for employing those who cannot make bread as manufacturers, and deserves well the attention of the legislature. The advantage of the spade is conspicuous with respect to war; it provides a multitude of robust men for recruiting the army, the want of whom may be supplied by the plough, till they return in peace to their former occupation. <116>

Progress of Property[1]

Among the senses inherent in man, the sense of property is eminent. That sense is the foundation of *yours* and *mine,* a distinction which no human being is ignorant of. By that sense, wild animals, caught with labour or art, are perceived to belong to the hunter or fisher: they become his *property.* There is the same perception of property with respect to wild animals tamed for use, with their progeny. A field separated from the common, and cultivated by a man for bread to himself and family, is equally perceived to be his property (*a*).

The sense of property is slower in its growth toward maturity than the external senses, which are perfect even in childhood; but it ripens more early than the sense of congruity, of symmetry, of dignity, of grace, and the other refined sen-<117>ses, which scarce make any figure before the age of manhood. Children discover a sense of property in distinguishing their own chair, and their own spoon. In them, however, it is faint and obscure, requiring time to ripen. The gradual progress of that sense, from its infancy among savages to its maturity among polished nations, is one of the most instructive articles that belong to the present undertaking. But as that article makes a part of Historical Law-tracts (*b*), nothing remains here but a few gleanings.

Man is by nature a hoarding animal, having an appetite for storing up things of use; and the sense of property is bestowed on men, for securing

(*a*) See Principles of Morality and Natural Religion, p. 77. edit. 2.
(*b*) Tract 3.
1. In 1st edition: "Progress of Men with respect to Property."

to them what they thus store up. Hence it appears, that things destined by Providence for our sustenance and accommodation, were not intended to be possessed in common. It is even probable, that in the earliest ages every man separately hunted for himself and his family. But chance prevails in that occupation; and it may frequently happen, that while some get more than enough, others must go supperless to bed. <118> Sensible of that inconvenience, it crept into practice, for hunting and fishing to be carried on in common.* We find, accordingly, the practice of hunting and fishing in common, even among gross savages. Those of New Holland, above mentioned, live upon small fish dug out of the sand when the sea retires. Sometimes they get plenty, sometimes very little; and all is <119> broiled and eat in common. After eating they go to rest: they return to their fishing next ebb of the tide, whether it be day or night, foul or fair; for go they must, or starve. In small tribes, where patriotism is vigorous, or in a country thinly peopled in proportion to its fertility, the living in common is agreeable: but in a large state where selfishness prevails, or in any state where great population requires extraordinary culture, the best method is to permit every man to shift for himself and his family: men wish to labour for themselves; and they labour more ardently for themselves, than for the public. Private property became more and sacred in the progress of arts and manufactures: to allow an artist of superior skill no profit above others, would be a sad discouragement to industry, and be scarce consistent with justice.

The sense of property is not confined to the human species. The beavers

---

* Inequalities of chance, which are great in a few trials, vanish almost entirely when an operation is frequently reiterated during a course of time. Did every man's subsistence depend on the fruits of his own field; many would die of hunger, while others wallowed in plenty. Barter and commerce among the inhabitants of a district, lessen the hazard of famine: the commerce of corn through a large kingdom, such as France or Britain, lessens it still more. Extend that commerce through Europe, through the world, and there will remain scarce a vestige of the inequalities of chance: the crop of corn may fail in one province, or in one kingdom; but that it should fail universally, is beyond the varieties of chance: the same observation holds in every other matter of chance: one's gain or loss at game for a night, for a week, may be considerable; but carry on the game for a year, and so little of chance remains, that it is almost the same whether one play for a guinea or for twenty. Hence a skilful insurer never ventures much upon one bottom, but multiplies his bargains as much as possible: the more bargains he is engaged in, the greater is the probability of gain.

perceive the timber they store up for food, to be their property; and the
bees seem to have the same perception with respect to their winter's provision of honey. Sheep know when they are in a trespass, and run to <120>
their own pasture on the first glimpse of a man. Monkies do the same when
detected in robbing an orchard. Sheep and horned cattle have a sense of
property with respect to their resting-place in a fold or inclosure, which
every one guards against the incroachments of others. He must be a sceptic
indeed, who denies that perception to rooks: thieves there are among them
as among men; but if a rook purloin a stick from another's nest, a council
is held, much chattering ensues, and the *lex talionis* is applied by demol-
ishing the nest of the criminal. To man are furnished rude materials only:
to convert these into food and clothing requires industry; and if he had not
a sense that the product of his labour belongs to himself, his industry would
be faint. In general, it is pleasant to observe, that the sense of property is
always given where it is useful, and never but where it is useful.

An ingenious writer, describing the inhabitants of Guiana, who continue hunters and fishers, makes an eloquent harangue upon the happiness
they enjoy, in having few wants and desires, and little notion of private
property.

The manners of these <121> Indians exhibit an amiable picture of pri-
meval innocence and happiness. The ease with which their few wants are
supplied, renders division of land unnecessary; nor does it afford any
temptation to fraud or violence. That proneness to vice, which among
civilized nations is esteemed a propensity of nature, has no existence in a
country where every man enjoys in perfection his native freedom and independence, without hurting or being hurt by others. A perfect equality
of rank, banishing all distinctions but of age and personal merit, promotes
freedom in conversation, and firmness in action, and suggests no desires
but what may be gratified with innocence. Envy and discontent cannot
subsist where there is perfect equality; we scarce even hear of a discon-
tented lover, as there is no difference of rank and fortune, the common
obstacles that prevent fruition. Those who have been unhappily accustomed to the refinements of luxury, will scarce be able to conceive, that
an Indian, with no covering but what modesty requires, with no shelter
that deserves that name of a <122> house, and with no food but of the

coarsest kind, painfully procured by hunting, can feel any happiness: and yet, to judge from external appearance, the happiness of these people may be envied by the wealthy of the most refined nations; and justly, because their ignorance of extravagant desires, and endless pursuits, that torment the great world, excludes every wish beyond the present. In a word, the inhabitants of Guiana are an example of what Socrates justly observes, that they who want the least, approach the nearest to the gods, who want nothing.[2]

It is admitted, that the innocence of such savages, here painted in fine colours, is in every respect more amiable than the luxury of the opulent. But is our author unacquainted with a middle state more suitable than either extreme to the dignity of human nature? The appetite for property is not bestowed upon us in vain: it has given birth to many arts: it is highly beneficial by furnishing opportunity for gratifying the most dignified natural affections; for without private property, what place <123> would there be for benevolence or charity (a)? Without private property there would be no industry; and without industry, men would remain savages for ever.

The appetite for property, in its nature a great blessing, degenerates, I acknowledge, into a great curse when it transgresses the bounds of moderation. Before money was introduced, the appetite seldom was immoderate, because plain necessaries were its only objects. But money is a species of property, of such extensive use as greatly to inflame the appetite. Money prompts men to be industrious; and the beautiful productions of industry and art, rousing the imagination, excite a violent desire for grand houses, fine gardens, and for every thing gay and splendid. Habitual wants multiply: luxury and sensuality gain ground: the appetite for property becomes headstrong, and must be gratified, even at the expence of justice and honour. Examples of this progress are without number; and yet the following history deserves to be kept in memory, as a striking and lamentable illustration. Hispaniola was that part of A-<124>merica which Columbus first discovered *anno* 1497. He landed upon the territory of Guacanaric, one of the principal Cacics of the island. That prince, who had nothing barbarous

(a) Historical Law Tracts, Tract 3.
2. Kames is quoting from Bancroft's *Essay on the Natural History of Guiana.*

in his manners, received his guests with cordiality, and encouraged his people to vie with one another in obliging them. To gratify the Spanish appetite
for gold, they parted freely with their richest ornaments; and, in return,
were satisfied with glass beads, and such baubles. The Admiral's ship having
been dashed against the rocks in a hurricane, Guacanaric was not wanting
to his friend on that occasion: he convened a number of men to assist in
unloading the ship; and attended himself till the cargo was safely lodged.
The Admiral having occasion to return to Spain, left a part of his crew
behind; who, forgetting the lessons of moderation he had taught them,
turned licentious. The remonstrances of Guacanaric were fruitless: they
seized upon the gold and wives of the Indians; and in general treated them
with great cruelty. Such enormities did not long pass unresented: the rapacious Spaniards, after much bloodshed, were shut up in <125> their fort,
and reduced to extremity. Unhappily a reinforcement arrived from Spain:
a long and bloody war ensued, which did not end till the islanders were
entirely subdued. Of this island, about 200 leagues in length, and between
sixty and eighty in breadth, a Spanish historian bears witness, that the inhabitants amounted to a million when Columbus landed.* The Spaniards,
relentless in their cruelty, forced these poor people to abandon the culture
of their fields, and to retire to the woods and mountains. Hunted like wild
beasts even in these retreats, they fled from mountain to mountain, till hunger and fatigue, which destroyed more than the sword, made them deliver
themselves up to their implacable enemies. There remained at that time but
60,000, who were divided among the Spaniards as slaves. Excessive fatigue
in the mines, and want even of necessaries, reduced them in five years to
14,000. Considering them to be only beasts of burden, they would have
yielded more profit had they been <126> treated with less inhumanity. Avarice frequently counteracts its own end: by grasping too much, it loses all.
The Emperor Charles resolved to apply some remedy; but being retarded
by various avocations, he got intelligence that the poor Indians were totally
extirpated. And they were so in reality, a handful excepted, who lay hid in
the mountains, and subsisted as by a miracle in the midst of their enemies.

---

* The numbers possibly are exaggerated. But whether a million, or a half of that
number, the moral is the same.

That handful were discovered many years after by some hunters, who treated them with humanity, regreting perhaps the barbarity of their fore-fathers. The poor Indians, docile and submissive, embraced the Christian religion, and assumed by degrees the manners and customs of their masters. They still exist, and live by hunting and fishing.

Affection for property! Janus double-faced, productive of many blessings, but degenerating often to be a curse. In thy right hand, Industry, a cornucopia *of plenty:* in thy left, Avarice, a Pandora's box *of deadly poison.*

<127>

Origin and Progress of Commerce

The few wants of men in the first stage of society, are supplied by barter in its rudest form. In barter, the rational consideration is, what is wanted by the one, and what can be spared by the other. But savages are not always so clear-sighted: a savage who wants a knife, will give for it any thing that is less useful to him at the time, without considering either the present wants of the person he is dealing with, or his own future wants. An inhabitant of Guiana will for a fish-hook give more at one time, than at another he will give for a hatchet, or for a gun. Kempfer reports, that an inhabitant of Puli Timor, an island adjacent to Malacca, will, for a bit of coarse linen not worth three-halfpence, give provisions worth three or four shillings. But people improve by degrees, attending to what is wanted on the one side, and to what can be spared on the other; and in that lesson, <128> the American savages in our neighbourhood are not a little expert.

Barter or permutation, in its original form, proved miserably deficient when men and their wants multiplied. That sort of commerce cannot be carried on at a distance; and, even among neighbours, it does not always happen that the one can spare what the other wants. Barter is somewhat enlarged by covenants: a bushel of wheat is delivered to me, upon my promising an equivalent at a future time. But what if I have nothing that my neighbour may have occasion for? or what if my promise be not relied on? Thus barter, even with the aid of covenants, proves still defective. The numberless wants of men cannot readily be supplied, without some commodity in general estimation, which will be gladly accepted in exchange for every other. That commodity ought not to be bulky, nor be expensive in keeping, nor be consumeable by time. Gold and silver are metals that possess these

74

properties in an eminent degree. They are at the same time perfectly ho-
mogeneous in whatever country produced: two masses of pure gold or of
pure silver <129> are always equal in value, provided they be of the same
weight. These metals are also divisible into small parts, convenient to be
given for goods of small value.*

Gold and silver, when introduced into commerce, were probably bartered, like other commodities, by bulk merely. Rock-salt in Ethiopia, white
as snow, and hard as stone, is to this day bartered in that manner with other
goods. It is dug out of the mountain Lafta, formed into plates a foot long,
and three inches broad and thick; and a portion is broken off equivalent
in value to the thing wanted. But more ac-<130>curacy came to be introduced into the commerce of gold and silver: instead of being given loosely
by bulk, every portion was weighed in scales: and this method of barter is
practised in China, in Ethiopia, and in many other countries. Even weight
was at length discovered to be an imperfect standard. Ethiopian salt may
be proof against adulteration; but weight is no security against mixing gold
and silver with base metals. To prevent that fraud, pieces of gold and silver

* Origo emendi vendendique à permutationibus coepit. Olim enim non ita erat num-
mus: neque aliud *merx,* aliud *pretium* vocabatur; sed unusquisque, secundum necessi-
tatem temporum, ac rerum, utilibus inutilia permutabat, quando plerumque evenit, ut
quod alteri superest, alteri desit. Sed quia non semper, nec facile concurrebat, ut, cum
tu haberes quod ego desiderarem, invicem haberem, quod tu accipere velles, electa materia est, cujus publica ac perpetua aestimatio difficultatibus permutationum, aequalitate
quantitatis subveniret: ea [que] materia forma publica percussa, usum dominiumque non
tam ex substantia praebet, quam ex quantitate; nec ultra *merx* utrumque, sed alterum
pretium vocatur; *l.* 1. *Digest, De contrahenda emptione.* [["The origin of purchase and
sale is derived from exchanges, for formerly money was not known, and there was no
name for merchandise or the price of anything, but every one, in accordance with the
requirements of the time and circumstances, exchanged articles which were useless to
him for other things which he needed; for it often happens that what one has a super-
abundance of, another lacks. But, for the reason that it did not always or readily happen
that you had what I wanted, or, on the other hand, that I had what you were willing to
take, a substance was selected whose public and perpetual value, by its uniformity as a
medium of exchange, overcame the difficulties arising from barter, and this substance,
having been coined by public authority, represented use and ownership, not so much on
account of the material itself as by its value, and both articles were no longer designated
merchandise, but one of them was called the price of the other": *The Civil Law: Digest,*
bk. XVIII, Title 1 ("Concerning the contract of purchase"); *Civil Law,* trans. Scott, vol.
5, p. 3. Note added in 2nd edition.]]

are impressed with a public stamp, vouching both the purity and quantity; and such pieces are termed *coin*. This was a notable improvement in commerce; and was probably at first thought complete. It was not foreseen, that these metals wear by much handling in the course of circulation; and consequently, that in time the public stamp is reduced to be a voucher of the purity only, not of the quantity. Hence proceed manifold inconveniencies; for which no other remedy occurs, but to restore the former method of weighing, trusting to the stamp for the purity only. This proves an embarrassment in commerce, which is remedied by the use of paper-<131>money. And paper-money is attended with another advantage, that of preventing the loss of much gold and silver by wearing. Formerly in China, gold and silver were coined as among us; but the wearing of coin by handling obliged them to recur to scales; and now weight alone is relied on for determining the quantity. Copper is the only metal that is circulated among them without weighing; and it is with it that small debts are paid, and small purchases made.[1]

When gold or silver in bullion is exchanged with other commodities, such commerce passes under the common name of *barter* or *permutation:* when current coin is exchanged, such commerce is termed *buying* and *selling;* and the money exchanged is termed *the price of the goods.*

As commerce cannot be carried on to any extent without a standard for comparing goods of different kinds, and as every commercial country is possessed of such a standard, it seems difficult to say by what means the standard has been established. It is plainly not founded on nature; for the different kinds of goods have naturally no common measure by <132> which they can be valued: two quarters of wheat can be compared with twenty; but what rule have we for comparing wheat with broad cloth, or either of them with gold, or gold with silver or copper? Several ingenious writers have endeavoured to account for the comparative value of commodities, by reducing them all to the labour employed in raising food; which labour is said to be a standard for measuring the value of all other labour, and consequently of all things produced by labour. "If, for example, a bushel of wheat and an ounce of silver be produced by the same quantity

1. "And paper-money is . . . small purchases made": added in 2nd edition.

of labour, will they not be equal in value?" This standard is imperfect in many respects. I observe, first, that to give it a plausible appearance, there is a necessity to maintain, contrary to fact, that all materials on which labour is employed are of equal value. It requires as much labour to make a brass candlestick as one of silver, tho' far from being of the same value. A bushel of wheat may sometimes equal in value an ounce of silver; but an ounce of gold does not always require more labour than a bushel of wheat; and yet they <133> differ widely in value. The value of labour, it is true, enters into the value of every thing produced by it; but is far from making the whole value. If an ounce of silver were of no greater value than the labour of procuring it, that ounce would go for payment of the labour, and nothing be left to the proprietor of the mine: such a doctrine will not relish with the King of Spain; and as little with the Kings of Golconda and Portugal, proprietors of diamond-mines. Secondly, The standard under review supposes every sort of labour to be of equal value, which however will not be maintained. An useful art in great request may not be generally known: the few who are skilful will justly demand more for their labour than the common rate. An expert husbandman bestows no more labour in raising a hundred bushels of wheat, than his ignorant neighbour in raising fifty: if labour be the only standard, the two crops ought to afford the same price. Was not Raphael entitled to a higher price for one of his fine pictures, than a dunce is for a tavern-sign, supposing the labour to have been equal? Lastly, As this standard is applicable to things <134> only that require labour, what rule is to be followed with respect to natural fruits and other things that require no labour?

Where a pound of one commodity gives the same price with a pound of another, these commodities are said to be of equal value; and therefore, whatever rule can be given for the price of commodities, that rule determines also their comparative values. Montesquieu (*a*) attempts to account for the price as follows. He begins with supposing, that there is but one commodity in commerce, divisible like gold and silver into parts, the parts like those of gold and silver uniform and equally perfect. Upon that supposition, the price, says he, of the whole commodity collected into a mass,

(*a*) [[*De l'esprit des lois.*]] Liv. 22. ch. 7.

will be the whole current gold and silver; and the price of any particular quantity of the former, will be the corresponding quantity of the latter, the tenth or twentieth part of the one corresponding to the tenth or twentieth part of the other. He goes on to apply the same computation to all the variety of goods in commerce; and <135> concludes in general, that as the whole mass of goods in commerce corresponds to the whole mass of gold and silver in commerce as its price, so the price of the tenth or twentieth part of the former will be the tenth or twentieth part of the latter. According to this computation, all different goods must give the same price, or, which is the same, be of equal value, provided their weight or measure be the same. Our author certainly did not intend such an absurdity; and yet I can draw no other inference from his reasoning. In the very next chapter he admits the negroes on the coast of Afric to be an exception from the general rule, who, says he, value commodities according to the use they have for them. But, do not all nations value commodities in the same manner?[2]

Rejecting, then, the foregoing attempts to account for the comparative value of commodities, I take a hint from what was last said to maintain, that it is the demand chiefly which fixes the value of every commodity. Quantity beyond the demand renders even necessaries of no value; of which water is an instance. It may be <136> held accordingly as a general rule, That the value of goods in commerce depends on a demand beyond what their quantity can satisfy; and rises in proportion to the excess of the demand above the quantity. Even water becomes valuable in countries where the demand exceeds the quantity: in arid regions, springs of water are highly valued; and, in old times, were frequently the occasion of broils and bloodshed. Comparing next different commodities with respect to value, that commodity of which the excess of the demand above the quantity is the greater, will be of the greater value. Were utility or intrinsic value only to be considered, a pound of iron would be worth ten pounds of gold; but as the excess of the demand for gold above its quantity is much greater than that of iron, the latter is of less value in the market. A pound of opium, or of Jesuits bark, is, for its salutary effects, more valuable than gold; and yet, for the reason given, a pound of gold will purchase many pounds of

2. Paragraph added in 2nd edition.

these drugs. Thus, in general, the excess of the demand above the quantity is the standard that chiefly fixes the mercantile value of <137> commodities.* Interest is the price or premium given for the loan of money; and the rate of interest, like the price of other commodities, is regulated by the demand. Many borrowers and few lenders produce high interest: many lenders and few borrowers produce low interest.†3

The causes that make a demand seem not so easily ascertained. One thing is evident, that the demand for necessaries in any country, must depend on the number of its inhabitants. This rule holds not so strictly in articles of convenience; because some people are more greedy of conveniencies than others. As to articles of taste and luxury, the demand appears so <138> arbitrary as not to be reducible to any rule. A taste for beauty is general, but so different in different persons, as to make the demand extremely variable: the faint representation of any plant in an agate, is valued by some for its rarity; but the demand is far from being universal. Savages are despised for being fond of glass beads; but were such toys equally rare among us, they would be coveted by many: a copper coin of the Emperor Otho is of no intrinsic value, and yet, for its rarity, would draw a great price.

The value of gold and silver in commerce, like that of other commodities, was at first, we may believe, both arbitrary and fluctuating; and, like other commodities, they found in time their value in the market. With respect to value, however, there is a great difference between money and other commodities. Goods that are expensive in keeping, such as cattle, or that are impaired by time, such as corn, will always be first offered in exchange for what is wanted; and when such goods are offered to sale, the vender must be contented with the current price: in making the bargain,

---

* In a voyage to Arabia Foelix, ann. 1708, the King of the territory where the crew landed, gave them an ox weighing a thousand or twelve hundred pounds for a fusee, and three score pound-weight of rice for twenty-eight ounces of gun-powder. The goods bartered were estimated according to the wants of each party, or, in other words, according to the demand above the quantity.

† From what is said in the treatise *Des corps politiques* [[by Jean Charles de Lavie]], (liv. 6. ch. 8.) it appears doubtful whether high or low interest be the most friendly to commerce.

3. "Interest is the . . . produce low interest": added in 2nd edition.

the <139> purchaser has the advantage; for he suffers not by reserving his money to a better market. And thus commodities are brought down by money, to the lowest value that can afford any profit. At the same time, gold and silver sooner find their value than other commodities. The value of the latter depends both on the quantity and on the demand; the value of the former depends on the quantity only, the demand being unbounded: and even with respect to quantity, these precious metals are less variable than other commodities.

Gold and silver, being thus sooner fixed in their value than other commodities, become a standard for valuing every other commodity, and consequently for comparative values. A bushel of wheat, for example, being valued at five shillings, a yard of broad cloth at fifteen, their comparative values are as one to three.

A standard of values is essential to commerce; and therefore where gold and silver are unknown, other standards are established in practice. The only standard among the savages of North America is the skin of a beaver. Ten of these are <140> given for a gun, two for a pound of gunpowder, one for four pounds of lead, one for six knives, one for a hatchet, six for a coat of woollen cloth, five for a petticoat, and one for a pound of tobacco. Some nations in Africa employ shells, termed *couries,* for a standard.

As my chief view in this sketch is, to examine how far industry and commerce are affected by the quantity of circulating coin, I premise the following plain propositions. Supposing, first, the quantity of money in circulation, and the quantity of goods in the market, to continue the same, the price will rise and fall with the demand. For when more goods are demanded than the market affords, those who offer the highest price will be preferred: as, on the other hand, when the goods brought to market exceed the demand, the venders have no resource but to entice purchasers by a low price. The price of fish, flesh, butter, and cheese, is much higher than formerly; for these being now the daily food even of the lowest people, the demand for them is greatly increased. <141>

Supposing a fluctuation in the quantity of goods only, the price falls as the quantity increases, and rises as the quantity decreases. The farmer whose quantity of corn is doubled by a favourable season, must sell at half the usual price; because the purchaser, who sees a superfluity, will pay no more

for it. The contrary happens upon a scanty crop: those who want corn must
starve, or give the market-price, however high. The manufactures of wool,
flax, and metals, are much cheaper than formerly; for though the demand
has increased, yet by skill and industry the quantities produced have increased in a greater proportion. More pot-herbs are consumed than formerly: and yet by skilful culture the quantity is so much greater in proportion, as to have lowered the price to less than one half of what it was
eighty years ago.

It is easy to combine the quantity and demand, supposing a fluctuation
in both. Where the quantity exceeds the usual demand, more people will
be tempted to purchase by the low price; and where the demand rises considerably above the quantity, the price will rise in proportion. <142> In
Mathematical language, these propositions may be thus expressed, that the
price is *directly* as the demand, and *inversely* as the quantity.

A variation in the quantity of circulating coin is the most intricate circumstance; because it never happens without making a variation in the
demand for goods, and frequently in the quantity. I take the liberty, however, to suppose that there is no variation but in the quantity of circulating
coin; for though that cannot happen in reality, yet the result of the supposition will throw light upon what really happens: the subject is involved,
and I wish to make it plain. I put a simple case, that the half of our current
coin is at once swept away by some extraordinary accident. This at first will
embarrass our internal commerce, as the vender will insist for the usual
price, which now cannot be afforded. But the error of such demand will
soon be discovered; and the price of commodities, after some fluctuation,
will settle at the one half of what it was formerly. At the same time, there
is here no downfal in the value of commodities, which cannot happen while
<143> the quantity and demand continue unvaried. The purchasing for a
sixpence what formerly cost a shilling, makes no alteration in the value of
the thing purchased; because a sixpence is equal in value to what a shilling
was formerly. In a word, when money is scarce, it must bear a high value:
it must in particular go far in the purchase of goods; which we express by
saying, that goods are cheap. Put next the case, that by some accident our
coin is instantly doubled: the result must be, not instantaneous indeed, to
double the price of commodities. Upon the former supposition, a sixpence

is in effect advanced to be a shilling: upon the present supposition, a shilling has in effect sunk down to a sixpence. And here again it ought to be observed, that though the price is augmented, there is no real alteration in the value of commodities. A bullock that, some years ago, could have been purchased for ten pounds, will at present yield fifteen. The vulgar ignorantly think, that the value of horned cattle has arisen in that proportion. The advanced price may, in some degree, be occasioned by a greater consumption; but it is chiefly occasioned <144> by a greater quantity of money in circulation.[4]

Combining all the circumstances, the result is, that if the quantity of goods and of money continue the same, the price will be in proportion to the demand. If the demand and quantity of goods continue the same, the price will be in proportion to the quantity of money. And if the demand and quantity of money continue the same, the price will fall as the quantity increases, and rise as the quantity diminishes.

These speculative notions will enable us with accuracy to examine, how industry and commerce are affected by variations in the quantity of circulating coin. It is evident, that arts and manufactures cannot be carried on to any extent without coin. Persons totally employed in any art or manufacture require wages daily or weekly, because they must go to market for every necessary of life. The clothier, the taylor, the shoemaker, the gardener, the farmer, must employ servants to prepare their goods for the market; to whom, for that reason, wages ought to be regularly paid. In a word, commerce among <145> an endless number of individuals, who depend on each other even for necessaries, would be inextricable without a quantity of circulating coin. Money may be justly conceived to be the oil, that lubricates

4. In the 1st edition the following note is appended to this paragraph: "It is commonly thought, that the rate of interest depends on the quantity of circulating coin; that interest will be high when money is scarce, and low when money abounds. But whatever be the cause of high or low interest, I am certain that the quantity of circulating coin can have no influence. Supposing, as above, the half of our money to be withdrawn, a hundred pounds lent ought still to afford but five pounds as interest; because if the principal be doubled in value, so is also the interest. If, on the other hand, the quantity of our money be doubled, the five pounds of interest will continue to bear the same proportion to the principal as formerly" [1:76].

all the springs and wheels of a great machine, and preserves it in motion.*
Supposing us now to be provided with no more of that precious oil than
is barely sufficient for the easy motion of our industry and manufactures,
a diminution of the necessary quantity must retard them: our industry and
manufactures must decay; and if we do not confine the expence of living
to our present circumstances, which seldom happens, the balance of trade
with foreign nations will turn against us, and leave us no resource for making the balance equal but to export our gold and sil-<146>ver. And when
we are drained of these metals, farewell to arts and manufactures: we shall
be reduced to the condition of savages, which is, that each individual must
depend entirely on his own labour for procuring every necessary of life.
The consequences of the balance turning for us, are at first directly opposite: but at the long-run come to be the same: they are sweet in the mouth,
but bitter in the stomach. An influx of riches by this balance, rouses our
activity. Plenty of money elevates our spirits, and inspires an appetite for
pleasure: we indulge a taste for show and embellishment, become hospitable, and refine upon the arts of luxury. Plenty of money is a prevailing
motive even with the most sedate, to exert themselves in building, in husbandry, in manufactures, and in other solid improvements. Such articles
require both hands and materials, the prices of which are raised by the
additional demand. The labourer now whose wages are thus raised, is not
satisfied with mere necessaries, but insists for conveniencies, the price of
which also is raised by the new demand. In short, increase of money raises
the price <147> of every commodity; partly from the greater quantity of
money, and partly from the additional demand for supplying artificial
wants. Hitherto a delightful view of prosperous commerce: but behold the
remote consequences. High wages at first promote industry, and double the
quantity of labour: but the utmost exertion of labour is limited within
certain bounds; and a perpetual influx of gold and silver will not for ever

* Money cannot be justly said to be deficient where there is sufficiency to purchase
every commodity, and to pay for every kind of labour that is wanted. Any greater quantity
is hurtful to commerce, as will be seen afterward. But to be forced to contract debt even
when one deals prudently and profitably, and consequently to be subjected to legal execution, is a proof, by no means ambiguous, of scarcity of money, which till of late was
remarkably the case in Scotland.

be attended with a proportional quantity of work: The price of labour will
rise in proportion to the quantity of money; but the produce will not rise
in the same proportion; and for that reason our manufactures will be dearer
than formerly. Hence a dismal scene. The high price at home of our manufactures will exclude us from foreign markets; for if the merchant cannot
draw there for his goods what he paid at home, with some profit, he must
abandon foreign commerce altogether. And, what is still more dismal, we
shall be deprived even of our own markets; for in spite of the utmost vig-
ilance, foreign commodities, cheaper than our own, will be poured in upon
us. The last scene <148> is to be deprived of our gold and silver, and reduced
to the same miserable state as if the balance had been against us from the
beginning.

However certain it may be, that an addition to the quantity of money
must raise the price of labour and of manufactures, yet there is a fact that
seems to contradict the proposition, which is, that in no other country are
labour and manufactures so cheap as in the two peninsulas on the right and
left of the Ganges, though in no other country is there such plenty of
money. To account for this singular fact, political writers say, that money
is there amassed by the nabobs, and withdrawn from circulation. This is
not satisfactory: the chief exportation from these peninsulas is their manufactures, the price of which comes first to the merchant and manufacturer;
and how can that happen without raising the price of labour? Rice, it is
true, is the food of their labouring poor; and an acre of rice yields more
food than five acres of wheat: but the cheapness of necessaries, though it
hath a considerable influence in keeping down the price of labour, cannot
keep it constantly down, <149> in opposition to an overflowing current of
money. The populousness of these two countries is a circumstance totally
overlooked. Every traveller is amazed how such swarms of people can find
bread, however fertile the soil may be. Let us examine that circumstance.
One thing is evident, that, were the people fully employed, there would
not be a demand for the tenth part of their manufactures. Here, then, is a
country where hand-labour is a drug for want of employment. The people,
at the same time, sober and inclining to industry, are glad to be employed
at any rate; and whatever pittance is gained by labour, makes always some
addition. Hence it is, that in these peninsulas, superfluity of hands over-

balancing both the quantity of money and the demand for their manufactures, serves to keep the price extremely low.

What is now said discovers an exception to the proposition above laid down. It holds undoubtedly in Europe, and in every country where there is work for all the people, that an addition to the circulating coin raises the price of labour and of manufactures: but such addition has <150> no sensible effect in a country where there is a superfluity of hands, who are always disposed to work when they find employment.

From these premises it is evident, that, unless there is a superfluity of hands, manufactures can never flourish in a country abounding with mines of gold and silver. This in effect is the case of Spain: a constant influx of these metals, raising the price of labour and manufactures, has deprived the Spaniards of foreign markets, and also of their own: they are reduced to purchase from strangers even the necessaries of life. What a dismal condition will they be reduced to, when their mines come to be exhausted! The Gold coast in Guinea has its name from the plenty of gold that is found there. As it is washed from the hills with the soil in small quantities, every one is on the watch for it; and the people, like gamesters, despise every other occupation. They are accordingly lazy and poor. The kingdom of Fidah, in the neighbourhood, where there is no gold, is populous: the people are industrious, deal in many branches of manufacture, and are all in easy circumstances.[5] <151>

To illustrate this observation, which is of great importance, I enter more minutely into the condition of Spain. The rough materials of silk, wool, and iron, are produced there more perfect than in any other country; and yet flourishing manufactures of these, would be ruinous to it in its present state. Let us only suppose, that Spain itself could furnish all the commodities that are demanded in its American territories, what would be the consequence? The gold and silver produced by that trade would circulate in Spain: money would become a drug: labour and manufactures would rise to a high price; and every necessary of life, not excepting manufactures of silk, wool, and iron, would be smuggled into Spain, the high price there being sufficient to overbalance every risk: Spain would be left without in-

---

5. "The Gold coast . . . in easy circumstances": added in 2nd edition.

dustry, and without people. Spain was actually in the flourishing state here supposed when America was discovered: the American gold and silver mines enflamed the disease, and consequently was the greatest misfortune that ever befel that once potent kingdom. The exportation of our silver coin to the East Indies, so <152> loudly exclaimed against by shallow politicians, is to us, on the contrary, a most substantial blessing: it keeps up the value of silver, and consequently lessens the value of labour and of goods, which enable us to maintain our place in foreign markets. Were there no drain for our silver, its quantity in our continent would sink its value so much as to render the American mines unprofitable. Notwithstanding the great flow of money to the East Indies, many mines in the West Indies are given up, because they afford not the expence of working; and were the value of silver in Europe brought much lower, the whole silver mines in the West Indies would be abandoned. Thus our East-India commerce, which is thought ruinous by many, because it is a drain to much of our silver, is for that very reason profitable to all. The Spaniards profit by importing it into Europe; and other nations profit, by receiving it for their manufactures.

How ignorantly do people struggle against the necessary chain of causes and effects! If money do not overflow, a commerce in which the imports exceed <153> in value the exports, will soon drain a nation of money, and put an end to its industry. Commercial nations for that reason struggle hard for the balance of trade; and they fondly imagine, that it cannot be too advantageous. If greatly advantageous to them, it must in the same proportion be disadvantageous to those they deal with; which proves equally ruinous to both. They foresee indeed, but without concern, immediate ruin to those they deal with; but they have no inclination to foresee, that ultimately it must prove equally ruinous to themselves. It appears the intention of Providence that all nations should benefit by commerce as by sun-shine; and it is so ordered, that an unequal balance is prejudicial to the gainers as well as to the losers: the latter are immediate sufferers; but no less so, ultimately, are the former. This is one remarkable instance, among many, of providential wisdom in conducting human affairs, independent of the will of man, and frequently against his will. An ambitious nation, placed advantageously for trade, would willingly engross all to themselves, and reduce their neighbours to be hewers of <154> wood and drawers of water. But an invincible bar is opposed to such ambition, making an overgrown commerce the means of its own destruction. The commercial balance held by the hand of Providence, is never permitted to preponderate much to one side; and every nation partakes, or may partake, of all the comforts of life. Engrossing is bad policy: men are prompted, both by interest and duty, to second the plan of Providence; and to preserve, as near as possible, equality in the balance of trade.

Upon these principles, a wise people, having acquired a stock of money sufficient for an extensive commerce, will tremble at a balance too advantageous: they will rest satisfied with an equal balance, which is the golden mean. A hurtful balance may be guarded against by industry and frugality: but by what means is a balance too favourable to be guarded against? With respect to that question, it is not the quantity of gold and silver in a country that raises the price of labour and manufactures, but the quantity in circulation; and may not that quantity be regulated by the state, permitting coinage as far only <155> as is beneficial to its manufactures? Let the registers of foreign mints be carefully watched, in order that our current coin may not exceed that of our industrious neighbours. There will always be a demand for the surplus of our bullion, either to be exported as a commodity, or to be purchased at home for plate; which cannot be too much encouraged, being ready at every crisis to be coined for public service. The senate of Genoa has wisely burdened porcelane with a heavy tax, being a foreign luxury; but it has no less wisely left gold and silver plate free; which we most unwisely have loaded with a duty.*

The accumulating money in the public treasury, anciently the practice of every prudent monarch, prevents superfluity. Lies there any good objection against that practice, in a trading nation where gold and silver flow in with impetuosity? A great sum locked up by a frugal King, Henry VII. of England for example, lessens the quantity of money in circulation: profusion in a successor, which was the <156> case with Henry VIII. is a spur to industry, similar to the influx of gold and silver from the new world. The canton of Bern, by locking up money in its treasury, possesses the

---

* That duty is wisely taken away by a late act.

miraculous art of reconciling immense weath with frugality and cheap labour. A climate not kindly, and a soil not naturally fertile, enured the inhabitants to temperance and to virtue. Patriotism is their ruling passion; they consider themselves as children of the republic; are fond of serving their mother; and hold themselves sufficiently recompensed by the privilege of serving her. The public revenue greatly exceeds the expence of government: they carefully lock up the surplus for purchasing land when a proper opportunity offers; which is a shining proof of their disinterestedness as well as of their wisdom. By that politic measure, much more than by war, the canton of Bern, from a very slender origin, is now far superior to any of the other cantons in extent of territory. But in what other part of the globe are there to be found ministers of state, moderate and disinterested like the citizens of Bern! In the hands of a British ministry, the <157> greatest treasure would vanish in the twinkling of an eye; and do more mischief by augmenting money in circulation above what is salutary, than formerly it did good by confining it within moderate bounds. But against such a measure there lies an objection still more weighty than its being an ineffectual remedy: in the hands of an ambitious prince it would prove dangerous to liberty.

If the foregoing measures be not relished, I can discover no other means for preserving our station in foreign markets, but a bounty on exportation. The sum would be great: but the preserving our industry and manufactures, and the preventing an influx of foreign manufactures, cannot be purchased too dear. At the same time, a bounty on exportation would not be an unsupportable load: on the contrary, superfluity of wealth, procured by a balance constantly favourable, would make the load abundantly easy. A proper bounty would balance the growing price of labour and materials at home, and keep open the foreign market. By neglecting that salutary measure, the Dutch have lost all their manufactures, a neglect that has <158> greatly benefited both England and France. The Dutch indeed act prudently in with-holding that benefit as much as possible from their powerful neighbours: to prevent purchasing from them, they consume the manufactures of India.

The manufactures of Spain, once extensive, have been extirpated by their gold and silver mines. Authors ascribe to the same cause the decline of their agriculture; but erroneously: on the contrary, superfluity of gold and silver is favourable to agriculture, by raising the price of its productions. It raises also, it is true, the price of labour; but that additional expence is far from balancing the profit made by high prices of whatever the ground produces. Too much wealth indeed is apt to make the tenant press into a higher rank: but that is easily prevented by a proper heightening of the rent, so as always to confine the tenant within his own sphere.

As gold and silver are essential to commerce, foreign and domestic, several commercial nations have endeavoured most absurdly to bar the exportation by penal laws; forgetting that gold and silver will <159> never be exported while the balance of trade is on their side, and that they must necessarily be exported when the balance is against them. Neither do they consider, that if a people continue industrious, they cannot be long afflicted with an unfavourable balance; for the value of money, rising in proportion to its scarcity, will lower the price of their manufactures, and promote exportation: the balance will turn in their favour; and money will flow in, till by plenty its value be reduced to a par with that of neighbouring nations.

It is an important question, Whether a bank, upon the whole, be friendly to commerce. It is undoubtedly a spur to industry, like a new influx of money: but then, like such influx, it raises the price of labour and of manufactures. Weighing these two facts in a just balance, the result seems to be, that in a country where money is scarce, a bank properly constituted is a great blessing, as it in effect increases the quantity of money, and promotes industry and manufactures; but that in a country which possesses money sufficient for extensive commerce, the only bank that will not injure foreign commerce, is what <160> is erected for supplying the merchant with ready money by discounting bills. At the same time, much caution and circumspection is necessary with respect to banks of both kinds. A bank erected for discounting bills, ought to be confined to bills really granted in the course of commerce; rejecting fictitious bills drawn merely for procuring a loan of money. And with respect to a bank purposely erected for lending money, there is great danger of extending credit too far; not only with respect to the bank itself, but with respect to the nation in general, by raising the price of labour and of manufactures, which is the never failing result of too great plenty of money, whether coin or paper.

The different effects of plenty and scarcity of money, have not escaped that penetrating genius, the sovereign of Prussia. Money is not so plentiful in his dominions as to make it necessary to withdraw a quantity by heaping up treasure. He indeed always retains in his treasury six or seven millions Sterling for answering unforeseen demands: but being sensible that the withdrawing from circulation any larger sum would be prejudicial to commerce, <161> every farthing saved from the necessary expence of government, is laid out upon buildings, upon operas, upon any thing rather than cramp circulation. In that kingdom, a bank established for lending money would promote industry and manufactures. <162>

Origin and Progress of Arts[1]

SECTION I

Useful Arts.

Some useful arts must be nearly coeval with the human race; for food, cloathing, and habitation, even in their original simplicity, require some art. Many other arts are of such antiquity as to place the inventors beyond the reach of tradition. Several have gradually crept into existence, without an inventor. The busy mind however, accustomed to a beginning in things, cannot rest till it find or imagine a beginning to every art. Bacchus is said to have invented wine; and Staphylus the mixing water with wine. The bow and arrow are ascribed by tradition to Scythos, son of Jupiter, though a weapon all the world over. Spinning is so useful, that it must be honoured with <163> some illustrious inventor: it was ascribed by the Egyptians to their goddess Isis; by the Greeks to Minerva; by the Peruvians to Mamma Ella, wife to their first sovereign Mango Capac; and by the Chinese to the wife of their Emperor Yao. Mark here by the way a connection of ideas: spinning is a female occupation, and it must have had a female inventor.*

In the hunter-state, men are wholly employed upon the procuring food, clothing, habitation, and other necessaries; and have no time nor zeal for

---

* The Ilinois are industrious above all their American neighbours. Their women are neat-handed: they spin the wool of their horned cattle, which is as fine as that of English sheep. The stuffs made of it are dyed black, yellow, or red, and cut into garments sewed with roe-buck sinews. After drying these sinews in the sun, and beating them, they draw out threads as white and fine as any that are made of flax, but much tougher.

1. In the 1st edition the arrangement of the argument of both sections of the present sketch differs slightly from that in the 2nd and 3rd editions.

studying conveniencies. The ease of the shepherd-state affords both time and inclination for useful arts; which are greatly promoted by numbers who are relieved by agriculture from bodily labour: the soil, by gradual improvements in husbandry, affords plenty with less labour than at first; and <164> the surplus hands are employed, first, in useful arts, and, next, in those of amusement. Arts accordingly make the quickest progress in a fertile soil, which produces plenty with little labour. Arts flourished early in Egypt and Chaldea, countries extremely fertile.

When men, who originally lived in caves like some wild animals, began to think of a more commodious habitation, their first houses were extremely simple; witness those of the Canadian savages, than which none can be more simple, even at present. Their houses, says Charlevoix, are built with less art, neatness, and solidity, than those of the beavers; having neither chimneys nor windows: a hole only is left in the roof, for admitting light and emitting smoke. That hole must be stopped when it rains or snows; and, of course, the fire is put out, that the inhabitants may not be stifled with smoke. To have passed so many ages in that manner without thinking of any improvement, shows how greatly men are influenced by custom. The blacks of Jamaica are still more rude in their buildings: their huts are erected without even a hole <165> in the roof; and, accordingly, at home they breathe nothing but smoke.

Revenge produced early hostile weapons. The club and the dart are obvious inventions: not so the bow and arrow; and for that reason it is not easy to say how that weapon came to be universal. As iron differs from other metals, being seldom found pure, it was a late discovery: at the siege of Troy, spears, darts, and arrows, were headed with brass. Menestheus, who succeeded Theseus in the kingdom of Athens, and led fifty ships to the siege of Troy, was reputed the first who marshalled an army in battle-array. Instruments of defence are made necessary by those of offence. Trunks of trees, interlaced with branches, and supported with earth, made the first fortifications; to which succeeded a wall finished with a parapet for shooting arrows at besiegers. As a parapet covers but half of the body, holes were left in the wall from space to space, no larger than to give passage to an arrow. Besiegers had no remedy but to beat down the wall: a battering ram was first used by Pericles the Athenian, and perfected by the Carthaginians at the siege of <166> Gades. To oppose that formidable machine, the wall was built with advanced parapets for throwing stones and fire upon the enemy, which kept him at a distance. A wooden booth upon wheels, and pushed close to the wall, secured the men who wrought the battering ram. This invention was rendered ineffectual, by surrounding the wall with a deep and broad ditch. Besiegers were reduced to the necessity of inventing engines for throwing stones and javelins upon those who occupied the advanced parapets, in order to give opportunity for filling up the ditch; and ancient histories expatiate upon the powerful operation of the catapulta and balista. These engines suggested a new invention for defence: instead of a circular wall, it was built with salient angles, like the teeth of a saw, in order that one part might flank another. That form of a wall was afterwards improved, by raising round towers upon the salient angles; and the towers were improved by making them square. The ancients had no occasion for any form more complete, being sufficient for defending against all the missile weapons at that time known. The invention <167> of cannon required a variation in military architecture. The first cannons were made of iron bars, forming a concave cylinder, united by rings of copper. The first cannon-balls were of stone, which required a very large aperture. A cannon was reduced to a smaller size, by using iron for balls instead of stone; and that destructive engine was perfected by making it of cast metal. To resist its force, bastions were invented, horn-works, crown-works, half-moons, &c. &c.; and military architecture became a system, governed by principles and general rules. But all in vain: it has indeed produced fortifications that have made sieges horridly bloody; but artillery, at the same time, has been carried to such perfection, and the art of attack so improved, that no fortification, it is thought, can be rendered impregnable. The only impregnable defence, is good neighbourhood among weak princes, ready to unite whenever one of them is attacked by a superior force. And nothing tends more effectually to promote such union, than constant experience that fortifications cannot be relied on. <168>

With respect to naval architecture, the first vessels were beams joined together, and covered with planks, pushed along with poles in shallow water, and in deep water drawn by animals on the shore. To these succeeded trunks of trees cut hollow, termed by the Greeks *monoxyles*. The next were

planks joined together in form of a monoxyle. The thought of imitating a
fish advanced naval architecture. A prow was constructed in imitation of
the head, a stern with a moveable helm in imitation of the tail, and oars in
imitation of the fins. Sails were at last added; which invention was so early
that the contriver is unknown. Before the year 1545, ships of war in England
had no port-holes for guns, as at present: they had only a few cannon placed
on the upper deck.

When Homer composed his poems, at least during the Trojan war, the
Greeks had not acquired the art of gelding cattle: they eat the flesh of bulls
and of rams. Kings and princes killed and cooked their victuals: spoons,
forks, table-cloths, napkins, were unknown. They fed sitting, the custom
of reclining upon beds being <169> afterward copied from Asia; and, like
other savages, they were great eaters. At the time mentioned, they had no
chimneys, nor candles, nor lamps. Torches are frequently mentioned by
Homer, but lamps never: a vase was placed upon a tripod, in which was
burnt dry wood for giving light. Locks and keys were not common at that
time. Bundles were secured with ropes intricately combined (a); and hence
the famous Gordian knot. Shoes and stockings were not early known
among them, nor buttons, nor saddles, nor stirrups. Plutarch reports, that
Gracchus caused stones to be erected along the highways leading from
Rome, for the convenience of mounting a horse; for at that time stirrups
were unknown in Rome, though an obvious invention. Linen for shirts was
not used in Rome for many years after the government became despotic.
Even so late as the eighth century, it was not common in Europe. We are
informed by Herodotus, that the Lydians were reputed to be the first who
coined gold and silver money. This was probably after the Trojan war; for
during that <170> war the Greeks and Trojans trafficked by barter, as Homer relates: Priam weighs out the ten talents of gold which were the ransom
of his son's body.[2]

Thales, one of the seven wise men of Greece, about six hundred years
before Christ, invented the following method for measuring the height of
an Egyptian pyramid. He watched the progress of the sun, till his body and

(a) Odyssey, b. 8. l. 483. Pope's translation.
2. "We are informed . . . his son's body": added in 2nd edition.

its shadow were of the same length; and at that instant measured the shadow of the pyramid, which consequently gave its height. Amasis King of Egypt, present at the operation, thought it a wonderful effort of genius; and the Greeks admired it highly. Geometry must have been in its cradle at that time. Anaximander, some ages before Christ, made the first map of the earth, as far as then known. About the end of the thirteenth century, spectacles for assisting the sight were invented by Alexander Spina, a monk of Pisa. So useful an invention cannot be too much extolled. At a period of life when the judgment is in maturity, and reading is of great benefit, the eyes begin to grow dim. One cannot help pitying the condition of bookish men <171> before that invention, many of whom must have had their sight greatly impaired, while their appetite for reading was in vigour.

The origin and progress of writing make a capital article in the history of arts. To write, or, in other words, to exhibit thoughts to the eye, was early attempted in Egypt by hieroglyphics. But these were not confined to Egypt: figures composed of painted feathers were used in Mexico to express ideas; and by such figures Montezuma received intelligence of the Spanish invasion: in Peru, the only arithmetical figures known were knots of various colours, which served to cast up accounts. The second step naturally in the progress of the art of writing, is, to represent each word by a mark, termed a *letter*, which is the Chinese way of writing: they have about 11,000 of these marks or letters in common use; and, in matters of science, they employ to the number of 60,000. Our way is far more easy and commodious: instead of marks or letters for words, which are infinite, we represent by marks or letters, the articulate sounds that compose words: these sounds <172> exceed not thirty in number; and consequently the same number of marks or letters are sufficient for writing. It was a lucky movement to pass at one step from hieroglyphics, the most imperfect mode of writing, to letters representing sounds, the most perfect; for there is no appearance that the Chinese mode was ever practised in this part of the world. With us, the learning to read is so easy as to be acquired in childhood; and we are ready for the sciences as soon as the mind is ripe for them: the Chinese mode, on the contrary, is an unsurmountable obstruction to knowledge; because, it being the work of a lifetime to read with ease, no time remains for studying the sciences. Our case was in some measure the same at the restoration of learning: it required an age to be familiarized with Greek and Latin; and too little time remained for gathering knowledge from books composed in these languages. The Chinese stand upon a more equal footing with respect to arts; for these may be acquired by imitation or oral instruction, without books.

The art of writing with letters representing sounds, is of all inventions the <173> most important, and the least obvious. The way of writing in China makes so naturally the second step in the progress of the art, that our good fortune in stumbling upon a way so much more perfect cannot be sufficiently admired, when to it we are indebted for our superiority in literature above the Chinese. Their way of writing will for ever continue an unsurmountable obstruction to science; for it is so rivetted by inveterate practice, that the difficulty would not be greater to make them change their language than their letters. Hieroglyphics were a sort of writing, so miserably imperfect, as to make every improvement welcome; but as the Chinese make a tolerable shift with their own letters, they never dream of any improvement. Hence it may be pronounced with great certainty, that in China, the sciences, though still in infancy, will never arrive at maturity.

There is no appearance that writing was known in Greece so early as the time of Homer; for in none of his works is there any mention of it. This, it is true, is but negative evidence; but negative evidence must always command our assent, <174> where no positive evidence stands in opposition. If it was known, it must have been newly introduced, and used probably to record laws, religious precepts, or other short compositions.[3] Cyphers, invented in Hindostan, were brought into France from Arabia about the end of the tenth century. The art of printing made a great revolution in learning. In the days of William the Conqueror, books were extremely scarce. Grace Countess of Anjou paid for a collection of homilies two hun-

---

3. In the 1st edition this paragraph begins: "The art of writing was known in Greece when Homer composed his two epics; for he gives somewhere a hint of it. It was at that time probably in its infancy, and used only for recording laws, religious precepts, or other short works" [1:93–94].

dred sheep, a quarter of wheat, another of rye, and a third of millet, beside a number of martre skins.[4]

Husbandry made a progress from Egypt to Greece, and from Afric to Italy. Mago, a Carthaginian general, composed twenty-eight books upon husbandry, which were translated into Latin by order of the Roman senate. From these fine and fertile countries, it made its way to colder and less kindly climates. According to that progress, agriculture must have been practised more early in France than in Britain; and yet the English, at present, make a greater figure in that art than the French, inferiority in soil and climate notwith-<175>standing. Before husbandry became an art in the northern parts of Europe, the French noblesse had deserted the country, fond of society in a town-life. Landed gentlemen in England, more rough, and delighting more in hunting and other country amusements, found leisure to practise agriculture. Skill in that art proceeded from them to their tenants, who now prosecute husbandry with success, though their landlords have generally betaken themselves to a town-life.

When Caesar invaded Britain, agriculture was unknown in the inner parts: the inhabitants fed upon milk and flesh, and were clothed with skins. Hollinshed, who wrote in the period of Queen Elisabeth, describes the rudeness of the preceding generation in the arts of life: "There were very few chimneys even in capital towns: the fire was laid to the wall, and the smoke issued out at the roof, or door, or window. The houses were wattled and plastered over with clay; and all the furniture and utensils were of wood. The people slept on straw-pallets, with a log of wood for a pillow." Henry II. of France, at <176> the marriage of the Duchess of Savoy, wore the first silk stockings that were made in France. Queen Elisabeth, the third year of her reign, received in a present a pair of black silk knit stockings; and Dr. Howel reports, that she never wore cloth hose any more. Before the conquest, there was a timber bridge upon the Thames between London and Southwark, which was repaired by King William Rufus, and was burnt by accident in the reign of Henry II. ann. 1176. At that time a stone bridge in place of it was projected, but not finished till the year 1212. The bridge

4. "The art of . . . of martre skins": added in 2nd edition.

of Notre-Dame over the Seine in Paris, was first of wood. It fell down anno 1499; and, as there was not in France a man who would undertake to rebuild it of stone, an Italian cordelier was employed, whose name was *Joconde,* the same upon whom Sanazarius made the following pun:

> *Jocondus geminum imposuit tibi, Sequana, pontem;*
> *Hunc tu jure potes dicere pontificem.* [5]

Two Genoese, Stephen Turquet and Bartholomew Narres, laid in 1536 the foundation of the silk manufacture at Lyons. The art of making glass was import-<177>ed from France into England *ann.* 674, for the use of monasteries. Glass windows in private houses were rare even in the twelfth century, and held to be great luxury. King Edward III. invited three clockmakers of Delft in Holland to settle in England. In the former part of the reign of Henry VIII. there did not grow in England cabbage, carrot, turnip, or other edible root; and it has been noted, that even Queen Catharine herself could not command a salad for dinner, till the King brought over a gardener from the Netherlands. About the same time, the artichoke, the apricot, the damask rose, made their first appearance in England. Turkeys, carps, and hops, were first known there in the year 1524. The currant-shrub was brought from the island of Zant *ann.* 1533; and in the year 1540, cherry-trees from Flanders were first planted in Kent. It was in the year 1563 that knives were first made in England. Pocket-watches were brought there from Germany *ann.* 1577. About the year 1580, coaches were introduced; before which time Queen Elisabeth, on public occasions, rode behind her chamberlain. A saw-mill <178> was erected near London *ann.* 1633, but afterward demolished, that it might not deprive the labouring poor of employment. How crude was the science of politics even in that late age? Coffee-houses were opened in London no sooner than the year 1652. [6]

People who are ignorant of weights and measures fall upon odd shifts to supply the defect. Howel Dha Prince of Wales, who died in the year 948, was a capital lawgiver. One of his laws is, "If any one kill or steal the cat

---

5. "Jocondus gave you an identical bridge [*pontem*], Sequana; you can rightly call this one a high priest [*pontificem*]." *Sequana* is the Latin name for the Seine; a cordelier is a strict Franciscan friar.

6. "Coffee-houses were . . . the year 1652": added in 2nd edition.

that guards the Prince's granary, he forfeits a milch ewe with her lamb; or
as much wheat as will cover the cat when suspended by the tail, the head
touching the ground." By the same lawgiver a fine of twelve cows is enacted
for a rape committed upon a maid, eighteen for a rape upon a matron. If
the fact be proved after being denied, the criminal for his falsity pays as
many shillings as will cover the woman's posteriors. The measure of the
mid stream for salmon among our forefathers is not less risible. It is, that
the mid stream shall be so wide as that a swine may turn itself in <179> it,
without touching either side with its snout or tail.[7]

The negroes of the kingdom of Ardrah, in Guinea, have made great
advances in arts. Their towns, for the most part, are fortified, and connected
by great roads, kept in good repair. Deep canals from river to river are commonly filled with canoes, for pleasure some, and many for business. The
vallies are pleasant, producing wheat, millet, yams, potatoes, lemons, or-
anges, cocoa-nuts, and dates. The marshy grounds near the sea are drained;
and salt is made by evaporating the stagnating water. Salt is carried to the
inland countries by the great canal of Ba, where numberless canoes are daily
seen going with salt, and returning with gold dust or other commodities.

In all countries where the people are barbarous and illiterate, the progress
of arts is wofully slow. It is vouched by an old French poem, that the virtues
of the loadstone were known in France before 1180. The mariner's compass
was exhibited at Venice *ann.* 1260 by Paulus Venetus, as his own invention.
John Goya of Amalphi was the first who, many years <180> afterward, used
it in navigation; and also passed for being the inventor. Though it was used
in China for navigation long before it was known in Europe, yet to this day
it is not so perfect as in Europe. Instead of suspending it in order to make
it act freely, it is placed upon a bed of sand, by which every motion of the
ship disturbs its operation. Hand-mills, termed *querns,* were early used for
grinding corn; and when corn came to be raised in greater quantity, horse-
mills succeeded. Water-mills for grinding corn are described by Vitruvius
(*a*). Wind-mills were known in Greece and in Arabia as early as the seventh
century; and yet no mention is made of them in Italy till the fourteenth

(*a*) L. 10. cap. 10.
7. "The measure of . . . snout or tail": added in 2nd edition.

century. That they were not known in England in the reign of Henry VIII.
appears from a household-book of an Earl of Northumberland, cotem-
porary with that King, stating an allowance for three mill-horses, "two to
draw in the mill, and one to carry stuff to the mill and fro." Water-mills
for corn must in England have been of a later <181> date. The ancients had
mirror-glasses, and employed glass to imitate crystal vases and goblets: yet
they never thought of using it in windows. In the thirteenth century, the
Venetians were the only people who had the art of making crystal glass for
mirrors. A clock that strikes the hours was unknown in Europe till the end
of the twelth century. And hence the custom of employing men to proclaim
the hours during night, which to this day continues in Germany, Flanders,
and England. Galileo was the first who conceived an idea that a pendulum
might be useful for measuring time; and Hughens was the first who put
the idea in execution, by making a pendulum clock. Hook, in the year 1660,
invented a spiral spring for a watch, though a watch was far from being a
new invention. Paper was made no earlier than the fourteenth century; and
the invention of printing was a century later. Silk manufactures were long
established in Greece before silk-worms were introduced there. The manufacturers were provided with raw silk from Persia: but that commerce being frequently interrupted by war, two monks, in the <182> reign of Justinian, brought eggs of the silk-worm from Hindostan, and taught their
countrymen the method of managing them. The art of reading made a
very slow progress. To encourage that art in England, the capital punishment for murder was remitted, if the criminal could but read, which in
law-language is termed *benefit of clergy.* One would imagine that the art
must have made a very rapid progress when so greatly favoured: but there
is a signal proof of the contrary; for so small an edition of the Bible as six
hundred copies, translated into English in the reign of Henry VIII. was
not wholly sold off in three years. The people of England must have been
profoundly ignorant in Queen Elisabeth's time, when a forged clause added
to the twentieth article of the English creed passed unnoticed till about
forty years ago.* The Emperor Rodol-<183>phus, *anno* 1281, appointed all

---

* In the act 13th Elisabeth, *anno* 1571, confirming the thirty-nine articles of the church
of England, these articles are not engrossed, but referred to as comprised in a printed

public acts to be written in the German language, instead of Latin as formerly. This was imitated in France, but not till the year 1539. In Scotland to this day charters, seisins, precepts of *Clare constat,* and some other land-titles, continue to be in Latin, or rather in a sort of jargon. Ignorance is the mother of devotion, to the church and to lawyers.[8]

The discoveries of the Portuguese in the west coast of Africa, is a remarkable instance of the slow progress of arts. In the beginning of the fifteenth century, they were totally ignorant of that coast beyond Cape Non, 28 deg. north latitude. In 1410, the celebrated Prince Henry of Portugal fitted out a fleet for discoveries, <184> which proceeded along the coast to Cape Bojadore, in 26 deg. but had not courage to double it. In 1418 Tristan Vaz discovered the island Porto Santo; and the year after, the island Madeira was discovered. In 1439 a Portuguese captain doubled Cape Bojadore; and the next year the Portuguese reached Cape Blanco, lat. 20 deg. In 1446 Nuna Tristan doubled Cape Verd, lat. 14° 40′. In 1448 Don Gonzallo Vallo took possession of the Azores. In 1449 the islands of Cape Verd were discovered for Don Henry. In 1471 Pedro d'Escovar discovered the island St. Thomas and Prince's island. In 1484 Diego Cam discovered the kingdom of Congo. In 1486 Bartholomew Diaz, employed by John II. of Portugal, doubled the Cape of Good Hope, which he called *Cabo Tormentoso,* from the tempestuous weather he found in the passage.

More arts have been invented by accident than by investigation. The art of porcelain is more intricate than that of glass. The Chinese, however, have possessed the former many ages, without knowing any thing of the latter till they were taught by Europeans.[9] <185>

The exertion of national spirit upon any particular art, promotes activity

---

book, intitled, *Articles agreed to by the whole clergy in the convocation holden at London* 1562. The forged clause is, "The church has power to decree rites and ceremonies, and authority in controversies of faith." That clause is not in the articles referred to; nor the slightest hint of any authority with respect to matters of faith. In the same year 1571, the articles were printed both in Latin and English, precisely as in the year 1562. But soon after came out spurious editions, in which the said clause was foisted into the twentieth article, and continues so to this day. A forgery so impudent would not pass at present; and its success shows great ignorance in the people of England at that period.

8. "The Emperor Rodolphus . . . and to lawyers": added in 2nd edition.
9. Paragraph added in 2nd edition.

to prosecute other arts. The Romans, by constant study, came to excel in the art of war, which led them to improve upon other arts. Having in the progress of society acquired some degree of taste and polish, a talent for writing broke forth. Nevius composed in verse seven books of the Punic war, beside comedies, replete with bitter raillery against the nobility (*a*). Ennius wrote annals, and an epic poem (*b*). Lucius Andronicus was the father of dramatic poetry in Rome (*c*). Pacuvius wrote tragedies (*d*). Plautus and Terence wrote comedies. Lucilius composed satires, which Cicero esteems to be slight, and void of erudition (*e*). Fabius Pictor, Cincius Alimentus, Piso Frugi, Valerius Antias, and Cato, were rather annalists than historians, confining themselves to naked facts, ranged in order of time. The genius of the Romans for the fine arts was much in-<186>flamed by Greek learning, when free intercourse between the two nations was opened. Many of those who made the greatest figure in the Roman state commenced authors, Caesar, Cicero, &c. Sylla composed memoirs of his own transactions, a work much esteemed even in the days of Plutarch.

The progress of art seldom fails to be rapid, when a people happen to be roused out of a torpid state by some fortunate change of circumstances: prosperity contrasted with former abasement, gives to the mind a spring, which is vigorously exerted in every new pursuit. The Athenians made no figure under the tyranny of Pisistratus; but upon regaining freedom and independence, they became heroes. Miletus, a Greek city of Ionia, being destroyed by the King of Persia, and the inhabitants made slaves, the Athenians, deeply affected with the misery of their brethren, boldly attacked that King in his own dominions, and burnt the city of Sardis. In less than ten years after, they gained a signal victory over him at Marathon; and under Themistocles, made head against a prodigious army, with <187> which Xerxes threatened utter ruin to Greece. Such prosperity produced its usual effect: arts flourished with arms, and Athens became the chief theatre for sciences as well as fine arts. The reign of Augustus Caesar, which put an

(*a*) Titus Livius, lib. 7. c. 2.
(*b*) Quintilian, lib. 10. c. 17.
(*c*) Cicero De oratore, lib. 2. N° 72.
(*d*) —— De oratore, lib. 2. N° 193.
(*e*) —— De finibus, lib. 1. N° 7.

end to the rancour of civil war, and restored peace to Rome with the comforts of society, proved an auspicious aera for literature; and produced a cloud of Latin historians, poets, and philosophers, to whom the moderns are indebted for their taste and talents. One who makes a figure rouses emulation in all: one catches fire from another, and the national spirit flourishes: classical works are composed, and useful discoveries made in every art and science. This fairly accounts for the following observation of Velleius Paterculus (*a*), that eminent men generally appear in the same period of time. "One age," says he, "produced Eschylus, Sophocles, and Euripides, who advanced tragedy to a great height. In another age the old comedy flourished under Eupolis, Cratinus, and Aristophanes; and the new was inven-<188>ted by Menander, and his cotemporaries Diphilus and Philemon, whose compositions are so perfect that they have left to posterity no hope of rivalship. The philosophic sages of the Socratic school, appeared all about the time of Plato and Aristotle. And as to rhetoric, few excelled in that art before Isocrates, and as few after the second descent of his scholars." The historian applies the same observation to the Romans, and extends it even to grammarians, painters, statuaries, and sculptors. With regard to Rome, it is true that the Roman government under Augustus was in effect despotic: but despotism, in that single instance, made no obstruction to literature, it having been the politic of that reign to hide power as much as possible. A similar revolution happened in Tuscany about three centuries ago. That country was divided into many small republics, which, by mutual hatred, usual between nations in close neighbourhood, became ferocious and bloody. These republics being united under the Great Duke of Tuscany, enjoyed the sweets of peace in a mild government. That comfortable revolution, which made <189> the deeper impression by a retrospect to recent calamities, roused the national spirit, and produced ardent application to arts and literature. The restoration of the royal family in England, which put an end to a cruel and envenomed civil war, promoted improvements of every kind: arts and industry made a rapid progress among the people, though left to themselves by a weak and fluctuating administration. Had the nation, upon that favourable turn of fortune, been

(*a*) Historia Romana, lib. 1. in fine.

blessed with a succession of able and virtuous princes, to what a height might not arts and sciences have been carried! In Scotland, a favourable period for improvements was the reign of the first Robert, after shaking off the English yoke: but the domineering spirit of the feudal system rendered abortive every attempt. The restoration of the royal family, mentioned above, animated the legislature of Scotland to promote manufactures of various kinds: but in vain; for the union of the two crowns had introduced despotism into Scotland, which sunk the genius of the people, and rendered them heartless and indolent. Liberty, indeed, and many other advantages, were <190> procured to them by the union of the two kingdoms; but these salutary effects were long suspended by mutual enmity, such as commonly subsists between neighbouring nations. Enmity wore away gradually, and the eyes of the Scots were opened to the advantages of their present condition: the national spirit was roused to emulate and to excel: talents were exerted, hitherto latent; and Scotland, at present, makes a figure in arts and sciences, above what it ever made while an independent kingdom.*

Another cause of activity and animation, is the being engaged in some important action of doubtful event, a struggle for liberty, the resisting a potent invader, or the like. Greece, divided into small states, <191> frequently at war with each other, advanced literature and the fine arts to unrivalled perfection. The Corsicans, while engaged in a perilous war for defence of their liberties, exerted a vigorous national spirit: they founded an university for arts and sciences, a public library, and a public bank. After a long stupor during the dark ages of Christianity, arts and literature revived among the turbulent states of Italy. The royal society in London, and the academy of sciences in Paris, were both of them instituted after civil wars that had animated the people, and roused their activity.

---

* In Scotland, an innocent bankrupt imprisoned for debt, obtains liberty by a process termed *cessio bonorum.* From the year 1694 to the year 1744, there were but twenty-four processes of that kind, which shows how languidly trade was carried on while the people remained ignorant of their advantages by the union. From that time to the year 1771, there have been thrice that number every year, taking one year with another; an evident proof of the late rapid progress of commerce in Scotland. Every one is roused to venture his small stock, though every one cannot be successful.

An useful art is seldom lost, because it is in constant practice. And yet, though many useful arts were in perfection during the reign of Augustus Caesar, it is amazing how ignorant and stupid men became, after the Roman empire was shattered by northern barbarians: they degenerated into savages. So ignorant were the Spanish Christians during the eighth and ninth centuries, that Alphonsus the Great, King of Leon, was necessitated to employ Mahometan preceptors for educating his eldest son. Even Charlemagne could not sign <192> his name: nor was he singular in that respect, being kept in countenance by several neighbouring princes.

As the progress of arts and sciences toward perfection is greatly promoted by emulation, nothing is more fatal to an art or science than to remove that spur, as where some extraordinary genius appears who soars above rivalship. Mathematics seem to be declining in Europe: the great Newton, having surpassed all the ancients, has not left to the moderns even the faintest hope of equalling him; and what man will enter the lists who despairs of victory?

In early times, the inventors of useful arts were remembered with fervent gratitude. Their history became fabulous by the many incredible exploits attributed to them. Diodorus Siculus mentions the Egyptian tradition of Osiris, that with a numerous army he traversed every inhabited part of the globe, in order to teach men the culture of wheat and of the vine. Beside the impracticability of supporting a numerous army where husbandry is unknown, no army could enable Osiris to introduce wheat or wine among stupid savages who live by hunting and fishing; which <193> probably was the case, in that early period, of all the nations he visited.

In a country thinly peopled, where even necessary arts want hands, it is common to see one person exercising more arts than one: in several parts of Scotland, the same man serves as a physician, surgeon, and apothecary. In a very populous country, even simple arts are split into parts, and there is an artist for each part: in the populous towns of ancient Egypt, a physician was confined to a single disease. In mechanic arts, that mode is excellent. As a hand confined to a single operation becomes both expert and expeditious, a mechanic art is perfected by having its different operations distributed among the greatest number of hands: many hands are employed in making a watch; and a still greater number in manufacturing a web of woollen cloth. Various arts or operations carried on by the same man, envigorate his mind, because they exercise different faculties; and, as he cannot be equally expert in every art or operation, he is frequently reduced to supply want of skill by thought and invention. Constant application, on the contrary, to a single ope-<194>ration, confines the mind to a single object, and excludes all thought and invention: in such a train of life, the operator becomes dull and stupid, like a beast of burden. The difference is visible in the manners of the people: in a country where, from want of hands, several occupations must be carried on by the same person, the people are knowing and conversable: in a populous country where manufactures flourish, they are ignorant and unsociable. The same effect is visible in countries where an art or manufacture is confined to a certain class of men. It is visible in Hindostan, where the people are divided into *casts,* which never mix even by marriage, and where every man follows his father's trade. The Dutch lint-boors are a similar instance: the same families carry on the trade from generation to generation, and are accordingly ignorant and brutish even beyond other Dutch peasants. The inhabitants of Buckhaven, a sea-port in the county of Fife, were originally a colony of foreigners, invited hither to teach our people the art of fishing. They continue fishers to this day, marry among themselves, have little intercourse with their <195> neighbours, and are dull and stupid to a proverb.*

A gentleman of a moderate fortune passed his time while husbandry was asleep, like a Birmingham workman who hammers a button from morning to evening. A certain gentleman, for example, who lived on his estate, issued forth to walk as the clock struck eleven. Every day he trod the same path, leading to an eminence which opened a view of the sea. A rock on the summit was his seat, where, after resting an hour, he returned home at leisure. It is not a little singular, that this exercise was repeated day after day for forty-three years, without interruption for the last twenty years of the gentleman's life. And though he has been long dead, the impression of his

---

* Population has one advantage not commonly thought of, which is, that it banishes ghosts and apparitions. Such imaginary beings are never seen but by solitary persons in solitary places. In great towns they are unknown: you never hear of such a thing in Holland, which in effect is one great town. [[Note added in 2nd edition.]]

heels in the sod remains visible to this day. Men by inaction degenerate into oysters.[10] <196>

SECTION II

Progress of Taste and of the fine Arts.

The sense by which we perceive right and wrong in actions, is termed the *moral sense:* the sense by which we perceive beauty and deformity in objects, is termed *taste.* Perfection in the moral sense consists in perceiving the minutest differences between right and wrong: perfection in taste consists in perceiving the minutest differences between beauty and deformity; and such perfection is termed *delicacy of taste* (*a*).

The moral sense is born with us; and so is taste: yet both of them require much cultivation. Among savages, the moral sense is faint and obscure; and taste still more so.* Even in the most enlightened ages, it requires in a judge both education and experience to perceive accurately <197> the various modifications of right and wrong: and to acquire delicacy of taste, a man must grow old in examining beauties and deformities. In Rome, abounding with productions of the fine arts, an illiterate shopkeeper is a more correct judge of statues, of pictures, and of buildings, than the best educated citizen of London (*b*). Thus taste goes hand in hand with the moral sense in their progress toward maturity; and they ripen equally by the same sort of culture. Want, a barren soil, cramps the growth of both: sensuality, a soil too fat, corrupts both: the middle state, equally distant from dispiriting poverty and luxurious sensuality, is the soil in which both of them flourish.

As the fine arts are intimately connected with taste, it is impracticable, in tracing their progress, to separate them by accurate limits. I join therefore the progress of the fine arts to that of taste, where the former depends

---

* Some Iroquois, after seeing all the beauties of Paris, admired nothing but the street De la Houchette, where they found a constant supply of eatables.

(*a*) Elements of Criticism, vol. 1. p. 112. edit. 5.

(*b*) Elements of Criticism, chap. 25.

10. Paragraph added in 2nd edition.

entirely on the latter; and I handle separately the progress of the fine arts, where that progress is influenced by other circumstances beside taste. <198>

During the infancy of taste, imagination is suffered to roam, as in sleep, without control. Wonder is the passion of savages and of rustics; to raise which, nothing is necessary but to invent giants and magicians, fairy-land and inchantment. The earliest exploits recorded of warlike nations, are giants mowing down whole armies, and little men overcoming giants; witness Joannes Magnus, Torfeus, and other Scandinavian writers. Hence the absurd romances that delighted the world for ages, which are now sunk into contempt every where. The more supernatural the facts related are, the more is wonder raised; and in proportion to the degree of wonder, is the tendency to belief among the vulgar (*a*). Madame de la Fayette led the way to novels in the present mode. She was the first who introduced sentiments instead of wonderful adventures, and amiable men instead of bloody heroes. In substituting distresses to prodigies, she made a discovery, that persons of taste and feeling are more attached by compassion than by wonder. <199>

By the improvement of our rational faculties, truth and nature came to bear sway: incredible fictions were banished: a remaining bias, however, for wonder paved the way to bombast language, turgid similes, and forced metaphors. The Song of Solomon, and many other Asiatic compositions, afford examples without end of such figures. These are commonly attributed to force of imagination in a warm climate; but a more extensive view will show this to be a mistake. In every climate, hot and cold, the figurative style is carried to extravagance, during a certain period in the progress of writing; a style that is relished by all at first, and continues to delight many, till it yield to a taste polished by long experience (*b*). Even in the bitter-cold country of Iceland, we are at no loss for examples. A rainbow is termed *Bridge of the gods:* gold, *Tears of Frya:* the earth is termed *Daughter of Night,* the *vessel that floats upon Ages;* and herbs and plants are her *hair,* or her *fleece.* Ice is termed *the great bridge:* a ship, *horse of the floods.* Many authors

---

(*a*) Elements of Criticism, vol. 1. p. 163. edit. 5.
(*b*) Elements of Criticism, vol. 2. pp. 184. 284. edit. 5.

foolishly conjecture, that the Hurons and some other <200> neighbouring nations, are of Asiatic extraction; because, like the Asiatics, their discourse is highly figurative.

The national progress of morality is slow: the national progress of taste is slower. In proportion as a nation polishes and improves in the arts of peace, taste ripens. The Chinese had long enjoyed a regular system of government, while the Europeans were comparatively in a chaos; and accordingly literary compositions in China were brought to perfection more early than in Europe. In their poetry they indulge no incredible fables, like those of Ariosto or the Arabian Tales; but commonly select such as afford a good moral. Their novels, like those of the most approved kind among us, treat of misfortunes unforeseen, unexpected good luck, and persons finding out their real parents. The Orphan of China, composed in the fourteenth century, surpasses far any European play of that early period. But good writing has made a more rapid progress with us; not from superiority of talents, but from the great labour the Chinese must undergo, in learning to read and write their own language. The Chinese <201> tragedy is indeed languid, and not sufficiently interesting, which M. Voltaire ascribes to want of genius. With better reason he might have ascribed it to the nature of their government, so well contrived for preserving peace and order, as to afford few examples of surprising events, and little opportunity for exerting manly talents.

A nation cannot acquire a taste for ridicule till it emerges out of the savage state. Ridicule, however, is too rough for refined manners: Cicero discovers in Plautus a happy talent for ridicule, and peculiar delicacy of wit; but Horace, who figured in the court of Augustus, eminent for delicacy of taste, declares against the low roughness of that author's raillery (a). The same Cicero, in a letter to Papirius Poetus, complains that by the influx of foreigners the true Roman humour was lost. It was not the influx of foreigners, but the gradual progress of manners from the rough to the polished.[11] The high burlesque style prevails commonly in the period between barbarity and politeness, in <202> which a taste somewhat improved dis-

(a) Elements of Criticism, chap. 2. part 2.
11. "The same Cicero . . . to the polished": added in 2nd edition.

covers the ridicule of former manners. Rabelais in France, and Butler in England, are illustrious examples. Dr. Swift is our latest burlesque writer, and probably is the last.

Emulation among a multitude of small states in Greece, was enflamed by their public games: by that means taste ripened, and the fine arts were promoted. Taste refines gradually, and is advanced toward perfection by a diligent study of beautiful productions. Rome was indebted to Greece for that delicacy of taste which figured during the reign of Augustus, especially in literary compositions. But taste could not long flourish in a despotic government: so low had the Roman taste fallen in the reign of the Emperor Hadrian, that nothing would please him but to suppress Homer, and in his place to install a silly Greek poet, named *Antimachus.*

The northern barbarians who desolated the Roman empire, and revived in some measure the savage state, occasioned a woful decay of taste. Pope Gregory the Great, struck with the beauty of some Saxon youths exposed to sale in Rome, <203> asked to what country they belonged. Being told they were Angles, he said that they ought more properly to be denominated angels; and that it was a pity so beautiful a countenance should cover a mind devoid of grace. Hearing that the name of their province was *Deïri,* a division of Northumberland, "Deïri!" replied he, "excellent: they are called to the mercy of God from his anger [*de ira*]." Being also told, that Alla was the king of that province, "Alleluia," cried he, "we must endeavour that the praises of God be sung in their country." Puns and conundrums passed in ignorant times for sterling wit.[12] Pope Gregory VII. *anno* 1080, presented to the Emperor Rodolph a crown of gold, with the following inscription, *Petra dedit Petro, Petrus diadema Rodolpho.*[13] Miserably low must taste have been in that period, when a childish play of words was relished as a proper decoration for a serious solemnity.

Pope Innocent III. *anno* 1207, made a present of jewels to John King of England, accompanied with the following letter, praised by Pere Orleans as full of spirit and beauty.

12. "Pope Gregory the . . . for sterling wit": added in 2nd edition.
13. "The rock (i.e., Christ) gave the crown to Peter, and Peter gives it to Rudolf."

Consider this present with <204> respect to form, number, matter, and colour. The circular figure of the ring denotes eternity, which has neither beginning nor end. And by that figure your mind will be elevated from things terrestrial to things celestial. The number of four, making a square, denotes the firmness of a heart, proof against both adversity and prosperity, especially when supported by the four cardinal virtues, justice, strength, prudence, and temperance. By the gold, which is the metal of the ring, is denoted wisdom, which excels among the gifts of Heaven, as gold does among metals. Thus it is said of the Messiah, that the spirit of wisdom shall rest upon him: nor is there any thing more necessary to a king, which made Solomon request it from God preferably to all other goods. As to the colour of the stones, the green of the emerald denotes faith; the purity of the saphire, hope; the red of the granite, charity; the clearness of the topaz, good works. You have therefore in the emerald what will increase your faith; in the saphire, what will encourage you to hope; in the granite, what <205> will prompt you to love; in the topaz, what will excite you to act; till, having mounted by degrees to the perfection of all the virtues, you come at last to see the God of gods in the celestial Sion.[14]

The famous golden bull of Germany, digested *anno* 1356 by Bartolus, a celebrated lawyer, and intended for a master-piece of composition, is replete with wild conceptions, without the least regard to truth, propriety, or connection. It begins with an apostrophe to Pride, to Satan, to Choler, and to Luxury: it asserts, that there must be seven electors for opposing the seven mortal sins: the fall of the angels, terrestrial paradise, Pompey, and Caesar, are introduced; and it is said, that Germany is founded on the Trinity, and on the three theological virtues. What can be more puerile! A sermon preached by the Bishop of Bitonto, at the opening of the council of Trent, excels in that mode of composition. He proves that a council is necessary; because several councils have extirpated heresy, and deposed kings and emperors; because the poets assemble councils of the gods; because Moses writes, that at the creation of man, and at confounding <206> the language of the giants, God acted in the manner of a council; because religion has three heads, doctrine, sacraments, and charity, and that these three are termed *a council.* He exhorts the members of the council to strict unity,

14. Paragraph added in 2nd edition.

like the heroes in the Trojan horse. He asserts, that the gates of paradise
and of the council are the same; that the holy fathers should sprinkle their
dry hearts with the living water that flowed from it; and that otherwise the
Holy Ghost would open their mouths like those of Balaam and Caiaphas
(*a*). James I. of Britain dedicates his Declaration against Vorstius to our
Saviour, in the following words: "To the honour of our Lord and Saviour
Jesus Christ, the eternal Son of the eternal Father, the only Theanthropos,
mediator, and reconciler of mankind; in sign of thankfulness, his most
humble and obliged servant, James, by the grace of God, King of Great
Britain, France, and Ireland, Defender of the Faith, doth dedicate and consecrate this his Declaration." Funeral orations were some time ago in fashion. Regnard, who was in Stockholm about the year 1680, <207> heard a
funeral oration at the burial of a servant-maid. The priest, after mentioning
her parents and the place of her birth, praised her as an excellent cook, and
enlarged upon every ragout that she made in perfection. She had but one
fault, he said, which was the salting her dishes too much; but that she
showed thereby her prudence, of which salt is the symbol; a stroke of wit
that probably was admired by the audience. Funeral orations are out of
fashion: the futility of a trite panegyric purchased with money, and indecent flattery in circumstances that require sincerity and truth, could not
long stand against improved taste. The yearly feast of the ass that carried
the mother of God into Egypt, was a most ridiculous farce, highly relished
in the dark ages of Christianity. See the description of that feast in Voltaire's
General History (*b*).

The public amusements of our forefathers, show the grossness of their
taste after they were reduced to barbarism by the Goths and Vandals. The
plays termed *Mysteries,* because they were borrowed from the scriptures,
indicate gross man-<208>ners, as well as infantine taste; and yet in France,
not farther back than three or four centuries, these Mysteries were such
favourites as constantly to make a part at every public festival. In a Spanish
play or mystery, Jesus Christ and the devil, ridiculously dressed, enter into

(*a*) Father Paul's history of Trent, lib. 1. [[Fra Paolo Sarpi's *Istoria del Concilio
Tridentino.*]]
(*b*) [[*Essai sur l'histoire générale,*]] Chap. 78.

a dispute about some point of controversy, are enflamed, proceed to blows, and finish the entertainment with a saraband. The reformation of religion, which roused a spirit of inquiry, banished that amusement, not only as low but as indecent. A sort of plays succeeded, termed *Moralities,* less indecent indeed, but little preferable in point of composition. These Moralities have also been long banished, except in Spain, where they still continue in vogue. The devil is commonly the hero: nor do the Spaniards make any difficulty, even in their more regular plays, to introduce supernatural and allegorical beings upon the same stage with men and women. The Cardinal Colonna carried into Spain a beautiful bust of the Emperor Caligula. In the war about the succession of Spain, after the death of its king Charles II., Lord Gallway, upon a painful search, found <209> that bust serving as a weight to a church-clock.

In the days of our unpolished forefathers, who were governed by pride as well as by hatred, princes and men of rank entertained a changeling, distinguished by the name of *fool;* who being the butt of their silly jokes, flattered their self-conceit. Such amusement, no less gross than inhuman, could not show its face even in the dawn of taste: it was rendered less insipid and less inhuman, by entertaining one of real wit, who, under disguise of a fool, was indulged in the most satirical truths. Upon a further purification of taste, it was discovered, that to draw amusement from folly, real or pretended, is below the dignity of human nature. More refined amusements were invented, such as balls, public spectacles, gaming, and society with women. Parasites, described by Plautus and Terence, were of such a rank as to be permitted to dine with gentlemen; and yet were so despicable as to be the butt of every man's joke. They were placed at the lower end of the table; and the guests diverted themselves with daubing their faces, and even kicking and <210> cuffing them; all which was patiently borne for the sake of a plentiful meal. They resembled the fools and clowns of later times, being equally intended to be laughed at: but the parasite profession shows grosser manners; it being shockingly indelicate in a company of gentlemen to abuse one of their own number, however contemptible in point of character.

Pride, which introduced fools, brought dwarfs also into fashion. In Italy, that taste was carried to extravagance. "Being at Rome in the year 1566," says a French writer, "I was invited by Cardinal Vitelli to a feast, where we were served by no fewer than thirty-four dwarfs, most of them horribly distorted." Was not the taste of that Cardinal horribly distorted? The same author adds, that Francis I. and Henry II. Kings of France, had many dwarfs: one named *Great John,* was the least ever had been seen, except a dwarf at Milan, who was carried about in a cage.

In the eighth and ninth centuries, no sort of commerce was carried on in Europe but in markets and fairs. Artificers and < 211 > manufacturers were dispersed through the country, and so were monasteries; the towns being inhabited by none but clergymen, and those who immediately depended on them. The nobility lived on their estates, unless when they followed the court. The low people were not at liberty to desert the place of their birth: the *villain* was annexed to the estate, and the *slave* to the person of his lord. Slavery fostered rough manners; and there could be no improvement in manners, nor in taste, where there was no society. Of all the polite nations in Europe, the English were the latest of taking to a town-life; and their progress in taste and manners has been proportionally slow.[15]

Our celebrated poet Ben Johnson lived at a time, when turgid conceptions and bombast language were highly relished; and his compositions are in the perfection of that taste, witness the quotations from him in Elements of Criticism (*a*). He was but too faithfully imitated by Beaumont and Fletcher, and other writers of that age. We owe to Dryden the dawn of a better < 212 > taste. For though the mode of writing in his time led him to the bombast, yet a just imitation of nature frequently breaks forth, especially in his later compositions. And, as nature will always at last prevail, the copies of nature given by that eminent writer were highly relished, produced many happy imitations, and in time brought about a total revolution of taste, which kept pace with that of government, both equally happy for

(*a*) Vol. 1. p. 244. edit. 5.

15. The 1st edition adds: "By no audience in the neighbouring kingdoms, would the following passage in one of Dryden's plays have been endured. 'Jack Sauce! if I say it is a tragedy, it shall be a tragedy in spite of you: teach your grandam how to piss.' These plays are full of such coarse stuff, and yet continued favourites down to the Revolution. For a long time after the revival of the arts and sciences, Lucan was ranked above Virgil by every critic."

this nation. Here is a fair deduction of the progress of taste in Britain. But, according to that progress, what shall be said of the immortal Shakespeare, in whose works is displayed the perfection of taste? Was not his appearance at least a century too early? Such events happen sometimes contrary to the ordinary progress. This was the case of Roger Bacon, as well as of Shakespeare: they were blazing stars that gave but a temporary lustre, and left the world as void of light as before.[16] Ben Johnson, accordingly, and even Beaumont and Fletcher, were greater national favourites than Shakespeare; and, in the same manner, the age before, Lucan was ranked above Virgil by every critic. By the same bad <213> taste, the true sublime of Milton was little relished for more than half a century after Paradise Lost was published. Ill-fated Shakespeare! who appeared in an age unworthy of him. That divine writer, who, merely by force of genius, so far surpassed his cotemporaries, how far would he have surpassed even himself, had he been animated with the praises so justly bestowed on him in later times?[17] We have Dryden's authority, that taste in his time was considerably refined:

> They who have best succeeded on the stage,
> Have still conform'd their genius to their age.
> Thus Johnston did mechanic humour show,
> When men were dull, and conversation low.
> Then comedy was faultless, but 'twas coarse:
> Cobb's Tankard was a jest, and Otter's Horse.
> Fame then was cheap, and the first comer sped:
> And they have kept it since by being dead.
> But were they now to write, when critics weigh
> Each line and ev'ry word throughout a play,
> None of them, no not Johnson in his height,
> Could pass without allowing grains for weight.
> If love and honour now are higher rais'd,
> It's not the poet, but the age is prais'd:
> Wit's now arriv'd to a more high degree,
> Our native language more refin'd and free.

16. "Our celebrated poet . . . light as before": added in 2nd edition.
17. "Ill-fated Shakespeare! . . . in later times": added in 2nd edition.

> Our ladies and our men now speak more wit
> In conversation, than those poets writ.[18] <214>

The high opinion Dryden had of himself and of his age, breaks out in every line. Johnson probably had the same opinion of himself and of his age: the present age is not exempted from that bias; nor will the next age be, though probably maturity in taste will be still later. We humble ourselves before the ancients, who are far removed from us; but not to soar above our immediate predecessors, would be a sad mortification. Many scenes in Dryden's plays, if not lower than Cobb's Tankard or Otter's Horse, are more out of place. In the *Wild Gallant,* the hero is a wretch constantly employed, not only in cheating his creditors, but in cheating his mistress, a lady of high rank and fortune. And how absurd is the scene, where he convinces the father of his mistress, that the devil had got him with child! The character of Sir Martin Marall is below contempt. The scenes in the same play, of a bawd instructing one of her novices how to behave to her gallants, and of the novice practising her lessons, are perhaps not lower than Cobb's Tankard or Otter's Horse, but surely they are less innocent. <215>

It is common to see people fond of a new fashion, vainly imagining that taste is greatly improved. Disguised dishes are a sort of bastard wit, like turrets jutting out at the top of a building. Such dishes were lately in high fashion, without having even the slender merit of being a new fashion. They prevailed in the days of Charles II. as we learn from one of Dryden's plays. "Ay, it look'd like variety, till we came to taste it; there were twenty several dishes to the eye, but in the palate nothing but spices. I had a mind to eat of a pheasant; and, so soon as I got it into my mouth, I found I was chewing a limb of cinnamon; then I went to cut a piece of kid, and no sooner it had touched my lips, but it turn'd to red pepper: at last I began to think myself another kind of Midas, that every thing I had touched should be turned to spice."[19]

Portugal was rising in power and splendor when Camoens wrote the Lusiad; and, with respect to the music of verse, it has merit. The author, however, is far from shining in point of taste. He makes a strange jumble

18. Epilogue to Part II of *The Conquest of Granada by the Spaniards,* ll. 1–18.
19. Paragraph added in 2nd edition.

of Heathen and Christian Deities. "Gama," observes Voltaire, <216> "in a storm addresses his prayers to Christ, but it is Venus who comes to his relief."[20] Voltaire's observation is but too well founded. In the first book, Jove summons a council of the gods, which is described at great length, for no earthly purpose but to show that he favoured the Portuguese. Bacchus, on the other hand, declares against them upon the following account, that he himself had gained immortal glory, as conqueror of the Indies; which would be eclipsed if the Portuguese should also conquer them. A Moorish commander having received Gama with smiles, but with hatred in his heart, the poet brings down Bacchus from heaven to confirm the Moor in his wicked purposes; which would have been perpetrated, had not Venus interposed in Gama's behalf. In the second canto, Bacchus feigns himself to be a Christian, in order to deceive the Portuguese; but Venus implores her father Jupiter to protect them. And yet, after all, I am loth to condemn an early writer for introducing Heathen Deities as actors in a real history, when, in the age of Lewis XIV. celebrated for refinement of taste, we find French writers, Boileau <217> in particular, guilty sometimes of the same absurdity (a).

At the meeting *ann.* 1520 near Calais between Francis I. of France and Henry VIII. of England, it is observed by several French writers, that the French nobility displayed more magnificence, the English more taste. If so, the alteration is great since that time: France at present gives the law to the rest of Europe in every matter of taste, gardening alone excepted.[21] At the same time, though taste in France is more correct than in any other country, it will bear still some purification. The scene of a clyster-pipe in Moliere is too low even for a farce; and yet to this day it is acted, with a few softenings, before the most polite audience in Europe.*

---

* No nation equals the French in dress, household furniture, watches, snuff-boxes, and in toys of every kind. The Italians have always excelled in architecture and painting, the English in gardening. How are such national differences to be explained? A nation, like an individual, may be disposed to grand objects, which swell the mind. A nation, like an individual, may relish things neat, pretty, and elegant. And if a taste of any kind happen once to prevail among men of figure, it soon turns general. The verdure of the fields in England invites a polishing hand.

(a) Elements of Criticism, chap. 22.

20. Voltaire criticizes Camoens in the *Essai sur la poèsie épique.*

21. "At the meeting . . . gardening alone excepted": added in 2nd edition.

In Elements of Criticism (*a*) several cau-<218>ses are mentioned that
may retard taste in its progress toward maturity, and that may give it a retrograde motion when it is in maturity. There are many biasses, both natural
and acquired, that tend to mislead persons even of the best taste. Of the
latter, instances are without number. I select one or two, to show what influence even the slightest circumstances have on taste. The only tree beautiful at all seasons is the holly: in winter, its deep and shining green entitles
it to be the queen of the grove: in summer, this colour completes the har-
monious mixture of shades, so pleasing in that season! Mrs. D—— is lively
and sociable. She is eminent above most of her sex for a correct taste, displayed not only within doors but in the garden and in the field. Having
become mistress of a great house by matrimony, the most honourable of
all titles, a group of tall hollies, which had long obscured one of the capital
rooms, soon attracted her eye. <219> She took an aversion to a holly, and
was not at ease till the group was extirpated. Such a bias is perfectly harmless. What follows is not so. The Oxonians disliked the great Newton, because he was educated at Cambridge; and they favoured every book writ
against him. That bias, I hope, has not come down to the present time.

Refinement of taste in a nation, is always accompanied with refinement
of manners: people accustomed to behold order and elegance in public
buildings and public gardens, acquire urbanity in private. But it is irksome
to trudge long in a beaten track, familiar to all the world; and therefore,
leaving what is said above, like a statue curtailed of legs and arms, I hasten
to the history of the fine arts.

Useful arts paved the way to fine arts. Men upon whom the former had
bestowed every convenience, turned their thoughts to the latter. Beauty was
studied in objects of sight; and men of taste attached themselves to the fine
arts, which multiplied their enjoyments and improved their benevolence.
Sculpture and painting made an early figure in Greece; which <220> afforded plenty of beautiful originals to be copied in these imitative arts.
Statuary, a more simple imitation than painting, was sooner brought to
perfection: the statue of Jupiter by Phidias, and of Juno by Polycletes,
though the admiration of all the world, were executed long before the art

(*a*) Chap. 25.

of light and shade was known. Appollodorus, and Zeuxis his disciple, who flourished in the fifteenth Olympiad, were the first who figured in that art. Another cause concurred to advance statuary before painting in Greece, namely, a great demand for statues of their gods. Architecture, as a fine art, made a slower progress. Proportions, upon which its elegance chiefly depends, cannot be accurately ascertained but by an infinity of trials in great buildings: a model cannot be relied on; for a large and a small building, even of the same form, require different proportions. Gardening made a still slower progress than architecture: the palace of Alcinoous, in the seventh book of the Odyssey, is grand, and highly ornamented; but his garden is no better than what we term a kitchen-garden. Gardening has made a great progress in England. In France, na-<221>ture is sacrificed to conceit. The gardens of Versailles deviate from nature no less than the hanging gardens at Babylon. In Scotland, a taste is happily commenced for neat houses and ornamented fields; and the circumstances of the people make it probable, that taste there will improve gradually till it arrive at perfection. Few gentlemen in Scotland can afford the expence of London; and supposing them to pass the winter in a provincial town, they return to the occupations of the country with redoubled ardor. As they are safe from the corruption of opulence, nature will be their guide in every plan; and the very face of their country will oblige them to follow nature; being diversified with hills and plains, rocks and rivers, that require nothing but polishing. It is no unpleasing prospect, that Scotland may in a century, or sooner, compare with England; not, indeed, in magnificence of country-seats, but in sweetness and variety of concordant parts.[22]

The ancient churches in this island cannot be our own invention, being unfit for a cold climate. The vast space they occupy, quantity of stone, and gloominess <222> by excluding the sun, afford a refreshing coolness, and fit them for a hot climate. It is highly probable that they have been copied from the mosques in the south of Spain, erected there by the Saracens. Spain, when possessed by that people, was the centre of arts and sciences, and led the fashion in every thing beautiful and magnificent.

From the fine arts mentioned, we proceed to literature. It is agreed

22. "Gardening has made . . . of concordant parts": added in 2nd edition.

among all antiquaries, that the first writings were in verse, and that prose
was of a much later date. The first Greek who wrote in prose, was Pherecides
Syrus: the first Roman, was Appius Caecus, who composed a declamation
against Pyrrhus. The four books of Chatah Bhade, the sacred book of Hindostan, are composed in verse stanzas; and the Arabian compositions in
prose followed long after those in verse. To account for that singular fact,
many learned pens have been employed; but without success. By some it
has been urged, that as memory is the only record of events where writing
is unknown, history originally was composed in verse for the sake of memory. This is not satisfactory. To <223> undertake the painful task of composing in verse for the sake of memory, would require more foresight than
ever was exerted by a barbarian; not to mention that other means were used
for preserving the memory of remarkable events, a heap of stones, a pillar,
or other object that catches the eye. The account given by Longinus is more
ingenious. In a fragment of his treatise on verse, the only part that remains,
he observes, "that measure or verse belongs to poetry, because poetry represents the various passions with their language; for which reason the ancients, in their ordinary discourse, delivered their thoughts in verse rather
than in prose." Longinus thought, that anciently men were more exposed
to accidents and dangers, than when they were protected by good government and by fortified cities. But he seems not to have considered, that fear
and grief, inspired by dangers and misfortunes, are better suited to humble
prose than to elevated verse. I add, that however natural poetical diction
may be when one is animated with any vivid passion, it is not supposable
that the ancients never wrote nor spoke <224> but when excited by passion.
Their history, their laws, their covenants, were certainly not composed in
that tone of mind.

An important article in the progress of the fine arts, which writers have
not sufficiently attended to, will, if I mistake not, explain this mystery. The
article is the profession of a bard, which sprung up in early times before
writing was known, and died away gradually as writing turned more and
more common. The curiosity of men is great with respect to the transactions of their forefathers; and when such transactions are described in verse,
accompanied with music, the performance is enchanting. An ear, a voice,
skill in instrumental music, and above all a poetical genius, are requisite to

excel in that complicated art. As such talents are rare, the few that possessed them were highly esteemed; and hence the profession of a bard, which, beside natural talents, required more culture and exercise than any other known art. Bards were capital persons at every festival and at every solemnity. Their songs, which, by recording the atchievements of kings and heroes, a-<225>nimated every hearer, must have been the entertainment of every warlike nation. We have Hesiod's authority, that in his time bards were as common as potters or joiners, and as liable to envy. Demodocus is mentioned by Homer as a celebrated bard (*a*); and Phemius, another bard, is introduced by him deprecating the wrath of Ulysses, in the following words:

> O king! to mercy be thy soul inclin'd,
> And spare the poet's ever-gentle kind.
> A deed like this thy future fame would wrong,
> For dear to gods and men is sacred song.
> Self-taught I sing: by heav'n, and heav'n alone,
> The genuine seeds of poesy are sown;
> And (what the gods bestow) the lofty lay,
> To gods alone, and godlike worth, we pay.
> Save then the poet, and thyself reward;
> 'Tis thine to merit, mine is to record.

Cicero reports, that at Roman festivals anciently, the virtues and exploits of their great men were sung (*b*). The same custom prevailed in Peru and Mexico, as we learn from Garcilasso and other authors. <226> Strabo (*c*) gives a very particular account of the Gallic bards. The following quotation is from Ammianus Marcellinus (*d*). "Bardi quidem fortia virorum illustrium facta, heroicis composita versibus, cum dulcibus lyrae modulis, cantitarunt."[23] We have for our authority Father Gobien, that even the inhabitants of the Marian islands have bards, who are greatly admired, because

---

(*a*) Odyssey, b. 8.
(*b*) Tusculan Questions, lib. 4. N° 3. & 4.
(*c*) Lib. 4.
(*d*) Lib. 15. cap. 9.
23. "The Bards sang to the sweet strains of the lyre the valorous deeds of famous men composed in heroic verse."

in their songs are celebrated the feats of their ancestors. There are traces of the same kind among the Apalachites in North America.* And we shall see afterward (*a*), that in no other part of <227> the world were bards more honoured than in Britain and Scandinavia.

Bards were the only historians before writing was introduced. Tacitus (*b*) says, that the songs of the German bards were their only annals. And Joannes Magnus, Archbishop of Upsal, acknowledges, that in compiling his history of the ancient Goths, he had no other records but the songs of the bards. As these songs made an illustrious figure at every festival, they were conveyed in every family by parents to their children; and in that manner were kept alive before writing was known.

The invention of writing made a change in the bard-profession. It is now an agreed point, that no poetry is fit to be accompanied with music, but what is <228> simple: a complicated thought or description requires the utmost attention, and leaves none for the music; or if it divide the attention, it makes but a faint impression (*c*). The simple operas of Quinault bear away the palm from every thing of the kind composed by Boileau or Racine. But when a language, in its progress to maturity, is enriched with variety of phrases fit to express the most elevated thoughts, men of genius aspire to the higher strains of poetry, leaving music and song to the bards: which distinguishes the profession of a poet from that of a bard. Homer,

---

* The first seal that a young Greenlander catches is made a feast for the family and neighbours. The young champion, during the repast, descants upon his address in catching the animal: the guests admire his dexterity, and extol the flavour of the meat. Their only music is a sort of drum, which accompanies a song in praise of seal-catching, in praise of their ancestors, or in welcoming the sun's return to them. Here are the rudiments of the bard-profession. The song is made for a chorus, as many of our ancient songs are. Take the following example:

> The welcome sun returns again,
> Amna ajah, ajah, ah-hu!
> And brings us weather fine and fair,
> Amna ajah, ajah, ah-hu!

The bard sings the first and third lines, accompanying it with his drum, and with a sort of dance. The other lines, termed the burden of the song, are sung by the guests.

(*a*) Sketch 6. Progress of Manners.
(*b*) De Moribus Germanorum, cap. 2.
(*c*) See Elements of Criticism, vol. 2. Appendix, article 33.

in a lax sense, may be termed a bard; for in that character he strolled from feast to feast. But he was not a bard in the original sense: he indeed recited his poems to crowded audiences; but his poems are too complex for music, and he probably did not sing them, nor accompany them with the lyre. The Trovadores of Provence were bards in the original sense; and made a capital figure in days of ignorance, when few could read, and fewer write. In later times the <229> songs of the bards were taken down in writing, which gave every one access to them without a bard; and the profession sunk by degrees into oblivion. Among the highlanders of Scotland, reading and writing in their own tongue is not common even at present; and that circumstance supported long the bard-profession among them, after being forgot among neighbouring nations. Ossian was the most celebrated bard in Caledonia, as Homer was in Greece.*

From the foregoing historical deduction, the reader will discover without my assistance why the first writings were in verse. The songs of the bards, being universal favourites, were certainly the first compositions that writing was employed upon: they would be carefully collected by the <230> most skilful writers, in order to preserve them in perpetual remembrance. The following part of the progress is equally obvious. People acquainted with no written compositions but what were in verse, composed in verse their laws, their religious ceremonies, and every memorable transaction. But when subjects of writing multiplied, and became more and more involved, when people began to reason, to teach, and to harangue, they were obliged to descend to humble prose: for to confine a writer or speaker to verse in handling subjects of that nature, would be a burden unsupportable.

The prose compositions of early historians are all of them dramatic. A writer destitute of art is naturally prompted to relate facts as he saw them performed: he introduces his personages as speaking and conferring; and

---

* The multitude are struck with what is new and splendid, but seldom continue long in a wrong taste. Voltaire holds it to be a strong testimony for the Gierusaleme Liberata, that even the gondoliers in Venice have it mostly by heart; and that one no sooner pronounces a stanza than another carries it on. Ossian has the same testimony in his favour: there are not many highlanders, even of the lowest rank, but can repeat long passages out of his works.

relates only what was acted and not spoken.* The historical books of the Old Testament are composed in that mode; and so addicted to the dra-<231>matic are the authors of these books, that they frequently introduce God himself into the dialogue. At the same time, the simplicity of that mode is happily suited to the poverty of every language in its early periods. The dramatic mode has a delicious effect in expressing sentiments, and every thing that is simple and tender (*a*). Take the following instance of a low incident becoming by that means not a little interesting. Naomi having lost her husband and her two sons in foreign parts, and purposing to return to the land of her forefathers, said to her two daughters-in-law,

> Go, return each to her mother's house: the LORD deal kindly with you, as ye have dealt with the dead, and with me. The LORD grant you that you may find rest, each of you in the house of her husband. Then she kissed them: and they lift up their voice and wept. And they said unto her, Surely we will return with thee unto thy people. And Naomi said, Turn again, my daughters: why will ye go with me? are there yet any more husbands in my womb, that they may be your husbands? Turn again, <232> my daughters, go your way, for I am too old to have an husband: if I should say, I have hope, if I should have a husband also to night, and should also bear sons; would ye tarry for them till they were grown? would ye stay for them from having husbands? nay, my daughters; for it grieveth me much for your sakes, that the hand of the LORD is gone out against me. And they lift up their voice and wept again: and Orpah kissed her mother-in-law, but Ruth clave unto her. And she said, Behold, thy sister-in-law is gone back unto her people, and unto her gods: return thou after thy sister-in-law. And Ruth said, Intreat me not to leave thee, or to return from following after thee: for whither thou goest, I will go; and where thou lodgest I will lodge: thy people shall be my people, and thy God my God: where thou diest, will I die, and there will I be buried: the LORD do so to me, and more also, if ought but death part thee and me. When she saw that she was stedfastly minded to go with her, then she left speaking unto her.

* Low people to this day tell their story in dialogue, as ancient writers did, and for the same reason. They relate things as they saw and heard them. [[Note added in 2nd edition.]]

(*a*) See Elements of Criticism, chap. 22.

So they two went until they came to <233> Beth-lehem. And it came to pass when they were come to Beth-lehem, that all the city was moved about them, and they said, Is this Naomi? And she said unto them, Call me not Naomi, call me Mara: for the Almighty hath dealt very bitterly with me. I went out full, and the Lord hath brought me home again empty: why then call ye me Naomi, seeing the Lord hath testified against me, and the Almighty hath afflicted me? So Naomi returned, and Ruth the Moabitess her daughter-in-law with her, which returned out of the country of Moab: and they came to Beth-lehem in the beginning of barley-harvest.

And Naomi had a kinsman of her husband's, a mighty man of wealth, of the family of Elimelech; and his name was Boaz. And Ruth the Moabitess said unto Naomi, Let me now go to the field, and glean ears of corn after him in whose sight I shall find grace. And she said unto her, Go, my daughter. And she went, and came, and gleaned in the field after the reapers: and her hap was to light on a part of the field <234> belonging unto Boaz, who was of the kindred of Elimelech.

And behold, Boaz came from Beth-lehem, and said unto the reapers, The Lord be with you: and they answered him, The Lord bless thee. Then said Boaz unto his servant that was set over the reapers, Whose damsel is this? And the servant that was set over the reapers answered and said, It is the Moabitish damsel that came back with Naomi, out of the country of Moab: and she said, I pray you, let me glean, and gather after the reapers, amongst the sheaves: so she came, and hath continued even from the morning until now, that she tarried a little in the house. Then said Boaz unto Ruth, Hearest thou not, my daughter? Go not to glean in another field, neither go from hence, but abide here fast by my maidens. Let thine eyes be on the field that they do reap, and go thou after them: have I not charged the young men, that they shall not touch thee? and when thou art athirst, go unto the vessels, and drink of that which the young men have drawn. Then she fell <235> on her face, and bowed herself to the ground, and said unto him, Why have I found grace in thine eyes, that thou shouldst take knowledge of me, seeing I am a stranger? And Boaz answered and said unto her, It hath fully been shewed me all that thou hast done unto thy mother-in-law since the death of thine husband: and how thou hast left thy father and thy mother, and the land of thy nativity, and art come unto a people which thou knewest not heretofore. The Lord

recompense thy work, and a full reward be given thee of the LORD God
of Israel, under whose wings thou art come to trust. Then she said, Let
me find favour in thy sight, my lord, for that thou hast comforted me, and
for that thou hast spoken friendly unto thine handmaid, though I be not
like unto one of thine handmaidens. And Boaz said unto her, At meal-
time come thou hither, and eat of the bread, and dip thy morsel in the
vinegar. And she sat beside the reapers: and he reached her parched corn,
and she did eat, and was sufficed, and left. And when she was risen up to
<236> glean, Boaz commanded his young men, saying, Let her glean even
among the sheaves, and reproach her not. And let fall also some of the
handfuls of purpose for her, and leave them, that she may glean them, and
rebuke her not. So she gleaned in the field until even, and beat out that
she had gleaned: and it was about an ephah of barley.

And she took it up, and went into the city: and her mother-in-law saw
what she had gleaned: and she brought forth, and gave to her that she had
reserved, after she was sufficed. And her mother-in-law said unto her,
Where hast thou gleaned to day? and where wroughtest thou? blessed be
he that did take knowledge of thee. And she shewed her mother-in-law
with whom she had wrought, and said, The man's name with whom I
wrought to day, is Boaz. And Naomi said unto her daughter-in-law,
Blessed be he of the LORD, who hath not left off his kindness to the living
and to the dead. And Naomi said unto her, The man is near of kin unto
us, one of our next kinsmen. And Ruth the Moabitess said, He said unto
me al-<237>so, Thou shalt keep fast by my young men, until they have
ended all my harvest. And Naomi said unto Ruth her daughter-in-law, It
is good, my daughter, that thou go out with his maidens, that they meet
thee not in any other field. So she kept fast by the maidens of Boaz to
glean, unto the end of barley-harvest, and of wheat-harvest; and dwelt
with her mother-in-law.

Then Naomi her mother-in-law said unto her, My daughter, shall I not
seek rest for thee, that it may be well with thee? And now is not Boaz of
our kindred, with whose maidens thou wast? Behold, he winnoweth barley
to night in the threshing-floor. Wash thyself therefore, and anoint thee,
and put thy raiment upon thee, and get thee down to the floor: but make
not thyself known unto the man, until he shall have done eating and
drinking. And it shall be when he lieth down, that thou shalt mark the
place where he shall lie, and thou shalt go in, and uncover his feet, and lay

thee down, and he will tell thee what thou shalt do. And she <238> said unto her, All that thou sayest unto me, I will do.

And she went down unto the floor, and did according to all that her mother-in-law bade her. And when Boaz had eaten and drunk, and his heart was merry, he went to lie down at the end of the heap of corn: and she came softly, and uncovered his feet, and laid her down.

And it came to pass at midnight, that the man was afraid, and turned himself: and behold, a woman lay at his feet. And he said, Who art thou? And she answered, I am Ruth thine handmaid: spread therefore thy skirt over thine handmaid, for thou art a near kinsman. And he said, Blessed be thou of the LORD, my daughter: for thou hast shewed more kindness in the latter end, than at the beginning, inasmuch as thou followedst not young men, whether poor or rich. And now, my daughter, fear not, I will do to thee all that thou requirest: for all the city of my people doth know, that thou art a virtuous woman. And now it is true, that I am thy near kinsman: howbeit <239> there is a kinsman nearer than I. Tarry this night, and it shall be in the morning, that if he will perform unto thee the part of a kinsman, well, let him do the kinsman's part; but if he will not do the part of a kinsman to thee, then will I do the part of a kinsman to thee, as the LORD liveth: lie down until the morning.

And she lay at his feet until the morning: and she rose up before one could know another. And he said, Let it not be known that a woman came into the floor. Also he said, Bring the vail that thou hast upon thee, and hold it. And when she held it, he measured six measures of barley, and laid it on her: and she went into the city. And when she came to her mother-in-law, she said, Who art thou, my daughter? And she told her all that the man had done to her. And she said, These six measures of barley gave he me; for he said to me, Go not empty unto thy mother-in-law. Then said she, Sit still, my daughter, until thou know how the matter will fall: for the man will not be in rest, <240> until he have finished the thing this day.

Then went Boaz up to the gate, and sat him down there: and behold, the kinsman of whom Boaz spake, came by; unto whom he said, Ho, such a one, turn aside, sit down here. And he turned aside, and sat down. And he took ten men of the elders of the city, and said, Sit ye down here. And they sat down. And he said unto the kinsman, Naomi that is come again out of the country of Moab, selleth a parcel of land, which was our brother

Elimelech's. And I thought to advertise thee, saying, Buy it before the inhabitants, and before the elders of my people. If thou wilt redeem it, redeem it; but if thou wilt not redeem it, then tell me, that I may know: for there is none to redeem it beside thee, and I am after thee. And he said, I will redeem it. Then said Boaz, What day thou buyest the field of the hand of Naomi, thou must buy it also of Ruth the Moabitess, the wife of the dead, to raise up the name of the dead upon his inheritance. And the kinsman said, I cannot redeem <241> it for myself, lest I mar mine own inheritance: redeem thou my right to thy self, for I cannot redeem it. Now this was the manner in former time in Israel, concerning redeeming, and concerning changing, for to confirm all things: A man plucked off his shoe, and gave it to his neighbour: and this was a testimony in Israel. Therefore the kinsman said unto Boaz, Buy it for thee: so he drew off his shoe. And Boaz said unto the elders, and unto all the people, Ye are witnesses this day, that I have bought all that was Elimelech's, and all that was Chilion's, and Mahlon's, of the hand of Naomi. Moreover, Ruth the Moabitess, the wife of Mahlon, have I purchased to be my wife, to raise up the name of the dead upon his inheritance, that the name of the dead be not cut off from among his brethren, and from the gate of his place: ye are witnesses this day. And all the people that were in the gate, and the elders said, We are witnesses: The LORD make the woman that is come into thine house, like Rachel, and like Leah, which two did build the house of Israel: and do thou <242> worthily in Ephratah, and be famous in Beth-lehem. And let thy house be like the house of Pharez (whom Tamar bare unto Judah) of the seed which the LORD shall give thee of this young woman.

So Boaz took Ruth, and she was his wife: and when he went in unto her, the LORD gave her conception, and she bare a son. And the women said unto Naomi, Blessed be the LORD, which hath not left thee this day without a kinsman, that his name may be famous in Israel. And he shall be unto thee a restorer of thy life, and a nourisher of thine old age: for thy daughter-in-law which loveth thee, which is better to thee than seven sons, hath born him. And Naomi took the child, and laid it in her bosom, and became nurse unto it (*a*).

(*a*) Ruth i. 8.–iv. 16.

The dramatic mode is far from being so agreeable in relating bare historical facts. Take the following example.

Wherefore Nathan spake unto Bath-sheba the mother of Solomon, saying, Hast thou not heard that Adonijah the <243> son of Haggith doth reign, and David our lord knoweth it not? Now therefore come, let me, I pray thee, give thee counsel, that thou mayst save thine own life, and the life of thy son Solomon. Go, and get thee in unto king David, and say unto him, Didst not thou, my lord O king, swear unto thine handmaid, saying, Assuredly Solomon thy son shall reign after me, and he shall sit upon my throne? Why then doth Adonijah reign? Behold, while thou yet talkest there with the king, I will also come in after thee, and confirm thy words.

And Bath-sheba went in unto the king, into the chamber: and the king was very old; and Abishag the Shunammite ministered unto the king. And Bath-sheba bowed, and did obeisance unto the king: and the king said, What wouldst thou? And she said unto him, My lord, thou swarest by the LORD thy God unto thine handmaid, saying, Assuredly Solomon thy son shall reign after me, and he shall sit upon my throne: and now behold, Adonijah reigneth; and now my lord the king, thou know-<244>est it not. And he hath slain oxen, and fat cattle, and sheep in abundance, and hath called all the sons of the king, and Abiathar the priest, and Joab the captain of the host: but Solomon thy servant hath he not called. And thou, my lord O king, the eyes of all Israel are upon thee, that thou shouldst tell them who shall sit on the throne of my lord the king after him. Otherwise it shall come to pass, when my lord the king shall sleep with his fathers, that I and my son Solomon shall be counted offenders.

And lo, while she yet talked with the king, Nathan the prophet also came in. And they told the king, saying, Behold, Nathan the prophet. And when he was come in before the king, he bowed himself before the king with his face to the ground. And Nathan said, my lord O king, hast thou said, Adonijah shall reign after me, and he shall sit upon my throne? For he is gone down this day, and hath slain oxen, and fat cattle, and sheep in abundance, and hath called all the king's sons, and the captains of the host, and Abiathar the priest; <245> and behold, they eat and drink before him, and say, God save king Adonijah. But me, even me thy servant, and Zadok the priest, and Benaiah the son of Jehoiada, and thy servant Solomon hath he not called. Is this thing done by my lord the king, and thou hast not shewed it unto thy servant who should sit on the throne of my lord the king after him?

Then king David answered and said, Call me Bath-sheba: and she came into the king's presence, and stood before the king. And the king sware, and said, As the LORD liveth, that hath redeemed my soul out of all distress, even as I sware unto thee by the LORD God of Israel, saying, Assuredly Solomon thy son shall reign after me, and he shall sit upon my throne in my stead; even so will I certainly do this day. Then Bath-sheba bowed with her face to the earth, and did reverence to the king, and said, Let my lord king David live for ever.

And king David said, Call me Zadok the priest, and Nathan the prophet, and Benaiah the son of Jehoiada. And they <246> came before the king. The king also said unto them, Take with you the servants of your lord, and cause Solomon my son to ride upon mine own mule, and bring him down to Gihon. And let Zadok the priest, and Nathan the prophet, anoint him there king over Israel: and blow ye with the trumpet, and say, God save king Solomon. Then ye shall come up after him, that he may come and sit upon my throne; for he shall be king in my stead: and I have appointed him to be ruler over Israel, and over Judah. And Benaiah the son of Jehoiada answered the king, and said, Amen: the LORD God of my lord the king say so too. As the LORD hath been with my lord the king, even so be he with Solomon, and make his throne greater than the throne of my lord king David. So Zadok the priest, and Nathan the prophet, and Benaiah the son of Jehoiada, and the Cherethites and the Pelethites, went down and caused Solomon to ride upon king David's mule, and brought him to Gihon. And Zadok the priest took an horn of oyl out of the tabernacle, and anointed <247> Solomon: and they blew the trumpet, and all the people said, God save king Solomon. And all the people came up after him, and the people piped with pipes, and rejoyced with great joy, so that the earth rent with the sound of them.

And Adonijah, and all the guests that were with him, heard it, as they had made an end of eating: and when Joab heard the sound of the trumpet, he said, Wherefore is this noise of the city, being in an uprore? And while he yet spake, behold, Jonathan the son of Abiathar the priest came, and Adonijah said unto him, Come in, for thou art a valiant man, and bringest good tidings. And Jonathan answered and said to Adonijah, Verily our lord king David hath made Solomon King. And the king has sent with him Zadok the priest, and Nathan the prophet, and Benaiah the son of Jehoiada, and the Cherethites, and the Pelethites, and they have caused him to ride upon the king's mule. And Zadok the priest, and Nathan the prophet have anointed him king in Gihon: and they are come up from thence <248> rejoycing, so that the city rang again: this is the noise that ye have heard. And also Solomon sitteth on the throne of the kingdom. And moreover the king's servants came to bless our lord king David, saying, God make the name of Solomon better than thy name, and make his throne greater than thy throne: and the king bowed himself upon the bed. And also thus said the king, Blessed be the LORD God of Israel, which hath given one to sit on my throne this day, mine eyes even seeing it. And all the guests that were with Adonijah were afraid, and rose up, and went every man his way (*a*).

In the example here given are found frequent repetitions; not however by the same person, but by different persons who have occasion in the course of the incidents to say the same things; which is natural in the dramatic mode, where things are represented precisely as they were transacted. In that view, Homer's repetitions are a beauty, not a blemish; for they are confined to the dramatic part, and never occur in the narrative. In the <249> 24th chapter of Genesis, there is a repetition precisely in the manner of Homer.

But the dramatic mode of composition, however pleasing, is tedious and intolerable in a long history. In the progress of society, new appetites and new passions arise; men come to be involved with each other in various connections; incidents and events multiply, and history becomes intricate by an endless variety of circumstances. Dialogue, accordingly, is more sparingly used, and in history plain narration is mixed with it. Narration is as it were the ground-work, and dialogue is raised upon it, like flowers in embroidery. Homer is admitted by all to be the great master in that mode of composition. Nothing can be more perfect in that respect than the Iliad. The Odyssey is far inferior; and to guard myself against the censure of the undistinguishing admirers of Homer, a tribe extremely formidable, I call

(*a*) I Kings, i. II.–49.

to my aid a celebrated critic, whose superior taste and judgment never was disputed. "The Odyssey," says Longinus, "shows how natural it is for a writer of a great genius, in his declining age, to sink down to fabulous narration; for <250> that Homer composed the Odyssey after the Iliad, is evident from many circumstances. As the Iliad was composed while his genius was in its greatest vigour, the structure of that work is dramatic and full of action; the Odyssey, on the contrary, is mostly employed in narration, proceeding from the coldness of old age. In that later composition, Homer may be compared to the setting sun, which has still the same greatness, but not the same ardor or force. We see not in the Odyssey that sublime of the Iliad, which constantly proceeds in the same animated tone, that strong tide of motions and passions flowing successively like waves in a storm. But Homer, like the ocean, is great, even when he ebbs, and loses himself in narration and incredible fictions; witness his description of tempests, the adventures of Ulysses with Polyphemus the Cyclops, and many others."*
<251>

The narrative mode came in time so to prevail, that in a long chain of history, the writer commonly leaves off dialogue altogether. Early writers of that kind appear to have had very little judgment in distinguishing capital facts from minute circumstances, such as can be supplied by the reader without being mentioned. The history of the Trojan war by Dares Phrygius is a curious instance of that cold and creeping manner of composition. Take the following passage. Hercules having made a descent upon Troy, slew King Laomedon, and made a present of Hesione, the king's daughter, to Telamon his companion. Priamus, who succeeded to the kingdom of Troy upon the death of his father Laomedon, sent Antenor to demand his sister Hesione. Our author proceeds in the following manner:

> Antenor, as commanded by Priamus, took shipping, and sailed to Magnesia, where Peleus resided. Peleus entertained him hospitably three days, and the fourth day de-<252>manded whence he came. Antenor said, that

---

* The *Pilgrim's Progress,* and *Robinson Crusoe,* great favourites of the vulgar, are composed in a style, enlivened like that of Homer, by a proper mixture of the dramatic and narrative; and upon that account, chiefly, have been translated into several European languages.

he was ordered by Priamus to demand from the Greeks, that they should restore Hesione. When Peleus heard this he was angry, because it concerned his family, Telamon being his brother; and ordered the ambassador to depart. Antenor, without delay, retired to his ship, and sailed to Salamis, where Telamon resided, and demanded of him, that he should restore Hesione to her brother Priamus, as it was unjust to detain so long in servitude a young woman of royal birth. Telamon answered, that he had done nothing to Priamus; and that he would not restore what he had received as a reward for his valour; and ordered Antenor to leave the island. Antenor went to Achaia; and sailing from thence to Castor and Pollux, demanded of them to satisfy Priamus, by restoring to him his sister Hesione. Castor and Pollux denied that they had done any injury to Priamus, but that Laomedon had first injured them; ordering Antenor to depart. From thence he sailed to Nestor in Pylus, telling him the cause of his coming; which when Nestor <253> heard, he begun to exclaim, how Antenor durst set his foot in Greece, seeing the Greeks were first injured by the Phrygians. When Antenor found that he had obtained nothing, and that Priamus was contumeliously treated, he went on shipboard, and returned home.

The Roman histories before the time of Cicero are chronicles merely. Cato, Fabius Pictor, and Piso, confined themselves to naked facts (*a*). In the *Augustae Historiae scriptores* we find nothing but a jejune narrative of facts, commonly very little interesting, concerning a degenerate people, without a single incident that can rouse the imagination, or exercise the judgment. The monkish histories are all of them composed in the same manner.* <254>

The dry narrative manner being very little interesting or agreeable, a taste for embellishment prompted some writers to be copious and verbose. Saxo Grammaticus, who in the 12th century composed in Latin a history of Denmark, surprisingly pure for that early period, is extremely verbose, and full

---

* Euripides, in his Phoenicians, introduces Oedipus, under sentence of banishment, and blind, calling for his staff, his daughter Antigone putting it in his hand, and directing every step, to keep him from stumbling. Such minute circumstances, like what are frequent in Richardson's novels, tend indeed to make the reader conceive himself to be a spectator (*b*): but whether that advantage be not more than overbalanced by the languor of a creeping narrative, may be justly doubted.

(*a*) Cicero de Oratore, lib. 2. N° 5.
(*b*) See Elements of Criticism, ch. 2. part 1. sect. 7.

of tautologies. Such a style, at any rate unpleasant, is intolerable in a modern tongue, before it is enriched with a stock of phrases for expressing aptly the great variety of incidents that enter into history. Take the following example out of an endless number. Henry VII. of England, having the young Queen of Naples in view for a wife, deputed three men, in character of ambassadors, to visit her, *and to answer certain questions contained in curious and exquisite instructions for taking a survey of her person, complexion, &c.* as expressed by Bacon in his life of that prince. One of the instructions was, to procure a picture of the Queen, which one would think could not require many words, yet behold the instruction itself.

> The King's said servants shall also, at their comyng to the parties of Spayne, diligently enquere for some conynge paynter having <255> good experience in making and paynting of visages and portretures, and suche oon they shall take with them to the place where the said Quuins make their abode, to the intent that the said paynter maye draw a picture of the visage and semblance of the said young Quine, as like unto her as it can or may be conveniently doon, which picture and image they shall substantially note, and marke in every pounte and circumstance, soo that it agree in similitude and likenesse as near as it may possible to the veray visage, countenance, and semblance of the said Quine; and in case they may perceyve that the paynter, at the furst or second making thereof, hath not made the same perfaite to her similytude and likenesse, or that he hath omitted any feiture or circumstance, either in colours, or other proporcions of the said visage, then they shall cause the same paynter, or some other the most conyng paynter that they can gete soo oftentimes to renewe and reforme the same picture, till it be made perfaite, and agreeable in every behalfe, with the very image and visage of the said <256> Quine.*

After this specimen so much approved by his Lordship, one will not be surprised at the flatness of the historical style during that period. By that

---

* The following passage, copied from an Edinburgh news-paper, may almost rival this eloquent piece. After observing that the frost was intense, which, says the writer, renders travelling very dangerous either in town or country, he proceeds thus: "We would therefore recommend it to shopkeepers, and those whose houses are close upon the streets or lanes, to scatter ashes opposite to their doors, as it may be a means of preventing passengers from falling, which they are in great danger of doing at present, from the slippiness of the streets, where that practice is not followed."

flatness of style Lord Bacon's history of Henry VII. sinks below the gravity
and dignity of history; particularly in his similes, metaphors, and allusions,
no less distant than flat. Of Perkin Warbeck and his followers, he says, "that
they were now like sand without lime, ill bound together." Again, "But
Perkin, advised to keep his fire, which hitherto burned as it were upon green
wood, alive with continual blowing, sailed again into Ireland." Again, "As
in the tides of people once up, there want <257> not commonly stirring
winds to make them more rough, so this people did light upon two ring-
leaders or captains." Again, speaking of the Cornish insurgents, and of the
causes that inflamed them, "But now these bubbles by much stirring began
to meet, as they used to do on the top of water." Again, speaking of Perkin,
"And as it fareth with smoak, that never loseth itself till it be at the highest,
he did now before his end raise his stile, intytling himself no more Richard
Duke of York, but Richard the Fourth, King of England." He descends
sometimes so low as to play upon words; witness the following speech made
for Perkin to the King of Scotland. "High and mighty King! your Grace
may be pleased benignly to bow your ears to hear the tragedy of a young
man that by right ought to hold in his hand the ball of a kingdom, but by
fortune is made himself a ball, tossed from misery to misery, and from place
to place." The following is a strangely forced allusion. Talking of Margaret
Duchess of Burgundy, who had patronized Lambert Simnel and Perkin
Warbeck, he says, "It <258> is the strangest thing in the world, that the
Lady Margaret should now, when other women give over child-bearing,
bring forth two such monsters, being, at birth, not of nine or ten months,
but of many years. And whereas other natural mothers bring furth children
weak, and not able to help themselves, she bringeth furth tall striplings,
able, soon after their coming into the world, to bid battle to mighty kings."
I should not have given so many instances of puerilities in composition,
were they not the performance of a great philosopher. Low indeed must
have been the taste of that age, when it infected its greatest genius.

The perfection of historical composition, which writers at last attain to
after wandering through various imperfect modes, is a relation of interesting facts connected with their motives and consequences. A history of that
kind is truly a chain of causes and effects. The history of Thucydides, and
still more that of Tacitus, are shining instances of that mode. There was

not a book written in France correct in its style before the year 1654, when the *Lettres Provinciales* appeared; nor a book in < 259 > a good historical style before the history of the conspiracy against Venice by the Abbé St. Real.[24]

A language in its original poverty, being deficient in strength and variety, has nothing at command for enforcing a thought but to redouble the expression. Instances are without number in the Old Testament. "And they say, How doth God know, and is there knowledge in the Most High?" Again, "Thus shalt thou say to the house of Jacob, and tell to the children of Israel." Again, "I will be an enemy unto thine enemies, and an adversary unto thine adversaries." Again, "To know wisdom and instruction, to perceive the words of understanding, to receive the instruction of wisdom." "She layeth her hands to the spindle, and her hands hold the distaff." "Put away from thee a froward mouth, and perverse lips put far from thee. Let thine eyes look right on, and let thine eye-lids look straight before thee."

Eloquence was of a later date than the art of literary composition; for till the latter was improved, there were no models < 260 > for studying the former. Cicero's oration for Roscius is composed in a style diffuse and highly ornamented; which, says Plutarch, was universally approved, because at that time the style of Asia, introduced into Rome with its luxury, was in high vogue. But Cicero, in a journey to Greece, where he leisurely studied Greek authors, was taught to prune off superfluities, and to purify his style, which he did to a high degree of refinement. He introduced into his native tongue a sweetness, a grace, a Majesty, that surprised the world, and even the Romans themselves. Cicero observes with great regret, that if ambition for power had not drawn Julius Caesar from the bar to command legions, he would have become the most complete orator in the world. So partial are men to the profession in which they excel. Eloquence triumphs in a popular assembly, makes some figure in a court of law composed of many judges; very little where there is but a single judge, and none at all in a despotic government. Eloquence flourished in the republics of Athens and of Rome; and makes some figure at present in a British House of Commons. < 261 >

In Athens eloquence could not but flourish. In an assembly of the peo-

24. "There was not . . . Abbé St. Real": added in 2nd edition.

ple, consisting of 5000 and upward, where every individual was entitled to give his opinion, the certainty of employing the talent of eloquence, was a strong motive with every young man of ambition to study that art. In Britain, very few are certain of obtaining a seat in the house of Commons; and that man must have great perseverance who can bestow years in acquiring an art that he may never have occasion to exercise. The eldest sons of peers have indeed a nearer prospect of a seat in the upper house: but young men of quality are commonly too much addicted to pleasure; and many of them come not to be peers till the fire of youth is spent. I am sorry to add another reason. Eloquence can never make a capital figure, but where patriotism is the ruling passion; for what can it avail among men who are deaf to every motive but what contributes to the interest or ambition of their party? When Demosthenes commenced his career of eloquence, patriotism made a figure in Athens, though it was on the decline. Had that great orator appeared more early, his <262> authority in Athens would have been supreme.*[25]

The Greek stage has been justly admired among all polite nations. The tragedies of Sophocles and Euripides in particular are by all critics held to be perfect in their kind, excellent models for imitation, but far above rivalship. If the Greek stage was so early brought to maturity, it is a phenomenon not a little singular in the progress of arts. The Greek tragedy made a rapid progress from Thespes to Sophocles and Euripides, whose compositions are indeed the most complete that ever were exhibited in Greece: but whether they be really such masterpieces as is generally thought, will admit some doubt. The subject is curious: and the candid reader will give attention. <263>

No human voice could fill the Greek theatre, which was so spacious as to contain several thousands without crowding. A brass pipe was invented

---

* Eloquence is necessary to those only who request, not to those who command. The Spartans, a bold and firm people, were decisive in their resolutions, and of few words; whence the laconic style. Take a modern instance of that style. In the year 1487, causes of discontent arising between O'Neal and Tirconnel, two Irish chieftains, the former wrote to the latter, "Send me tribute, or else." The latter answered, "I owe you none, and if."

25. Paragraph added in 2nd edition.

to strengthen the voice; but that invention destroyed the melody of pronunciation, by confining the voice to a harsh monotony. The pipe was not
the only unpleasant circumstance: every actor wore a mask; for what end
or purpose is not explained. It may be true, that the expressions of the
countenance could not be distinctly seen by those who occupied the back
rows; and a mask possibly was thought necessary in order to put all the
citizens upon a level. But without prying into the cause, let us only figure
an actor with a mask and a pipe. He may represent tolerably a simple incident or plain thought, such as are the materials of an Italian opera; but
the voice, countenance, and gestures, are indispensable in expressing refined
sentiments, and the more delicate tones of passion.

Where then lies the charm in ancient tragedies that captivated all ranks
of men? Greek tragedies are more active than sentimental: they contain
many judicious reflections on morals, manners, and upon <264> life in
general; but no sentiments except what are plain and obvious. The subjects
are of the simplest kind, such as give rise to the passions of hope, fear, love,
hatred, envy, and revenge, in their most ordinary exertions: no intricate nor
delicate situation to occasion any singular emotion; no gradual swelling and
subsiding of passion; and seldom any conflict between different passions.
I would not however be understood as meaning to depreciate Greek tragedies. They are indeed wonderful productions of genius, considering that
the Greeks at that period were but beginning to emerge from roughness
and barbarity into a taste for literature. The compositions of Eschylus,
Sophocles, and Euripides, must have been highly relished among a people
who had no idea of any thing more perfect: we judge by comparison, and
every work is held to be perfect that has no rival. It ought at the same time
to be kept in view, that it was not the dialogue which chiefly enchanted the
Athenians, nor variety in the passions represented, nor perfection in the
actors, but machinery and pompous decoration, accompanied with exquisite music. That <265> these particulars were carried to the greatest height,
we may with certainty conclude from the extravagant sums bestowed on
them: the exhibiting a single tragedy was more expensive to the Athenians
than their fleet or their army in any single campaign.

One would imagine, however, that these compositions are too simple to
enchant for ever; as without variety in action, sentiment, and passion, the
stage will not continue long a favourite entertainment: and yet we find not

a single improvement attempted after the days of Sophocles and Euripides. This may appear a matter of wonder at first view. But the wonder vanishes upon considering, that the manner of performance prevented absolutely any improvement. A fluctuation of passion and refined sentiments would have made no figure on the Greek stage. Imagine the discording scene between Brutus and Cassius, in Julius Caesar, to be there exhibited, or the handkerchief in the Moor of Venice: how slight would be their effect, when pronounced in a mask, and through a pipe? The workings of nature upon the countenance and the flections of voice <266> expressive of various feelings, so deeply affecting in modern representation, would have been entirely lost. If a great genius had arisen with talents for composing a pathetic tragedy in perfection, he would have made no figure in Greece. An edifice must have been erected of a moderate size: new players must have been trained to act without a mask, and to pronounce in their own voice. And, after all, there remained a greater miracle still to be wrought, namely, a total reformation of taste in the people of Athens. In one word, the simplicity of the Greek tragedy was suited to the manner of acting, and that manner excluded all improvements.

In composing a tragedy, the Grecian writers seem to have had no aim but to exhibit on the stage some known event as it was supposed to have happened. To give a distinct notion of the event beforehand, a person introduced on the stage related every incident to the audience; and that person sometimes gave a particular account of all that was to happen during the action, which seems to me a very idle thing. This speech was termed *the prologue.* There was no notion of an in-<267>vented fable, by which the audience might be kept in suspense during the action. In a word, a Greek tragedy resembles in every respect a history-picture, in which is represented some event known to all the world. Thus we see the same subject handled by different tragic writers, each showing his genius in the manner of representing it. Shakespeare's historical plays are all of the same kind. But the entertainment afforded by such a composition is far inferior to what arises from an unknown story, where every incident is new, where the hopes and fears of the audience are kept in constant agitation, and where all is suspended till the final conclusion.[26]

26. Paragraph added in 2nd edition.

From these premises an inference may with certainty be drawn, that delicacy of taste and feeling were but faintly known among the Greeks, even when they made the greatest figure. Music, indeed, may be successfully employed in a sentimental tragedy; but pomp and splendour avail nothing. A spectator deeply affected is regardless of decoration. I appeal to the reproving scene between Hamlet and the Queen his mother: does any man of taste <268> give the slightest attention to the beauty of the scenery? It would, however, be rash to involve in the same censure every Athenian. Do not pantomime-show, rope-dancing, and other such fashionable spectacles, draw multitudes from the deepest tragedies? And yet among us there are persons of taste, not a few, who despise such spectacles as fit only for the mob, persons who never bowed the knee to Baal. And, if there were such persons in Athens, of which we have no reason to doubt, it evinces the superiority of their taste: they had no example of more refined compositions than were exhibited on their stage; we have many.

With respect to comedy, it does not appear that the Greek comedy surpassed the tragedy, in its progress toward perfection. Horace mentions three stages of Greek comedy. The first was well suited to the rough and coarse manners of the Greeks when Eupolis, Cratinus, and Aristophanes wrote. These authors were not ashamed to represent on the stage real persons, not even disguising their names; of which we have a striking instance in a comedy of Aristophanes, called *The Clouds,* where So-<269>crates is introduced, and most contemptuously treated. This sort of comedy, sparing neither gods nor men, was restrained by the magistrates of Athens forbidding persons to be named on the stage. This led writers to do what is imitated by us: the characters and manners of known persons were painted so much to the life, that there could be no mistake. The satire was indeed heightened by this regulation, as every one contributed to the satire by detecting the persons who were meant in the representation. This was termed the *middle comedy.* But, as there still remained too great scope for obloquy and licentiousness, a law was made, prohibiting real events or incidents to be introduced upon the stage. This law happily banished satire against individuals, and confined it to manners and customs in general. Obedient to this law are the comedies of Menander, Philemon, and Diphilus, who flourished about 300 years before the Christian aera. And this is termed the *third stage* of Greek comedy. The comedies of Aristophanes, which still remain, err no less against taste than against decency. But we have good ground to believe, that <270> the Greek comedy was considerably refined by Menander and his cotemporaries; tho' we must rely upon collateral evidence, having very few remains of them. Their works, however, were far from perfection, if we can draw any conjecture from their imitator Plautus, who wrote about a century later. Plautus was a writer of genius; and it may reasonably be supposed that his copies did not fall greatly short of the originals, in matters at least that can be faithfully copied. At that rate, they must have been extremely defective in their subjects, as well as in the conduct of their pieces; for he shows very little art in either. With respect to the former, his plots are wondrous simple, very little varied, and very little interesting. The subject of almost every piece is a young man in love with a music-girl, desiring to purchase her from the procurer, and employing a favourite slave to cheat his father out of the price; and the different ways of accomplishing the cheat, is all the variety we find. In some few of his comedies, the story rises to a higher tone, the music-girl being discovered to be the daughter of a free man, which removes every obstruc-<271>tion to a marriage between her and her lover. With respect to the conduct of his pieces, there is a miserable defect of art. Instead of unfolding the subject in the progress of the action, as is done by Terence and by every modern writer, Plautus introduces an actor, for no better purpose than to explain the story to the audience. In one of his comedies, a household-god is so obliging as not only to unfold the subject, but to relate beforehand every particular that is to be represented, not excepting the catastrophe. Did not Plautus know, that it is pleasant to have our curiosity raised about what will happen next? In the course of the action, persons are frequently introduced who are heard talking to themselves on the open street. One would imagine the Greeks to have been great babblers, when they could not refrain soliloquies even in public. Could Plautus have been so artless in the conduct of his pieces, had a more perfect model been exhibited to him by Menander or the other authors mentioned?

It is observed in Elements of Criticism (*a*), that when a language has re-

(*a*) Chap. 13.

<272>ceived some polish, and the meaning of words is tolerably ascertained, then it is that a play of words comes to be relished. At that period of the Roman language, Plautus wrote. His wit consists almost entirely in a play of words, an eternal jingle, words brought together that have nearly the same sound, with different meanings, and words of different sounds that have the same meaning. As the Greek language had arrived to its perfection many years before, such false wit may be justly ascribed to Plautus himself, not to the Greeks from whom he copied. What was the period of that bastard wit in Greece, I know not; but it appears not to have been antiquated in Homer's days, witness the joke in the Odyssey, where Ulysses imposed upon Polyphemus, by calling him *Houtis* or *No-man.* Nor seems it to have been antiquated in the days of Euripides, who in his Cyclops repeats the same silly joke. The Roman genius soon purged their compositions of such infantine beauties; for in Terence, who wrote about fifty years later than Plautus, there is scarce a vestige of them. The dialogue beside of Terence is more natural and correct, not a word <273> but to the purpose: Plautus is full of tautologies, and digressions very little to the purpose. In a word, considering the slow progress of arts, the Roman theatre, from the time of Plautus to that of Terence, made as rapid a progress as perhaps ever happened in any country. Aristotle defines comedy to be an imitation of light and trivial subjects provoking laughter. The comedies of Plautus correspond accurately to that definition: those of Terence rise to a higher tone.

Beside the disadvantages of the mask and pipe mentioned above, there are two causes that tended to keep back the Greek and Roman comedy from the perfection of its kind. The first is the slow progress of society among these nations, occasioned by separating from the female sex. Where women are excluded from society, it never can arrive at any degree of refinement, not to talk of perfection. In a society of men and women, every one endeavours to shine: every latent talent, and every variety of character, are brought to light. To judge from ancient writers, man was a very plain being. Tacitus wrote when society between the sexes was abundantly <274> free; and in no author before him is to be found any thing beyond the outlines of character. In ancient comedies there are misers, lovers, parasites, procurers; but the individuals of each class are cast in the same mould. In the Rudens of Plautus, it is true, a miser is painted with much anxiety about his hidden treasure, every trifling incident being converted by him into a cause of suspicion; but he is still the same miser that is painted by others, without any shade or singularity in the character. Homer is the only ancient that deserves to be excepted: his heroes have all courage; but courage in each is clearly of a distinct kind. Knowledge of an endless variety of character in the human species, acquired from unrestrained society, has enabled the moderns to enrich the theatre with new characters without end. What else is it but defect of knowledge in the dispositions of men, that has confined the comedies of Plautus and Terence, like those of Italy, to a very few characters?

Nothing is more evident, than the superiority of Terence above Plautus in the art of writing; and, considering that Terence is a later writer, nothing would ap-<275>pear more natural, if they did not copy the same originals. It may be owing to genius that Terence excels in purity of language, and propriety of dialogue; but how account for his superiority over Plautus in the construction and conduct of a play? It will not certainly be thought, that Plautus would copy the worst models, leaving the best to future writers. This difficulty has not occurred to any of the commentators, as far as I can recollect.[27] If it be fair to judge of Menander and of his cotemporaries from Plautus their imitator, the talents of Terence must have been great, to excel all of them so much both in the construction and conduct of his plays.

Homer, for more than two thousand years, has been held the prince of poets. Such perfection in an author who flourished when arts were far short of maturity, would be surprising, would be miraculous. An author of genius (*a*) has endeavoured to account for this extraordinary phaenomenon; and I willingly acknowledge, that he has exerted much industry, as well as invention; but, in my apprehension, with-<276>out giving satisfaction. The new light that is thrown above upon the Greek theatre, has emboldened me to attempt a criticism on the Iliad, in order to judge whether Ho-

(*a*) [[Thomas Parnell,]] Essay on the life and writings of Homer.

27. In the 1st edition the paragraph ends: "Had the works of Menander and of his cotemporaries been preserved, they probably would have explained the mystery; which for want of that light will probably remain a mystery for ever."

mer has so far anticipated the ordinary progress of nature, as in a very early period to have arrived at the perfection of his art.

To form a good writer, genius and judgment must concur. Nature supplies the former; but, to the latter, instruction and imitation are essential. Shakespeare lived in an age that afforded him little opportunity to cultivate or improve his judgment; and, though inimitable in every article that depends on genius, there are found many defects in the conduct of his plays, and in other particulars, that require judgment ripened by experience. Homer lived in a rude age, little advanced in useful arts, and still less in civilization and enlarged benevolence. The nations engaged in the Trojan war, are described by him as in a progress from the shepherd-state to that of agriculture. In the Iliad, many eminent men are said to be shepherds. Andromaché, in particular (a), <277> mentions seven of her brethren, who were slain by Achilles as they tended their father's flocks and herds. In that state, garments of woollen cloth were used; but the skins of beasts, the original clothing, were still worn as an upper garment: every chief in the Iliad appears in that dress. Such, indeed, was the simplicity of this early period, that a black ewe was promised by each chief to the man who would undertake to be a spy. In such times, literature could not be far advanced; and it is a great doubt, whether there was at that time a single poem of the epic kind, for Homer to imitate or improve upon. Homer is undoubtedly a wonderful genius, perhaps the greatest that ever existed: his fire, and the boldness of his conceptions, are inimitable. But, in that early age, it would fall little short of a real miracle, to find such ripeness of judgment and correctness of execution, as in modern writers are the fruits of long experience and progressive improvements, during the course of many centuries. Homer is far from being so ripe, or so correct. I shall mention but two or three particulars; for, to dwell upon the imperfections of so il-<278>lustrious an author, is not pleasant. The first is, that he reduces his heroes to be little better than puppets. Not one of them performs an action of eclat, but with the assistance of some deity: even Achilles himself is every where aided by superior powers. It is Jupiter who inspires Hector with boldness to perform the heroic actions so finely described in the 15th book; and it is

(a) Book 6.

Jupiter who, changing sides, fills his heart with dismay. Glaucus, desperately wounded, supplicates Apollo, is miraculously healed, and returns to the battle perfectly sound. Hector, struck to the ground with a stone, and at the point of giving up the ghost, is cured by Apollo, and sent back to the battle with redoubled vigour. Homer resembles a sect of Christians, who hold, that a man can do nothing of himself, and that he is merely an instrument which God employs, as we do a spade or a hatchet. Can Homer's admirers be so blind as not to perceive, that this sort of machinery detracts from the dignity of his heroes, renders them less interesting, and less worthy of admiration? Homer, however, is deservedly such a favourite, that we are prone to admit any <279> excuse. In days of ignorance, people are much addicted to the marvellous. Homer himself, it may be justly supposed, was infected with that weakness; and he certainly knew, that his hearers would be enchanted with every thing wonderful, and out of the common course of nature. Another particular is his digressions without end, which draw our attention from the principal subject. I wish some apology could be made for them. Diomedes (*a*), for instance, meeting with Glaucus in the field of battle, and doubting, from his majestic air, whether he might not be an immortal, inquires who he was, declaring that he would not fight with a god. Glaucus lays hold of this very slight opportunity, in the heat of action, to give a long history of his family. In the mean time, the reader's patience is put to a trial, and his ardor cools. Agamemnon (*b*) desiring advice how to resist the Trojans, Diomedes springs forward; but, before he offers advice, gives the history of all his progenitors, and of their characters, in a long train. And, after all, what was the sage advice that required such a preface? <280> It was, that Agamemnon should exhort the Greeks to fight bravely. At any rate, was Diomedes so little known, as to make it proper to suspend the action at so critical a juncture for a genealogical history! A third particular, is an endless number of minute circumstances, especially in the description of battles, where they are the least tolerable. One capital beauty of an epic poem, is the selection of such incidents and circumstances as make a deep impression, keeping out of

(*a*) Book 6.
(*b*) Book 14.

view every thing low or familiar (*a*). An account of a single battle employs the whole fifth book of the Iliad, and a great part of the sixth: yet in the whole there is no general action; but warriors, whom we never heard of before, killed at a distance with an arrow or a javelin; and every wound described with anatomical accuracy. The whole seventeenth book is employed in the contest about the dead body of Patroclus, stuffed with minute circumstances below the dignity of an epic poem: the reader fatigued, has nothing to relieve him but the melody of Homer's versification. Gratitude would prompt an apology <281> for an author who affords so much entertainment: Homer had no good models to copy after; and, without good models, we cannot expect maturity of judgment. In a word, Homer was a blazing star, and the more to be admired, because he blazed in an obscure age. But that he should, in no degree, be tainted with the imperfections of such an age, is a wild thought: it is scarce possible, but by supposing him to be more than man.

Particular causes that advance the progress of fine arts, as well as of useful arts, are mentioned in the first part of this Sketch, and to these I refer.

Having traced the progress of the fine arts toward maturity in a summary way, the decline of these arts comes next in order. A useful art seldom turns retrograde, because every one has an interest to preserve it in perfection. Fine arts depend on more slender principles than those of utility; and therefore the judgment formed of them is more fluctuating. The variety of form that is admitted into the fine arts by such fluctuation of judgment, excites artists to indulge their love of no-<282>velty.[28] Restless man knows no golden mean, but will be attempting innovations without end. Such innovations do well in an art distant from perfection: but they are commonly the cause of degeneracy in arts that are in perfection; for an artist ambitious

---

(*a*) Elements of Criticism, vol. 1. p. 232. edit. 5.

28. "A useful art . . . love of novelty": added in 2nd edition. In 1st edition: "An art, in its progress towards maturity, is greatly promoted by emulation; and after arriving at maturity, its downfal is not less promoted by it. It is difficult to judge of perfection but by comparison; and an artist, ambitious to outstrip his predecessors, cannot submit to be an imitator, but must strike out something new, which in an art advanced to ripeness, seldom fails to be a degeneracy. This cause of the decline of the fine arts, I shall endeavour to illustrate by various instances."

to excel, aims always to be an original, and cannot submit to be an imitator. This is the plain meaning of a florid passage of Velleius Paterculus (Roman history, lib. 1). "Naturaque, quod summo studio petitum est, ascendit in summum; difficilisque in perfecto mora est; naturaliterque, quod procedere non potest, recedit."[29] Which may pass in a learned language, but will never do in our own tongue. "The idea," says Winckelmann, "of beauty could not be made more perfect; and those arts that cannot advance farther, become retrograde, by a fatality attending all human things, that if they cannot mount, they must fall down, because stability is not a quality of any created thing." I shall endeavour to illustrate the cause assigned by me above for decline of the fine arts, beginning with architecture. The Ionic was the favourite order when archi-<283>tecture was in its height of glory. The Corinthian order came next; which, in attempting greater perfection, has deviated from the true simplicity of nature: and the deviation is still greater in the Composite order (a).

With respect to literary productions, the first essays of the Romans were very imperfect. We may judge of this from Plautus, whose compositions are abundantly rude, though much admired by his cotemporaries, being the best that existed at that time in Rome. The exalted spirit of the Romans hurried them on to the grand and beautiful; and literary productions of all kinds were in perfection when Augustus reigned. In attempting still greater perfection, the Roman compositions became a strange jumble of inconsistent parts: they were tumid and pompous, and at the same time full of antitheses, conceit, and tinsel wit. Every thing new in a fine art pleases; and, for that reason, such compositions were relished. We see not by what gradual steps writers after the time of Augustus devia-<284>ted from the patterns that were before them; for no book of any moment, from the death of that Emperor, is preserved till we come down to Seneca, in whose works nature and simplicity give place to quaint thought, and bastard wit. He was a great corrupter of the Roman taste; and after him nothing was relished but brilliant strokes of fancy, with very little regard to sentiment: even Virgil

(a) Elements of Criticism, vol. 1. p. 206. edit. 5.

29. "And in the nature of things, that which is cultivated with the highest zeal advances to the highest perfection; but it is difficult to continue to the point of perfection, and naturally that which cannot advance must recede."

and Cicero made no figure in comparison. Lucan has a strained elevation of thought and style, very difficult to be supported: he sinks often into puerile reflections; witness his encomium on the river Po, which, says he, would equal the Danube, had it the same number of tributary streams. Quintilian, a writer of true and classical taste, who was protected and encouraged by Vespasian, attempted to stem the tide of false writing. His rhetoric is composed in an elegant style; and his observations contain every delicacy of the critical art. At the same time flourished Tacitus, possessing a more extensive knowledge of human nature than any other author ancient or modern, if Shakespeare be not excepted. His style is original, concise, com-<285>pact, and comprehensive; and, in what is properly called his history, perfectly correct and beautiful. He has been imitated by several, but never equalled by any. Brutus is said to be the last of the Romans for love of liberty: Quintilian and Tacitus may be said to be the last of the Romans for literary genius. Pliny the younger is no exception: his style is affected, turgid, and full of childish brilliancy. Seneca and Pliny are proper examples of writers who study show more than substance, and who make sense yield to sound.[30]

Whether music be or be not on the decline, seems a doubtful point, as the virtuosi are divided about it. In Greece, celebrated for taste, music was a theatrical entertainment, and had a dignified office, that of enlivening or enforcing the impressions made on the audience by the action. In that office, harmony being of little use, was little cultivated: nor did the musical instruments at that time known, afford great scope for harmony. Among us, harmony is brought to perfection; and, in modern compositions, it commonly is the chief part. To have melody <286> and harmony both in perfection, they can never be united in the same piece. The heart, swoln by a melancholy strain, is regardless of harmony; and, when subdued by a delightful strain of whatever kind, it has no leisure for complicated harmony. Rich harmony, on the other hand, engrossing the whole attention, leaves

30. In the 1st edition the paragraph continues: "Music among the Greeks limited itself to the employment to which it is destin'd by nature, viz. to be the handmaid of sense, to enforce, enliven, or sweeten, a sentiment. In the Italian opera the mistress is degraded to be the handmaid; and harmony triumphs, with very little regard to sentiment" [1:53].

the heart in a measure vacant.* The Greeks excelled in melody: the moderns excel in harmony. A just comparison between these, with respect to their effects on the hearer, will give instruction, and perhaps may enable us to determine whether music be or be not on the decline.

Nature, kindly to its favourite man, has furnished him with five external senses, not only for supporting animal life, but for procuring to him variety of enjoyments. A towering hill as an object of sight, a blushing rose as an object of smell, a pine-apple as an object of taste, a fine fur as an object of touch, do every one of them <287> produce a pleasant feeling. With respect to the sense of hearing in particular, certain sounds heard at the same instant raise a pleasant feeling; and certain sounds heard in succession raise another pleasant feeling; the former termed *harmony,* the latter *melody.* Harmony, like the pleasure of tasting or of smelling, affects us at the organ of sense only, and ceases when its object is removed. But melody is not confined to the organ of sense: it pierces to the heart, and produces different emotions, according to the nature of the modulation. An emotion so raised, such as that of gaiety, of melancholy, of pity, of courage, of benevolence, subsists after the music ceases, and even swells into a passion where it meets with a proper object. An air, sweet and melting, raises an emotion in the tone of love, and readily is elevated to the passion of love on the sight of a beautiful object. An air, slow and plaintive, produces an emotion in the tone of pity or grief, which, on the appearance of a person in distress, becomes a passion. A lively and animating strain produces an emotion of courage: the hearer exalted to <288> a hero, longs for an opportunity to exert his prowess.

> *Spumantemque dari, pecora inter inertia, votis*
> *Optat aprum, aut fulvum descendere monte leonem.* [31]

Can harmony produce an effect in any degree similar? The greatest admirer of harmony will not affirm that it can. The emotion raised by harmony

---

* Corelli excels in combining harmony with melody. His melody could not be richer without impoverishing his harmony; nor his harmony richer without impoverishing his melody.

31. "And prays that amid the timorous herds a foaming boar may be granted to his vows or a tawny lion come down from the mountains": Virgil, *Aeneid,* bk. IV, ll. 158–59.

has no affinity to passion or sentiment, more than the smell of a tuberose, or the taste of an ortolan; and it vanishes instantaneously with the concordant sounds that produced it.

Hence it may fairly be concluded, that, as far as melody is superior to harmony, as far was Greek music superior to the generality of what is now in practice. Exceptions there are undoubtedly that rival whatever could be performed by the ancients: but they are not many in number; the talent of composing music in the tone of a passion, seems in a great measure to lie dormant. The Italian opera resembles in form the Greek tragedy, from which evidently it is copied, but very little in substance. In the latter, the dialogue maintains its superior station; and music, confined to its proper place, has the strong-<289>est effect that music can produce. In the former, music usurping the superior station, commands attention by a storm of sound, leaving the dialogue languid and uninteresting. This unnatural disjunction of sound from sense, has introduced a sort of bastard music, termed *recitative*. Suffering the words to pass, though abundantly flat and languid,* I object to the execution, an unnatural movement between pronouncing and singing, that cannot be agreeable but to those who have been long accustomed to it. Of one thing I am certain, that graceful pronunciation, whether in the calm narrative tone, or in the warm tone of passion, is far more pleasant. What puts the preference of the Greek model far beyond a doubt, is, that the tragedies of Sophocles and Euripides were for a long course of time the delight of the most refined nation that ever existed: an Italian opera, on the contrary, never runs above a season; and, after being once laid aside, is never revived. But this slight and superficial taste for harmony above melody, can-<290>not be lasting: nature may be wrested, but soon or late resumes its empire. Sentimental music will be seriously cultivated, and restored to the place in the theatre it anciently possessed with dignity and propriety. Then it is that we may hope to rival the Greeks in music as in other arts. Upon the whole, music undoubtedly is much improved with respect to its theory;

---

* No person will suspect that under this censure is comprehended the celebrated Metastasio.

but, with respect to the practical part, there appears as little doubt of a woeful degeneracy.[32]

I lay hold of this opportunity to add a short article concerning the history of music, which regard to my native country will not suffer me to omit. We have in Scotland a multitude of songs tender and pathetic, expressive of love in its varieties, of hope, fear, success, despondence, and despair. The style of the music is wild and irregular, extremely pleasing to the natives, but little relished by the bulk of those who are accustomed to the regularity of the Italian style. None but men of genius, who follow nature and break loose from the thraldom of custom, esteem that music. It was a favourite of the late Geminiani, whose compositions show deli-<291>cacy of taste equal to the superiority of his genius; and it is warmly praised by Alessandro Tassoni, the celebrated author of Secchia Rapita. Discoursing of ancient and modern music, and quoting from various authors the wonderful effects produced by some modern compositions, he subjoins the following passage. "Noi ancora possiamo connumerar trà nostri, Iacopo Rè de Scozia, che non pur cose sacre compose in tanto, ma trovò da sestesso una nuovo musica lamentevole e mesta, differente da tutte l'atre. Nel che poi è stato imitato da Carlo Gesualdo Principe di Venosa, che in questa nostra età ha illustrata anch' egli la musica con nuova mirabili invenzioni" (a).* The king mentioned must be James I. of Scotland, the only one of our kings who seems to <292> have had any remarkable taste in the fine arts; and the music can be no other than the songs mentioned above. These are commonly attributed to David Rizzio, because he was an Italian and a musician; but erroneously, as we now discover from Tassoni. Our James I. was eminent for poetry no less than for music. He is praised for the former by Bishop Leslie, one of our historians, in the following words: "Patrii carminis gloria

---

* "We may reckon among the composers of the moderns James King of Scotland, who not only composed sacred songs, but was himself the inventor of a new style of music, plaintive and pathetic, different from all others. In this manner of composition, he has been imitated in our times by Carlo Gesualdo Prince of Venosa, who has illustrated that style of music with new and wonderful invention."

(a) Pensieri diversi, lib. 10. cap. 23.

32. This and the preceding two paragraphs added in 2nd edition.

nulli secundus."[33] We have many poems ascribed by tradition to that king; one in particular, *Christ's kirk on the green,* is a ludicrous poem, describing low manners with no less propriety than sprightliness.

Another cause that precipitates the downfal of every fine art, is despotism. The reason is obvious; and there was a dismal example of it in Rome, particularly with regard to eloquence. We learn from a dialogue accounting for the corruption of the Roman eloquence, that, in the decline of the art, it became fashionable to stuff harangues with impertinent poetical quotations, without any view but ornament merely; and this also was long fashionable in France. It happened unluckily for <293> the Romans, and for the world, that the fine arts were at their height in Rome, and not much upon the decline in Greece, when despotism put an end to the republic. Augustus, it is true, retarded their fall, particularly that of literature; it being the policy of his reign to hide despotism, and to give his government an air of freedom. His court was a school of urbanity, where people of genius acquired that delicacy of taste, that elevation of sentiment, and that purity of expression, which characterize the writers of his time. He honoured men of learning, admitted them to his table, and was bountiful to them. It would be painful to follow the decline of the fine arts in Rome to their total extirpation. The tyranny of Tiberius and of subsequent emperors, broke at last the elevated and independent spirit of the brave Romans, reduced them to abject slavery, and left not a spark of genius.* The science of law is <294> the only exception, as it flourished even in the worst of times: the Roman

---

* A singular persecution was carried on by Pope Gregory, most improperly surnamed the Great, against the works of Cicero, Titus Livius, and Cornelius Tacitus, which in every corner of Christendom were publicly burnt; and from that time, there has not been seen a complete copy of any of these authors. This happened in the sixth century: so soon had the Romans fallen from the perfection of taste and knowledge to the most humbling barbarity. Nor was that the only persecution of books on the score of religion. Many centuries before, a similar instance happened in China, directed by a foolish emperor. The Alexandrian library was twice consumed by fire, once in the time of Julius Caesar, and once in the time of the Calif Omar. What a profusion of knowledge was lost past redemption! And yet, upon the whole, it seems doubtful, whether the moderns have suffered by these events. At what corner of a library shall a man begin where he sees an infinity of books, choice ones too? He will turn his back to the library, and begin at no corner.

33. "Second to none in the glory of the songs of the Father."

lawyers were a respectable body, and less the object of jealousy than men of power and extensive land property. Among the Greeks also, a conquered people, the fine arts decayed, but not so rapidly as at Rome: the Greeks, farther removed from the seat of government, were less within the reach of a Roman tyrant. During their depression, they were guilty of the most puerile conceits; witness verses composed in the form of an axe, an egg, wings, and such like. The style of Greek writers in the reign of the Emperor Hadrian, is unequal, obscure, <295> stiff, and affected. Lucian is the only exception I am acquainted with.

We need scarce look for any other cause but despotism, to account for the decline of statuary and painting in Greece. These arts had arrived at their utmost perfection about the time of Alexander the Great: from that time they declined gradually along with the vigour of a free people; for Greece was now enslaved by the Macedonian power. It may in general be observed, that when a nation becomes stationary in that degree of power and eminence which it acquires from its constitution and situation, the national spirit subsides, and men of talents become rare. It is still worse with a nation that is sunk below its former power and eminence; and worst of all when it is reduced to slavery. Other causes concurred to accelerate the downfal of the arts mentioned. Greece, in the days of Alexander, was filled with statues of excellent workmanship; and there being little demand for more, the later statuaries were reduced to heads and busts. At last the Romans put a total end both to statuary and painting in Greece, by plundering it of its finest pieces; and <296> the Greeks, exposed to the avarice of the conquerors, bestowed no longer any money on the fine arts.[34]

The decline of the fine arts in Rome, is by a writer of taste and elegance ascribed to a cause different from any above mentioned, a cause equally destructive to manhood and to the fine arts; and that is opulence, joined with its constant attendants avarice and luxury. It would be doing injustice to that author to quote him in any words but his own.

---

34. In the 1st edition the paragraph continues: "Winckelmann, overlooking the causes mentioned, borrows from Velleius Paterculus a reason for the decline of the fine arts in Greece, not a little ridiculous" [1:55].

Priscis temporibus, quum adhuc nuda virtus placeret, vigebant artes in-
genuae; summumque certamen inter homines erat, ne quid profuturum
seculis diu lateret. Itaque, Hercules! omnium herbarum succos Democritus expressit: et ne lapidum virgultorumque vis lateret, aetatem inter ex-
perimenta consumpsit. Eudoxus quidem in cacumine excelsissimi montis
consenuit, ut astrorum coelique motus deprehenderet: et Chrysippus, ut
ad inventionem sufficiret, ter helleboro animum detersit. Verum ut ad
plastas convertar, Lysippum statuae unius lineamentis inhaerentem inopia
extinxit: et Myron, qui penè hominum <297> animas ferarumque aere
comprehenderat, non invenit heredem. At nos, vino scortisque demersi,
ne paratas quidem artes audemus cognoscere; sed accusatores antiquitatis,
vitia tantum docemus, et discimus. Ubi est dialectica? ubi astronomia? ubi
sapientiae consultissima via? Quis unquam venit in templum, et votum
fecit si ad eloquentiam pervenisset? quis, si philosophiae fontem invenis-
set? Ac ne bonam quidem mentem, aut bonam valetudinem, petunt: sed
statim, antequam limen capitolli tangunt, alius donum promittit si pro-
pinquum divitem extulerit; alius, si thesaurum effoderit; alius, si ad tre-
centies H——S. salvus pervenerit. Ipse senatus, recti bonique praeceptor,
mille pondo auri capitolio promittere solet: et ne quis dubitet pecuniam
concupiscere, Jovem quoque peculio exorat. Nolito ergo mirari, si pictura
defecit, quum omnibus diis hominibusque formosior videatur massa auri,
quam quidquid Apelles Phidiasve fecerunt (a).* <298>

(a) Petronius Arbiter.
* "In ancient times, when naked virtue had her admirers, the liberal arts were in their
highest vigour; and there was a generous contest among men, that nothing of real and
permanent advantage should long remain undiscovered. Democritus extracted the juice
of every herb and plant; and, lest the virtue of a single stone or twig should escape him,
he consumed a lifetime in experiments. Eudoxus, immersed in the study of astronomy,
spent his age upon the top of a mountain. Chrysippus, to stimulate his inventive faculty,
thrice purified his genius with hellebore. To turn to the imitative arts: Lysippus, while
labouring on the forms of a single statue, perished from want. Myron, whose powerful
hand gave to the brass almost the soul of man, and animals,—at his death found not an
heir! Of us of modern times what shall we say? Immersed in drunkenness and debauchery, we want the spirit to cultivate those arts which we possess. We inveigh against the
manners of antiquity; we study vice alone; and vice is all we teach. Where now is the art
of reasoning? where astronomy? where is the right path of wisdom? What man now a-
days is heard in our temples to make a vow for the attainment of eloquence, or for the
discovery of the fountain of true philosophy? Nor do we even pray for health of body,
or a sound understanding. One, while he has scarce entered the porch of the temple,

In England, the fine arts are far from such perfection as to suffer by opulence. They are in a progress, it is true, toward ma-<299>turity; but, gardening alone excepted, they proceed in a very slow pace.

There is a particular cause that never fails to undermine a fine art in a country where it is brought to perfection, abstracting from every one of the causes above mentioned. In the first part of the present sketch it is remarked, that nothing is more fatal to an art or to a science, than a performance so much superior to all of the kind, as to extinguish emulation. This remark is exemplified in the great Newton, who, having surpassed all the ancients, has not left to his countrymen even the faintest hope of rivalling him; and to that cause is attributed the visible decline of mathematical knowledge in Great Britain. The same cause would have been <300> fatal to the arts of statuary and painting among the Greeks, even though they had continued a free people. The decay of painting in modern Italy, is probably owing to the same cause: Michael Angelo, Raphael, Titian, &c. are lofty oaks that keep down young plants in their neighbourhood, and intercept from them the sunshine of emulation. Had the art of painting made a slower progress in Italy, it might have there continued in vigour to this day. Velleius Paterculus says judiciously, "Ut primo ad consequendos quos priores ducimus accendimur; ita, ubi aut praeteriri aut aequari eos posse desperavimus, studium cum spe senescit; et quod adsequi non potest, sequi desinit: praeteritoque eo in quo eminere non possimus, aliquid in quo nitamur conquirimus."* <301>

The decline of an art or science proceeding from the foregoing cause, is the most rapid where a strict comparison can be instituted between the

---

devotes a gift in the event of the death of a rich relation; another prays for the discovery of a treasure; a third for a ministerial fortune. The senate itself, the exemplary preceptor of what is good and laudable, has promised a thousand pounds of gold to the capitol; and, to remove all reproach from the crime of avarice, has offered a bribe to Jupiter himself. How should we wonder that the art of painting has declined, when, in the eyes both of the gods and men, there is more beauty in a mass of gold, than in all the works of Phidias and Apelles?"

* "As at first we are excited to emulate those superior models, so, when once we have lost the hope of excelling, or even of equalling them, our ambition fails us with our hopes: we cease to pursue what we cannot attain; and, neglecting that study in which we are debarred from arriving at excellence, we search for a different field of emulation."

works of different masters. The superiority of Newton above every other mathematician, can be ascertained with precision; and hence the sudden decline of that science in Great Britain. In Italy, a talent for painting continued many years in vigour; because no painter appeared with such superiority of genius, as to carry perfection into every branch of the art. As one surpassed in design, one in colours, one in graceful attitudes, there was still scope for emulation. But when, in the progress of the art, there was not a single perfection but had been seized by one or other master, from that period the art began to languish. Architecture continued longer in vigour than painting, because the principles of comparison in the former are less precise than in the latter. The artist who could not rival his predecessors in an established mode, sought out a new mode for himself, which, though perhaps less elegant or perfect, was for a time supported by novelty. <302>

Corruption of the Latin tongue makes a proper appendix to the decline of the fine arts in Rome. That the Latin tongue did not long continue in purity after the Emperor Augustus, is certain; and all writers agree, that the cause of its early corruption was a continual influx into Rome of men, to whom the Latin was a foreign language. The reason is plausible, but whether solid, may be doubted. In all countries, there are provincial dialects, which, however, tend not to corrupt the language of the capital, because they are carefully avoided by all who pretend to speak properly; and, accordingly, the multitude of provincials who flock to Paris and to London, have no influence to corrupt the language. The same probably was the case in old Rome, especially with respect to strangers whose native tongue was totally different from that of Rome: their imperfect manner of speaking Latin might be excused, but certainly was not imitated. Slaves in Rome had little conversation with their masters, except in receiving orders or reproof; which had no tendency to vitiate the Latin tongue. The corruption of that tongue, and at last its death <303> and burial as a living language, were the result of two combined causes; of which the early prevalence of the Greek language in Rome is the first. Latin was native to the Romans only, and to the inhabitants of Latium. The languages of the rest of Italy were numerous: the Messapian was the mother-tongue in Apulia, the Hetruscan in Tuscany and Umbria, the Greek in Magna Graecia, the Celtic in Lombardy and Liguria, &c. &c. Latin had arrived at its purity not many years before the reign of Augustus, and had not taken deep root in those parts of Italy where it was not the mother-tongue, when Greek became the fashionable language among people of rank, as French is in Europe at present. Greek, the storehouse of learning, prevailed in Rome even in Cicero's time; of which he himself bears testimony in his oration for the poet Archias: "Graeca leguntur in omnibus fere gentibus: Latina suis finibus, exiguis sane, continentur."[35] And, for that reason, Atticus is warmly solicited by him to write the history of his consulate in Greek. Thus Latin, justled by Greek out of its place, was left to inferiors, and probably would have sunk to utter <304> oblivion, even though the republic had continued in vigour. But the chief cause was the despotism of the Roman government, which proved the destruction of the fine arts, and of literature in particular. In a country of so many different languages, the Latin tongue could not be preserved in purity, but by constant perusal of Roman classics: but these were left to rot in libraries, a dark cloud of ignorance having overspread the whole empire. Every person carelessly spoke the language acquired in the nursery; and people of different tongues being mixed under one government, without a common standard, fell gradually into a sort of mixed language, which every one made a shift to understand. The irruption of many barbarous nations into Italy, several of whom settled there, added to the jargon. And that jargon, composed of many heterogeneous parts, was in process of time purified to the tongue that is now native to all the inhabitants of Italy.

In a history of the Latin tongue, it ought not to be overlooked, that it continued long in purity among the Roman lawyers. The science of law was in Rome <305> more cultivated than in any other country. The books written upon that science in Latin were numerous; and, being highly regarded, were the constant study of every man who aspired to be an eminent lawyer. Neither could such men have any bias to the Greek tongue, as law was little cultivated in Greece. Thus it happened, that the Latin tongue, as far as concerns law, was preserved in purity, even to the time of the Emperor Justinian.

---

35. "Greek literature is read in nearly every nation under heaven, while the vogue of Latin is confined to its own boundaries, and they are, we must grant, narrow."

Greek was preserved in purity much longer than Latin. The same language was spoken through all Greece, with some slight varieties in dialect. It was brought to great perfection and firmly rooted during the prosperous days of Greece. Its classics were numerous, and were studied by every person who pretended to literature.* Now, tho' the free and manly spirit of the Greeks yielded to Roman despotism, yet while any appetite for literature remained, their invaluable classics were a standard, which preserved the language in purity. But ignorance at length became <306> universal; and the Greek classics ceased to be a standard, being buried in libraries, as the Roman classics had been for centuries. In that state, the Greek tongue could not fail to degenerate among an ignorant and servile people, who had no longer any ambition to act well, write well, or speak well. And yet, after all, that beautiful tongue, far beyond a rival, has suffered less alteration than any other ever did in similiar circumstances; one cause of which is, that to this day the Greeks live separate from their masters the Turks, and have little commerce with them.

From the fate of the Latin tongue, an observation is drawn by many writers, that all languages are in a continual flux, changing from age to age without end. And such as are fond of fame, deplore it as a heavy misfortune, that the language in which they write will soon become obsolete and unintelligible. But it is a common error in reasoning, to found a general conclusion upon a single fact. In its progress toward perfection, a language is continually improving, and therefore continually changing. But supposing a language to have acquired its utmost perfec-<307>tion, I see nothing that should necessarily occasion any change: on the contrary, the classical books in that language become a standard for writing and speaking, to which every man of taste and figure conforms himself. Such was the case of the Greek tongue, till the Greeks were brutified by despotism. The Italian has continued in perfection more than three centuries, and the French more than one. The Arabic has continued without change more than a thousand years: there is no book in that language held to be in a style more pure or perfect

---

* There still remain about three thousand Greek books; of Latin books not above sixty.

than the Koran.* The English language has not yet acquired all the purity it is susceptible of; but, when there is no place for further improvements, there seems little doubt of its becoming stationary, like the languages mentioned. I bar always such a revolution as eradi-<308>cates knowledge, and reduces a people to a state of barbarity. In an event so dismal, the destruction of classical books and of a pure language, is not the greatest calamity: they will be little regretted in the universal wreck. In the mean time, to a writer of genius in a polished nation, it cannot but be a charming prospect, that his works will stand and fall with his country. To make such a writer exert his talents for purifying his mother-tongue, and for adding to the number and reputation of its classics, what nobler excitement, than the certainty of being transmitted to posterity, and admired by every person of taste through all ages!

As before the invention of printing, writers could have nothing in view but reputation and praise, they endeavoured to give the utmost perfection to their compositions. They at the same time studied brevity, in order that their works might pass through many hands; for the expence of transcribing great volumes, could not be afforded by every reader. The art of printing has made a great revolution: the opportunity it furnishes to mul-<309>tiply copies, has degraded writing to be a lucrative employment. Authors now study to swell their works, in order to raise the price; and being in a hurry for money, they reject the precept of Horace, *Nonum prematur in annum.*[36] Take for example the natural history of Aldrovandus, in many folio volumes. After filling his common-place book with passages from every author ancient and modern, to the purpose and not to the purpose; he sits down to compose, bent to transfuse into his book every article thus painfully collected. For example, when he introduces the ox, the cock, or any other

---

* I am far from thinking, that the language of the Arabians, an illiterate people in the days of their prophet Mahomet, was at that time carried to such purity and perfection as not to be susceptible of improvement. The fixing that language was undoubtedly owing to the Koran, which was held the word of God delivered to Mahomet by the angel Gabriel, and consequently was piously judged to be the standard of perfection. [[Note added in 2nd edition.]]

36. "Let it not be published until the ninth year": *Ars Poetica,* l. 388.

animal; far from confining himself to its natural history, he omits nothing
that has been said of it in books where it has been occasionally introduced,
not even excepting tales for amusing children: he mentions all the superstitious notions concerning it, every poetical comparison drawn from it,
the use it has served in hieroglyphics and in coats-armorial; in a word, all
the histories and all the fables in which it has been named. Take another
instance from a German or Dutch chronologer, whose name has escaped
me, and which I give <310> in a translation from the Latin, to prevent the
bias that one has for a learned language.

> Samson was the same with the Theban Hercules; which appears from the
> actions attributed to each of them, especially from the following, That
> Hercules, unarmed, is said to have suffocated the Nemean lion with a
> squeeze of his arms: Samson, unarmed, did the same, by tearing a lion to
> pieces: and Josephus says, that he did not tear the lion, but put out his
> breath with a squeeze; which could be done, and was done by Scutilius
> the wrestler, as reported by Suidas. David also, unarmed, tore to pieces a
> lion, 1 Samuel, chap. 17.; and Benaiah the son of Jehoiada also slew a lion,
> 2 Sam. chap. 23. ver. 20. Moreover we read, that Samson having caught
> three hundred foxes, tied lighted firebrands to their tails, and drove them
> into the standing corn of the Philistines, by which both the shocks and
> standing corn, with the vineyards and olives, were burnt up. Many think
> it incredible, that three hundred foxes should be caught by one man; as
> the fox, being the most cunning of all <311> animals, would not suffer
> itself to be easily taken. Accordingly Oppian, a Greek poet who writes
> upon hunting, asserts, that no fox will suffer itself to be taken in a gin or
> a net; though we are taught the contrary by Martial, lib. 10. epig. 37.

Hic olidum clamosus ages in retia vulpem. [37]

In India, eagles, hawks, and ravens, are taught to hunt foxes, as we are
informed by Olianus, Var. hist. lib. 9. cap. 26. They are also caught by
traps and snares, and in covered pits, as wolves are, and other large animals.
Nor is it wonderful that such a multitude of foxes were caught by Samson,
considering that Palestine abounded with foxes. He had hunters without

---

37. "Here you will clamorously drive a malodorous vixen into your toils."

number at command; and he was not confined in time. The fame of that
exploit was spread far and near. Even among the Romans there were ves-
tiges of it, as appears from Ovid, Fast. lib. 9. ver. 681. In one Roman festival, armed foxes were let loose in the circus; which Ovid, in the place
quoted, says was done in memory of the Carsiolan fox, which, <312> having destroyed many hens belonging to a country-woman, was caught by
her, and punished as follows. She wrapped up the fox in hay, which she
set fire to; and the fox being let go, fled through the standing corn and set
it on fire. There can be no doubt but that this festival was a vestige of
Samson's foxes, not only from congruity of circumstances, but from the
time of celebration, which was the month of April, the time of harvest
in Palestine. See more about foxes in Burman's works.

Not to mention the ridiculous arguments of this writer to prove Samson
to be the same with the Theban Hercules, nor the childish wanderings from
that subject; he has totally overlooked the chief difficulties. However well
fixed the fire-brands might be, it is not easily conceivable, that the foxes,
who would naturally fly to their lurking-holes, could much injure the corn,
or the olive-trees. And it is as little conceivable, what should have moved
Samson to employ foxes, when, by our author's supposition, he had men
at command, much better qualified than foxes for committing waste. This
author would have <313> saved himself much idle labour, had he embraced
a very probable opinion, that, if the translation be not erroneous, the original text must be corrupted. But enough, and more than enough, of these
writers. Maturity of taste has banished such absurdities; and at present,
happily, books are less bulky, and more to the purpose, than formerly.

It is observed above (*a*), that in a country thinly peopled, where the same
person must for bread undertake different employments, the people are
knowing and conversable; but stupid and ignorant in a populous country
where industry and manufactures abound. That observation holds not with
respect to the fine arts. It requires so much genius to copy even a single
figure, whether in painting or in sculpture, as to prevent the operator from
degenerating into a brute. The great exertion of genius, as well as of in-

---

(*a*) First section of the present Sketch.

vention, required in grouping figures, and in imitating human actions, tends to envigorate these faculties with respect to every subject, and of course to form a man of parts. <314>

Manners[1]

Some persons have a peculiar air, a peculiar manner of speaking or of acting, which, in opposition to the manners of the generality, are termed *their manners.* Such peculiarities in a whole nation, by which it differs from other nations or from itself at different periods, are termed *the manners of that nation.* Manners therefore signify a mode of behaviour peculiar to a certain person, or to a certain nation. The term is not applied to mankind in general; except perhaps in contradistinction to other beings.

Manners are distinguished from morals; but in what respect has not been clearly stated. Do not the same actions come under both? Certainly; but in different respects: an action considered as right or wrong, belongs to morals; considered as peculiar to a person or to a people, it belongs to manners.
<315>

The intention of the present sketch is, to trace out such manners only as appear to proceed immediately from the nature and character of a people, whether influenced by the form of government, or depending on the degree of civilization. I am far from regretting, that manners produced by climate, by soil, and by other permanent causes, fall not under my plan: I should indeed make a sorry figure upon a subject that has been acutely discussed by the greatest genius of the present age (*a*).

I begin with external appearance, being the first thing that draws attention. The human countenance and gestures have a greater variety of ex-

(*a*) Montesquieu [[*De l'esprit des lois,* pt. III]].
1. In the 1st edition, the order of this and Sketch VI is reversed: first comes "Progress of the Female Sex," then "Progress of Manners."

pressions than those of any other animal: and some persons differ widely
from the generality in these expressions, so as to be known by their manner
of walking, or even by so slight an action as that of putting on or taking
off a hat: some men are known even by the sound of their feet in walking.
Whole nations are distinguishable by such peculiarities. And yet there is
less variety in looks and gestures, than the different tones of mind would
produce, were men left to <316> the impulses of pure nature: man, an imitative animal, is prone to copy others; and by imitation, external behaviour
is nearly uniform among those who study to be agreeable; witness people
of fashion in France.² I rest upon these outlines: to enter fully into the
subject would be an endless work; disproportioned at any rate to the narrowness of my plan.

   Dress must not be omitted, because it enters also into external appearance. Providence hath clothed all animals that are unable to clothe themselves. Man can clothe himself; and he is endowed beside with an appetite
for dress, no less natural than an appetite for food. That appetite is proportioned in degree to its use: in cold climates it is vigorous; in hot climates,
faint. Savages must go naked till they learn to cover themselves; and they
soon learn where covering is necessary. The Patagonians, who go naked in
a bitter-cold climate, must be woefully stupid. And the Picts, a Scotch tribe,
who, it is said, continued naked down to the time of Severus, did not probably much surpass the Patagonians in the talent of invention. <317>

   Modesty is another cause for clothing: few savages expose the whole of
the body. It gives no high idea of Grecian modesty, that at the Olympic
games people wrestled and run races stark naked.

   There is a third cause for clothing, which is, the pleasure it affords. A
fine woman, seen naked once in her life, is made a desirable object by novelty. But let her go naked for a month, how much more charming will she
appear, when dressed with propriety and elegance! Clothing is so essential
to health, that to be less agreeable than nakedness would argue an incongruity in our nature. Savages probably at first thought of clothing as a pro-

   2. The 1st edition adds: "I am acquainted with a blind man, who, without moving
his feet, is constantly balancing from side to side, excited probably by some internal
impulse. Had he been endowed with eyesight, he would have imitated the manners of
others" [1:227].

tection only against the weather; but they soon discovered a beauty in dress: men led the way, and women followed. Such savages as go naked paint their bodies, excited by the same fondness for ornament that our women shew in their party-coloured garments. Among the Jews, the men wore ear-rings as well as the women (*a*). When Media was governed by its own kings, the men were sumptuous in dress: they wore loose robes, <318> floating in the air; had long hair covered with a rich bonnet, bracelets, chains of gold, and precious stones: they painted their faces, and mixed artificial hair with that of nature. As authors are silent about the women, they probably made no figure in that kingdom, being shut up, as at present, in seraglios. In the days of Socrates, married women in Greece were confined to be household drudges merely. Xenophon in his *Memorabilia Socratis,* introduces Ischoma-chus, an Athenian of great riches and reputation, discoursing to Socrates of his family affairs, "that he told his wife that his main object in marrying her was to have a person in whose discretion he could confide, who would take proper care of his servants, and lay out his money with oeconomy"; that one day he observed her face painted, and with high heeled shoes; that he chid her severely for such follies, "could she imagine to pass such silly tricks on a husband? If she wanted to have a better complection, why not weave at her loom standing upright, why not employ herself in baking and other family exercises, which would give her such a bloom as <319> no paint could imitate?" But when the Athenian manners came to be more polished, greater indulgence was given to the ladies in dress and ornament.[3] They consumed the whole morning at the toilette; employing paint, and every drug for cleaning and whitening the skin: they laid red even upon their lips, and took great care of their teeth: their hair, made up in buckles with a hot iron, was perfumed and spread upon the shoulders: their dress was elegant, and artfully contrived to set off a fine shape. Such is the influence of appetite for dress: vanity could not be the sole motive, as married ladies were

---

(*a*) Exod. xxxii. 2.

3. "In the days . . . dress and ornament": added in 3rd edition. In 1st and 2nd editions: "Very different was the case of Athenian ladies, after polygamy was banished from Greece" [1:228–29].

never seen in public.* We learn from St. Gregory, that women in his time dressed the head extremely high, environing it with many tresses of false hair, disposed in knots and buckles, so as to resemble a regular fortification. Josephus reports, that the Jewish ladies powdered their hair with gold dust; a fashion that was carried from Asia to Rome. The first <320> writer who mentions white powder for the hair, the same we use at present, is L'Etoile, in his journal for the year 1593. He relates, that nuns walked the streets of Paris curled and powdered. That fashion spread by degrees through Europe. For many years after the civil wars in France, it was a fashion in Paris to wear boots and spurs with a long sword: a gentleman was not in full dress without these accouttrements. The sword continues an article of dress, though it distinguishes not a gentleman from his valet. To show that a taste for dress and ornament is deeply rooted in human nature, savages display that taste upon the body, having no covering to display it upon. Seldom is a child of a savage left to nature: it is deprived of a testicle, a finger, a tooth; or its skin is engraved with figures.

Clothing hath no slight influence, even with respect to morals. I venture to affirm, at the hazard of being thought paradoxical, that nakedness is more friendly to chastity than covering. Adultery is unknown among savages, even in hot climates where they have scarce any covering.[4] Dress gives play to the imagination, <321> which pictures to itself many secret beauties which vanish when rendered familiar by sight: if a lady accidentally discover half a leg, imagination is instantly inflamed; tho' an actress appearing in breeches is beheld with indifference: a naked Venus makes not such an impression as when a garter only is discovered.

Cleanness is an article in external appearance. Whether cleanliness be inherent in the nature of man, or only a refinement of polished nations, may at first appear doubtful. What pleads for the former is, that cleanness is remarkable in several nations which have made little progress in the arts of life. The savages of the Caribbee islands, once a numerous tribe, were

* Young women in Athens appeared frequently in public, but always by themselves. In festivals, sacrifices, &c. they made part of the show, crowned with flowers, chanting hymns, and dancing in knots. [[Note added in 2nd edition.]]

4. The 1st edition adds: "A woman dressed with taste is a more desirable object than one who always goes naked" [1:230].

remarked by writers as neat and cleanly. In the island Otaheite, or King George's island, both sexes are cleanly: they bathe frequently, never eat nor drink without washing before and after, and their garments, as well as their persons, are kept free of spot or blemish. Ammianus Marcellinus, describing the Gauls, says, that they were cleanly; and that even the poorest women were never seen with dirty garments. The negroes, parti-<322>cularly those of Ardrah in the slave-coast, have a scrupulous regard to cleanness. They wash morning and evening, and perfume themselves with aromatic herbs. In the city of Benin, women are employed to keep the streets clean; and in that respect they are not outdone by the Dutch. In Corea, people mourn three years for the death of their parents; during which time they never wash. Dirtiness must appear dismal to that people, as to us.* But instances are no less numerous that favour the other side of the question. Ammianus Marcellinus reports of the Huns, that they wore a coat till it fell to pieces with dirt and rottenness. Plan Carpin, who visited the Tartars anno 1246, says, "That they never wash face nor hands; that they never clean a dish, a pot, nor a garment; that, like swine, they make food of every thing, not excepting the vermin that crawl on them." The present people of Kamskatka answer to that description in every article. The nasti-<323>ness of North-American savages, in their food, in their cabins, and in their garments, passes all conception. As they never change their garments till they fall to rags, nor ever think of washing them, they are eat up with vermin. The Esquimaux, and many other tribes, are equally nasty.

As cleanness requires attention and industry, the cleanness of some savages must be the work of nature, and the dirtiness of others must proceed from indolence counteracting nature. In fact, cleanness is agreeable to all, and nastiness disagreeable: no person prefers dirt; and even those who are the most accustomed to it are pleased with a cleanly appearance in others. It is true, that a taste for cleanness, like that for order, for symmetry, for congruity, is extremely faint during its infancy among savages. Its strongest antagonist is indolence, which savages indulge to excess: the great fatigue

---

* Many animals are remarkable for cleanness. Beavers are so, and so are cats. This must be natural. Though a taste for cleanness is not remarkable in dogs, yet, like men, they learn to be cleanly.

they undergo in hunting, makes them fond of ease at home; and dirtiness, when once habitual, is not easily conquered. But cleanness improves gradually with manners, and makes a figure in every industrious nation. Nor is a taste for clean-<324>ness bestowed on man in vain: its final cause is conspicuous, cleanness being extremely wholesome, and nastiness no less unwholesome.* <325>

Thus it appears, that a taste for cleanness is inherent in our nature. I say more: cleanness is evidently a branch of propriety, and consequently a self-duty. The performance is rewarded with approbation; and the neglect is punished with contempt (*a*).

A taste for cleanness is not equally distributed among all men; nor indeed is any branch of the moral sense equally distributed: and if, by nature, one person be more cleanly than another, a whole nation may be so. I judge that to be the case of the Japanese, so finically clean as to find fault even with the Dutch for dirtiness. Their inns are not an exception; nor their

---

* The plague, pestilential fevers, and other putrid diseases, were more frequent in Europe formerly than at present, especially in great cities, where multitudes were crowded together in small houses, separated by narrow streets. Paris, in the days of Henry IV. occupied not the third part of its present space, and yet contained nearly the same number of inhabitants; and in London the houses are much larger, and the streets wider, than before the great fire of 1666. There is also a remarkable alteration in point of diet. Formerly, people of rank lived on salt meat the greater part of the year: at present, fresh meat is common all the year round. Pot-herbs and roots are now a considerable article of food: about London, in particular, the consumption at the Revolution was not the sixth part of what it is now. Add the great consumption of tea and sugar, which I am told by physicians to be no inconsiderable antiseptics. But the chief cause of all is cleanness, which is growing more and more general, especially in the city of London. In Constantinople, putrid diseases reign as much as ever; not from unhealthiness in the climate, but from the narrowness and nastiness of the streets. How it comes that Turkish camps differ so much from the metropolis, I cannot say. Busbequius visited a Turkish camp in the days of Solyman the Magnificent. The ordure was carefully buried under ground; not any noisome smell; in every corner it was clean and neat. The excrements, which appear every where in our camps when stationary, create a sort of plague among the men. Captain Cook lately made a voyage round the world, and lost but a single man by disease, who at the same time was sickly when he entered the ship. One main article that preserved the health of the crew was cleanness. The Captain regularly one morning every week reviewed his ship's company, to see that every one of them had clean linen; and he bestowed the same care with respect to their clothes and bedding.

(*a*) Elements of Criticism, chap. 10.

little-houses, in which water is always at hand for washing after the operation. I judged it to be also the case of <326> the English, who, high and
low, rich and poor, are remarkable for cleanness all the world over; and I
have often amused myself with so singular a resemblance between islanders,
removed at the greatest distance from each other. But I was forced to abandon the resemblance, upon a discovery that the English have not always
been so clean as at present. Many centuries ago, as recorded in Monkish
history, one cause of the aversion the English had to the Danes was their
cleanness: they combed their hair, and put on a clean shirt once a-week. It
was reputed an extraordinary effort in Thomas a Becket, that he had his
parlor strewed every day with clean straw. The celebrated Erasmus, who
visited England in the reign of Henry VIII. complains of the nastiness and
slovenly habits of its people; ascribing to that cause the frequent plagues
which infested them. "Their floors," says he, "are commonly of clay strewed
with rushes, under which lies unmolested a collection of beer, grease, frag-
ments, bones, spittle, excrements of dogs and cats, and of every thing that
is nauseous" (a). And the strewing a <327> floor with straw or rushes was
common in Queen Elisabeth's time, not excepting even her presence-
chamber. A change so extraordinary in the taste and manners of the English, rouses our curiosity; and I flatter myself that the following cause will
be satisfactory. A savage, remarkably indolent at home, though not insensible of his dirtiness, cannot rouse up activity sufficient to attempt a serious
purgation; and would be at a loss where to begin. The industrious, on the
contrary, are improved in neatness and propriety, by the art or manufacture
that constantly employs them: they are never reduced to purge the stable
of Augeas; for being prone to action, they suffer not dirt to rest unmolested.
Industrious nations, accordingly, all the world over, are the most cleanly.
Arts and industry had long flourished in Holland, where Erasmus was born
and educated: the people were clean above all their neighbours, because
they were industrious above all their neighbours; and, upon that account,
the dirtiness of England could not fail to strike a Hollander. At the period
mentioned, industry was as great a stranger to England as cleanness: <328>
from which consideration, may it not fairly be inferred, that the English

(a) Epist. 432.

are indebted for their cleanliness to the great progress of industry among them in later times? If this inference hold, it places industry in an amiable light. The Spaniards, who are indolent to a degree, are to this day as dirty as the English were three centuries ago. Madrid, their capital, is nauseously nasty: heaps of unmolested dirt in every street, raise in that warm climate a pestiferous steam, which threatens to knock down every stranger. A purgation was lately set on foot by royal authority. But people habituated to dirt are not easily reclaimed: to promote industry is the only effectual remedy.* The nastiness of the <329> streets of Lisbon before the late earthquake, was intolerable; and so is at present the nastiness of the streets of Cadiz.

Though industry be the chief promoter of cleanness, yet it is seldom left to operate alone: other causes mix, some to accelerate the progress, some to retard it. The moisture of the Dutch climate has a considerable influence in promoting cleanliness; and, joined with industry, produces a surprising neatness and cleanness among people of business: men of figure and fashion, who generally resort to the Hague, the seat of government, are not so cleanly. On the other hand, the French are less cleanly than the English, though not less industrious. But the lower classes of people being in England more at their ease than in France, have a greater taste for living well, and in particular for keeping themselves clean.† <330>

A beard gives to the countenance a rough and fierce air, suited to the manners of a rough and fierce people. The same face without a beard appears milder; for which reason, a beard becomes unfashionable in a polished

---

* Till the year 1760 there was not a privy in Madrid, though it is plentifully supplied with water. The ordure, during night, was thrown from the windows into the street, where it was gathered into heaps. By a royal proclamation, privies were ordered to be built. The inhabitants, though long accustomed to an arbitrary government, resented this proclamation as an infringement of the common rights of mankind, and struggled vigorously against it. The physicians were the most violent opposers: they remonstrated, that, if the filth was not thrown into the streets, a fatal sickness would ensue; because the putrescent particles of air, which the filth attracted, would be imbibed by the human body.

† In a country thinly peopled, cleanness seldom prevails. The incitement is wanting of appearing agreeable to others, and the natural inclination for cleanness yields to indolence. In the high country between Derby and Matlock, thinly peopled, the inhabitants are as dirty as in the wildest parts of Scotland. [[Note added in 3rd edition.]]

nation. Demosthenes, the orator, lived in the same period with Alexander the Great, at which time the Greeks began to leave off beards. A bust, however, of that orator, found in Herculaneum, has a beard, which must either have been done for him when he was young, or from reluctance in an old man to a new fashion. Barbers were brought to Rome from Sicily the 454th year after the building of Rome. And it must relate to a time after that period what Aulus Gellius says (*a*), that people accused of any crime, were prohibited to shave their beards till they were absolved. From Hadrian downward, the Roman Emperors wore beards. Julius Capitolinus reproaches the Emperor Verus for cutting his beard at the instigation of a concubine. All the Roman generals wore beards in Justinian's <331> time (*b*). The Pope shaved his beard, which was held a manifest apostasy by the Greek church, because Moses, Jesus Christ, and even God the Father, were always drawn with beards by the Greek and Latin painters. Upon the dawn of smooth manners in France, the beaus cut the beard into shapes, and curled the whiskers. That fashion produced a whimsical effect: men of gravity left off beards altogether. A beard, in its natural shape, was too fierce even for them; and they could not for shame copy after the beaus. This accounts for a regulation, *anno* 1534, of the University of Paris, forbidding the professors to wear a beard.[5]

Language, when brought to any perfection among a polished people, may justly be considered as one of the fine arts; and, in that view, is handled above. But, considered as a branch of external behaviour, it belongs to the present sketch. Every part of external behaviour is influenced by temper and disposition, and speech more than any other part. In Elements of Criticism (*c*) it is observed, that an emotion <332> in many instances bears a resemblance to its cause. The like holds universally in all the natural sounds prompted by passion. Let a passion be bold, rough, cheerful, tender, or humble, still it holds, that the natural sounds prompted by it, are in the same tone: and hence the reason why these sounds are the same in all languages. Some slight resemblance of the same kind is discoverable in many

(*a*) Lib. 3. cap. 4.
(*b*) Procopii Historia Vandalica, lib. 2.
(*c*) Chap. 2. part 6.
5. "This accounts for . . . wear a beard": added in 2nd edition.

artificial sounds. The language of a savage is harsh; of polite people, smooth; and of women, soft and musical. The tongues of savage nations abound in gutturals, or in nasals: yet one would imagine that such words, being pronounced with difficulty, should be avoided by savages, as they are by children. But temper prevails, and suggests to savages harsh sounds, conformable to their roughness. The Esquimaux have a language composed of the harshest gutturals; and the languages of the northern European nations are not remarkably smoother. The Scotch peasants are a frank and plain people; and their dialect is in the tone of their character. The Huron tongue hath stateliness and energy <333> above most known languages, which is more conformable to the elevation of their sentiments, than to their present low condition. Thus the manners of a people may, in some measure, be gathered from their language. Nay, manners may frequently be gathered from single words. The Hebrew word LECHOM signifies both *food* and *fighting;* and TEREPH signifies both *food* and *plunder.* KARAB signifies *to draw near to one,* and signifies also *to fight.* The Greek word LEIA, which signified originally *spoil procured by war or piracy,* came to signify *wealth.* And the great variety of Greek words signifying *good* and *better,* signified originally *strong* and *violent.*

Government, according to its different kinds, hath considerable influence in forming the tone of a language. Language in a democracy is commonly rough and coarse; in an aristocracy, manly and plain; in a monarchy, courteous and insinuating; in despotism, imperious with respect to inferiors, and humble with respect to superiors. The government of the Greek empire is well represented in <334> Justinian's edicts, termed *Novellae Constitutiones;* the style of which is stiff, formal, and affectedly stately, but destitute of order, of force, and of ligament. About three centuries ago, Tuscany was filled with small republics, whose dialect was manly and plain. Its rough tones were purged off by their union under the Great Duke of Tuscany; and the Tuscan dialect has arrived nearer to perfection than any other in Italy. The tone of the French language is well suited to the nature of its government: every man is politely submissive to those above him; and this tone forms the character of the language in general, so as even to regulate the tone of the few who have occasion to speak with authority. The freedom of the English government forms the manners of the people: the English language is accordingly more manly and nervous than the French, and abounds more with rough sounds. The Lacedemonians of old, a proud and austere people, affected to talk with brevity, in the tone of command more than of advice; and hence the Laconic style, dry but masculine. The Attic <335> style is more difficult to be accounted for: it is sweet and copious, and had a remarkable delicacy above the style of any other nation. And yet the democracy of Athens produced rough manners; witness the comedies of Aristophanes, and the orations of Eschines and Demosthenes. We are not so intimately acquainted with the Athenians, as to account for the difference between their language and their manners. We are equally at a loss about the Russian tongue, which, notwithstanding the barbarity of the people, is smooth and sonorous: and, though the Malayans are the fiercest people in the universe, their language is the softest of all that are spoken in Asia. All that can be said is, that the operation of a general cause may be disturbed by particular circumstances. Languages resemble tides: the influence of the moon, which is the general cause of tides, is in several instances overbalanced by particular causes acting in opposition.

There may be observed in some savage tribes a certain refinement of language that might do honour to a polished people. The Canadians never give a man his proper <336> name, in speaking to him. If he be a relation, he is addressed to in that quality: if a stranger, the speaker gives him some appellation that marks affection; such as brother, cousin, friend.

In early times, people lived in a very simple manner, ignorant of such habitual wants as are commonly termed luxury. Rebecca, Rachel, and the daughters of Jethro, tended their father's flocks: they were really shepherdesses. Young women of fashion drew water from the well with their own hands. The joiner who made the bridal bed of Ulysses, was Ulysses himself (*a*). The Princess Nausicaa washes the family-clothes; and the Princes her brothers, upon her return, unyoke the car, and carry in the clothes (*b*). Queens, and even female deities, are employed in spinning (*c*). Is it from

(*a*) Odyssey, book 23.
(*b*) Book 6. & 7.
(*c*) Book 10.

this fashion that young women in England are denominated *spinsters?* Telemachus goes to council with no attendants but two dogs: <337>

> Soon as in solemn form th' assembly sat,
> From his high dome himself descends in state;
> Bright in his hand a pond'rous jav'lin shin'd;
> Two dogs, a faithful guard, attend behind.
>
> ODYSSEY, *book* 2.

Priam's car is yoked by his own sons, when he goes to redeem from Achilles the body of his son Hector. Telemachus yokes his own car (*a*). Homer's heroes kill and dress their own victuals (*b*). Achilles entertaining Priam, slew a snow-white sheep; and his two friends flea'd and dressed it. Achilles himself divided the roasted meat among his guests.* The story of Ruth is a pleasing instance of simplicity in ancient times; and her laying herself down to sleep at the feet of Boaz, a no less pleasing instance of innocence in these times.[6] No people lived more innocently than the ancient Germans, though men and women lived together without <338> reserve. They slept promiscuously round the walls of their houses; and yet we never read of adultery among them. The Scotch Highlanders to this day live in the same manner. In Sparta, men and women lived familiarly together: public baths were common to both; and in certain games, they danced and combated together naked as when born. In a later period, the Spartan dames were much corrupted; occasioned, as authors say, by a shameful freedom of intercourse between the sexes. But remark, that corruption was not confined to the female sex, men having degenerated as much from their original manhood as women from their original chastity; and I have no difficulty to maintain, that gold and silver, admitted contrary to the laws of Lycurgus, were what corrupted both sexes. Opulence could not fail to have the same effect there that it has every where; which is to excite luxury and every

---

* Pope, judging it below the dignity of Achilles to act the butcher, suppresses that article, imposing the task upon his two friends. Pope did not consider, that from a lively picture of ancient manners, proceeds one of the capital pleasures we have in perusing Homer.

(*a*) Odyssey, book 15.

(*b*) Odyssey, book 19. & 20.

6. "The story of . . . in these times": added in 2nd edition.

species of sensuality. The Spartans accordingly, renouncing austerity of manners, abandoned themselves to pleasure: the most expensive furniture, the softest beds, superb tapestry, precious vases, exquisite wines, delicious viands, were not <339> now too delicate for an effeminate Spartan, once illustrious for every manly virtue. Lycurgus understood human nature better than the writers do who carp at him. It was his intention, to make his countrymen soldiers, not whining lovers: and he justly thought, that familiar intercourse between the sexes, would confine their appetites within the bounds of nature; an useful lesson to women of fashion in our days, who expose their nakedness in order to attract and enflame lovers. What justifies this reasoning is, the ascendant that Spartan dames had over their husbands while the laws of Lycurgus were in vigour: they in effect ruled the state as well as their own families. Such ascendant cannot be obtained nor preserved but by strict virtue: a woman of loose manners may be the object of loose desire; but seldom will she gain an ascendant over any man, and never over her husband.

Not to talk of gold, silver was scarce in England during the reign of the third Edward. Rents were paid in kind; and what money they had, was locked up in the coffers of the great barons. Pieces of <340> plate were bequeathed even by kings of England, so trifling in our estimation, that a gentleman of a moderate fortune would be ashamed to mention such in his will.

Next of action. Man is naturally prone to motion; witness children, who are never at rest but when asleep. Where reason governs, a man restrains that restless disposition, and never acts without a motive. Savages have few motives to action when the belly is full; their huts require little work, and their covering of skins still less. Hunting and fishing employ all their activity. After much fatigue in hunting, rest is sweet; which the savage prolongs, having no motive to action till the time of hunting returns. Savages accordingly, like dogs, are extremely active in the field, and extremely indolent at home.* Sava-<341>ges in the torrid zone are indolent above all

---

* Quotiens bella non ineunt, non multum venatibus, plus per otium, transigunt, dediti somno, ciboque. Fortissimus quisque ac bellicosissimus nihil agens, delegata domus et penatium et agrorum cura feminis senibusque, et infirmissimo cuique ex familia,

others: they go naked; their huts cost them no trouble; and vegetables, that grow spontaneously, are their only food. The Spaniards who first landed in Hispaniola, were surprised at the manners of the inhabitants. They are described as lazy, and without ambition; passing part of their time in eating and dancing, and the rest in sleep; having no great share of memory, and still less of understanding. The character given of these savages belongs to all, especially to savages in hot climates. The imperfection of their memory and judgement is occasioned by want of exercise. The same imperfection was remarkable in the people of Paraguay, when under Jesuit government; of which afterward (a). <342>

We now take under consideration, the progress of such manners as are more peculiarly influenced by internal disposition; preparing the reader by a general view, before entering into particulars. Man is by nature a timid animal, having little ability to secure himself against harm: but he becomes bold in society, and gives vent to passion against his enemies. In the hunter-state, the daily practice of slaughtering innocent animals for food, hardens men in cruelty: more savage than bears or wolves, they are cruel even to their own kind.* The calm and sedentary life of <343> a shepherd, tends

---

ipsi hebent; mira diversitate naturae, cum iidem homines sic ament inertiam, et oderint quietem. *Tacitus, De moribus Germanorum, cap.* 15.—[*In English thus:* "While not engaged in war, they do not often spend their time in hunting, but chiefly in indolence, minding nothing but their sleep and food. The bravest and most warlike among them, having nothing to do, pass the time in a sluggish stupidity, committing the care of the house, the family, and the culture of the lands, to women, old men, and to the most weakly. Such is the wonderful diversity of their nature, that they are at once the most indolent of beings, and the most impatient of rest."]

(a) Book 2. sketch 1.

* Though it is beyond the reach of conception, that blood, flesh, fibres, or bones, can be a *substratum* for thought, for will, for passion, or for any mental quality; yet certain philosophers boldly undertake to derive even the noblest principles from external circumstances relative to the body only. Thus courage and cowardice are held to depend on the climate by the celebrated Montesquieu and several others. Sir William Temple ascribes these qualities to food, maintaining, that no animal which lives on vegetables is endowed with courage, the horse and cock alone excepted. I relish not doctrines that tend to degrade the most refined mental principles into bodily properties. With respect to the point under consideration, a very acute philosopher, taking a hint from Sir William Temple, derives from the difference of food the mental qualities of cruelty and hu-

to soften the harsh manners of hunters; and agriculture, requiring the union of many hands in one operation, improves benevolence. But here <344> the hoarding appetite starts up to disturb that auspicious commencement of civilization. Skilful husbandry, producing the necessaries of life in plenty, paves the way <345> to arts and manufactures. Fine houses, splendid gardens, and rich apparel, are desirable objects: the appetite for property becomes headstrong, and to obtain gratification tramples down

---

manity. (*a*) "Certain it is, (says that author), that the people who subsist mostly on animal food are cruel and fierce above others. The barbarity of the English is well known: the Gaures, who live wholly on vegetables, are the sweetest-tempered of all men. Wicked men harden themselves to murder by drinking blood." Even the most acute thinkers are not always on their guard against trivial analogies. Blood and slaughter are the limits of cruelty; and hence it is rashly inferred, that the drinking blood and eating flesh tend to inspire cruelty. The Carribees, in the same way of thinking, abstain from swines flesh; "which (say they), would make our eyes small like those of swine." Before venturing on a general rule, one ought to be prepared by an extensive induction of particulars. What will M. Rousseau say as to the Macassars, who never taste animal food, and yet are acknowledged to be the fiercest of mortals? And what will he say as to the negroes of New Guinea, remarkably brutal and cruel? A favourite dog, companion to his master, lives commonly on the refuse of his table, and yet is remarkably gentle. The English are noted for love of liberty: they cannot bear oppression; and they know no bounds to resentment against oppressors. He may call this cruelty if he be so disposed: others more candid will esteem it a laudable property. But to charge a nation in general with cruelty and ferocity, can admit no excuse but stubborn truth. Ignorance cannot be admitted; and yet he shows gross ignorance, as no people are more noted for humanity: in no other nation do sympathetic affections prevail more: none are more ready in cases of distress to stretch out a relieving hand. Did not the English, in abolishing the horrid barbarity of torture, give an illustrious example of humanity to all other nations? Nay his instance that butchers are prohibited from being put upon a jury, the only particular instance he gives of their cruelty, is on the contrary a proof of their humanity. For why are butchers excluded from being judges in criminal trials? for no other reason than that being inured to the blood of animals, they may have too little regard to the lives of their fellow subjects.

Flesh is composed of particles of different kinds. In the stomach, as in a still, it is resolved into its component particles, and ceases to be flesh before it enters the lacteals. Will M. Rousseau venture to say, which of these component particles it is that generates a cruel disposition? Man, from the form of his teeth, and from other circumstances, is evidently fitted by his maker for animal as well as vegetable food; and it would be an imputation on providence, that either of them should have any bad effect on his mind more than on his body. [[Note added in 2nd edition.]]

(*a*) Emile, liv. 1.

every obstacle of justice or honour (*a*). Differences arise, fomenting discord and resentment: war springs up, even among those of the same tribe; and while it was lawful for a man to take revenge at his own hand (*b*), that fierce passion swallowed up all others. Inequality of rank and fortune fostered dissocial passions; witness pride in particular, which produced a custom, once universal among barbarians, of killing men, women, dogs, and horses, for the use of a chieftain in the other world. Such complication of hateful and violent passions, rendering society uncomfortable, cannot be stemmed by any human means, other than wholesome laws: a momentary obstacle inflames desire; but perpetual restraint deadens even the most fervid passion. The authority of good government <346> gave vigour to kindly affections; and appetite for society, which acts incessantly, though not violently, gave a currency to mutual good offices. A circumstance concurred to blunt the edge of dissocial passions: the first societies were small; and small states in close neighbourhood engender discord and resentment without end: the junction of many such states into a great kingdom, removes people farther from their enemies, and renders them more gentle (*c*). In that situation, men have leisure and sedateness to relish the comforts of social life: they find that selfish and turbulent passions are subversive of society; and through fondness for social intercourse, they patiently undergo the severe discipline, of restraining passion and smoothing manners. Violent passions that disturb the peace of society have subsided, and are now seldom heard of: humanity is in fashion, and social affections prevail. Men improve in urbanity by conversing with women; and, however selfish at heart, they conciliate favour by assuming an air of disinterestedness. Selfishness, <347> thus refined, becomes an effectual cause of civilization. But what follows? Turbulent and violent passions are buried, never again to revive; leaving the mind totally ingrossed by self-interest. In the original state of hunters, there being little connection among individuals, every man minds his own concerns, and selfishness governs. The discovery that hunting is best carried on in company, promotes some degree of society in that

(*a*) See sketch 3.
(*b*) See Historical Law-tracts, tract 1.
(*c*) See this more fully handled, book 2. sketch 1.

state: it gains ground in the shepherd state, and makes a capital figure where husbandry and commerce flourish. Private concord is promoted by social affection; and a nation is prosperous in proportion as the *amor patriae* prevails. But wealth, acquired whether by conquest or commerce, is productive of luxury, and every species of sensuality. As these increase, social affections decline, and at last vanish. This is visible in every opulent city that has long flourished in extensive commerce. Selfishness becomes the ruling passion: friendship is no more; and even blood-relation is little regarded. Every man studies his own interest: opulence and sensual pleasure are idols worshipped by all. And thus, in the progress of manners, <348> men end as they began: selfishness is no less eminent in the last and most polished state of society, than in the first and most rude state.

From a general view of the progress of manners we descend to particulars. And the first scene that presents itself is, cruelty to strangers, extended, in process of time, against members of the same tribe. Anger and resentment are predominant in savages, who never think of restraining passion. But this character is not universal: some tribes are remarkable for humanity, as mentioned in the first sketch. Anger and resentment formed the character of our European ancestors, and rendered them fierce and cruel. The Goths were so prone to blood, that, in their first inroads into the Roman territories, they massacred man, woman, and child. Procopius reports, that in one of these inroads they left Italy thin of inhabitants. They were however an honest people; and by the polish they received in the civilized parts of Europe, they became no less remarkable for humanity, than formerly for cruelty. Totila, their king, having mastered Rome after a long and bloody <349> siege, permitted not a single person to be killed in cold blood, nor the chastity of any woman to be attempted. One cannot without horror think of the wanton cruelties exercised by the Tartars against the nations invaded by them under Gengizcan and Timor Bec.

A Scythian, says Herodotus, presents the king with the heads of the enemies he has killed in battle; and the man who brings not a head, gets no share of the plunder. He adds, that many Scythians clothe themselves with the skins of men, and make use of the skulls of their enemies to drink out of. Diodorus Siculus reports of the Gauls, that they carry home the heads of their enemies slain in battle; and after embalming them, deposit them

in chests as their chief trophy; bragging of the sums offered for these heads
by the friends of the deceased, and refused. In similar circumstances, men
are the same all the world over. The scalping of enemies, in daily use among
the North-American savages, is equally cruel and barbarous.

No savages are more cruel than the Greeks and Trojans were, as described
by Homer; men butchered in cold blood, <350> towns reduced to ashes,
sovereigns exposed to the most humbling indignities, no respect paid to age
nor to sex. The young Adrastus (*a*), thrown from his car, and lying in the
dust, obtained quarter from Menelaus. Agamemnon upbraided his brother
for lenity: "Let none from destruction escape, not even the lisping infant
in the mother's arms: all her sons must with Ilium fall, and on her ruins
unburied remain." He pierced the supplicant with his spear; and setting his
foot on the body, pulled it out. Hector, having stripped Patroclus of his
arms, drags the slain along, vowing to lop the head from the trunk, and to
give the mangled corse a prey to the dogs of Troy. And the seventeenth
book of the Iliad is wholly employed in describing the contest about the
body between the Greeks and Trojans. Beside the brutality of preventing
the last duties from being performed to a deceased friend, it is a low scene,
unworthy of heroes. It was equally brutal in Achilles to drag the corse of
Hector to the ships tied to his car. In a scene be-<351>tween Hector and
Andromache (*b*), the treatment of vanquished enemies is pathetically described; sovereigns massacred, and their bodies left a prey to dogs and vul-
tures; sucking infants dashed against the pavement; ladies of the first rank
forced to perform the lowest acts of slavery. Hector doth not dissemble,
that if Troy should be conquered, his poor wife would be condemned to
draw water like the vilest slave. Hecuba, in Euripides, laments that she was
chained like a dog at Agamemnon's gate; and the same savage manners are
described in many other Greek tragedies. Prometheus makes free with the
heavenly fire, in order to give life to man. As a punishment for bringing
rational creatures into existence, the gods decree, that he be chained to a
rock, and abandoned to birds of prey. Vulcan is introduced by Eschylus
rattling the chain, nailing one end to a rock, and the other to the breast-

(*a*) Book 6. of the Iliad.
(*b*) Iliad, book 6.

bone of the criminal. Who but an American savage can at present behold such a spectacle and not be shocked? A scene representing a woman murdered by her children would be hissed <352> by every modern audience; and yet that horrid scene was represented with applause in the Electra of Sophocles. Stoboeus reports a saying of Menander, that even the gods cannot inspire a soldier with civility: no wonder that the Greek soldiers were brutes and barbarians, when war was waged, not only against the state, but against every individual. At present, humanity prevails among soldiers as among others; because we make war only against a state, not against individuals. The Greeks are the less excusable for their cruelty, as they appear to have been sensible that humanity is a cardinal virtue. Barbarians are always painted by Homer as cruel; polished nations as tender and compassionate:

> Ye Gods! (he cried) upon what barren coast,
> In what new region is Ulysses tost?
> Possess'd by wild barbarians fierce in arms,
> Or men whose bosom tender pity warms?
>
> ODYSSEY, *book* 13. 241.

Cruelty is inconsistent with true heroism; and, accordingly, very little of the latter is discoverable in any of Homer's warriors. So much did they retain of the savage character, as, even without blushing, to fly from an enemy superior in bo-<353>dily strength. Diomedes, who makes an illustrious figure in the fifth book of the Iliad, retires when Hector appears: "Diomedes beheld the chief, and shuddered to his inmost soul." Antilochus, son of Nestor, having slain Melanippus (*a*), rushed forward, eager to seize his bright arms. But seeing Hector, he fled like a beast of prey who shuns the gathering hinds. And the great Hector himself shamefully turns his back upon the near approach of Achilles: "Periphetes, endowed with every virtue, renowned in the race, great in war, in prudence excelling his fellows, gave glory to Hector, covering the chief with renown." One would expect a fierce combat between these two bold warriors. Not so, Periphetes

(*a*) Book 15.

stumbling, fell to the ground; and Hector was not ashamed to transfix with his spear the unresisting hero.

In the same tone of character, nothing is more common among Homer's warriors than to insult a vanquished foe. Patroclus, having beat Cebriones to the ground with a huge stone, derides his fall in the following words: <354>

> Good heav'ns! what active feats yon artist shows,
> What skilful divers are our Phrygian foes!
> Mark with what ease they sink into the sand.
> Pity! that all their practice is by land.[7]

The Greeks are represented (*a*) one after another stabbing the dead body of Hector: "Nor stood an Argive near the chief who inflicted not a wound. Surely now, said they, more easy of access is Hector, than when he launched on the ships brands of devouring fire."

When such were the manners of warriors at the siege of Troy, it is no surprise to find the heroes on both sides no less intent on stripping the slain than on victory. They are every where represented as greedy of spoil.

The Jews did not yield to the Greeks in cruelty. It is unnecessary to give instances, as the historical books of the Old Testament are in the hands of every one. I shall select one instance for a specimen, dreadfully cruel without any just provocation: "And David gathered all the people together, and went to Rabbah, and fought against it, and took it. And he <355> brought forth the people that were therein, and put them under saws, and under harrows of iron, and under axes of iron, and made them pass through the brick-kiln: and thus did he unto all the cities of the children of Ammon" (*b*).

That cruelty was predominant among the Romans, is evident from every one of their historians. If a Roman citizen was found murdered in his own house, his whole household slaves, perhaps two or three hundred, were put to death without mercy, unless they could detect the murderer. Such a law, cruel and unjust, could never have been enacted among a people of any

(*a*) Book 22.
(*b*) 2 Samuel, xii. 29.
7. *Iliad,* bk. XVI, ll. 903–6 (trans. Pope).

humanity. Brutality to their offspring was glaring. Children were held, like cattle, to be the father's property: and so tenacious was the *patria potestas,* that if a son or daughter sold to be a slave was set free, he or she fell again under the father's power, to be sold a second time, and even a third time. The power of life and death over children was much less unnatural, while no public tribunal existed for punishing crimes. A <356> son, being a slave, could have no property of his own. Julius Caesar was the first who privileged a son to retain for his own use spoils acquired in war. When law became a lucrative profession, what a son gained in that way was declared to be his property. In Athens, a man had power of life and death over his children; but, as they were not slaves, what they acquired belonged to themselves. So late as the days of Dioclesian, a son's marriage did not dissolve the Roman *patria potestas* (*a*). But the power of selling children wore out of use (*b*). When powers so unnatural were given to men over their children, and exercised so tyranically, can there be any doubt of their cruelty to others?* <357> During the second triumvirate, horrid cruelties were every day perpetrated without pity or remorse. Antony, having ordered Cicero to be beheaded, and the head to be brought to him, viewed it with savage pleasure. His wife Fulvia laid hold of it, struck it on the face, uttered many bitter execrations, and, having placed it between her knees, drew out the tongue, and pierced it with a bodkin. The delight it gave the Romans to

---

* The effect of such unnatural powers was to eradicate natural affection between a man and his children. And, indeed, so little of nature was left in this connection, that a law was found necessary prohibiting a man to disinherit his children, except for certain causes specified, importing gross ingratitude in the latter; which was done by Justinian the Emperor in one of his Novels. But behold what follows. A prohibition to exheredate children renders them independent; and such independence produces an effect still more pernicious than despotic power in a father. Awe and reverence to parents make the only effectual check against the headstrong passions of youth: remove that check, and young men of fortune will give the rein to every vice. It deserves to be seriously pondered, whether the same encouragement be not given to vice, by a practice general in England among men of fortune in their marriage-articles; which is, to vest the estate in trustees, for behoof of the heir of the marriage.

(*a*) l. 1. Cod. cap. De patria potestate. [[*Codex,* bk. I, title IX, "Concerning Paternal Authority," sec. 1.]]

(*b*) l. 10. cod. [[Ibid., sec. 10.]]

see wild beasts set loose against one another in their circus, is a proof not
at all ambiguous of their taste for blood, even at the time of their highest
civilization. The Edile Scaurus sent at one time to Rome 150 panthers, Pompey 410, and Augustus 420, for the public spectacles. Their gladiato-
<358>rian combats are a less evident proof of their ferocity: the courage
and address exerted in these combats gave a manly pleasure, that balanced
in some measure the pain of seeing these poor fellows cut and slash one
another. And, that the Romans were never cured of their thirst for blood,
appears from Caligula, Nero, and many other monsters, who tormented
the Romans after Augustus. There is no example in modern times of such
monsters in France, though an absolute monarchy, nor even in Turkey.

Ferocity was, in the Roman empire, considerably mollified by literature
and other fine arts; but it acquired new force upon the irruption of the
barbarous nations who crushed that empire. In the year 559, Clotaire, King
of the Franks, burnt alive his son, with all his friends, because they had
rebelled against him. Queen Brunehaud, being by Clotaire II. condemned
to die, was dragged through the camp at a horse's tail, till she gave up the
ghost. The ferocity of European nations became boundless during the anarchy of the feudal system. Many peasants in the northern provinces of
France being <359> sorely oppressed in civil wars carried on by the nobles
against each other, turned desperate, gathered together in bodies, resolving
to extirpate all the nobles. A party of them, *anno* 1358, forced open the castle
of a knight, hung him upon a gallows, violated in his presence his wife and
daughters, roasted him upon a spit, compelled his wife and children to eat
of his flesh, and terminated that horrid scene with massacring the whole
family, and burning the castle. When they were asked, says Froissard, why
they committed such abominable actions, their answer was, "That they did
as they saw others do; and that all the nobles in the world ought to be
destroyed." The nobles, when they got the upper hand, were equally cruel.
They put all to fire and sword, and massacred every peasant who came in
the way, without troubling themselves to separate the innocent from the
guilty. The Count de Ligny encouraged his nephew, a boy of fifteen, to kill
with his own hand some prisoners who were his countrymen; in which,
says Monstrelet, the young man took great delight. How much worse than
brutal must have been <360> the manners of that age! for even a beast of

prey kills not but when instigated by hunger. The third act of stealing from the lead-mines in Derby was, by a law of Edward I. punished in the following manner. A hand of the criminal was nailed to a table; and, in that condition, he was left without meat or drink, having no means for freedom but to employ the one hand to cut off the other. The barbarity of the English at that period made severe punishments necessary: but the punishment mentioned goes beyond severity; it is brutal cruelty. The barbarous treatment of the Jews during the dark ages of Christianity, gives pregnant evidence, that Christians were not short of Pagans in cruelty. Poisoning and assassination were most licentiously perpetrated no farther back than the last century. Some pious men made vigorous efforts in more than one general council to have assassination condemned, as repugnant to the law of God; but in vain.* <361>

I wish to soften the foregoing scene: it may be softened a little. Among barbarians, punishments must be sanguinary, as their bodies only are sensible of pain, not their minds.†

The restoration of arts and sciences in Europe, and a reformation in religion, had a wonderful effect in sweetening manners, and promoting the interests of society. Of all crimes high treason is the most involved in circumstances, and the most difficult to be defined or circumscribed. And yet, for that crime are reserved the most exquisite torments. In England, the punishment is, to cut up the criminal a-<362>live, to tear out his heart, to dash it about his ears, and to throw it into the flames. The same punishment continues in form, not in reality: the heart indeed is torn out, but not till the criminal is strangled. Even the virulence of religious zeal is considerably

---

* It required the ferocity and cruelty of a barbarous age to give currency to a Mahometan doctrine, That the sword is the most effectual means of converting men to a dominant religion. The establishment of the Inquisition will not permit me to say, that Christians never put in practice a doctrine so detestable: on the contrary, they surpassed the Mahometans, giving no quarter to heretics either in this life, or in that to come. The eternity of hell-torments is a doctrine no less inconsistent with the justice of the Deity, than with his benevolence.

† The Russians are far from refinement either in manners or feelings. The Baron de Manstein, talking of the severity of Count Munich's military discipline, observes, that it is indispensible in Russia, where mildness makes no impression; and that the Russians are governed by fear, not by love. [[Note added in 2nd edititon.]]

abated. Savonarola was condemned to the flames as an impious impostor; but he was first privately strangled. The fine arts, which humanize manners, were in Italy at that time accelerating toward perfection. The famous Latimer was in England condemned to be burnt for heresy: but bags of gunpowder were put under his arms, that he might be burnt with the least pain. Even Knox, a violent Scotch reformer, acknowledges, that Wishart was strangled before he was thrown into the flames for heresy. So bitter was the late persecution against the Jesuits, that not only were their persons proscribed, but in many places their books, not even excepting books upon mathematics, and other abstract subjects. That persecution resembled in many particulars the persecution against the knights-templars: fifty-nine of the latter were burnt alive: the former were really less inno-<363>cent; and yet such humanity prevails at present, that not a drop of Jesuit-blood has been shed. A bankrupt in Scotland, if he have not suffered by unavoidable misfortune, is by law condemned to wear a party-coloured garment. That law is not now put in execution, unless where a bankrupt deserves to be stigmatized for his culpable misconduct.

Whether the following late instance of barbarity do not equal any of those above mentioned, I leave to the reader. No traveller who visited Petersburgh during the reign of the Empress Elizabeth can be ignorant of Madam Lapouchin, the great ornament of that court. Her intimacy with a foreign ambassador having brought her under suspicion of plotting with him against the government, she was condemned to undergo the punishment of the knout. At the place of execution, she appeared in a genteel undress, which heightened her beauty. Of whatever indiscretion she might have been guilty, the sweetness of her countenance and her composure, left not in the spectators the slightest suspicion of guilt. Her youth also, her beauty, her life and spirit pleaded for her. <364> But all in vain: she was deserted by all, and abandoned to surly executioners; whom she beheld with astonishment, seeming to doubt whether such preparations were intended for her. The cloak that covered her bosom being pulled off, modesty took the alarm, and made her start back: she turned pale, and burst into tears. One of the executioners stripped her naked to the waste, seized her with both hands, and threw her on his back, raising her some inches from the ground. The other executioner laying hold of her delicate limbs with his rough fists, put her in a posture for receiving the punishment. Then laying hold of the knout, a sort of whip made of a leathern strap, he with a single stroke tore off a slip of skin from the neck downward, repeating his strokes till all the skin of her back was cut off in small slips. The executioner finished his task with cutting out her tongue; after which she was banished to Siberia.* <365>

The native inhabitants of the island Amboyna are Malayans. Those on the sea-coast are subject to the Dutch: those in the inland parts are their declared enemies, and never give quarter. A Dutch captive, after being confined five days without food, is ripped up, his heart cut out, and the head severed from the body, is preserved in spice for a trophy. Those who can show the greatest number of Dutch heads are the most honourable.

In early times, when revenge and cruelty trampled on law, people formed associations for securing their lives and their possessions. These were common in Scandinavia and in Scotland. They were also common in England during the Anglo-Saxon government, and for some ages after the Conquest. But, instead of support-<366>ing justice, they contributed more than any other cause to confusion and anarchy, the members protecting each other, even in robbery and murder. They were suppressed in England by a statute of Richard II.; and in Scotland by reiterated statutes.

Roughness and harshness of manners are generally connected with cruelty; and the manners of the Greeks and Trojans are accordingly represented in the Iliad as remarkably rough and harsh. When the armies were ready to engage (*a*), Menestheus King of Athens, and Ulysses of Ithaca, are bitterly reproached by Agamemnon for lingering, while others were more forward. "Son of Peleus," he said, "and thou versed in artful deceit, in mischief only wise, why trembling shrink ye back from the field; why wait till others

---

* The present Empress has laid an excellent foundation for civilizing her people; which is a Code of laws, founded on principles of civil liberty, banishing slavery and torture, and expressing the utmost regard for the life, property, and liberty, of all her subjects, high and low. Peter I. reformed many bad customs: but being rough in his own manners, he left the manners of his people as he found them. If this Empress happen to enjoy a long and prosperous reign, she may possibly accomplish the most difficult of all undertakings, that of polishing a barbarous people. No task is too arduous for a woman of such spirit.

(*a*) Book 4.

engage in fight? You it became, as first in rank, the first to meet the flame of war. Ye first to the banquet are called, when we spread the feast. Your delight is to eat, to regale, to quaff unstinted the generous wine." In the fifth book, Sarpedon upbraids Hector <367> for cowardice. And Tlepolemus, ready to engage with Sarpedon, attacks him first with reviling and scurrilous words. Because Hector was not able to rescue the dead body of Sarpedon from the Greeks, he is upbraided by Glaucus, Sarpedon's friend, in the following words: "Hector, though specious in form, distant art thou from valour in arms. Undeserved hast thou fame acquired, when thus thou shrinkest from the field. Thou sustainest not the dreadful arm, not even the sight of godlike Ajax. Thou hast shunned his face in the fight: thou darest not approach his spear."

Rough and harsh manners produced slavery; and slavery fostered rough and harsh manners, by giving them constant exercise. The brutality of the Spartans to the Helots, their slaves, is a reproach to the human species. Beside suffering the harshest usage, they were prevented from multiplying by downright murder and massacre. Why did not such barbarity render the Spartans detestable, instead of being respected by their neighbours as the most virtuous people in Greece? There can be but one reason, that the Greeks <368> were all of them cruel, the Spartans a little more perhaps than the rest. In Rome, a slave, chained at the gate of every great house, gave admittance to the guests invited to a feast: could any but barbarians behold such a spectacle without pain?

Whence the rough and harsh manners of our West-Indian planters, but from the unrestrained licence of venting ill humour upon their negro slaves?* Why art car-<369>ters a rugged set of men? Plainly because horses,

---

* C'est de cet esclavage des negres, que les Créoles tirent peut-être en partie un certain caractere, qui les fait paroître bizzarres, fantasques, et d'une société peu goûtée en Europe. A peine peuvent ils marcher dans l'enfance, qu'ils voient autour d'eux des hommes grands et robustes, destinés à deviner, à prevenir leur volonté. Ce premier coup d'oeil doit leur donner d'eux mêmes l'opinion la plus extravagante. Rarement exposés à trouver de la résistance dans leurs fantaisies même injustes, ils prennent un esprit de présomption, de tyrannie, et de mépris extrême, pour une grande portion du genre humain. Rien n'est plus insolent que l'homme qui vit presque toujours avec ses inferieurs; mais quand ceux-ci sont des esclaves, accoutumés à servir des enfans, à craindre jusqu' à des cris qui doivent leur attirer des châtiments que peuvent devenir des maitres qui n'ont jamais obéi, des

their slaves, submit without resistance. An ingenious writer, describing Guiana in the southern continent of America, observes, that the negroes, who are more numerous than the whites, must be kept in awe by severity of discipline.[8] And he endeavours to justify the practice; ur-<370>ging, that beside contributing to the safety of the white inhabitants, it makes the slaves themselves less unhappy. "Impossibility of attainment," says he, "never fails to annihilate desire of enjoyment; and rigid treatment, suppressing every hope of liberty, makes them peaceably submit to slavery." Sad indeed must be the condition of slaves, if harsh treatment contribute to make them less unhappy. Such reasoning may be relished by rough European planters, intent upon gain: I am inclined, however, to believe, that the harsh treatment of these poor people is more owing to the avarice of their masters than to their own perverseness.* That slaves in all ages have been harshly treated, is a melancholy truth. One exception I know, and but one, which I gladly mention in honour of the Mandingo negroes. Their slaves, who are numerous, <371> receive very gentle treatment; the women

_____

méchans qui n'ont jamais été punis, des foux qui mettent des hommes à la chaîne? [[Abbé Raynal,]] *Histoire Philosophique et Politique des etablissements des Européens dans les Deux Indes, l. 4. p. 201.*—[*In English thus:* "It is from the slavery of the negroes that the Creoles derive in a great measure that character which makes them appear capricious and fantastical, and of a style of manners which is not relished in Europe. Scarcely have the children learned to walk, when they see around them tall and robust men, whose province it is to guess their inclinations, and to prevent their wishes. This first observation must give them the most extravagant opinion of themselves. From being seldom accustomed to meet with any opposition, even in their most unreasonable whims, they acquire a presumptuous and tyrannical disposition, and entertain an extreme contempt for a great part of the human race. None is so insolent as the man who lives almost always with his inferiors; but when these inferiors are slaves accustomed to serve infants, and to fear even their crying, for which they must suffer punishment, what can be expected of those masters who have never obeyed, profligates who have never met with chastisement, and madmen who load their fellow-creatures with chains?"]

* In England, slavery subsisted so late as the sixteenth century. A commission was issued by Queen Elisabeth, anno 1574, for inquiring into the lands and goods of all her bondmen and bondwomen in the counties of Cornwall, Devon, Somerset, and Glocester, in order to compound with them for their manumission or freedom, that they might enjoy their own lands and goods as free men.

8. Presumably Kames means Edward Bancroft.

especially, who are generally so well dressed as not to be distinguishable from those who are free.

Many political writers are of opinion, that for crimes instigated by avarice only, slavery for life, and hard work, would be a more adequate punishment than death. I would subscribe to that opinion but for the following consideration, that the having such criminals perpetually in view, would harden our hearts, and eradicate pity, a capital moral passion. Behold the behaviour of the Dutch in the island of Amboyna. A native who is found guilty of theft, is deprived of his ears and nose, and made a slave for life. William Funnel, who was there anno 1705, reports, that 500 of these wretches were secured in prison, and never suffered to go abroad but in order to saw timber, to cut stone, or to carry heavy burdens. Their food is a pittance of coarse rice boiled in water, and their bed the hard ground. What is still worse, poor people who happen to run in debt are turned over to the servants of the East India company, who send them to work among their slaves, with a daily al-<372>lowance of two-pence, which goes to the creditor. A nation must be devoid of bowels who can establish such inhumanity by law. But time has rendered that practice so familiar to the Dutch, that they behold with absolute indifference the multiplied miseries of their fellow creatures. It appears, indeed, that such a punishment would be more effectual than death to repress theft; but can any one doubt, that society would suffer more by eradicating pity and humanity, than it would gain by punishing capitally every one who is guilty of theft? At the same time, the Dutch, however cruel to the natives, are extremely complaisant to one another: seldom is any of them punished but for murder: a small sum will procure pardon for any other crime.

Upon the brutality and harsh manners of savages, was founded an opinion universally prevalent, that man is an obdurate being who must be governed by fear, not by love. It was the politic of princes to keep their subjects in awe; and every subject became a creeping slave. Hence the universal practice of never appearing before a sovereign or a prince but with a <373> splendid present, in order to deprecate his wrath or soften his temper. Philosophy has in time banished these crude notions of human nature, and taught us that man is a social being, upon whom benevolence has a more powerful influence than fear. Benevolence, accordingly, has become the ruling principle in society; and it is now the glory of princes to bestow favours and to receive none. This change of manners governs equally the worship paid to the Deity. Among rude nations, the Deity is represented as an angry God, visiting the sins of the fathers upon the children; and hence oblations, offerings, sacrifices, not even excepting human victims. Happy it is for us to have received more refined notions of the Deity. The opinion, justly founded, that benevolence is his prime attribute, has banished oblations, sacrifices, and such trumpery; and we depend on the goodness of the Deity, without any retribution but that of a grateful heart.

A degree of coarseness and indelicacy is connected with rough manners. The manners of the Greeks, as copied by Plautus and Terence from Menander and other Greek writers, were extremely coarse; such <374> as may be expected from a people living among their slaves, without any society with virtuous women. The behaviour of Demosthenes and Eschines to each other in their public harangues is wofully coarse. But Athens was a democracy; and a democracy, above all other governments, is rough and licentious. In the Athenian comedy, neither gods nor men are spared. The most respectable persons of the republic are ridiculed by name in the comedies of Aristophanes, which wallow in looseness and detraction. In the third act of Andromaché, a tragedy of Euripides, Peleus and Menelaus, Kings of Thessaly and Sparta, fall into downright ribaldry; Menelaus swearing that he will not give up his victim, and Peleus threatening to knock him down with his staff. The manners of Jason, in the tragedy of Medea by Euripides, are wofully indelicate. With unparallelled ingratitude to his wife Medea, he, even in her presence, makes love to the King of Corinth's daughter, and obtains her in marriage. Instead of blushing to see a person he had so deeply injured, he coolly endeavours to excuse himself, "that he was an exile like herself, without support; and <375> that his marriage would acquire powerful friends to them and to their children." Could he imagine that such frigid reasons would touch a woman of any spirit? A most striking picture of indelicate manners is exhibited in the tragedy of Alcestes. Admetus prevails upon Alcestes, his loving and beloved wife, to die in his stead. What a barbarian must the man be who grasps at life upon such a condition? How ridiculous is the bombast flourish of Admetus, that, if he were Orpheus, he would pierce to hell, brave the three-headed Cerberus,

and bring his wife to earth again! and how indecently does he scold his
father for refusing to die for him! What pretext could the monster have to
complain of his father, when he himself was so disgracefully fond of life,
as even to solicit his beloved spouse to die in his stead! What stronger instance, after all, would one require of indelicacy in the manners of the
Greeks, than that they held all the world except themselves to be barbarians?
In that particular, however, they are not altogether singular. Though the
Tartars, as mentioned above, were foul feeders, and hoggishly nasty, yet they
were extremely proud, despising, like <376> the Greeks, every other nation.
The people of Congo think the world to be the work of angels, except their
own country, which they hold to be the handiwork of the supreme archi-
tect. The Greenlanders have a high conceit of themselves; and in private
make a mock of the Europeans, or Kablunets, as they call them. Despising
arts and sciences, they value themselves on their skill in catching seals, con-
ceiving it to be the only useful art. They hold themselves to be the only
civilized and well-bred people; and when they see a modest stranger, they
say, "he begins to be a man"; that is, to be like one of themselves. Sometimes, however, sparks of light are perceived breaking through the deepest
gloom. When the Athenians were at war with Philip King of Macedon,
they intercepted some letters addressed by him to his ministers. These they
opened for intelligence: but one to his Queen Olympias they left with the
messenger untouched. This was done not by a single person, but by authority of the whole people.[9]

So coarse and indelicate were Roman manners, that whipping was a punishment inflicted on the officers of the army, <377> not even excepting
centurions (a). Doth it not show extreme grossness of manners to express
in plain words the parts that modesty bids us conceal? and yet this is common in Greek and Roman writers. In the Cyclops of Euripides, there is
represented a scene of the vice against nature, grossly obscene, without the
least disguise. How wofully indelicate must the man have been, who could
sit down gravely to compose such a piece! and how dissolute must the spectators have been who could behold such a scene without hissing! Next to

(a) Julius Capitolinus, in the life of Albinus.
9. "Sometimes, however, sparks . . . the whole people": added in 2nd edition.

the indecency of exposing one's nudities in good company, is the talking of them without reserve. Horace is extremely obscene, and Martial no less. But I censure neither of them, and as little the Queen of Navarre for her tales; for they wrote according to the manners of the times: it is the manners I censure, not the writers. In Rome, a woman taken in adultery was prostituted on the public street to all comers, a bell ringing the whole time. This abominable practice was abolished by the Emperor Theodosius (*a*). <378>

The manners of Europe, before the revival of letters, were no less coarse than cruel. In the Cartularies of Charlemagne, judges are forbidden to hold courts but in the morning, with an empty stomach. It would appear, that men in those days were not ashamed to be seen drunk, even in a court of justice. It was customary, both in France and Italy, to collect for sport all the strumpets in the neighbourhood, and to make then run races. Several feudal tenures give evidence of manners both low and coarse. Struvius mentions a tenure, binding the vassal, on the birth-day of his lord, to dance and fart before him. The cod-piece, which, a few centuries ago, made part of a man's dress, and which swelled by degrees to a monstrous size, testifies shamefully-coarse manners; and yet it was a modest ornament, compared with one used in France during the reign of Lewis XI. which was the figure of a man's privy parts fixed to the coat of breeches. In the same period, the judgment of Paris was a favourite theatrical entertainment: three women stark-naked represented the three goddesses, Juno, Venus, and Minerva. Nick-names, so com-<379>mon not long ago, are an instance of the same coarseness of manners; for to fix a nick-name on a man, is to use him with contemptuous familiarity. In the thirteenth century, many clergymen refused to administer the sacrament of the Lord's supper, unless they were paid for it.* In the tenth century, Edmond King of England, at a festival in the county of Gloucester, observed Leolf, a notorious robber under sentence of banishment, sitting at table with the King's attendants. Enraged at this insolence, he ordered Leolf to leave the room. On his refusing to obey, the King leaped on him, and seized him by the hair. The ruffian drew

* Corpus Christi tenentes in manibus, (says the canon), ac si dicerent, Quid mihi vultus dare, et ego eum vobis tradam?—[*In English thus:* "Holding the body of Christ in their hands, as if they said, What will you give me for this?"]

(*a*) Socrates, Hist. Eccl. liv. 5. cap. 18.

his dagger, and gave the King a wound, of which he immediately expired. How lamentable would be our condition, were we as much persecuted as our forefathers were with omens, dreams, prophesies, astrologers, witches, and apparitions? Our forefathers were robust both in mind and body, and <380> could bear without much pain what would totally overwhelm us.

Even after the revival of letters, the European manners were a long time coarse and indelicate. In the year 1480, the Cardinal Bibiena exhibited the *Calendra,* a comedy of intrigue upon a good model, but extremely licentious, as all compositions of that age were. The *Mandragora* of Machiavel is equally licentious; and, considering the author, the Queen of Navarre's tales, worst of all.[10]

Swearing as an expletive of speech, is a violent symptom of rough and coarse manners. It prevails among all barbarous nations. Even women in Plautus use it fluently. It prevailed in Spain and in France, till it was banished by polite manners. Our Queen Elisabeth was a bold swearer;* and the English populace, who are rough beyond their neighbours, <381> are noted by strangers for that vice. John King of England swore commonly "by the teeth of God." Charles VIII. of France "by God's day." Francis I. "upon the faith of a gentleman." And the oath of Lewis XII. was "may the devil take me."[11] Though swearing, in order to enforce an expression, is not in itself immoral; it is, however, hurtful in its consequences, rendering sacred names too familiar. God's beard, the common oath of William Rufus, suggests an image of our Maker as an old man with a long beard. In vain have acts of parliament been made against swearing: it is easy to evade the penalty, by coining new oaths; and, as that vice proceeds from an overflow of spirits, people in that condition brave penalties. Polished manners are the only effectual cure for that malady.

When a people begin to emerge out of barbarity, loud mirth and rough

---

* Writing to her sister the Queen, begging that she might not be imprisoned in the Tower, she concludes her letter thus: "As for that traitor Wyat, he might peradventure write me a letter: but on my faith I never received any from him. And, as for the copy of my letter sent to the French King, I pray God confound me eternally if ever I sent him word, message, token, or letter."

10. "In the tenth . . . worst of all": added in 2nd edition.

11. "John King of . . . devil take me": added in 2nd edition.

jokes come in place of rancour and resentment. About a century ago, it was usual for the servants and retainers of the Court of Session in Scotland, to break out into riotous mirth and uproar the last day of every term, throwing bags, dust, sand, or stones, <382> all around. We have undoubted evidence of that disorderly practice from an act of the Court, prohibiting it under a severe penalty, as dishonourable to the Court, and unbecoming the civility requisite in such a place (*a*).

And this leads to the lowness of ancient manners; plainly distinguishable from simplicity of manners: the latter is agreeable, not the former. Among the ancient Egyptians, to cram a man was an act of high respect. Joseph, the King's first minister, in order to honour Benjamin above his brethren, gave him a five-fold mess (*b*). The Greeks, in their feasts, distinguished their heroes by a double portion (*c*). Ulysses cut a fat piece out of the chine of a wild boar for Demodocus the bard (*d*). The same respectful politeness is practised at present among the American savages; so much are all men alike in similar circumstances. Telemachus (*e*) complains bitterly of Penelope's suitors, that they were gluttons, and consumed his beef and <383> mutton. The whole 14th book of the Odyssey, containing the reception of Ulysses by Eumaeus the swine-herd, is miserably low. Manners must be both gross and low, where common beggars are admitted to the feasts of princes, and receive scraps from their hands (*f*). In Rome every guest brought his own napkin to a feast. A slave carried it home, filled with what was left from the entertainment. Sophocles, in his tragedy of Iphigenia in Aulis, represents Clytemnestra, stepping down from her car, and exhorting her servants to look after her baggage, with the anxiety and minuteness of a lady's waiting-woman. In the tragedy of Ion, this man, a servant in the temple of Delphos, is represented cleaning the temple, and calling out to a flock of birds, each by name, threatening to pierce them with his arrows

(*a*) Act of Sederunt, 21st February 1663. [[An Act of Sederunt is an ordinance for regulating the forms of procedure before the Court of Session.]]

(*b*) Gen. xliii. 34.

(*c*) Odyssey, b. 8. v. 513. b. 15. v. 156.

(*d*) Odyssey, b. 8. v. 519.

(*e*) Odyssey, b. 2.

(*f*) See 17th & 18th books of the Odyssey.

if they dunged upon the offerings. Homer paints in lively colours the riches of the Phoeacians, their skill in navigation, the magnificence of the King's court, of his palace, and of the public buildings. But, with the same breath, he describes Nausicaa, the King's daughter, travelling <384> to the river on a waggon of greasy clothes, to be washed by her and her maids. Possibly it may be urged, that such circumstances, however low in our opinion, did not appear low in Greece, as they were introduced by their chief poet, and the greatest that ever existed. I acknowledge the force of this argument: but what does it prove, more than that the Greeks were not sensible of the lowness of their manners? Is any nation sensible of the lowness of their own manners? The manners of the Greeks did not correspond to the delicacy of their taste in the fine arts: nor can it be expected, when they were strangers to that polite society with women, which refines behaviour, and elevates manners. The first kings in Greece, as Thucydides observes, were elective, having no power but to command their armies in time of war; which resembles the government that obtains at present in the isthmus of Darien. The Greeks had no written laws, being governed by custom merely. To live by plunder was held honourable; for it was their opinion, that the rules of justice are not intended for restraining the powerful. All strangers were accounted <385> enemies, as among the Romans; and inns were unknown, because people lived at home, having very little intercourse even with those of their own nation. Inns were unknown in Germany, and to this day are unknown in the remote parts of the highlands of Scotland; but for an opposite reason, that hospitality prevailed greatly among the ancient Germans, and continues to prevail so much among our highlanders, that a gentleman takes it for an affront if a stranger pass his door. At a congress between Francis I. of France and Henry VIII. of England, among other spectacles for public entertainment, the two Kings had a wrestling-match. Had they forgot that they were sovereign princes?

   One would imagine war to be a soil too rough for the growth of civilization; and yet it is not always an unkindly soil. War between two small tribes is fierce and cruel: but a large state mitigates resentment, by directing it not against individuals, but against the state. We know no enemies but those who are in arms: we have no resentment against others, but rather find a pleasure in treating <386> them with humanity.* Cruelty, having thus in war few individuals for its object, naturally subsides; and magnanimity in its stead transforms soldiers from brutes to heroes. Some time ago, it was usual in France to demand battle; and it was held dishonourable to decline it, however unequal the match. Before the battle of Pavia, Francis I. wrote to the Marquis Pescara, the Imperial General, "You will find me before Pavia, and you ought to be here in six days: I give you twenty. Let not the superiority of my forces serve for an excuse; I will fight you with equal numbers." Here was heroism without prudence; but, in all reformations, it is natural to go from one extreme to the other. While the King of England held any possessions in France, war was perpetual between the two nations, which was commonly carried on <387> with more magnanimity than is usual between inveterate enemies. It became customary to give prisoners their freedom, upon a simple parole to return with their ransom at a day named. The same was the custom in the border-wars between the English and Scots, before their union under one monarch. But parties found their account equally in such honourable behaviour. Edward Prince of Wales, in a pitched battle against the French, took the illustrious Bertrand du Gueselin prisoner. He long declined to accept a ransom; but, finding it whispered that he was afraid of that hero, he instantly set him at liberty without a ransom. This may be deemed impolitic or whimsical: but is love of glory less praise-worthy than love of conquest? The Duke of Guise, victor in the battle of Dreux, rested all night in the field of battle; and gave the Prince of Condé, his prisoner, a share of his bed, where they lay like brothers. The Chevalier Bayard, commander of a French army *anno* 1524, being mortally wounded in retreating from the Imperialists, placed himself under a tree, his face, however, to the enemy. The Marquis de Pescara, ge-<388>neral of the Imperialists, finding him dead in that posture, behaved with the generosity of a gallant adversary: he directed his body to

---

* The constable du Gueselin, the greatest warrior of his time, being on deathbed, *anno* 1380, and bidding adieu to his veteran officers who had served under him forty years, entreated them not to forget what he had said to them a thousand times, "that in whatever country they made war, churchmen, women, infants, and the poor people, were not their enemies." [[Note added in 2nd edition.]]

be embalmed, and to be sent to his relations in the most honourable manner. Magnanimity and heroism, in which benevolence is an essential ingredient, are inconsistent with cruelty, perfidy, or any grovelling passion. Never was gallantry in war carried to a greater height, than between the English and Scotch borderers before the crowns were united. The night after the battle of Otterburn, the victors and vanquished lay promiscuously in the same camp, without apprehending the least danger one from the other. The manners of ancient warriors were very different. Homer's hero, though superior to all in bodily strength, takes every advantage of his enemy, and never feels either compassion or remorse. The policy of the Greeks and Romans in war, was to weaken a state by plundering its territory, and destroying its people. Humanity with us prevails even in war. Individuals not in arms are secure, which saves much innocent blood. Prisoners were set at liberty upon paying a ransom; and, by later im-<389>provements in manners, even that practice is left off as too mercantile, a more honourable practice being substituted, namely, a cartel for exchange of prisoners. Humanity was carried to a still greater height, in our late war with France, by an agreement between the Duke de Noailes and the Earl of Stair, That the hospitals for the sick and wounded soldiers should be secure from all hostilities. The humanity of the Duke de Randan in the same war, makes an illustrious figure even in the present age, remarkable for humanity to enemies. When the French troops were compelled to abandon their conquests in the electorate of Hanover, their Generals every where burnt their magazines, and plundered the people. The Duke de Randan, who commanded in the city of Hanover, put the magistrates in possession of his magazines, requesting them to distribute the contents among the poor; and he was, beside, extremely vigilant to prevent his soldiers from committing acts of violence.* <390> I relish not the brutality exercised in the present war be-

---

* Such kindness in an enemy from whom nothing is expected but mischief, is an illustrious instance of humanity. And a similar instance will not make the less figure that it was done by a man of inferior rank. When Mons. Thurot, during our late war with France, appeared on the coast of Scotland with three armed vessels; the terror he at first spread, soon yielded to admiration of his humanity. He paid a full price for every thing; and, in general, behaved with so much affability, that a countryman ventured to complain to him of an officer who had robbed him of fifty or sixty guineas. The officer acknowl-

tween the Turks and Russians. The latter, to secure their winter <391> quarters on the left hand of the Danube, laid waste a large territory on the right. To reduce so many people to misery merely to prevent a surprise, which can be more effectually done by strict discipline, is a barbarous remedy. But the peace concluded between these great powers, has given an opening to manners very different from what were to be expected from the fact now mentioned. This peace has been attended with signal marks not only of candour, but of courtesy. The Grand Signior, of his own accord, has dismissed from chains every Christian taken prisoner <392> during the war; and the Empress of Russia has set at liberty 3000 Turks, with an order to set at liberty every Turk within her dominions.[12] The necessity of fortifying towns to guard from destruction the innocent and defenceless, affords convincing evidence of the savage cruelty that prevailed in former times. By the growth of humanity, such fortifications have become less frequent: and they serve no purpose at present, but to defend against invasion; in which view a small fortification, if but sufficient for the garrison, is greatly pref-

---

edged the fact, but said, that he had divided the money among his men. Thurot ordered the officer to give his bill for the money, which, he said, should be stopped out of his pay, if they were so fortunate as to return to France. Compare this incident with that of the great Scipio, celebrated in Roman story, who restored a beautiful young woman to her bridegroom, and it will not suffer by the comparison. Another instance is no less remarkable. One of his officers gave a bill upon a merchant in France, for the price of provisions purchased by him. Thurot having accidentally seen the bill, informed the countryman that it was of no value, reprimanded the officer bitterly for the cheat, and compelled him to give a bill upon a merchant who he knew would pay the money. At that very time, Thurot's men were in bad humour, and disposed to mutiny. In such circumstances, would not Thurot have been excused for winking at a fraud to which he was not accessory? But he acted all along with the strictest honour, even at the hazard of his life. Common honesty to an enemy is not a common practice in war. Thurot was strictly honest in circumstances that made the exertion of common honesty an act of the highest magnanimity. These incidents ought to be held up to princes as examples of true heroism. War carried on in that manner, would, from desolation and horror, be converted into a fair field for acquiring true military glory, and for exercising every manly virtue. I feel the greatest satisfaction, in paying this tribute of praise to the memory of that great man. He will be kept in remembrance by every true-hearted Briton, though he died fighting against us. But he died in the field of honour, fighting for his country.

12. "I relish not . . . within her dominions": added in 2nd edition.

erable, being constructed at a much less expence, and having the garrison only to provide for.

In the progress of society, there is commonly a remarkable period, when social and dissocial passions seem to bear equal sway, prevailing alternately. In the history of Alexander's successors, there are frequent instances of cruelty, equalling that of American savages; and instances no less frequent of gratitude, of generosity, and even of clemency, that betoken manners highly polished. Ptolemy of Egypt, having gained a complete victory over Demetrius, son of Antigonus, restored <393> to him his equipage, his friends, and his domestics, saying, that "they ought not to make war for plunder, but for glory." Demetrius having defeated one of Ptolemy's generals, was less delighted with the victory, than with the opportunity of rivalling his antagonist in humanity. The same Demetrius having restored liberty to the Athenians, was treated by them as a demi-god; and yet afterward, in his adversity, found their gates shut against him. Upon a change of fortune, he laid siege to Athens, resolving to chastise that rebellious and ungrateful people. He assembled the inhabitants in the theatre, surrounding them with his army, as preparing for a total massacre. Their terror was extreme, but short: he pronounced their pardon, and bestowed on them 100,000 measures of wheat. Ptolemy, the same who is mentioned above, having, at the siege of Tyre, summoned Andronicus the governour to surrender, received a provoking and contemptuous answer. The town being taken, Andronicus gave himself up to despair: but the King, thinking it below his dignity to resent an injury done to him by an inferior, now his prisoner, not only o-<394>verlooked the injury, but courted Andronicus to be his friend. Edward, the Black Prince, is an instance of refined manners, breaking, like a spark of fire, through the gloom of barbarity. The Emperor Charles V. after losing 30,000 men at the siege of Metz, made an ignominious retreat, leaving his camp filled with sick and wounded, dead and dying. Though the war between him and the King of France was carried on with unusual rancour, yet the Duke of Guise, governour of the town, exerted, in those barbarous times, a degree of humanity that would make a splendid figure even at present. He ordered plenty of food for those who were dying of hunger, appointed surgeons to attend the sick and wounded, removed to the adjacent villages those who could bear motion, and admitted the remainder into the hospitals that he had fitted up for his own soldiers: those who recovered their health were sent home, with money to defray the expence of the journey.

In the period that intervenes between barbarity and humanity, there are not wanting instances of opposite passions in the same person, governing alternately; <395> as if a man could this moment be mild and gentle, and next moment harsh and brutal. To vouch the truth of this observation, I beg leave to introduce two rival monarchs, who for many years distressed their own people, and disturbed Europe, the Emperor Charles, and the French King Francis. The Emperor, driven by contrary winds on the coast of France, was invited by Francis, who happened to be in the neighbourhood, to take shelter in his dominions, proposing an interview at Aigues-Mortes, a sea-port town. The Emperor instantly repaired there in his galley; and Francis, relying on the Emperor's honour, visited him on shipboard, and was received with every expression of affection. Next day the Emperor repaid the confidence reposed in him: he landed at Aigues-Mortes with as little precaution, and found a reception equally cordial. After twenty years of open hostilities or of secret enmity, after having formally given the lie and challenged each other to single combat, after the Emperor had publicly inveighed against Francis as void of honour, and Francis had accused the Emperor as murderer of his <396> own son; a behaviour so open and frank will scarce be thought consistent with human nature. But these monarchs lived in a period verging from cruelty to humanity; and such periods abound with surprising changes of temper and behaviour. In the present times, changes so violent are unknown.

Conquest has not always the same effect upon the manners of the conquered. The Tartars who subdued China in the thirteenth century, adopted immediately the Chinese manners: the government, laws, customs, continued without variation. And the same happened upon their second conquest of China in the seventeenth century. The barbarous nations also who crushed the Roman empire, adopted the laws, customs, and manners, of the conquered. Very different was the fate of the Greek empire when conquered by the Turks. That warlike nation introduced every where their own laws and manners: even at this day they continue a distinct people as much as ever. The Tartars, as well as the barbarians who overthrew the Roman empire, were all of them rude and illiterate, destitute of laws, and igno-<397>rant of government. Such nations readily adopt the laws and manners of a civilized people, whom they admire. The Turks had laws, and a regular government; and the Greeks, when subdued by them, were reduced by sensuality to be objects of contempt, not of imitation.

Manners are deeply affected by persecution. The forms of procedure in the Inquisition enable the inquisitors to ruin whom they please. A person accused is not confronted with the accuser: every sort of accusation is welcome, and from every person: a child, a common prostitute, one branded with infamy, are reputable witnesses: a man is compelled to give evidence against his father, and a woman against her husband. Nay, the persons accused are compelled to inform against themselves, by guessing what sin they may have been guilty of. Such odious, cruel, and tyrannical proceedings, made all Spain tremble: every man distrusted his neighbour, and even his own family: a total end was put to friendship, and to social freedom. Hence the gravity and reserve of a people, who have naturally all the vivacity arising from a tem-<398>perate clime and bountiful soil.* Hence the profound ignorance of that people, while other European nations are daily improving in every art and in every science. Human nature is reduced to its lowest state, when governed by superstition clothed with power.

We proceed to another capital article in the history of manners, namely, the selfish and social branches of our nature, by which manners are greatly influenced. Selfishness prevails among savages; because corporeal pleasures are its chief objects, and of these every savage is perfectly sensible. Benevolence and kindly affection are too refined for a savage, unless of the simplest kind, such as the ties of blood. While artificial wants were unknown, selfishness, tho' prevalent, made no capital figure: the means of gratifying the calls of nature were in plenty; and men who are not afraid of ever being in want, never think of providing against it; and far less do they think of co-<399>veting what belongs to another. The Caribbeans, who know no wants but what nature inspires, are amazed at the industry of the Europeans

---

* The populace of Spain, too low game for the Inquisition, are abundantly chearful, perhaps more so than those of France. And I am credibly informed, that the Spanish women are perpetually dancing, singing, laughing, or talking.

in amassing wealth. Listen to one of them expostulating with a Frenchman in the following terms: "How miserable art thou, to expose thy person to tedious and dangerous voyages, and to suffer thyself to be oppressed with anxiety about futurity! An inordinate appetite for wealth is thy bane; and yet thou art no less tormented in preserving the goods thou hast acquired, than in acquiring more: fear of robbery or shipwreck suffers thee not to enjoy a quiet moment. Thus thou growest old in thy youth, thy hair turns gray, thy forehead is wrinkled, a thousand ailments afflict thy body, a thousand distresses surround thy heart, and thou movest with painful hurry to the grave. Why art thou not content with what thy own country produceth? Why not contemn superfluities, as we do?"[13] But men are not long contented with simple necessaries: an unwearied appetite to be more and more comfortably provided, leads them from necessaries to <400> conveniencies, and from these to every sort of luxury. Avarice turns headstrong; and locks and bars, formerly unknown, become necessary to protect people from the rapacity of their neighbours. When the goods of fortune, money in particular, come to be prized, selfishness soon displays itself. In Madagascar, a man who makes a present of an ox or a calf, expects the value in return; and scruples not to say, "You my friend, I your friend; you no my friend, I no your friend; I salamanca you, you salamanca me" (*a*). Admiral Watson being introduced to the King of Baba, in Madagascar, was asked by his Majesty, What presents he had brought? Hence the custom, universal among barbarians, of always accosting a king, or any man of high rank, with presents. Sir John Chardin says, that this custom goes through all Asia. It is reckoned an honour to receive presents: they are received in public; and a time is chosen when the croud is greatest. It is a maxim too refined for the potentates of Asia, that there is more honour in bestowing than in receiving.[14] <401>

The peculiar excellence of man above all other animals, is the capacity he has of improving by education and example. In proportion as his faculties refine, he acquires a relish for society, and finds a pleasure in benev-

(*a*) Salamanca means, the making a present.
13. "The Caribbeans . . . as we do": added in 2nd edition.
14. "Sir John Chardin . . . than in receiving": added in 2nd edition.

olence, generosity, and in every other kindly affection, far above what self-ishness can afford. How agreeable is this scene! Alas, too agreeable to be lasting. Opulence and luxury inflame the hording appetite; and selfishness at last prevails as it did originally. The selfishness, however, of savages differs from that of pampered people. Luxury confining a man's whole views to himself, admits not of friendship, and scarce of any other social passion. But where a savage takes a liking to a particular person, the whole force of his social affection being directed to a single object, becomes extremely fervid. Hence the unexampled friendship between Achilles and Patroclus in the Iliad; and hence many such friendships among savages.

But there is much more to be said of the influence of opulence on manners. Rude and illiterate nations are tenacious < 402 > of their laws and manners; for they are governed by custom, which is more and more rivetted by length of time. A people, on the contrary, who are polished by having passed through various scenes, are full of invention, and constantly thinking of new modes. Manners, in particular, can never be stationary in a nation refined by prosperity and the arts of peace. Good government will advance men to a high degree of civilization; but the very best government will not preserve them from corruption, after becoming rich by prosperity. Opulence begets luxury, and envigorates the appetite for sensual pleasure. The appetite, when inflamed, is never confined within moderate bounds, but clings to every object of gratification, without regard to propriety or decency. When Septimius Severus was elected Emperor, he found on the roll of causes depending before the judges in Rome no fewer than three thousand accusations of adultery. From that moment he abandoned all thoughts of a reformation. Love of pleasure is similar to love of money: the more it is indulged the more it is inflamed. Polygamy is an incentive to the < 403 > vice against nature; one act of incontinence leading to others without end. When the Sultan Achmet was deposed at Constantinople, the people, breaking into the house of one of his favourites, found not a single woman. It is reported of the Algerines, that in many of their seraglios there are no women. For the same reason polygamy is far from preventing adultery, a truth finely illustrated in Nathan's parable to David. What judgement then are we to form of the opulent cities London and Paris, where pleasure is the ruling passion, and where riches are coveted as instruments

of sensuality? What is to be expected but a pestiferous corruption of manners? Selfishness, ingrossing the whole soul, eradicates patriotism, and
leaves not a cranny for social virtue. If in that condition men abstain from
robbery or from murder, it is not love of justice that restrains them, but
dread of punishment. Babylon is arraigned by Greek writers for luxury,
sensuality, and profligacy. But Babylon represents the capital of every opulent kingdom, ancient and modern: the manners of all are the same; for
power and riches never fail to <404> produce luxury, sensuality, and profligacy.* Canghi, Emperor of China, who died in the year 1722, deserves to
be recorded in the annals of fame, for resisting the softness and effeminacy
of an Asiatic court. Far from abandoning himself to sensual pleasure, he
passed several months yearly in the mountains of Tartary, mostly on horseback, and declining no fatigue. Nor in that situation were affairs of state
neglected: many hours he borrowed from sleep, to hear his ministers, and
to issue orders. How few monarchs, bred up like Canghi in the downy
indolence of a seraglio, have resolution to withstand the temptations of
sensual pleasure!

In no other history is the influence of prosperity and opulence on manners so conspicuous as in that of old Rome. During the second Punic war,
when the Romans were reduced by Hannibal to fight *pro aris et focis,* Hiero,
King of Syracuse, <405> sent to Rome a large quantity of corn, with a
golden statue of victory weighing three hundred and twenty pounds, which
the senate accepted. But, though their finances were at the lowest ebb, they
accepted but the lightest of forty golden vases presented to them by the
city of Naples; and politely returned, with many thanks, some golden vases
sent by the city of Paestum, in Lucania: a rare instance of magnanimity.
But no degree of virtue is proof against the corruption of conquest and
opulence. Upon the influx of Asiatic riches and luxury, the Romans abandoned themselves to every vice: they became, in particular, wonderfully

---

* In Paris and London, people of fashion are incessantly running after pleasure, without ever attaining it. Dissatisfied with the present, they fondly imagine that a new pursuit
will relieve them. Life thus passes like a dream, with no enjoyment but what arises from
expectation. [[Note added in 2nd edition.]]

avaricious, breaking through every restraint of justice and humanity.* Spain in parti-<406>cular, which abounded with gold and silver, was for many years a scene, not only of oppression and cruelty, but of the basest treachery, practised against the natives by successive Roman generals, in order to accumulate wealth. Lucullus, who afterward made a capital figure in the Mithridatic war, attacked Cauca, a Celtiberian city, without the slightest provocation. Some of the principal citizens repaired to his camp with olive branches, desiring to be informed upon what conditions they could purchase his friendship. It was agreed that they should give hostages, with a hundred talents of silver. They also consented to admit a garrison of 2000 men, in order, said Lucullus, to protect them against their enemies. But how were they protected? The gates were opened by the garrison to the whole army; and the inhabitants were butchered, without distinction of sex or age. What other remedy had they, but to invoke the gods presiding over oaths and covenants, and to pour out execrations against the Ro-<407>mans for their perfidy? Lucullus, enriched with the spoils of the town, felt no remorse for leaving 20,000 persons dead upon the spot. Shortly after, having laid siege to Intercatia, he solicited a treaty of peace. The citizens reproaching him with the slaughter of the Cauceans, asked, Whether, in making peace, he was not to employ the same right hand, and the same faith, he had already pledged to their countrymen? Seroclius Galba, another Roman general, persuaded the Lusitanians to lay down their arms, promising them a fruitful territory instead of their own mountains; and having thus got them into his power, he ordered all of them to be murdered. Of the few that escaped, Viriatus was one, who, in a long and bloody war against the Romans, amply avenged the massacre of his countrymen. Our author Appian reports, that Galba, surpassing even Lucullus in covetousness, distributed but a small share of the plunder among the

---

* Postquam divitiae honori esse coeperunt, et eas gloria, imperium, potentia sequebatur; hebescere virtus, paupertas probro haberi, innocentia pro malevolentia duci, coepit. Igitur ex divitiis juventutem luxuria, atque avaritia, cum superbia invasere. *Sallust. Bell. Cat. c.* 12.—[*In English thus:* "After it had become an honour to be rich, and glory, empire, and power, became the attendants of riches, virtue declined apace, poverty was reckoned disgraceful, and innocence was held secret malice. Thus to the introduction of riches our youth owe their luxury, their avarice, and pride."]

soldiers, converting the bulk of it to his own use. He adds, that though
Galba was one of the richest men in Rome, yet he never scrupled at lies
nor perjury to procure money. But the corruption was general: <408>
Galba being accused of many misdemeanors, was acquitted by the senate
through the force of bribes. A tribe of the Celtiberians, who had long served
the Romans against the Lusitanians, had an offer made them by Titus Di-
dius of a territory in their neighbourhood, lately conquered by him. He
appointed them a day to receive possession; and having inclosed them in
his camp, under shew of friendship, he put them all to the sword; for which
mighty deed he obtained the honour of a triumph. The double-dealing
and treachery of the Romans, in their last war against Carthage, is beyond
example. The Carthaginians, suspecting that a storm was gathering against
them, sent deputies to Rome for securing peace at any rate. The senate, in
appearance, were disposed to amicable measures, demanding only hostages;
and yet, though three hundred hostages were delivered without loss of time,
the Roman army landed at Utica. The Carthaginian deputies attended the
Consuls there, desiring to know what more was to be done on their part.
They were required to deliver up their arms; which they chearfully did,
<409> imagining that they were now certain of peace. Instead of which,
they received peremptory orders to evacuate the city, with their wives and
children, and to make no settlement within eighty furlongs of the sea. In
perusing Appian's history of that memorable event, compassion for the
distressed Carthaginians is stifled by indignation at their treacherous oppressors. Could the monsters, after such treachery, have the impudence to
talk of *Punica fides?* The profligacy of the Roman people, during the triumvirate of Caesar, Pompey, and Crassus, is painted in lively colours by
the same author. "For a long time, disorder and confusion overspread the
commonwealth: no office was obtained but by faction, bribery, or criminal
service: no man was ashamed to buy votes, which were sold in open market.
One man there was, who, to obtain a lucrative office, expended eight hundred talents (*a*): ill men enriched themselves with public money, or with
bribes: no honest man would stand candidate for an office; and, into a situa-

(*a*) About L. 150,000 Sterling.

<410>tion so miserable was the commonwealth reduced, that once for eight months it had not a single magistrate." Cicero, writing to Atticus, that Clodius was acquitted by the influence of Crassus, expresses himself in the following words: "Biduo, per unum servum, et eum ex gladiatorio ludo, confecit totum negotium. Accersivit ad se, promisit, intercessit, dedit. Iam vero, O dii boni, rem perditam! etiam noctes certarum mulierum, atque adolescentulorum nobilium, introductiones nonnullis judicibus pro mercedis cumulo fuerunt" (*a*).* Ptolomy King of Egypt was dethroned by his subjects for tyranny. Having repaired to Rome for protection, he found means to poison the greater part of a hundred <411> Egyptians, his accusers, and to assassinate Dion, their chief. And yet these crimes, perpetrated in the heart of Rome, were suffered to pass with impunity. But he had secured the leading men by money, and was protected by Pompey. The following instance is, if possible, still more gross. Ptolomy, King of Cyprus, had always been a faithful ally to the Romans. But his gold, jewels, and precious moveables, were a tempting bait: and all was confiscated by a decree of the people, without even a pretext. Money procured by profligacy is not commonly hoarded up; and the Romans were no less voluptuous than avaricious. Alexander ab Alexandro mentions the Fanian, Orchian, Didian, Oppian, Cornelian, Ancian, and Julian laws, for repressing luxury of dress and of eating, all of which proved ineffectual. He adds, that Tiberius had it long at heart to contrive some effectual law against luxury, which now had surpassed all bounds, but that he found it impracticable to stem the tide. He concludes, that by tacit agreement among a corrupted people, all sumptuary laws were in effect abrogated; <412> and that the Roman people, abandoning themselves to vice, broke through every restraint of morality and religion (*b*). Tremble, O Britain, on the brink of a

---

* "In two days he completed the affair, by the means of one slave, a gladiator. He sent for him, and by promises, wheedling, and large gifts, he gained his point. Good God, to what an infamous height has corruption at length arrived! Some judges were rewarded with a night's lodging of certain ladies; and others, for an illustrious bribe, had some young boys of Noble family introduced to them."

(*a*) Lib. 1. epist. 13.
(*b*) Lib. 3. cap. 11.

precipice! how little distant in rapacity from Roman senators are the leaders of thy people!*

The free states of Italy, which had become rich by commerce, employed mer-<413>cenary troops to save their own people, who were more profitably employed at home. But, as mercenaries gained nothing by victory or bloodshed, they did very little execution against one another. They exhausted the states which employed them, without doing any real service. Our condition is in some degree similar. We employ generals and admirals, who, by great appointments, soon lose relish for glory, intent only to prolong a war for their own benefit. According to our present manners, where luxury and selfishness prevail, it appears an egregious blunder, to enrich a general or admiral during his command: have we any reason to expect, that he will fight like one whose fortune depends on his good behaviour? This single error against good policy has reduced Britain more than once to a low condition, and will prove its ruin at last.[15]

Riches produce another lamentable effect: they enervate the possessor, and degrade him into a coward. He who commands the labour of others, who eats without hunger, and rests without fatigue, becomes feeble in mind as well as in body, <414> has no confidence in his own abilities, and is reduced to flatter his enemies, because he hath not courage to brave them.

Selfishness among the rude and illiterate is rough, blunt, and undisguised. Selfishness, which in an opulent kingdom usurps the place of

---

* Down on your knees, my countrymen, down on your knees, and render God thanks from the bottom of your hearts, for a minister very different from his immediate predecessors. Untainted with luxury or avarice, his talents are dedicated to his King and his country. Nor was there ever a period in Britain, when prudence and discernment in a minister were more necessary than in the present year 1775. Our colonies, pampered with prosperity, aim at no less than independence, and have broken out into every extravagance. The case is extremely delicate, it appearing equally dangerous to pardon or to punish. Hitherto the most salutary measures have been prosecuted; and we have great reason to hope a happy issue, equally satisfactory to both parties. But tremble still, O Britain, on the brink of a precipice! Our hold of that eminent minister is sadly precarious; and, in a nation as deeply sunk in selfishness as formerly it was exalted by patriotism, how small is our chance of a successor equal to him! [[Note added in 2nd edition. Presumably Kames refers to the ministry of Lord North, which had begun in 1770 and was to end in 1782.]]

15. Paragraph added in 3rd edition.

patriotism, is smooth, refined, and covered with a veil. Pecuniary interest, a low object, must be covered with the thickest veil: ambition, less dishonourable, is less covered: but delicacy as to character and love of fame, are so honourable, that even the thinnest veil is held unnecessary. History justifies these observations. During the prosperity of Greece and Rome, when patriotism was the ruling passion, no man ever thought of employing a hostile weapon but against the enemies of his country: swords were not worn during peace, nor was there an instance of a private duel. The frequency of duels in modern times, is no slight symptom of degeneracy: regardless of our country, selfishness is exerted without disguise when reputation or character is in question; and a nice sense of honour prompts revenge for every imagined af-<415>front, without regard to justice. How much more manly and patriotic was the behaviour of Themistocles, when insulted by the Lacedemonian general in deliberating about the concerns of Greece! "Strike," says he, "but first hear me."* <416>

---

* Is duelling a crime by the law of nature? A distinction is necessary. If two men, bent to destroy each of them the other, meet armed, and one or both be slain, the act is highly criminal: it is murder in the strictest sense of the word. If they appoint time and place to execute their murderous purpose, such agreement will not be more innocent than an agreement among a band of robbers to attack every passenger: they will be abhorred as unfit for civil society. A duel which an affront forces a man upon for vindicating his honour, when no satisfaction is offered, or no proper satisfaction, is very different. I cannot see that the person affronted is guilty of any crime; and, if the person who gave the affront have offered what he thinks full satisfaction, I see no crime on either side. The parties have agreed to decide their quarrel in the honourable way, and no other person is hurt. If it be urged, that duelling is a crime against the state, which is interested in the lives of its subjects, I answer, that individuals are entitled to be protected by the state; but that if two men, waving that protection, agree to end the dispute by single combat, the state has no concern. There is nothing inconsistent with the laws of society, that men, in an affair of honour, should reserve the privilege of a duel; and, for that reason, the privilege may be justly understood as reserved by every man when he enters into society. I admit, that the using the privilege on every slight occasion, cannot be too much discouraged; but such discouragement, if duelling be not criminal, belongs to a court of police, not to a court of law. What then shall be said of our statutes, which punish with death and confiscation of moveables those who fight a single combat without the King's licence; and which punish even the giving or accepting a challenge with banishment and confiscation of moveables? Where a man thinks his honour at stake, fear of death will not deter him from seeking redress: nor is an alternative left him, as the bearing a gross affront is highly dishonourable in the opinion of all the world. Have

When a nation, formerly in prosperity, is depressed by luxury and self-ishness, what follows next? Let the Egyptians an-<417>swer the question. That unhappy people, having for many ages been a prey to every barbarous invader, are now become effe-<418>minate, treacherous, cruel, and cor-

---

we not instances without number, of men adhering to the supposed orthodoxy of their religious tenets, unawed by flames and gibbets? How absurd, then, is it in our legislature to punish a man for doing what is indispensable, if he wish to avoid contempt? Laws that contradict honest principles, or even honest prejudices, never are effectual: nature revolts against them. And, it is believed, that these statutes have never been effectual in any one instance, unless perhaps to furnish an excuse for declining a single combat.

As duelling falls under censorian powers, the proper censure for rashness or intemperance in duelling, is disgrace, not death or confiscation of moveables. In that view, the following or some such plan may be adopted. It appears from the statute first mentioned to be a branch of the royal prerogative to license a duel. Therefore, if an affront be so gross as in the person's opinion not to admit of any reparation but a duel, let him be entitled to apply to his Majesty for liberty to give a challenge. In Britain formerly, and through all Europe, single combat was a legal method of determining controversies, even in matters of right and wrong; and there is great reason for continuing that law, with respect to matters of honour. If the King have any doubt whether other reparation may not be sufficient, he is to name three military officers who have served with honour for twenty years; granting to them full powers as a court of honour to judge of the application; and upon calling the parties before them to pronounce sentence. If a duel be judged necessary, it must be done in presence of the court, with proper solemnities. Obedience will of course be given to this judgement; because to decline it would be attended with public infamy. If other reparation be enjoined, the party who stands out shall be declared infamous, unworthy for ever of the privilege of a duel; which ought to satisfy the other party, as he comes off with honour. If, notwithstanding the prohibition of the court, they afterward proceed to a duel, and both be killed, the public gains by having two quarrelsome men removed out of the way. If one of them be killed, the survivor shall be incapable of any public office, civil or military, shall be incapable of electing or being elected a member of parliament, shall be prohibited to wear a sword, shall forfeit his title of honour, and have his arms erazed out of the herald's register. If both survive, this censure shall reach both. Degrading censures which disgrace a man, are the only proper punishment in an affair of honour. The transgression of the act of parliament by fighting privately without licence from the King, shall be attended with the same degrading punishments.

It is a capital circumstance, that the court of honour has power to authorise a duel. A man grossly affronted will not be easily persuaded to submit his cause to a court that cannot decree him adequate reparation; and this probably is the cause, why the court of honour in France has fallen into contempt. But they must be perverse indeed or horribly obstinate, who decline a court which can decree them ample reparation. At the same time, the necessity of applying for a court of honour affords time for passion to subside, and for friends to bring about a reconciliation. [[Note added in 2nd edition.]]

rupted with every vice that debases humanity. A nation in its infancy, however savage, is susceptible of every improvement; but a nation worn out
with age and disease is susceptible of no improvement. There is no remedy,
but to let the natives die < 419 > out, and to repeople the country with better
men. Egypt has for many ages been in the same languid and servile state.
An Arabian author, who wrote the history of the great Saladin, observes,
that the Egyptians never thought of supporting the monarch in possession,
but tamely submitted to every conqueror. "It was," says he, "the custom in
Egypt at that time to deliver to the victor the ensigns of royalty, without
ever thinking of inquiring into his title." What better than a flock of sheep,
obedient to the call of the present shepherd!

I fly from a scene so dismal to one that will give no pain. Light is intended
by our Maker for action, and darkness for rest. In the fourteenth century,
the shops in Paris were opened at four in the morning: at present, a shopkeeper is scarce awake at seven. The King of France dined at eight in the
morning, and retired to his bed-chamber at the same hour in the evening;
an early hour at present for public amusements.* The Spaniards ad-
< 420 >here to ancient customs.† Their King to this day dines precisely at
noon, and sups no less precisely at nine in the evening. During the reign
of Henry VIII. fashionable people in England breakfasted at seven in the
morning, and dined at ten in the forenoon. In Elizabeth's time, the nobility,
gentry, and students, dined at eleven forenoon, and supped between five
and six afternoon. In the reign of Charles II. four in the afternoon was the
appointed hour for acting plays. At present, even dinner is at a later hour.
The King of Yeman, the greatest prince in Arabia Felix, dines at nine in
the morning, sups at five afternoon, and goes to rest at eleven. From this
short specimen it appears, that the occupations of day-light commence
gradually later and later; as if there were a tendency in polite nations, of
converting night into day, and day into night. No-< 421 >thing happens
without a cause. Light disposes to action, darkness to rest: the diversions

* Louis XII. of France after taking for his second wife Mary sister to Henry VIII. of
England, much under him in years, totally changed his manner of living. Instead of
dining at eight in the morning, he now dined at mid-day: instead of going to bed at six
in the evening, he now frequently sat up till midnight.
† Manners and fashions seldom change where women are locked up.

of day are tournaments, tennis, hunting, racing, and other active exercises: the diversions of night are sedentary; plays, cards, conversation. Balls are of a mixed nature, partly active in dancing, partly sedentary in conversing. Formerly, active exercises prevailed among a robust and plain people:* the milder pleasures of society prevail as manners refine. Hence it is, that candle-light amusements are now fashionable in France, and in other polished countries; and when such amusements are much relished, they banish the robust exercises of the field. Balls, I conjecture, were formerly more frequent in day-light: at present, candle-light is their favourite time: the active part is at that time equally agreeable; and the sedentary part, more so.

Gaming is the vice of idle people. Savages are addicted to gaming; and those of North America in particular are fond <422> to distraction of a game termed *the platter.* A losing gamester will strip himself to the skin; and some have been known to stake their liberty, though by them valued above all other blessings. Negroes in the slave-coast of Guinea, will stake their wives, their children, and even themselves. Tacitus (*a*), talking of gaming among the Germans, says, "Extremo ac novissimo jactu, de libertate et de corpore contendant."† The Greeks were an active and sprightly people, constantly engaged in war, or in cultivating the fine arts. They had no leisure for gaming, nor any knowledge of it. Happy for them was their ignorance; for no other vice tends more to render men selfish, dishonest, and, in the modish style, dishonourable. A gamester, a friend to no man, is a bitter enemy to himself. The luxurious of the present age, pass every hour in gaming that can be spared from sensual pleasure. Idleness is their excuse, as it is among savages; and they would in some degree <423> be excusable, were they never actuated by a more disgraceful motive.

Writers do not carefully distinguish particular customs from general manners. Formerly, women were not admitted upon the stage in France, Italy, or England: at that very time, none but women were admitted in

* The exercises that our forefathers delighted in were so violent as that in the days of Henry II. of England cock-fighting and horse-racing were despised as unmanly and childish amusements. [[Note added in 2nd edition.]]

† "For their last throw they stake their liberty and life."

(*a*) De moribus Germanorum, c. 24.

Spain. From that fashion it would be rash to infer, that women have more liberty in Spain than in the other countries mentioned; for the contrary is true. In Hindostan, established custom prompts women to burn themselves alive with the bodies of their deceased husbands; but from that singular custom, it would be a false inference, that the Hindow women are either more bold, or more affectionate to their husbands, than in other countries. The Polanders, even after they became Christians in the thirteenth century, adhered to the customs of their forefathers, the Sarmatians, in killing infants born deformed, and men debilitated by age; which would betoken horrid barbarity, if it were not a singular custom. Roman Catholics imagine, that there is no religion in England nor in Holland; because, from a spirit of civil liber-<424>ty, all sects are there tolerated. The encouragement given to assassination in Italy, where every church is a sanctuary, makes strangers rashly infer, that the Italians are all assassins. Writers sometimes fall into an opposite mistake, attributing to a particular nation, certain manners and customs common to all nations in one or other period of their progress. It is remarked by Heraclides Ponticus as peculiar to the Athamanes, that the men fed the flocks, and the women cultivated the ground. This has been the practice of all nations, in their progress from the shepherd-state to that of husbandry; and is at present the practice among American savages. The same author observes, as peculiar to the Celtae and Aphitaei, that they leave their doors open without hazard of theft. But that practice is common among all savages in the first stage of society, before the use of money is known.

Hitherto there appears as great uniformity in the progress of manners, as can reasonably be expected among so many different nations. There is one exception, extraordinary indeed if true, which is, the manners of the Caledonians described by <425> Ossian, manners so pure and refined as scarce to be parallelled in the most cultivated nations. Such manners among a people in the first stage of society, acquainted with no arts but hunting and making war, I acknowledge, miraculous. And yet to suppose these manners to be the invention of an illiterate savage, is really no less miraculous: I should as soon expect from a savage a performance equal to the elements of Euclid, or even to the *Principia* of Newton. One, at first view, will boldly declare the whole a modern fiction; for how is it credible, that a people, rude at present and illiterate, were, in the infancy of their society, highly refined in sentiment and manners? And yet, upon a more accurate inspection, many weighty considerations occur to balance that opinion.

From a thousand circumstances it appears, that the works of Ossian are not a late production. They are composed in an old dialect of the Celtic tongue; and as, till lately, they were known only in the highlands of Scotland, the author must have been a Caledonian. The translator (*a*) <426> saw, in the Isle of Sky, the first four books of the poem Fingal, written in a fair hand on vellum and bearing date in the year 1403. The natives believe that poem to be very ancient: every person has passages of it by heart, transmitted by memory from their forefathers. Their dogs bear commonly the name of *Luath, Bran,* &c. mentioned in these poems, as our dogs do of *Pompey* and *Caesar.** Many other particulars might be mentioned; but these are sufficient to prove, that the work must have existed at least three or four centuries. Taking that for granted, I proceed to certain considerations tending to evince, that the manners described in Ossian were Caledonian manners, and not a pure fiction. And, after perusing with attention these considerations, I am not afraid that even the most incredulous will continue altogether unshaken. <427>

It is a noted and well-founded observation, That manners are never painted to the life by any one to whom they are not familiar. It is not difficult to draw the outlines of imaginary manners; but to fill up the picture with all the variety of tints that manners assume in different circumstances, uniting all concordantly in one whole—*hic labor, hoc opus est.* Yet the manners here supposed to be invented, are delineated in a variety of incidents, of sentiments, of images, and of allusions, making one entire picture, without once deviating into the slightest incongruity. Every scene in Ossian relates

---

* In the Isle of Sky, the ruins of the castle of Dunscaich, upon an abrupt rock hanging over the sea, are still visible. That castle, as vouched by tradition, belonged to Cuchullin Lord of that Isle, whose history is recorded in the Poem of Fingal. Upon the green before the castle there is a great stone, to which, according to the same tradition, his dog Luath was chained.

(*a*) Mr. Macpherson. [[James Macpherson's editions of Ossian were first published between 1760 and 1763. A collected *Works of Ossian* appeared in 1765. A committee set up by the Highland Society of Scotland after Macpherson's death in 1796 decided that the poems were not translations of Gaelic originals—as some had suspected all along.]]

to hunting, to fighting, or to love, the sole occupations of men in the original state of society; there is not a single image, simile, or allusion, but what
is borrowed from that state, without a jarring circumstance.—Supposing
all to be mere invention, is it not amazing to find no mention of highland
clans, or of any name now in use? Is it not still more amazing, that there
is not the slightest hint of the Christian religion, not even in a metaphor
or allusion? Is it not equally amazing, that, in a work where deer's flesh is
frequently mentioned, <428> and a curious method of roasting it, there
should not be a word of fish as food, so common in later times? Very few
highlanders know that their forefathers did not eat fish; and, supposing it
to be known, it would require singular attention, never to let a hint of it
enter the poem. Can it be supposed, that a modern writer could be so constantly on his guard, as never to mention corn nor cattle? In a story so scanty
of poetical images, the sedentary life of a shepherd, and the industry of a
husbandman, would make a capital figure: the cloven foot would somewhere peep out. And yet, in all the works of Ossian, there is no mention
of agriculture; and but a slight hint of a herd of cattle in one or two allusions. I willingly give all advantages to the unbeliever: Supposing the author of Ossian to be a late writer, adorned with every refinement of modern
education; yet, even upon that supposition, he is a miracle, far from being
equalled by any other author ancient or modern.

But difficulties multiply when it is taken into the account, that the poems
of Ossian have existed three or four centuries at least. Our highlanders at
present are <429> rude and illiterate; and were in fact little better than
savages at the period mentioned. Now, to hold the manners described in
that work to be imaginary, is in effect to hold, that they were invented by
a highland savage, acquainted with the rude manners of his country, but
utterly unacquainted with every other system of manners. The manners of
different countries are now so well known as to make it an easy task to invent
manners by blending the manners of one country with those of another;
but to invent manners of which the author has no example, and yet neither
whimsical nor absurd, but congruous to human nature in its most polished
state, I pronounce to be far above the powers of man. Is it so much as
supposable, that such a work could be the production of a Tartar, or of a
Hottentot? From what source then did Ossian draw the refined manners

so deliciously painted by him? Supposing him to have been a traveller, of which we have not the slightest hint, the manners of France at that period, of Italy, and of other neighbouring nations, were little less barbarous than those of his own country. I can discover no source <430> but inspiration. In a word, whoever seriously believes the manners of Ossian to be fictitious, may well say, with the religious enthusiast, *"Credo quia impossible est:* I believe it because it is impossible."

But further: The uncommon talents of the author of this work will cheerfully be acknowledged by every reader of taste: he certainly was a great master in his way. Now, whether the work be late, or composed four centuries ago, a man of such talents inventing a historical fable, and laying the scene of action among savages in the hunter-state, would naturally frame a system of manners the best suited in his opinion to that state. What then could tempt him to adopt a system of manners, so opposite to any notion he could form of savage manners? The absurdity is so gross, that we are forced, however reluctantly, to believe, that these manners are not fictitious, but in reality the manners of his country, coloured perhaps, or a little heightened, according to the privilege of an epic poet. And once admitting that fact, there can be no hesitation in ascribing the work to Ossian, son of Fingal, <431> whose name it bears: we have no better evidence for the authors of several Greek and Roman books. Upon the same evidence, we must believe, that Ossian lived in the reign of the Emperor Caracalla, of whom frequent mention is made under the designation of *Caracul the Great King;* at which period, the shepherd-state was scarce known in Caledonia, and husbandry not at all. Had he lived so late as the twelfth century, when there were flocks and herds in that country, and some sort of agriculture, a poet of genius, such as Ossian undoubtedly was, would have drawn from these his finest images.

The foregoing considerations, I am persuaded, would not fail to convert the most incredulous; were it not for a consequence extremely improbable, that a people, little better at present than savages, were in their primitive hunter-state highly refined; for such Ossian describes them. And yet it is no less improbable, that such manners should be invented by an illiterate highland bard. Let a man chuse either side, the difficulty cannot be solved but by a sort of miracle. What shall we conclude upon the whole? for the

mind cannot for <432> ever remain in suspense. As dry reasoning has left
us in a dilemma, taste perhaps and feeling may extricate us. May not the
case be here as in real painting? A portrait drawn from fancy, may resemble
the human visage; but such peculiarity of countenance and expression as
serves to distinguish a certain person from every other, is always wanting.
Present a portrait to a man of taste, and he will be at no loss to say, whether
it be copied from life, or be the product of fancy. If Ossian paint from
fancy, the cloven foot will appear: but if his portraits be complete, so as to
express every peculiarity of character, why should we doubt of their being
copied from life? In that view, the reader, I am hopeful, will not think his
time thrown away in examining some of Ossian's striking pictures. I perceive not another resource.

Love of fame is painted by Ossian as the ruling passion of his countrymen
the Caledonians. Warriors are every where described, as esteeming it their
chief happiness to be recorded in the songs of the bards: that feature is never
wanting in <433> any of Ossian's heroes. Take the following instances.

"King of the roaring Strumon," said the rising joy of Fingal, "do I behold
thee in arms after thy strength has failed? Often hath Morni shone in battles, like the beam of the rising sun, when he disperses the storms of the
hill, and brings peace to the glittering fields. But why didst thou not rest
in thine age? Thy renown is in the song: the people behold thee, and bless
the departure of mighty Morni" (a). "Son of Fingal," he said, "why burns
the soul of Gaul? My heart beats high: my steps are disordered; and my
hand trembles on my sword. When I look toward the foe, my soul lightens
before me, and I see their sleeping host. Tremble thus the souls of the
valiant, in battles of the spear? How would the soul of Morni rise, if we
should rush on the foe! Our renown would grow in the song, and our steps
be stately in the eye of the brave" (b).* <434>

---

* Love of fame is a laudable passion, which every man values himself upon. Fame in
war is acquired by courage and candour, which are esteemed by all. It is not acquired by
fighting for spoil, because avarice is despised by all. The spoils of an enemy were displayed
at a Roman triumph, not for their own sake, but as a mark of victory. When nations at
war degenerate from love of fame to love of gain, stratagem, deceit, breach of faith, and
every sort of immorality, are never failing consequences.
    (a) Lathmon.
    (b) Lathmon.

That a warrior has acquired his fame is a consolation in every distress:

"Carril," said the King in secret, "the strength of Cuchullin fails. My days are with the years that are past; and no morning of mine shall arise. They shall seek me at Temora, but I shall not be found. Cormac will weep in his hall, and say, Where is Tura's chief? But my name is renowned, my fame in the song of bards. The youth will say, *O let me die as Cuchillin died: renown clothed him like a robe; and the light of his fame is great.* Draw the arrow from my side; and lay Cuchullin below that oak. Place the shield of Caithbat near, that they may behold me amid the arms of my fathers" (*a*).

Fingal speaks:

Ullin, my aged bard, take the ship of the King. Carry Oscar to Selma, and let the daughters of Morven weep. We shall fight in Erin for the race of fallen Cormac. The days of my years begin to fail: I feel the weakness of my arm. My fathers bend from their clouds to receive their gray-hair'd son. But, Trenmore! before I go hence, one beam of my fame shall rise: in fame shall my days end, as my years begun: my life shall be one stream of light to other times (*b*).

Ossian speaks:

Did thy beauty last, O Ryno! stood the strength <435> of car-borne Oscar!* Fingal himself passed away, and the halls of his fathers forgot his steps. And shalt thou remain, aged bard, when the mighty have failed? But my fame shall remain; and grow like the oak of Morven, which lifts its broad head to the storm, and rejoiceth in the course of the wind (*c*).

The chief cause of affliction when a young man is cut off in battle, is his not having received his fame:

---

* Several of Ossian's heroes are described as fighting in cars. The Britons, in general, fought in that manner. Britanni demicant non equitatu modo, aut pedite, verum et bigis et curribus; *Pomponius Mela, l.* 3.—[*In English thus:* "The Britons fight, not only with cavalry, or foot, but also with cars and chariots."]
(*a*) The death of Cuchillin.
(*b*) Temora.
(*c*) Berrathon.

"And fell the swiftest in the race," said the King, "the first to bend the bow? Thou scarce hast been known to me; why did young Ryno fall? But sleep thou softly on Lena, Fingal shall soon behold thee. Soon shall my voice be heard no more, and my footsteps cease to be seen. The bards will tell of Fingal's name; the stones will talk of me. But, Ryno! thou art low indeed, thou hast not received thy fame. Ullin, strike the harp for Ryno; tell what the chief would have been. Farewell thou first in every field. No more shall I direct thy dart. Thou that hast been so fair; I behold thee not.— Farewell" (*a*). "Cal-< 436 >thon rushed into the stream: I bounded forward on my spear: Teutha's race fell before us: night came rolling down. Dunthalmo rested on a rock, amidst an aged wood: the rage of his bosom burned against the car-borne Calthon. But Calthon stood in his grief; he mourned the fallen Colmar; Colmar slain in youth, before his fame arose" (*b*).

Lamentation for loss of fame. Cuchullin speaks:

But, O ye ghosts of the lonely Cromla! ye souls of chiefs that are no more! be ye the companions of Cuchullin, and talk to him in the cave of his sorrow. For never more shall I be renowned among the mighty in the land. I am like a beam that has shone; like a mist that fled away when the blast of the morning came, and brightened the shaggy side of the hill. Connal, talk of arms no more; departed is my fame. My sighs shall be on Cromla's wind, till my footsteps cease to be seen. And thou white bosom'd Bragéla, mourn over the fall of my fame; for, vanquished, never will I return to thee, thou sun-beam of Dunscaich (*c*).

Love of fame begets heroic actions, which go hand in hand with elevated sentiments: of the former there are examples in every page; of the latter take the following examples:

"And let him come," replied the King. "I love < 437 > a foe like Cathmor: his soul is great; his arm strong; and his battles full of fame. But the little soul is like a vapour that hovers round the marshy lake, which never rises on the green hill, lest the winds meet it there" (*d*).

(*a*) Fingal.
(*b*) Calthon and Colmar.
(*c*) Fingal.
(*d*) Lathmon.

Ossian speaks:

"But let us fly, son of Morni, Lathmon descends the hill." "Then let our
steps be slow," replied the fair-hair'd Gaul, "lest the foe say with a smile,
Behold the warriors of night: they are like ghosts, terrible in darkness; but
they melt away before the beam of the East" (*a*). "Son of the feeble hand,"
said Lathmon, "shall my host descend! They are but two, and shall a thousand lift their steel! Nuah would mourn in his hall for the departure of
Lathmon's fame: his eyes would turn from Lathmon, when the tread of
his feet approached. Go thou to the heroes, son of Dutha, for I behold
the stately steps of Ossian. His fame is worthy of my steel: let him fight
with Lathmon" (*b*). "Fingal does not delight in battle, though his arm is
strong. My renown grows on the fall of the haughty: the lightning of my
steel pours on the proud in arms. The battle comes; and the tombs of the
valiant rise; the tombs of my people rise, O my fathers! and I at last must
remain alone. But I will remain renowned, and the departure of my soul
shall be one stream of light" (*c*). "I raised my voice for Fovar-gormo, when
they laid the chief in earth. The aged Crothar was there, but his sigh was
not heard. He searched for the wound of his son, <438> and found it in
his breast: joy arose in the face of the aged: he came and spoke to Ossian:
'King of spears, my son hath not fallen without his fame: the young warrior did not fly, but met death as he went forward in his strength. Happy
are they who die in youth, when their renown is heard: their memory shall
be honoured in the song; the young tear of the virgin falls'" (*d*). "Cuchullin kindled at the sight, and darkness gathered on his brow. His hand
was on the sword of his fathers: his red-rolling eye on the foe. He thrice
attempted to rush to battle, and thrice did Connal stop him. 'Chief of
the isle of mist,' he said, 'Fingal subdues the foe: seek not a part of the
fame of the King'" (*e*).

The pictures that Ossian draws of his countrymen, are no less remarkable for tender sentiments, than for elevation. Parental affection is finely
couched in the following passage:

(*a*) Lathmon.
(*b*) Lathmon.
(*c*) Lathmon.
(*d*) Croma.
(*e*) Fingal.

"Son of Comhal," replied the chief, "the strength of Morni's arm has failed. I attempt to draw the sword of my youth, but it remains in its place: I throw the spear, but it falls short of the mark; and I feel the weight of my shield. We decay like the grass of the mountain, and our strength returns no more. I have a son, O Fingal! his soul has delighted in the actions of Morni's youth; but his sword has not been lifted against the foe, neither has his fame begun. I come with him to battle, to direct his arm. His renown will be a <439> sun to my soul, in the dark hour of my departure. O that the name of Morni were forgot among the people, that the heroes would only say, Behold the father of Gaul!" (*a*)

And no less finely touched is grief for the loss of children:

We saw Oscar leaning on his shield: we saw his blood around. Silence darkened on the face of every hero: each turned his back and wept. The King strove to hide his tears. He bends his head over his son; and his words are mixed with sighs. "And art thou fallen, Oscar, in the midst of thy course! The heart of the aged beats over thee. I see thy coming battles: I behold the battles that ought to come, but they are cut off from thy fame. When shall joy dwell at Selma? when shall the song of grief cease on Morven? My son falls by degrees, Fingal will be the last of his race. The fame I have received shall pass away: my age shall be without friends. I shall sit like a grey cloud in my hall: nor shall I expect the return of a son with his sounding arms. Weep, ye heroes of Morven; never more will Oscar rise" (*b*).

Crothar speaks:

Son of Fingal! dost thou not behold the darkness of Crothar's hall of shells? My soul was not dark at the feast, when my people lived. I rejoiced in the presence of strangers, when my son shone in the hall. But, Ossian, he is a beam <440> that is departed, and left no streak of light behind. He is fallen, son of Fingal, in the battles of his father.—Rothmar, the chief of grassy Tromlo, heard that my eyes had failed; he heard that my arms were fixed in the hall, and the pride of his soul arose. He came toward Croma; my people fell before him. I took my arms in the hall; but what

(*a*) Lathmon.
(*b*) Temora.

could sightless Crothar do? My steps were unequal; my grief was great. I wished for the days that were past, days wherein I fought and won in the field of blood. My son returned from the chace, the fair-hair'd Fovar-gormo. He had not lifted his sword in battle, for his arm was young. But the soul of the youth was great; the fire of valour burnt in his eyes. He saw the disordered steps of his father, and his sigh arose. "King of Croma," he said, "is it because thou hast no son; is it for the weakness of Fovar-gormo's arm that thy sighs arise? I begin, my father, to feel the strength of my arm; I have drawn the sword of my youth; and I have bent the bow. Let me meet this Rothmar with the youths of Croma: let me meet him, O my father; for I feel my burning soul." "And thou shalt meet him," I said, "son of the sightless Crothar! But let others advance before thee, that I may hear the tread of thy feet at thy return; for my eyes behold thee not, fair-hair'd Fovar-gormo!"—He went, he met the foe; he fell. The foe advances toward Croma. He who slew my son is near, with all his pointed spears (*a*).

The following sentiments about the shortness of human life are pathetic.

<441>

"Desolate is the dwelling of Moinna, silence in the house of her fathers. Raise the song of mourning over the strangers. One day we must fall; and they have only fallen before us.—Why dost thou build the hall, son of the winged days! Thou lookest from thy towers to day: soon will the blast of the desert come. It howls in thy empty court, and whistles over thy half-worn shield" (*b*). "How long shall we weep on Lena, or pour tears in Ullin! The mighty will not return; nor Oscar rise in his strength: the valiant must fall one day, and be no more known. Where are our fathers, O warriors, the chiefs of the times of old! They are set, like stars that have shone: we only hear the sound of their praise. But they were renowned in their day, and the terror of other times. Thus shall we pass, O warriors, in the day of our fall. Then let us be renowned while we may; and leave our fame behind us, like the last beams of the sun, when he hides his red head in the west" (*c*).

(*a*) Croma.
(*b*) Carthon.
(*c*) Temora.

In Homer's time, heroes were greedy of plunder; and, like robbers, were much disposed to insult a vanquished foe. According to Ossian, the ancient Caledonians had no idea of plunder: and as they fought for fame only, their humanity overflowed to the vanquished. American savages, it is true, are not addicted to plunder, and are ready to bestow on the <442> first comer what trifles they force from the enemy. But they have no notion of a pitched battle, nor of single combat: on the contrary, they value themselves upon slaughtering their enemies by surprise, without risking their own sweet persons. Agreeable to the magnanimous character given by Ossian of his countrymen, we find humanity blended with courage in all their actions.

Fingal pitied the white-armed maid: he stayed the uplifted sword. The tear was in the eye of the King, as bending forward he spoke: "King of streamy Sora, fear not the sword of Fingal: it was never stained with the blood of the vanquished; it never pierced a fallen foe. Let thy people rejoice along the blue waters of Tora: let the maids of thy love be glad. Why should'st thou fall in thy youth, King of streamy Sora!" (*a*)

Fingal speaks:

"Son of my strength," he said, "take the spear of Fingal: go to Teutha's mighty stream, and save the car-borne Colmar. Let thy fame return before thee like a pleasant gale; that my soul may rejoice over my son, who renews the renown of our fathers. Ossian! be thou a storm in battle, but mild where the foes are low. It was thus my fame arose, O my son; and be thou like Selma's chief. When the haughty come to my hall, my <443> eyes behold them not; but my arm is stretched forth to the unhappy, my sword defends the weak" (*b*). "O Oscar! bend the strong in arm, but spare the feeble hand. Be thou a stream of many tides against the foes of thy people, but like the gale that moves the grass to those who ask thy aid. Never search for the battle, nor shun it when it comes. So Trenmor lived; such Trathal was; and such has Fingal been. My arm was the support of the injured; and the weak rested behind the lightning of my steel" (*c*).

(*a*) Carric-thura.
(*b*) Calthon and Comal.
(*c*) Fingal, book 3.

Humanity to the vanquished is displayed in the following passages. After defeating in battle Swaran King of Lochlin, Fingal says,

"Raise, Ullin, raise the song of peace, and soothe my soul after battle, that my ear may forget the noise of arms. And let a hundred harps be near to gladden the King of Lochlin: he must depart from us with joy: none ever went sad from Fingal. Oscar, the lightening of my sword is against the strong; but peaceful it hangs by my side when warriors yield in battle" (*a*). "Uthal fell beneath my sword, and the sons of Berrathon fled. It was then I saw him in his beauty, and the tear hung in my eye. Thou art fallen, young tree, I said, with all thy budding beauties round thee. The winds come from the desert, and there is no sound in thy leaves. Lovely art thou in death, son of car-borne Lathmor" (*b*). <444>

After perusing these quotations, it will not be thought that Ossian deviates from the manners represented by him, in describing the hospitality of his chieftains:

"We heard the voice of joy on the coast, and we thought that the mighty Cathmor came; Cathmor, the friend of strangers, the brother of red-hair'd Cairbar. But their souls were not the same; for the light of heaven was in the bosom of Cathmor. His towers rose on the banks of Atha: seven paths led to his hall: seven chiefs stood on these paths, and called the stranger to the feast. But Cathmor dwelt in the wood, to avoid the voice of praise (*c*)." "Rathmor was a chief of Clutha. The feeble dwelt in his hall. The gates of Rathmor were never closed: his feast was always spread. The sons of the stranger came, and blessed the generous chief of Clutha. Bards raised the song, and touched the harp: joy brightened on the face of the mournful. Dunthalmo came in his pride, and rushed into combat with Rathmor. The chief of Clutha overcame. The rage of Dunthalmo rose: he came by night with his warriors; and the mighty Rathmor fell: he fell in his hall, where his feast had been often spread for strangers" (*d*).

(*a*) Fingal, book 6.
(*b*) Berrathon.
(*c*) Temora.
(*d*) Calthon and Colmal.

It seems not to exceed the magnanimity of his chieftains, intent upon glory only, <445> to feast even an enemy before a battle. Cuchullin, after the first day's engagement with Swaran, King of Lochlin or Scandinavia, says to Carril, one of his bards,

> Is this feast spread for me alone, and the King of Lochlin on Ullin's shore; far from the deer of his hills, and sounding halls of his feasts? Rise, Carril of other times, and carry my words to Swaran; tell him from the roaring of waters, that Cuchullin gives his feast. Here let him listen to the sound of my groves amid the clouds of night: for cold and bleak the blustering winds rush over the foam of his seas. Here let him praise the trembling harp, and hear the songs of heroes (a).

The Scandinavian King, less polished, refused the invitation. Cairbar speaks:

> "Spread the feast on Lena, and let my hundred bards attend. And thou, red-hair'd Olla, take the harp of the King. Go to Oscar, King of swords, and bid him to our feast. To-day we feast and hear the song; to-morrow break the spears" (b). "Olla came with his songs. Oscar went to Cairbar's feast. Three hundred heroes attend the chief, and the clang of their arms is terrible. The gray dogs bound on the heath, and their howling is frequent. Fingal saw the <446> departure of the hero: the soul of the King was sad. He dreads the gloomy Cairbar: but who of the race of Trenmor fears the foe?" (c)

Cruelty is every where condemned as an infamous vice. Speaking of the bards,

> "Cairbar feared to stretch his sword to the bards, tho' his soul was dark; but he closed us in the midst of darkness. Three days we pined alone: on the fourth the noble Cathmor came. He heard our voice from the cave, and turned the eye of his wrath on Cairbar. Chief of Atha, he said, how long wilt thou pain my soul? Thy heart is like the rock of the desert, and thy thoughts are dark. But thou art the brother of Cathmor, and he will fight thy battles. Cathmor's soul is not like thine, thou feeble hand of war.

(a) Fingal, book 1.
(b) Temora.
(c) Temora.

The light of my bosom is stained with thy deeds. The bards will not sing of my renown: they may say, Cathmor was brave, but he fought for gloomy Cairbar: they will pass over my tomb in silence, and my fame shall not be heard. Cairbar, loose the bards; they are the sons of other times: their voice shall be heard in other ages when the Kings of Temora have failed" (*a*). "Ullin raised his white sails: the wind of the south came forth. He bounded on the waves toward Selma's walls. The feast is spread on Lena: an hundred heroes reared the tomb of Cairbar; but no song is raised over the chief, for his soul had been dark and bloody. We remembered the <447> fall of Cormac; and what could we say in Cairbar's praise?" (*b*)

Genuine manners never were represented more to the life by a Tacitus nor a Shakespeare. Such painting is above the reach of pure invention: it must be the work of knowledge and feeling.

One may discover the manners of a nation from the figure their women make. Among savages, women are treated like slaves; and they acquire not the dignity that belongs to the sex, till manners be considerably refined (*c*). According to the manners above described, women ought to have made a considerable figure among the ancient Caledonians. Let us examine Ossian upon that subject, in order to judge whether he carries on the same tone of manners through every particular. That women were highly regarded, appears from the following passages.

"Daughter of the hand of snow! I was not so mournful and blind, I was not so dark and forlorn, when Everallin loved me, Everallin with the dark-brown hair, the white-bosomed love of <448> Cormac. A thousand heroes sought the maid, she denied her love to a thousand: the sons of the sword were despised; for graceful in her eyes was Ossian. I went in suit of the maid to Lego's sable surge; twelve of my people were there, sons of the streamy Morven. We came to Branno friend of strangers, Branno of the sounding mail.—From whence, he said, are the arms of steel? Not easy to win is the maid that had denied the blue-eyed sons of Erin. But blest be thou, O son of Fingal, happy is the maid that waits thee. Though twelve daughters of beauty were mine, thine were the choice, thou son of

(*a*) Temora.
(*b*) Temora.
(*c*) See the Sketch immediately following.

fame! Then he opened the hall of the maid, the dark-haired Everallin. Joy kindled in our breasts of steel, and blest the maid of Branno" (*a*). "Now Connal, on Cromla's windy side, spoke to the chief of the noble car. Why that gloom, son of Semo? Our friends are the mighty in battle. And renowned art thou, O warrior! many were the deaths of thy steel. Often has Bragela met thee with blue-rolling eyes of joy; often has she met her hero returning in the midst of the valiant, when his sword was red with slaughter, and his foes silent in the field of the tomb. Pleasant to her ears were thy bards, when thine actions rose in the song" (*b*). "But, King of Morven, if I shall fall, as one time the warrior must fall, raise my tomb in the midst, and let it be the greatest on Lena. And send over the dark-blue wave the sword of Orla, to the spouse of his love; that she may show it to her son, with tears, to kindle <449> his soul to war" (*c*). "I lifted my eyes to Cromla, and I saw the son of generous Semo.—Sad and slow he retired from his hill toward the lonely cave of Tura. He saw Fingal victorious, and mixed his joy with grief. The sun is bright on his armour, and Connal slowly followed. They sunk behind the hill, like two pillars of the fire of night, when winds pursue them over the mountain, and the flaming heath resounds. Beside a stream of roaring foam, his cave is in a rock. One tree bends above it; and the rushing winds echo against its sides. There rests the chief of Dunscaich, the son of generous Semo. His thoughts are on the battles he lost; and the tear is on his cheek. He mourned the departure of his fame, that fled like the mist of Cona. O Bragela, thou art too far remote to cheer the soul of the hero. But let him see thy bright form in his soul; that his thoughts may return to the lonely sun-beam of Dunscaich" (*d*). "Ossian King of swords," replied the bard, "thou best raisest the song. Long hast thou been known to Carril, thou ruler of battles. Often have I touched the harp to lovely Everallin. Thou, too, hast often accompanied my voice in Branno's hall of shells. And often amidst our voices was heard the mildest Everallin. One day she sung of Cormac's fall, the youth that died for her love. I saw the tears on her cheek, and on thine, thou chief of men. Her soul was touched for the unhappy, though she loved him not. How fair among a thousand maids, was the daughter of

(*a*) Fingal, book 4.
(*b*) Fingal, book 5.
(*c*) Fingal, book 5.
(*d*) Fingal, book 5.

the generous <450> Branno" (*a*). "It was in the days of peace," replied the great Clessammor, "I came in my bounding ship to Balclutha's walls of towers. The winds had roared behind my sails, and Clutha's streams received my dark-bosomed vessel. Three days I remained in Reuthamir's halls, and saw that beam of light, his daughter. The joy of the shell went round, and the aged hero gave the fair. Her breasts were like foam on the wave, and her eyes like stars of light: her hair was dark as the raven's wing: her soul was generous and mild. My love for Moina was great: and my heart poured forth in joy" (*b*). "The fame of Ossian shall rise: his deeds shall be like his father's. Let us rush in our arms, son of Morni, let us rush to battle. Gaul, if thou shalt return, go to Selma's lofty hall. Tell Everallin that I fell with fame: carry the sword to Branno's daughter: let her give it to Oscar when the years of his youth shall arise" (*c*).

Next to war, love makes the principal figure: and well it may; for in Ossian's poems it breathes every thing sweet, tender, and elevated.

"On Lubar's grassy banks they fought; and Grudar fell. Fierce Cairbar came to the vale of the echoing Tura, where Brassolis, fairest of his sisters, all alone raised the song of grief. She sung the actions of Grudar, the youth of her se-<451>cret soul: she mourned him in the field of blood; but still she hoped his return. Her white bosom is seen from her robe, as the moon from the clouds of night: her voice was softer than the harp, to raise the song of grief: her soul was fixed on Grudar, the secret look of her eye was his;—when wilt thou come in thine arms, thou mighty in the war? Take, Brassolis, Cairbar said, take this shield of blood: fix it on high within my hall, the armour of my foe. Her soft heart beat against her side: distracted, pale, she flew, and found her youth in his blood.—She died on Cromla's heath. Here rests their dust, Cuchullin; and these two lonely yews, sprung from their tombs, wish to meet on high. Fair was Brassolis on the plain, and Grudar on the hill. The bard shall preserve their names, and repeat them to future times" (*d*). "Pleasant is thy voice, O Carril, said the blue-eyed chief of Erin; and lovely are the words of other times: they are like the calm shower of spring, when the sun looks on the field, and the light

(*a*) Fingal, book 5.
(*b*) Carthon.
(*c*) Lathmon.
(*d*) Fingal, book 1.

cloud flies over the hill. O strike the harp in praise of my love, the lonely sun-beam of Dunscaich: strike the harp in praise of Bragela, whom I left in the isle of mist, the spouse of Semo's son.—Dost thou raise thy fair face from the rock to find the sails of Cuchullin? the sea is rolling far distant, and its white foam will deceive thee for my sails. Retire, my love, for it is night, and the dark winds sigh in thy hair: retire to the hall of my feasts, and think of times that are past; for I will not return till the storm of war cease. O Connal, speak of war and <452> arms, and send her from my mind; for lovely with her raven hair is the white-bosomed daughter of Sorglan" (*a*).

Malvina speaks.

"But thou dwellest in the soul of Malvina, son of mighty Ossian. My sighs arise with the beam of the east, my tears descend with the drops of the night. I was a lovely tree in thy presence, Oscar, with all my branches round me: but thy death came like a blast from the desert, and laid my green head low: the spring returned with its showers, but of me not a leaf sprung. The virgins saw me silent in the hall, and they touched the harp of joy. The tear was on the cheek of Malvina, and the virgins beheld my grief. Why art thou sad, they said, thou first of the maids of Lutha? Was he lovely as the beam of the morning, and stately in thy sight?" (*b*) "Fingal came in his mildness, rejoicing in secret over the actions of his son. Morni's face brightened with gladness, and his aged eyes looked faintly through tears of joy. We came to the halls of Selma, and sat round the feast of shells. The maids of the song came into our presence, and the mildly-blushing Everallin. Her dark hair spreads on her neck of snow, her eye rolls in secret on Ossian. She touches the harp of music, and we bless the daughter of Branno" (*c*).

Had the Caledonians made slaves of <453> their women, and thought as meanly of them as savages commonly do, Ossian could never have thought, even in a dream, of bestowing on them those numberless graces that exalt the female sex, and render many of them objects of pure and elevated affection. I say more: Supposing a savage to have been divinely

(*a*) Fingal, book 1.
(*b*) Croma.
(*c*) Lathmon.

inspired, manners so inconsistent with their own would not have been relished, nor even comprehended, by his countrymen. And yet that they were highly relished is certain, having been diffused among all ranks, and preserved for many ages by memory alone, without writing. Here the argument mentioned above strikes with double force, to evince, that the manners of the Caledonians must have been really such as Ossian describes.

Catharina Alexowna, Empress of Russia, promoted assemblies of men and women, as a means to polish the manners of her subjects. And in order to preserve decency in such assemblies, she published a body of regulations, of which the following are a specimen. "Ladies who play at forfeitures, questions and commands, &c. shall not be noisy nor riotous. No <454> gentleman must attempt to force a kiss, nor strike a woman in the assembly, under pain of exclusion. Ladies are not to get drunk upon any pretence whatever; nor gentlemen before nine." Compare the manners that required such regulations with those described above. Can we suppose, that the ladies and gentlemen of Ossian's poems ever amused themselves, after the age of twelve, with hide and seek, questions and commands, or such childish play. Can it enter into our thoughts, that Bragela or Malvina were so often drunk, as to require the reprimand of a public regulation? or that any hero of Ossian ever struck a woman of fashion in ire?

The immortality of the soul was a capital article in the Celtic creed, inculcated by the Druids (a). And in Valerius Maximus we find the following passage:—"Gallos, memoriae proditum est, pecunias mutuas, quae sibi apud inferos redderentur, dare: quia persuasum habuerint, animas hominum immortales esse. Dicerem stultos, nisi idem braccati sensissent quod palliatus Pythagoras <455> sensit" (b).* All savages have an impression of immortality; but few, even of the most enlightened before Christianity prevailed, had the least notion of any occupations in another life, but what they were accustomed to in this. Even Virgil, in his poetical fer-

---

* "It is reported, that the Gauls frequently lent money to be paid back in the infernal regions, from a firm persuasion that the souls of men were immortal. I would have called them fools, if those wearers of breeches had not thought the same as Pythagoras who wore a cloak."

(a) Pomponius Mela. Ammianus Marcellinus.

(b) Lib. 2.

vency, finds no amusements for his departed heroes, but what they were fond of when alive; the same love for war, the same taste for hunting, and the same affection to their friends. As we have no reason to expect more invention in Ossian, the observation may serve as a key to the ghosts introduced by him, and to his whole machinery, as termed by critics. His description of these ghosts is copied plainly from the creed of his country.

In a historical account of the progress of manners, it would argue gross insensibility to overlook those above mentioned. <456> The subject, it is true, has swelled upon my hands beyond expectation; but it is not a little interesting. If these manners be genuine, they are a singular phenomenon in the History of Man: if they be the invention of an illiterate bard, among savages utterly ignorant of such manners, the phenomenon is no less singular. Let either side be taken, and a sort of miracle must be admitted. In the instances above given, such a beautiful mixture there is of simplicity and dignity, and so much life given to the manners described, that real manners were never represented with a more striking appearance of truth. If these manners be fictitious, I say again, that the author must have been inspired: they plainly exceed the invention of a savage; nay, they exceed the invention of any known writer. Every man will judge for himself: it is perhaps fondness for such refined manners, that makes me incline to reality against fiction.

I am aware at the same time, that manners so pure and elevated, in the first stage of society, are difficult to be accounted for. The Caledonians were not an original tribe, who may be supposed to have <457> had manners peculiar to themselves: they were a branch of the Celtae, and had a language common to them with the inhabitants of Gaul, and of England. The manners probably of all were the same, or nearly so; and if we expect any light for explaining Caledonian manners, it must be from that quarter: we have indeed no other resource. Diodorus Siculus (*a*) reports of the Celtae, that, though warlike, they were upright in their dealings, and far removed from deceit and duplicity. Caesar (*b*), "Galli homines aperti minimeque insi-

---

(*a*) Lib. 5.
(*b*) De bello Africo.

diosi, qui per virtutem, non per dolum, dimicare consueverunt."* And though cruel to their enemies, yet Pomponius Mela (*a*) observes, that they were kind and compassionate to the supplicant and unfortunate. Strabo (*b*) describes the Gauls as studious of war, and of great alacrity in fighting; otherwise an innocent people, altogether void of malignity. He says, that they had three orders of <458> men, bards, priests, and druids; that the province of the bards was to study poetry, and to compose songs in praise of their deceased heroes; that the priests presided over divine worship; and that the druids, beside studying moral and natural philosophy, determined all controversies, and had some direction even in war. Caesar, less attentive to civil matters, comprehends these three orders under the name of *druids;* and observes, that the druids teach their disciples a vast number of verses, which they must get by heart. Diodorus Siculus says, that the Gauls had poets termed *bards,* who sung airs accompanied with the harp, in praise of some, and dispraise of others. Lucan, speaking of the three orders, says,

> Vos quoque, qui fortes animas, belloque peremptas,
> Laudibus in longum, vates, dimittitis aevum,
> Plurima securi sudistis carmina bardi.† <459>

With respect to the Celtic women in particular, it is agreed by all writers, that they were extremely beautiful (*c*); and no less remarkable for spirit than for beauty. If we can rely on Diodorus Siculus, the women in Gaul equalled the men in courage. Tacitus, in his life of Agricola, says, that the British

---

* "The Gauls are of an open temper, not at all insidious; and in fight they rely on valour, not on stratagem."

† You too, ye bards! whom sacred raptures fire,
  To chant your heroes to your country's lyre;
  Who consecrate in your immortal strain,
  Brave patriot souls, in righteous battle slain;
  Securely now the tuneful task renew,
  And noblest themes in deathless songs pursue.
                                        ROWE.

[[*Pharsalia,* bk. I, ll. 784–89. The Latin original is quoted by Macpherson on the title page of the *Works of Ossian.*]]

(*a*) Lib. 3.
(*b*) Lib. 4.
(*c*) Diodorus Siculus, lib. 5. Athenaeus, lib. 13.

women frequently joined with the men, when attacked by an enemy. And so much were they regarded, as to be thought capable of the highest command. "Neque enim sexum in imperiis discernunt,"* says the same author (*a*). And accordingly, during the war carried on by Caractacus, a gallant British King, against the Romans, Cartismandua was Queen of the Brigantes. Boadicea is recorded in Roman annals as a Queen of a warlike spirit. She led on a great army against the Romans; and in exhorting her people to behave with courage, she observed, that it was not unusual to see a British army led on to battle <460> by a woman; to which Tacitus adds his testimony: "Solitum quidem Britannis foeminarum ductu bellare" (*b*).† No wonder that Celtic women, so amply provided with spirit, as well as beauty, made a capital figure in every public entertainment (*c*).

The Gallic Celtae undoubtedly carried with them their manners and customs to Britain, and spread them gradually from south to north. And as the Caledonians, inhabiting a mountainous country in the northern parts of the island, had little commerce with other nations, they preserved long in purity many Celtic customs, particularly that of retaining bards. Arthur the last Celtic King of England, who was a hero in the defence of his country against the Saxons, protected the bards, and was immortalized by them. All the chieftains had bards in their pay, whose province it was to compose songs in praise of their ancestors, and to accom-<461>pany these songs with the harp. This entertainment enflamed their love for war, and at the same time softened their manners, which, as Strabo reports, were naturally innocent and void of malignity. It had beside a wonderful influence in forming virtuous manners: the bards, in praising deceased heroes, would naturally select virtuous actions, which are peculiarly adapted to heroic poetry, and tend the most to illustrate the hero of their song: vice may be flattered; but praise is never willingly nor successfully bestowed upon any atchievement but what is virtuous and heroic. It is accordingly observed by

---

* "They made no distinction of sex in conferring authority."
† "The Britons even followed women as leaders in the field."
(*a*) Vita Agricolae, cap. 16.
(*b*) Annalium, lib. 14.
(*c*) Athenaeus, lib. 10.

Ammianus Marcellinus (*a*), that the bards inculcated in their songs virtue and actions worthy of praise. The bards, who were in high estimation, became great proficients in poetry; of which we have a conspicuous instance in the works of Ossian. Their capital compositions were diligently studied by those of their own order, and admired by all. The songs of the bards, accompanied with the harp, made a deep impression on the young war- <462>rior, elevated some into heroes, and promoted virtue in every hearer.* Another circumstance, common to the Caledonians with every other nation in the first stage of society, concurred to form their manners; which is, that avarice was unknown among them. People in that stage, ignorant of habitual wants, and having a ready supply of all that nature requires, have little notion of property, and not the slightest desire of accumulating the goods of fortune; and for that reason are always found honest and disinterested. With respect to the female sex, who make an illustrious figure in Ossian's poems, if they were so eminent both for courage and beauty as they are represented by the best authors, it is no wonder to find them painted by Ossian as objects of love the <463> most pure and refined. Nor ought it to be overlooked, that the soft and delicate notes of the harp have a tendency to purify manners, and to refine love.

Whether the causes here assigned of Celtic manners be fully adequate, may well admit of a doubt; but if authentic history be relied on, we can entertain no doubt, that the manners of the Gallic and British Celtae, including the Caledonians, were such as are above described. And as the manners ascribed by Ossian to his countrymen the Caledonians, are in every particular conformable to those now mentioned, it clearly follows, that Ossian was no inventor, but drew his pictures of manners from real life. This is made highly probable from intrinsic evidence, the same that is so copi-

---

* Polydore Virgil says, *Hiberni sunt musicae peritissimi.*—[*In English thus:* "The Irish are most skilful in music."]—Ireland was peopled from Britain; and the music of that country must have been derived from British bards. The Welsh bards were the great champions of independence; and in particular promoted an obstinate resistance to Edward I. when he carried his arms into Wales. And hence the tradition, that the Welsh bards were all slaughtered by that King.

(*a*) Lib. 15.

ously urged above: and now by authentic history, that probability is so much heightened, as scarce to leave room for a doubt.

Our present highlanders are but a small part of the inhabitants of Britain; and they have been sinking in their importance, from the time that arts and sciences made a figure, and peaceable manners prevailed. And yet in that people are dis-<464>cernible many remaining features of their forefathers the Caledonians. They have to this day a disposition to war, and when disciplined make excellent soldiers, sober, active, and obedient. They are eminently hospitable; and the character given by Strabo of the Gallic Celtae, that they were innocent and devoid of malignity, is to them perfectly applicable. That they have not the magnanimity and heroism of the Caledonians, is easily accounted for. The Caledonians were a free and independent people, unawed by any superior power, and living under the mild government of their own chieftains; compared with their forefathers, the present highlanders make a very inconsiderable figure: their country is barren, and at any rate is but a small part of a potent kingdom; and their language deprives them of intercourse with their polished neighbours.

There certainly never happened in literature, a discovery more extraordinary than the works of Ossian. To lay the scene of action among hunters in the first stage of society, and to bestow upon such a people a system of manners that would do honour to the most polished state, seem-<465>ed at first an ill-contrived forgery. But if a forgery, why so bold and improbable? why not invent manners more congruous to the savage state? And as at any rate the work has great merit, why did the author conceal himself? These considerations roused my attention, and produced the foregoing disquisition; which I finished, without imagining that any more light could be obtained. But, after a long interval, a thought struck me, that as the Caledonians formerly were much connected with the Scandinavians, the manners of the latter might probably give light in the present inquiry. I cheerfully spread my sails in a wide ocean, not without hopes of importing precious merchandise. Many volumes did I turn over of Scandinavian history; attentive to those passages where the manners of the inhabitants in the first stage of society are delineated. And now I proceed to present my reader with the goods imported.

The Danes, says Adam of Bremen, are remarkable for elevation of mind:

the punishment of death is less dreaded by them than that of whipping. "The philosophy of the Cimbri," says Valerius Ma-<466>ximus, "is gay and resolute: they leap for joy in a battle, hoping for a glorious end; in sickness they lament, for fear of the contrary." What fortified their courage, was a persuasion, that those who die in battle fighting bravely are instantly translated to the hall of Odin, to drink beer out of the skull of an enemy. "Happy in their mistake," says Lucan, "are the people who live near the pole: persuaded that death is only a passage to long life, they are undisturbed by the most grievous of all fears, that of dying: they eagerly run to arms, and esteem it cowardice to spare a life they shall soon recover in another world." Such was their magnanimity, that they scorned to snatch a victory by surprise. Even in their piratical expeditions, instances are recorded of setting aside all the ships that exceeded those of the enemy, lest the victory should be attributed to superiority of numbers. It was held unmanly to decline a combat, however unequal; for courage, it was thought, rendered all men equal. The shedding tears was unmanly, even for the death of friends.

The Scandinavians were sensible in a <467> high degree to praise and reproach; for love of fame was their darling passion. Olave, King of Norway, placing three of his scalds or bards around him in a battle, "You shall not relate," said he, "what you have only heard, but what you are eye-witnesses of." Upon every occasion we find them insisting upon glory, honour, and contempt of death, as leading principles. The bare suspicion of cowardice was attended with universal contempt: a man who lost his buckler, or received a wound behind, durst never again appear in public. Frotho King of Denmark, made captive in a battle, obstinately refused either liberty or life. "To what end," says he, "should I survive the disgrace of being made a captive? Should you even restore to me my sister, my treasure, and my kingdom, would these benefits restore me to my honour? Future ages will always have to say, that Frotho was taken by his enemy" (a).

Much efficacy is above ascribed to the songs of Caledonian bards; and with satisfaction I find my observations justified <468> in every Scandinavian history. The Kings of Denmark, Norway, and Sweden, are repre-

(a) Saxo Grammaticus.

sented in ancient chronicles as constantly attended with scalds or bards, who were treated with great respect, especially by princes distinguished in war. Harold Harfager at his feasts placed them above all his other officers; and employed them in negociations of the greatest importance. The poetic art, held in great estimation, was cultivated by men of the first rank. Rogvald, Earl of Orkney, passed for an able poet. King Regnar was distinguished in poetry, no less than in war. It was the proper province of bards in Scandinavia, as in other countries, to celebrate in odes the atchievements of deceased heroes. They were frequently employed in animating the troops before a battle. Hacon, Earl of Norway, in his famous engagement against the warriors of Iomsburg, had five celebrated poets, each of whom sung an ode to the soldiers ready to engage. Saxo Grammaticus, describing a battle between Waldemar and Sueno, mentions a scald belonging to the former, who, advancing to the front of the <469> army, reproached the latter in a pathetic ode as the murderer of his own father.

The odes of the Scandinavian bards have a peculiar energy; which is not difficult to be accounted for. The propensity of the Scandinavians to war, their love of glory, their undaunted courage, and their warlike exploits, naturally produced elevated sentiments, and an elevated tone of language; both of which were displayed in celebrating heroic deeds. Take the following instances. The first is from the Edda, which contains the birth and genealogy of their Gods.

> The giant Rymer arrives from the east, carried in a chariot: the great serpent, rolling himself furiously in the waters, lifteth up the sea. The eagle screams, and with his horrid beak tears the dead. The vessel of the gods is set afloat. The black prince of fire issues from the south, surrounded with flames: the swords of the gods beam like the sun: shaken are the rocks, and fall to pieces. The female giants wander about weeping: men in crouds tread the paths of death. Heaven is split asunder, the sun darkened, and the earth sunk in <470> the ocean. The shining stars vanish: the fire rages: the world draws to an end; and the flame ascending licks the vault of heaven. From the bosom of the waves an earth emerges, clothed with lovely green: the floods retire: the fields produce without culture: misfortunes are banished from the world. Balder and his brother, gods of war, return to inhabit the ruin'd palace of Odin. A palace more resplendent

than the sun, rises now to view; adorned with a roof of gold: there good men shall inhabit; and live in joy and pleasure through all ages.

In a collection of ancient historical monuments of the north, published by Bioner, a learned Swede, there is the following passage. "Grunder, perceiving Grymer rushing furiously through opposing battalians, cries aloud, *Thou alone remainest to engage with me in single combat. It is now thy turn to feel the keenness of my sword.* Their sabres, like dark and threatening clouds, hang dreadful in the air. Grymer's weapon darts down like a thunderbolt: their swords furiously strike: they are bathed in gore. Grymer cleaves the <471> casque of his enemy, hews his armour in pieces, and pours the light into his bosom. Grunder sinks to the ground; and Grymer gives a dreadful shout of triumph." This picture is done with a masterly hand. The capital circumstances are judiciously selected; and the narration is compact and rapid. Indulge me with a moment's pause to compare this picture with one or two in Ossian's manner. "As Autumn's dark storms pour from two echoing hills; so to each other approach the heroes. As from high rocks two dark streams meet, and mix and roar on the plain; so meet Lochlin and Innis-fail, loud, rough, and dark in battle. Chief mixes his strokes with chief, and man with man; steel sounds on steel, helmets are cleft on high. Blood bursts, and smoaks around. Strings murmur on the polished yew. Darts rush along the sky. Spears fall like sparks of flame that gild the stormy face of night. As the noise of the troubled ocean when roll the waves on high, as the last peal of thundering heaven, such is the noise of battle. Tho' Cormac's hundred bards <472> were there, feeble were the voice of an hundred bards to send the deaths to future times; for many were the heroes who fell, and wide poured the blood of the valiant." Again, "As roll a thousand waves to the rocks, so came on Swaran's host: as meets a rock a thousand waves, so Innis-fail met Swaran. The voice of death is heard all around, and mixes with the sound of shields. Each hero is a pillar of darkness, and the sword a beam of fire in his hand. From wing to wing echoes the field, like a hundred hammers that rise by turns on the red sun of the furnace. Who are those on Lena's heath, so gloomy and dark? they are like two clouds, and their swords lighten above. Who is it but Ossian's son and the car-borne chief of Erin?" These two descriptions make a deeper impression, and swell the heart more than the former: they are more poetical by short similes finely interwoven; and the images are far more lofty. And yet Ossian's chief talent is sentiment, in which Scandinavian bards are far inferior: in the generosity, tenderness, <473> and humanity of his sentiments, he has not a rival.

The ancient Scandinavians were undoubtedly a barbarous people, compared with the southern nations of Europe; but that they were far from being gross savages, may be gathered from a poem still extant, named *Havamaal; or, The sublime discourse of Odin.* Tho' that poem is of great antiquity, it is replete with good lessons and judicious reflections; of which the following are a specimen.

> Happy he who gains the applause and good will of men.
>
> Love your friends, and love also their friends.
>
> Be not the first to break with your friend: sorrow gnaws the heart of him who has not a single friend to advise with.
>
> Where is the virtuous man that hath not a failing? Where is the wicked man that hath not some good quality?
>
> Riches take wing; relations die: you yourself shall die. One thing only is out of the reach of fate; which is, the judgement that passes on the dead.
>
> There is no malady more severe than the being discontented with one's lot. <474>
>
> Let not a man be overwise nor overcurious: if he would sleep in quiet, let him not seek to know his destiny.
>
> While we live, let us live well: a man lights his fire, but before it be burnt out death may enter.
>
> A coward dreams that he may live for ever: if he should escape every other weapon, he cannot escape old age.
>
> The flocks know when to retire from pasture: the glutton knows not when to retire from the feast.
>
> The lewd and dissolute make a mock of every thing, not considering how much they deserve to be mocked.
>
> The best provision for a journey, is strength of understanding: more useful than treasure, it welcomes one to the table of the stranger.

Hitherto the manners of the Scandinavians resemble in many capital circumstances those delineated in the works of Ossian. I lay not, however,

great stress upon that resemblance, because such manners are found among
several other warlike nations in the first stage of society. The circumstance
that has occasioned the greatest doubt about Ossian's system of <475>
manners, is the figure his women make. Among other savage nations, they
are held to be beings of an inferior rank; and as such are treated with very
little respect: in Ossian they make an illustrious figure, and are highly regarded by the men. I have not words to express my satisfaction, when I
discovered, that anciently among the barbarous Scandinavians, the female
sex made a figure no less illustrious. A resemblance so complete with respect
to a matter extremely singular among barbarians, cannot fail to convert the
most obstinate infidel, leaving no doubt of Ossian's veracity.—But I ought
not to anticipate. One cannot pass a verdict till the evidence be summed
up; and to that task I now proceed with sanguine hopes of success.

It is a fact ascertained by many writers, That women in the north of
Europe were eminent for resolution and courage. Caesar, in the first book
of his commentaries, describing a battle he fought with the Helvetii, says,
that the women with a warlike spirit exhorted their husbands to persist, and
placed the waggons in a line to prevent their flight. Florus and Taci-
<476>tus mention, that several battles of those barbarous nations were re-
newed by their women, presenting their naked bosoms, and declaring their
abhorrence of captivity. Flavius Vopiscus, writing of Proculus Caesar, says,
that a hundred Sarmatian virgins were taken in battle. The Longobard
women, when many of their husbands were cut off in a battle, took up
arms, and obtained the victory (a). The females of the Galactophagi, a
Scythian tribe, were as warlike as the males, and went often with them to
war (b). In former times, many women in Denmark applied themselves to
arms (c). Jornandes describes the women of the Goths as full of courage,
and trained to arms like the men. Joannes Magnus, Archbishop of Upsal,
says the same; and mentions in particular an expedition of the Goths to
invade a neighbouring country, in which more women went along with the
men than were left at home (d). Several Scandinavian women exercised

(a) Paulus Diaconus.
(b) Nicolaus Damascenus.
(c) Saxo Grammaticus.
(d) Book 1.

piracy (*a*). The Cimbri were always attended with their <477> wives even in their distant expeditions, and were more afraid of their reproaches than of the blows of the enemy. The Goths, compelled by famine to surrender to Belisarius the city of Ravenna, were bitterly reproached by their wives for cowardice (*b*). In a battle between Regner King of Denmark and Fro King of Sweden, many women took part with the former, Langertha in particular, who fought with her hair flowing about her shoulders. Regner, being victorious, demanded who that woman was who had behaved so gallantly; and finding her to be a virgin of noble birth, he took her to wife. He afterward divorced her, in order to make way for a daughter of the King of Sweden. Regner being unhappily engaged in a civil war with Harald, who aspired to the throne of Denmark; Langertha, overlooking her wrongs, brought from Norway a body of men to assist her husband; and behaved so gallantly, that, in the opinion of all, Regner was indebted to her for the victory.

To find women, in no considerable portion of the globe, rivalling men in <478> their capital property of courage, is a singular phenomenon. That this phenomenon must have had an adequate cause, is certain; but of that cause, it is better to acknowledge our utter ignorance, however mortifying, than to squeeze out conjectures that will not bear examination.

In rude nations, prophets and soothsayers are held to be a superior class of men: what a figure then must the Vandal women have made, when in that nation, as Procopius says, all the prophets and soothsayers were of the female sex? In Scandinavia, women are said to have been skilful in magic arts, as well as men. Tacitus informs us, that the Germans had no other physicians but their women. They followed the armies, to staunch the blood, and suck the wounds of their husbands.* He mentions a fact that sets the <479> German women in a conspicuous light, That female hos-

---

* The expression of Tacitus is beautiful: "Ad matres, ad conjuges, vulnera ferunt: nec illae numerare aut exfugere plagas pavent: cibosque et hortamina pugnantibus gestant."—[*In English thus:* When wounded, they find physicians in their mothers and wives, who are not afraid to count and suck their wounds. They carry provisions for their sons and husbands, and animate them in battle by their exhortations."]

(*a*) Olaus Magnus.

(*b*) Procopius, Historia Gothica, lib. 2.

tages bound the Germans more strictly to their engagements than male hostages. He adds, "Inesse quinetiam sanctum aliquid et providum putant: nec aut consilia earum aspernantur, aut responsa negliguntur."* The histories and romances of the north represent women, and even princesses, acting as physicians in war.

Polygamy sprung up in countries where women are treated as inferior beings: it can never take place where the two sexes are held to be of equal rank. For that reason, polygamy never was known among the northern nations of Europe. Saxo Grammaticus, who wrote the history of Denmark in the twelfth century, gives not the slightest hint of polygamy, even among kings and princes. Crantz, in his history of the Saxons (a), affirms, that polygamy was never known among the nor-<480>thern nations of Europe; which is confirmed by every other writer who gives the history of any of these nations. Scheffer in particular, who writes the history of Lapland, observes, that neither polygamy nor divorce were ever heard of in that country, not even during Paganism.

We have the authority of Procopius (b), that the women in those countries were remarkable for beauty, and that those of the Goths and Vandals were the finest that ever had been seen in Italy; and we have the authority of Crantz, that chastity was in high estimation among the Danes, Swedes, and other Scandinavians. When these facts are added to those above mentioned, it will not be thought strange, that love between the sexes, even among that rude people, was a pure and elevated passion. That it was in fact such, is certain, if history can be credited, or the sentiments of a people expressed in their poetical compositions. I begin with the latter, as evidence the most to be relied on. The ancient Poems of Scandinavia contain the warmest expressions of love and regard for the female sex. In an ode of King Regner <481> Lodbrog, a very ancient poem, we find the following sentiments. "We fought with swords upon a promontory of England, when I saw ten thousand of my foes rolling in the dust. A dew of blood distilled

* "They believe that there is something sacred in their character, and that they have a foresight of futurity: for this reason their counsels are always respected; nor are their opinions ever disregarded."
(a) Lib. I. cap. 3.
(b) Historia Gothica, lib. 3.

from our swords: the arrows, that flew in search of the helmets, hissed through the air. The pleasure of that day was like the clasping a fair virgin in my arms." Again, "A young man should march early to the conflict of arms; in which consists the glory of the warrior. He who aspires to the love of a mistress, ought to be dauntless in the clash of swords." These Hyperboreans, it would appear, had early learned to combine the ideas of love and of military prowess; which is still more conspicuous in an ode of Harald the Valiant, of a later date. That prince, who figured in the middle of the eleventh century, traversed all the seas of the north, and made piratical incursions even upon the coasts of the Mediterranean. In this ode he complains, that the glory he had acquired made no impression on Elissir, daughter to Jarislas, King of Russia. "I have made the tour of Sicily. My brown vessel, <482> full of mariners, made a swift progress. My course I thought would never slacken—and yet a Russian maiden scorns me. The troops of Drontheim, which I attacked in my youth, exceeded ours in number. Terrible was the conflict: I left their young king dead on the field—and yet a Russian maiden scorns me. Six exercises I can perform: I fight valiantly: firm is my seat on horseback: inured I am to swimming: swift is my motion on scates: I dart the lance: I am skilful at the oar—and yet a Russian maiden scorns me. Can she deny, this young and lovely maiden, that near a city in the south I joined battle, and left behind me lasting monuments of my exploits?—and yet a Russian maiden scorns me. My birth was in the high country of Norway, famous for archers: but ships were my delight; and, far from the habitations of men, I have traversed the seas from north to south—and yet a Russian maiden scorns me." In the very ancient poem of Havamaal, mentioned above, there are many expressions of love to the fair sex. "He who would gain the love <483> of a maiden, must address her with smooth speeches, and showy gifts. It requires good sense to be a skilful lover." Again, "If I aspire to the love of the chastest virgin, I can bend her mind, and make her yield to my desires." The ancient Scandinavian chronicles present often to our view young warriors endeavouring to acquire the favour of their mistresses, by boasting of their accomplishments, such as their dexterity in swimming and scating, their talent in poetry, their skill in chess, and their knowing all the stars by name. Mallet, in the introduction to his history of Denmark, mentions many ancient Scandinavian novels that turn upon love and heroism. These may be justly held as authentic evidence of the manners of the people: it is common to invent facts; but it is not common to attempt the inventing manners.

It is an additional proof of the great regard paid to women in Scandinavia, that in Edda, the Scandinavian Bible, female deities make as great a figure as male deities.

Agreable to the manners described, we <484> find it universally admitted among the ancient Scandinavians, that beauty ought to be the reward of courage and military skill. A warrior was thought entitled to demand in marriage any young woman, even of the highest rank, if he overcame his rivals in single combat: nor was it thought any hardship on the young lady, to be yielded to the victor. The ladies were not always of that opinion; for the stoutest fighter is not always the handsomest man, nor the most engaging. And in the histories of Denmark, Sweden, and Norway, many instances are related, of men generously interposing to rescue young beauties from brutes, destitute of every accomplishment but strength and boldness. Such stories have a fabulous air; and many of them probably are mere fables. Some of them, however, have a strong appearance of truth: men are introduced who make a figure in the real history of the country; and many circumstances are related that make links in the chain of that history, Take the following specimen. The ambassadors of Frotho, King of Denmark, commissioned to demand in marriage the daughter of a King <485> of the Huns, were feasted for three days, as the custom was in ancient times; and being admitted to the young Princess, she rejected the offer; "Because," says she, "your King has acquired no reputation in war, but passes his time effeminately at home." In Biorner's collection of ancient historical monuments, mentioned above, there is the following history. Charles King of Sweden kept on foot an army of chosen men. He had a daughter named *Inguegerda,* whose lively and graceful accomplishments were admired still more than her birth and fortune. The breast of the King overflowed with felicity. Grymer, a youth of noble birth, knew to dye his sword in the blood of his enemies, to run over craggy mountains, to wrestle, to play at chess, and to trace the motions of the stars. He studied to show his skill in the apartment of the damsels, before the lovely Inguegerda. At length he ventured to open his mind. "Wilt thou, O fair Princess! accept of me for a husband, if I obtain the King's consent?" "Go," says she, "and supplicate my father." The courtly youth respectfully addressing the King, said, "O <486> King! give me in marriage thy beautiful daughter." He answered sternly, "Thou hast learned to handle thy arms: thou hast acquired some honourable distinctions: but hast thou ever gained a victory, or given a banquet to savage beasts that rejoice in blood?" "Where shall I go, O King! that I may dye my sword in crimson, and render myself worthy of being thy son-in-law?"—"Hialmar, son of Harec," said the King, "who governs Biarmland, has become terrible by a keen sword: the firmest shields he hews in pieces, and loads his followers with booty. Go, and prove thy valour by attacking that hero: cause him to bite the dust, and Inguegerda shall be thy reward." Grymer, returning to his fair mistress, saluted her with ardent looks of love. "What answer hast thou received from the King?" "To obtain thee I must deprive the fierce Hialmar of life." Inguegerda exclaimed with grief, "Alas! my father hath devoted thee to death." Grymer selected a troop of brave warriors, eager to follow him. They launch their vessels into the wide ocean: they unfurl the sails, <487> which catch the springing gale: the shrouds rattle: the waves foam, and dash against the prows: they steer their numerous vessels to the shore of Gothland; bent to glut the hungry raven, and to gorge the wolf with prey. Thus landed Grymer on Gothland! and thus did a beauteous maiden occasion the death of many heroes. Hialmar demanded who the strangers were. Grymer told his name; adding, that he had spent the summer in quest of him. "May your arrival," replied Hialmar, "be fortunate; and may health and honour attend you. You shall partake of my gold, with the unmixed juice of the grape." "Thy offers," said Grymer, "I dare not accept. Prepare for battle; and let us hasten to give a banquet to beasts of prey." Hialmar laid hold of his white cuirass, his sword, and his buckler. Grymer, with a violent blow of his sabre, transfixes Hialmar's shield, and cuts off his left hand. Hialmar enraged, brandishes his sword, and striking off Grymer's helmet and cuirass, pierces his breast and sides: an effusion of blood follows. Grymer raising his sabre with both hands, lays <488> Hialmar prostrate on the ground; and he himself sinks down upon the dead body of his adversary. He was put on shipboard, and when landed seemed to be at the last period of life. The distressed Princess undertook his cure; and restored him to health. They were married with great solemnity; and the beauteous bride of Grymer filled the heart of her hero with unfading joy.

According to the rude manners of those times, a lover did not always wait for the consent of his mistress. Joannes Magnus, Archbishop of Upsal, observes in his history of the Goths, that ravishing of women was of old no less frequent among the Scandinavians than among the Greeks. He relates, that Gram, son to the King of Denmark, carried off the King of Sweden's daughter, whose beauty was celebrated in verses remembered even in his time. Another instance he gives, of Nicolaus King of Denmark (*a*), who courted Uluilda, a noble and beautiful Norvegian lady, and obtained her consent. Nothing remained but the celebration of the nuptials, when she was carried off by Suercher, <489> King of Sweden. We have the authority of Saxo Grammaticus, that Skiold, one of the first Kings of Denmark, fought a duel for a beautiful young woman, and obtained her for a wife. That author relates many duels of the same kind. It was indeed common among the Scandinavians, before they became Christians, to fight for a wife, and to carry off the desired object by force of arms. No cause of war between neighbouring kings was more frequent. Fridlevus King of Denmark sent a solemn embassy to Hasmundus King of Norway, to demand in marriage his daughter. Hasmundus had a rooted aversion to the Danes, who had done much mischief in his country. "Go," says he to the ambassadors, "and demand a wife where you are less hated than in Norway." The young lady, who had no aversion to the match, intreated leave to speak. "You seem," said she, "not to consult the good of your kingdom in rejecting so potent a son-in-law, who can carry by force what he is now applying for by intreaties." The father continuing obstinate, dismissed the ambassadors. Fridlevus sent other ambassadors, redoubling <490> his intreaties for a favourable answer. Hasmundus said, that one refusal might be thought sufficient; and in a fit of passion put the ambassadors to death. Fridlevus invaded Norway with a potent army; and, after a desperate battle, carried off the lady in triumph.

The figure that women made in the north of Europe by their courage, their beauty, and their chastity, could not fail to produce mutual esteem

(*a*) Book 18.

and love between the sexes: nor could that love fail to be purified into the most tender affection, when their rough manners were smoothed in the progress of society. If love between the sexes prevail in Lapland as much as any where, which is vouched by Scheffer in his history of that country, it must be for a reason very different from that now mentioned. The males in Lapland, who are great cowards, have no reason to despise the females for their timidity; and in every country where the women equal the men, mutual esteem and affection naturally take place. Two Lapland odes communicated to us by the author mentioned, leave no doubt of this fact, being full of the tenderest sentiments <491> that love can inspire. The following is a literal translation.

FIRST ODE

I

Kulnasatz my rain-deer,
We have a long journey to go;
The moors are vast,
And we must haste;
Our strength, I fear,
Will fail if we are slow;
And so
Our songs will do.

II

Kaigé, the watery moor,
Is pleasant unto me,
Though long it be;
Since it doth to my mistress lead,
Whom I adore:
The Kilwa moor
I ne'er again will tread.

III

Thoughts fill'd my mind
Whilst I thro' Kaigé past
Swift as the wind,

And my desire,
Wing'd with impatient fire,
My rain-deer let us haste.

IV

So shall we quickly end our pleasing pain:
Behold my mistress there,
With decent motion walking o'er the plain.
Kulnasatz my rain-deer, <492>
Look yonder, where
She washes in the lake:
See while she swims,
The waters from her purer limbs
New clearness take.

SECOND ODE

I

With brightest beams let the sun shine
On Orra moor
Could I be sure
That from the top o' th' lofty pine
I Orra moor might see,
I to its highest bow would climb,
And with industrious labour try
Thence to descry
My mistress, if that there she be.

II

Could I but know, amid what flowers,
Or in what shade she stays,
The gaudy bowers,
With all their verdant pride,
Their blossoms and their sprays,
Which make my mistress disappear,
And her in envious darkness hide,
I from the roots and bed of earth would tear.

III

Upon the raft of clouds I'd ride,
Which unto Orra fly:
O' th' ravens I would borrow wings,
And all the feather'd inmates of the sky:
But wings, alas, are me deny'd,
The stork and swan their pinions will not lend, <493>
There's none who unto Orra brings,
Or will by that kind conduct me befriend.

IV

Enough, enough! thou hast delay'd
So many summers days,
The best of days that crown the year,
Which light upon the eye-lids dart,
And melting joy upon the heart:
But since that thou so long hast stay'd,
They in unwelcome darkness disappear.
Yet vainly dost thou me forsake;
I will pursue and overtake.

V

What stronger is than bolts of steel?
What can more surely bind?
Love is stronger far than it;
Upon the head in triumph she doth sit;
Fetters the mind,
And doth control
The thought and soul.

VI

A youth's desire is the desire of wind;
All his essays
Are long delays:
No issue can they find.
Away fond counsellors, away,
No more advice obtrude:
I'll rather prove

The guidance of blind love;
To follow you is certainly to stray:
One single counsel, tho' unwise, is good.

In the Scandinavian manners here described, is discovered a striking re-
sem-<494>blance to those described by Ossian. And as such were the manners of the Scandinavians in the first stage of society, it no longer remains
a wonder, that the manners of Caledonia should be equally pure in the
same early period. And now every argument above urged for Ossian as a
genuine historian has its full weight, without the least counterpoise. It is
true, that Caledonian manners appear from Ossian to have been still more
polished and refined than those of Scandinavia; but that difference may
have proceeded from accidents which time has buried in oblivion.

I make no apology for insisting so largely on Scandinavian manners; for
they tend remarkably to support the credit of Ossian; and consequently to
ascertain a fact not a little interesting, that our forefathers were not such
barbarians as they are commonly held to be. All the inhabitants of Britain
were of Celtic extraction; and there is reason to believe, that the manners
of Caledonia were the manners of every part of the island, before the inhabitants of the plains were inslaved by the Romans. The only circumstance peculiar to the Caledonians, is their moun-<495>tainous situation:
being less exposed to the oppression of foreigners, and farther removed
from commerce, they did longer than their southern neighbours preserve
their manners pure and untainted.

I have all along considered the poems of Ossian in a historical view
merely. In the view of criticism they have been examined by a writer of
distinguished taste (*a*); and however bold to enter a field where he hath
reaped laurels, I imagine that there still remain some trifles for me to glean.
Two of these poems, Fingal and Temora, are regular epic poems; and perhaps the single instances of epic poetry moulded into the form of an opera.
We have in these two poems both the *Recitativo* and *Aria* of an Italian
opera; dropped indeed in the translation, from difficulty of imitation. Ossian's poems were all of them composed with a view of music; though in

(*a*) Doctor Blair, Professor of Rhetoric in the college of Edinburgh. [[See *A Critical
Dissertation on the Poems of Ossian.*]]

the long poems mentioned, it is probable that the airs only were accompanied with the harp, the recitative being left to the voice. The poems of Ossian are singular in another respect, being probably the only regular <496> work now remaining that was composed in the hunter-state. Some songs of that early period may possibly have escaped oblivion; but no other poem of the epic kind. One may advance a step farther, and pronounce, with a high degree of probability, that Fingal and Temora are the only epic poems that ever were composed in that state. How great must have been the talents of the author, beset with every obstruction to genius, the manners of his country alone excepted; a cold unhospitable climate; the face of the country so deformed as scarce to afford a pleasing object; and he himself absolutely illiterate! One may venture boldly to affirm, that such a poem as Fingal or Temora never was composed in any other part of the world, under such disadvantageous circumstances.

Tho' permanent manners enter not regularly into the present sketch, I am however tempted to add a few words concerning the influence of soil upon the manners of men. The stupidity of the inhabitants of New Holland, mentioned above, is occasioned by the barrenness of their soil, yielding nothing that can be food for man <497> or beast. Day and night they watch the ebb of the tide, in order to dig small fish out of the sand; and sleep in the intervals, without an hour to spare for any other occupation. People in that condition, must for ever remain ignorant and brutish. Were all the earth barren like New Holland, all men would be ignorant and brutish, like the inhabitants of New Holland. On the other hand, were every portion of this earth so fertile as spontaneously to feed all its inhabitants, which is the golden age figured by poets, what would follow? Upon the former supposition, man would be a meagre, patient, and timid animal: upon the latter supposition, he would be pampered, lazy, and effeminate. In both cases, he would be stupidly ignorant, and incapable of any manly exertion, whether of mind or body. But the soil of our earth is in general more wisely accommodated to man, its chief inhabitant. It is neither so fertile as to supersede labour, nor so barren as to require the utmost labour. The laborious occupation of hunting for food, produced originally some degree of industry: and though all the industry of man was at first necessary for procuring <498> food, cloathing, and habitation; yet the soil, by skill in agriculture, came to produce plenty with less labour; which to some afforded time for thinking of conveniencies. A habit of industry thus acquired, excited many to bestow their leisure hours upon the arts, proceeding from useful arts to fine arts, and from these to sciences. Wealth, accumulated by industry, has a wonderful influence upon manners: feuds and war, the offspring of wealth, call forth into action friendship, courage, heroism, and every social virtue, as well as many selfish vices. How like brutes do we pass our time, without once reflecting on the wisdom of Providence visible even in the soil we tread upon!

Diversity of manners, at the same time, enters into the plan of Providence, as well as diversity of talents, of feelings, and of opinions. Our Maker hath given us a taste for variety; and he hath provided objects in plenty for its gratification. Some soils, naturally fertile, require little labour: some soils, naturally barren, require much labour. But the advantages of the latter are more than sufficient to counterbalance its barrenness: the inha-<499>bitants are sober, industrious, vigorous; and consequently courageous, as far as courage depends on bodily strength.* The disadvantages of a fertile soil, on the contrary, are more than sufficient to counterbalance its advantages: the inhabitants are rendered indolent, weak, and cowardly. Hindostan may seem to be an exception; for though it be extremely fertile, the people are industrious, and export manufactures in great abundance at a very low price. But Hindostan properly is not an exception. The Hindows, who are prohibited by their religion to kill any living creature, must abandon to animals for food a large proportion of land; which obliges them to cultivate what remains with double industry, in order to procure <500> food for themselves. The populousness of their country contributes also to make them industrious. Aragon was once the most limited monarchy in

---

* That a barren country is a great spur to industry, appears from Venice and Genoa in Italy, Nuremberg in Germany, and Limoges in France. The sterility of Holland required all the industry of its inhabitants for procuring the necessaries of life; and by that means chiefly they became remarkably industrious. Camden ascribes the success of the town of Halifax in the cloth-manufacture, to its barren soil. A sect of pampered Englishmen, it is to be hoped not many in number, who centre all their devotion in a luxurious board, despise Scotland for its plain fare; and in bitter contumely, characterize it as a poor country.

Europe, England not excepted: the barrenness of the soil was the cause, which rendered the people hardy and courageous. In a preamble to one of their laws, the states declare, that, were they not more free than other nations, the barrenness of their country would tempt them to abandon it. Opposed to Aragon stands Egypt, the fertility of which renders the inhabitants soft and effeminate, and consequently an easy prey to every invader.* The fruitfulness of the province of Quito in Peru, and the low price of every necessary, occasioned by its <501> distance from the sea, have plunged the inhabitants into supine indolence, and excessive luxury. The people of the town of Quito in particular, have abandoned themselves to every sort of debauchery: the time they have to spare from wine and women, is employed in excessive gaming. In other respects also the manners of a people are influenced by the country they inhabit. A great part of Calabria, formerly populous and fertile, is at present covered with trees and shrubs, like the wilds of America; and the ferocity of its inhabitants corresponds to the rudeness of the fields. The same is visible in the inhabitants of Mount Etna in Sicily: the country and its inhabitants are equally rugged.

END of the FIRST VOLUME

* Fear impressed by strange and unforeseen accidents, is the most potent cause of superstition. No other country is less liable to strange and unforeseen accidents than Egypt: no thunder, scarce any rain, perfect regularity in the seasons, and in the rise and fall of the river. So little notion had the Egyptians of variable weather, as to be surprised that the rivers in Greece did not overflow like the Nile. They could not comprehend how their fields were watered: rain, they said, was very irregular; and what if Jupiter should take a conceit to send them no rain? What then made the antient Egyptians so superstitious? The fertility of the soil, and the inaction of the inhabitants during the inundation of the river, enervated both mind and body, and rendered them timid and pusillanimous. Superstition was the offspring of this character in Egypt, as it is of strange and unforeseen accidents in other countries.

SKETCHES

OF THE

HISTORY OF MAN.

CONSIDERABLY ENLARGED
BY THE LAST ADDITIONS
AND CORRECTIONS
OF THE AUTHOR.

IN FOUR VOLUMES.

VOLUME II.

EDINBURGH:

PRINTED FOR A. STRAHAN AND T. CADELL, LONDON;
AND FOR WILLIAM CREECH, EDINBURGH.

M,DCC,LXXXVIII.

CONTENTS[1]

1. The original page numbers from the 1788 edition are retained here.

BOOK I

Progress of Men Independent of Society

Progress of the Female Sex

The progress of the female sex, a capital branch of the history of man, comprehends great variety of matter, curious, and interesting. But sketches are my province, not complete histories; and I propose in the present sketch to trace the gradual progress of wo-<2>men, from their low state in savage tribes, to their elevated state in civilized nations.

With regard to the outlines, whether of internal disposition or of external figure, men and women are the same. Nature, however, intending them for mates, has given them dispositions different but concordant, so as to produce together delicious harmony. The man, more robust, is fitted for severe labour and for field-exercises: the woman, more delicate, is fitted for sedentary occupations; and particularly for nursing children. That difference is remarkable in the mind, no less than in the body. A boy is always running about; delights in a top or a ball, and rides upon a stick as a horse. A girl has less inclination to move: her first amusement is a baby; which she delights to dress and undress. I have seen oftener than once a female child under six getting an infant in its arms, caressing it, singing, and walking about staggering under the weight. A boy never thinks of such a pastime. The man, bold and vigorous, is qualified for being a protector: the

woman, delicate and timid, requires pro-<3>tection.* The man, as a protector, is directed by nature to govern: the woman, conscious of inferiority,
is disposed to obey. Their intellectual powers correspond to the destination
of nature: men have penetration and solid judgement to fit them for governing: women have sufficient understanding to make a decent figure under
good government; a greater proportion would excite dangerous rivalship.
Women have more imagination and more sensibility than men; and yet
none of them have made an eminent figure in any of the fine arts. We hear
of no sculptor nor statuary among them; and none of them have risen
above a mediocrity in poetry or painting. Nature has avoided rivalship between the sexes, by giving them different talents. Add another capital difference of disposition: the gentle and insinuating manners of the female
sex, tend to soften the roughness of the other sex; and where-ever women
are indulged <4> with any freedom, they polish sooner than men.†

These are not the only particulars that distinguish the sexes. With respect
to matrimony, it is the privilege of the male, as superior and protector, to
make a choice; the female preferred has no privilege but barely to consent
or to refuse. Nature fits them for these different parts: the male is bold, the
female bashful. Hence among all nations it is the practice for men to court,
and for women to be courted: which holds also among many other animals,
probably among all that pair.

Another distinction is equally visible: The master of a family is immediately connected with his country; his wife, his <5> children, his servants,
are immediately connected with him, and with their country through him
only. Women accordingly have less patriotism than men; and less bitterness
against the enemies of their country.

---

* From which it appears to proceed, that women naturally are more careful of their
reputation than men, and more hurt by obloquy. [[Note added in 2nd edition.]]

† The chief quality of women, says Rousseau, is sweetness of temper. Made by nature
for submission in the married state, they ought to learn to suffer wrong, even without
complaining. Sourness and stubborness serve but to increase the husband's unkindness
and their own distresses. It was not to indulge bad humour, that Heaven bestowed on
them manners insinuating and persuasive: they were not made weak in order to be imperious: a sweet voice suits ill with scolding; delicate features ought not to be disfigured
with passion. They frequently may have reason for complaints; but never, to utter them
publicly. [[Note added in 2nd edition.]]

The peculiar modesty of the female sex, is also a distinguishing circumstance. Nature hath provided them with it as a defence against the artful solicitations of the other sex before marriage, and also as a support of conjugal fidelity.[1]

A fundamental article in the present sketch is matrimony; and it has been much controverted, whether it be an appointment of nature, or only of municipal law. Many writers have exercised their talents in that controversy, but without giving satisfaction to a judicious inquirer. If I mistake not, it may be determined upon solid principles; and as it is of importance in the history of man, the reader, I am hopeful, will not be disgusted at the length of the argument.

Many writers hold that women were originally common; that animal love was gratified as among horses and horned cattle; and that matrimony was not <6> known, till nations grew in some degree to be orderly and refined. I select Cicero as an author of authority: "Nam fuit quoddam tempus, cum in agris homines passim, bestiarum more, vagabantur, et sibi victu ferino vitam propagabant: nec ratione animi quicquam sed pleraque viribus corporis administrabant. Nondum divinae religionis non humani officii ratio colebatur. Nemo legitimas viderat nuptias, non certos quisquam inspexerat liberos (*a*)."*—Pliny, in support of that doctrine, informs us, that the Garamantes, an African nation, male and female lived promiscuously together, without any notion of matrimony. Among the Auses, a people of Libya, as Herodotus says, matrimony was not known, and men cohabited with women indifferently, like other <7> animals. A boy educated by his mother was at a certain age admitted to an assembly of men, and the man he clung to was reputed his father. Justin and other authors report, that before Cecrops, who reigned in Attica about 1600 years before Christ, mar-

---

* "For there was a time, when men, like the brutes, roamed abroad over the earth, and fed like wild beasts upon other animals. Then reason bore no sway, but all was ruled by superior strength. The ties of religion, and the obligations of morality, were then unfelt. Lawful marriage was unknown, and no father was certain of his offspring."

(*a*) De Inventione, lib. 1.

1. The 1st edition adds: "It is held to be their capital virtue; and a woman who surrenders her chastity is universally despised; tho' in a man chastity is scarce held to be a virtue, except in the married state. But of that more fully afterwards" [1:169].

riage was not known in Greece; and that the burden of children lay upon the mother.

Before entering directly into the matter, it is proper to remove, if possible, the bias of these great names. The practice of the Garamantes and of the Auses is mentioned by Pliny and Herodotus as singular; and, were it even well vouched, it would avail very little against the practice of all other nations. Little weight can be laid upon Pliny's evidence in particular, considering what he reports in the same chapter of the Blemmyans, that they had no head, and that the mouth and eyes were in the breast. Pliny at the same time, as well as Herodotus, being very deficient in natural knowledge, were grossly credulous; and cannot be relied on with respect to any thing strange or uncommon. As to what is reported of ancient Greece, Cecrops possibly prohibited polygamy, or introdu-<8>ced some other matrimonial regulation, which by writers might be mistaken for a law appointing matrimony. However that be, one part of the report is undoubtedly erroneous; for it will be made evident afterward, that in the hunter-state, or even in that of shepherds, it is impracticable for any woman, by her own industry alone, to rear a numerous issue. If this be at all possible, it can only be in the torrid zone, where people live on fruits and roots, which are produced in plenty with very little labour. Upon that account, Diodorus Siculus is less blameable for listening to a report, that the inhabitants of Taprobana, supposed to be the island of Ceylon, never marry, but that women are used promiscuously. At the same time, as there is no such custom at present in the East Indies, there is no good ground to believe, that it ever was customary; and the East Indies were so little known to the ancient Greeks, that their authors cannot be much relied on, in the accounts they give of that distant region. The authority of Cicero, however respectable in other matters, will not be much regarded upon the present question, when <9> the passage above quoted is dissected. How crude must his notions be of the primitive state of man, when he denies to savages any sense of religion or of moral duty! Ought we to rely more on him, when he denies that they have any notion of matrimony? Caesar's account of the ancient Britons approaches the nearest to a loose commerce with women, tho' in the main it is good evidence against Cicero. It was common, he says, for a

number of brothers, or other near relations, to use their wives promiscuously. The offspring however were not common; for each man maintained
the children that were produced by his own wife. Herodotus reports the
same of the Massagetae.

Laying thus aside the great names of Cicero, Herodotus, and Pliny, the
field lies open to a fair and impartial investigation. And as the means provided by nature for continuing the race of other animals, may probably
throw light upon the oeconomy of nature with respect to man; I begin with
that article, which has not engaged the attention of naturalists so much as
it ought to have done. With respect to animals whose nourishment is <10>
grass, pairing would be of no use: the female feeds herself and her young
at the same instant; and nothing is left for the male to do. On the other
hand, all brute animals whose young require the nursing care of both parents, are directed by nature to pair; nor is that connection dissolved till the
young can provide for themselves. Pairing is indispensable to wild birds
that build on trees; because the male must provide food for his mate while
she is hatching the eggs. And as they have commonly a numerous issue, it
requires the labour of both to pick up food for themselves and for their
young. Upon that account it is so ordered, that the young are sufficiently
vigorous to provide for themselves, before a new brood is produced.

What I have now opened suggests the following question, Whether, according to the oeconomy above displayed, are we to presume, or not, that
man is directed by nature to matrimony? If analogy can be relied on, the
affirmative must be held, as there is no other creature in the known world
to which pairing is so necessary. Man is an animal of long life, and is pro-
<11>portionally slow in growing to maturity: he is a helpless being before
the age of fifteen or sixteen; and there may be in a family ten or twelve
children of different births, before the eldest can shift for itself. Now in the
original state of hunting and fishing, which are laborious occupations, and
not always successful, a woman, suckling her infant, is not able to provide
food even for herself, far less for ten or twelve voracious children. Matrimony, therefore, or pairing, is so necessary to the human race, that it must
be natural and instinctive. When such ample means are provided for continuing every other animal race, is it supposable that the chief race is ne-

glected? Providential care descends even to vegetable life: every plant bears a profusion of seed; and in order to cover the earth with vegetables, some seeds have wings, some are scattered by means of a spring, and some are so light as to be carried about by the wind. Brute animals which do not pair, have grass and other food in plenty, enabling the female to feed her young without needing any assistance from the male. But where the young require the nursing care <12> of both parents, pairing is a law of nature. When other races are so amply provided for, can it be seriously thought, that Providence is less attentive to the human race? If men and women were not impelled by nature to matrimony, they would be less fitted for continuing the species, than even the humblest plant. Have we not then reason fairly to conclude, that matrimony in the human race is an appointment of nature? Can that conclusion be resisted by any one who believes in Providence, and in final causes.*

To confirm this doctrine, let the consequences of a loose commerce between the sexes be examined. The carnal appetite, when confined to one object, seldom transgresses the bounds of temperance. But were it encouraged to roam, like a bee sucking honey from every flower, every new object would inflame the imagina-<13>tion; and satiety with respect to one, would give new vigour with respect to others: a generic habit would be formed of intemperance in fruition (a); and animal love would become the ruling passion. Men, like the hart in rutting-time, would all the year round fly with impetuosity from object to object, giving no quarter even to women suckling their infants: and women, abandoning themselves to the same appetite, would become altogether regardless of their offspring. In that state, the continuance of the human race would be a miracle. In the savage state, as mentioned above, it is beyond the power of any woman to provide food for a family of children; and now it appears, that intem-

---

* It appears a wise appointment of Providence, that women give over child-bearing at fifty, while they are still in vigour of mind and body to take care of their offspring. Did the power of procreation continue in women to old age as in men, children would often be left in the wide world, without a mortal to look after them.

(a) Elements of Criticism, chap. 14.

perance in animal love would render a woman careless of her family, however easy it might be to provide for it.* <14>

I say more. The promiscuous use of women would unqualify them in a great measure to procreate. The carnal appetite in man resembles his appetite for food: each of them demands gratification, after short intervals. Where the carnal appetite is felt but a short space annually, as among animals who feed on grass, the promiscuous use of females is according to the order of nature: but such a law in man, where the carnal appetite is always awake, would be an effectual bar to procreation; it being an undoubted truth, that women <15> who indulge that appetite to excess, seldom have children; and if all women were common, all women would in effect be common prostitutes.

If undisguised nature show itself any where, it is in children. So truly is matrimony an appointment of nature, as to be understood even by children. They often hear, it is true, people talking of matrimony; but they also hear of logical, metaphysical, and commercial matters, without understanding a syllable. Whence then their notion of marriage but from nature? Marriage is a compound idea, which no instruction could bring within the comprehension of a child, did not nature co-operate.

That the arguments urged above against a promiscuous use of women, do not necessarily conclude against polygamy, or the union of one man

---

* I have often been tempted to blame Providence for bringing to perfection in early youth the carnal appetite, long before people have acquired any prudence or self-command. It rages the most when young men should be employed in acquiring knowledge, and in fitting themselves for living comfortably in the world. I have set this thought in various lights; but I now perceive that the censure is without foundation. The early ripeness of this appetite, proves it to be the intention of Providence that people should early settle in matrimony. In that state the appetite is abundantly moderate, and gives no obstruction to education. It never becomes unruly, till a man, forgetting the matrimonial tie, wanders from object to object. Pride and luxury are what dictate late marriages: industry never fails to afford the means of living comfortably, provided men confine themselves to the demands of nature. A young man, at the same time, who has the care of a family upon him, is impelled to be active in order to provide food for them. And supposing him to have a sufficiency without labour, attention to his wife and children produces a habit of doing good, which is regularly extended to all around. And married men become thus good citizens; and some of them eminent patriots. [["A young man . . . them eminent patriots": added in 3rd edition.]]

with a plurality of women, will not escape an attentive reader. St. Augustin and other fathers admit, that polygamy is not prohibited by the law of nature; and the learned Grotius professes the same opinion (*a*). But great names <16> terrify me not; and I venture to maintain, that pairing in the strictest sense is a law of nature among men as among wild birds; and that polygamy is a gross infringement of that law. My reasons follow.

I urge, in the first place, the equal number of males and females, as a clear indication that Providence intends every man to be confined to one wife, and every woman to one husband. That equality, which has subsisted in all countries and at all times, is a signal instance of over-ruling Providence; for the chances against it are infinite. All men are by nature equal in rank: no man is privileged above another to have a wife; and therefore polygamy is contradictory to the plan of Providence. Were ten women born for one man, as is erroneously reported to be the case in Bantam, polygamy might be the intention of Providence; but from the equality of males and females, it is clearly the voice of nature, as well as of the sacred scripture, "That a man shall leave his father and mother, and cleave to his wife; and they shall be one flesh." <17>

Consider, in the next place, that however plausible polygamy may appear in the present state of things, where inequality of rank and of fortune have produced luxury and sensuality; yet that the laws of nature were not contrived by our Maker for a forced state, where numberless individuals are degraded below their natural rank, for the benefit of a few who are elevated above it. To form a just notion of polygamy, we must look back to the original state of man, where all are equal. In that state, every man cannot have two wives; and consequently no man is entitled to more than one, till every other be upon an equal footing with him. At the same time, the union of one man with one woman is much better calculated for continuing the race, than the union of one man with many women. Think of a savage who may have fifty or sixty children by different wives, all depending for food upon his industry: chance must turn out much in his favour, if the half of them perish not by hunger. How much a better chance for life have infants who are distributed more equally in different families? <18>

(*a*) De jure belli ac pacis, lib. 2. cap. 5. § 9.

Polygamy has an effect still more pernicious, with respect to children even of the most opulent families. Unless affection be reciprocal and equal, there can be no proper society in the matrimonial state, no cordiality, nor due care of offspring. But such affection is inconsistent with polygamy: a woman in that state, far from being a companion to her husband, is degraded to the rank of a servant, a mere instrument of pleasure and propagation. Among many wives there will always be a favourite: the rest turn peevish; and if they resent not the injury against their husband, and against their children as belonging to him, they will at least be disheartened, and turn negligent of them. At the same time, fondness for the favourite wife and her children, makes the husband indifferent about the rest; and woful is the condition of children who are neglected by both parents (a). To produce such an effect, is certainly not the purpose of nature.

It merits peculiar attention, that Providence has provided for an agreeable union, among all creatures who are taught by <19> nature to pair. Animal love among creatures who pair not, is confined within a narrow space of time: while the dam is occupied about her young, animal love lies dormant, that she may not be abstracted from her duty. In pairing animals, on the contrary, animal love is always awake: frequent enjoyment endears a pair to each other, and makes constancy a pleasure. Such is the case of the human race; and such is the case of wild birds (b). Among the wild birds that build on trees, the male, after feeding his mate in the nest, plants himself upon the next spray, and cheers her with a song.* There is still greater enjoyment provided for the human race in the matrimonial state, and stronger incitements to constancy. Sweet is the society of a pair fitted for each other, in whom are collected the affections of husband, wife, lover, friend, the tenderest affections of human nature. Public government is in perfection, when the sovereign commands with humanity, <20> and the subjects are cordial in their obedience. Private government in conjugal society arrives at still greater perfection, where husband and wife govern and

* A male canary bird, singing to his mate on her nest in a breeding cage, fell down dead. The female alarmed left her nest and pecked at him: finding him immoveable, she refused nourishment and died at his side. [[Note added in 2nd edition.]]
(a) [[Montesquieu,]] L'esprit des loix, liv. 16. chap. 6.
(b) Buffon, liv. 5. p. 359. octavo edition.

are governed reciprocally, with entire satisfaction to both. The man bears rule over his wife's person and conduct; she bears rule over his inclinations: he governs by law: she by persuasion. Nor can her authority ever fail, where it is supported by sweetness of temper, and zeal to make him happy.* <21>

The God of nature has enforced conjugal society, not only by making it agreeable, but by the principle of chastity inherent in our nature. To animals that have no instinct for pairing, chastity is utterly unknown; and to them it would be useless. The mare, the cow, the ewe, the she-goat, re-ceive the male without ceremony, and admit the first that comes in the way without distinction. Neither have tame fowl any notion of chastity: they pair not; and the female gets no food from the male, even during incuba-tion. But chastity and mutual fidelity are essen-<22>tial to all pairing ani-mals; for wandering inclinations would render them negligent in nursing their young. While birds pair; and they are by instinct faithful to each other, while their young require nurture. Chastity is essential to the human race; enforced by the principle of chastity, a branch of the moral sense. Chastity is essential even to the continuation of the human race. As the carnal ap-

---

* L'empire de la femme est un empire de douceur, d'addresse, et de complaisance; ses ordres sont des caresses, ses menaces sont des pleurs. Elle doit regner dans la maison comme un ministre dans l'etat, en se faisant commander ce qu'elle veut faire. En ce sens il est constant que les meilleurs ménages sont ceux où la femme a le plus d'autorité. Mais quand elle meconnoit la voix du chef, qu'elle veut usurper ses droits et commander elle-même; il ne resulte jamais de ce desordre, que misere, scandale, et dishonneur; *Rousseau, Emile, liv.* 5. *p.* 96.—[*In English thus:* "The empire of the woman is an empire of softness, of address, of complacency; her commands are caresses, her menaces are tears. She ought to reign in the family like a minister in the state, by making that which is her inclination be enjoined to her as her duty: Thus it is evident, that the best domestic oeconomy is that where the wife has most authority. But when she is insensible to the voice of her chief, when she tries to usurp his prerogative, and to command alone, what can result from such disorder, but misery, scandal, and dishonour?"]—The Empress Livia being questioned by a married lady, how she had obtained such ascendent over her husband Augustus, answered, "By being obedient to his commands, by not wishing to know his secrets, and by hiding my knowledge of his amours." The late Queen of Spain was a woman of singular prudence, and of solid judgement. A character of her, published after her death, contains the following passage: "She had a great ascendency over the King, founded on his persuasion of her superior sense, which she showed in a perfect sub-mission to his commands; the more easily obeyed, as they were commonly, though to him imperceptibly, dictated by herself. She cured him of many foibles, and, in a word, was his Minerva, under the appearance of Mentor."

petite is always alive, the sexes would wallow in pleasure, and be soon rendered unfit for procreation, were it not for the restraint of chastity.[2]

Nor is chastity confined to the matrimonial state. Matrimony is instituted by nature for continuing the species; and it is the duty of man to abstain from animal enjoyment, except in that state. The ceremonies of marriage and the causes of separation and divorce, are subjected to municipal law: but, if a man beget children, it is his duty to unite with the mother in taking care of them; and such union is matrimony according to the law of nature. Hence it is, that the first acts of incontinence, where enjoyment only is in view, are always attended with shame, and with <23> a degree of remorse.* At the same time, as chastity in persons who are single is only a self-duty, it is not so strongly enforced by the moral sense as chastity is in married persons, who owe fidelity to each other. Deviations accordingly from the former make a less figure than from the latter: we scarce ever hear of adultery among savages; though among them incontinence before marriage is not uncommon. In Wales, even at present, and in the highlands of Scotland, it is scarce a disgrace for a young woman to have a bastard. In the country last mentioned, the first instance known of a bastard-child being destroyed by its mother through shame, is a late one. The virtue of chastity appears to be there gaining ground; as the only temptation a woman can have to destroy her child, is to conceal her frailty. The principle of chastity, like that of propriety or of decency, is faint among <24> savages; and has little of that influence which prevails among polished nations before they are corrupted by luxury. We shall have occasion to see afterward, that even the great duty of justice is faint among barbarians; and that it

---

* Quand enfin cette aimable jeunesse vient à se marier, les deux époux se donnant mutuellement les premices de leur personne, en sont plus chers l'un à l'autre; des multitudes d'enfans sains et robustes deviennent le gage d'une union que rien n'altere; *Rousseau, Emile.* [["When at last those delightful young people marry, they bestow on each other the first fruits of their person, and are all the dearer therefore. Swarms of strong and healthy children are the pledges of a union which nothing can change" (bk. IV, p. 212). Note added in 2nd edition.]]

2. "Chastity is essential . . . restraint of chastity": added in 2nd edition.

yields readily to every irregular impulse, before the moral sense has arrived to maturity.[3]

Chastity is a restraint upon nature; and, therefore, if shame be removed by making it lawful to obey the appetite, nature will prevail. In the year 1707, a contagious distemper having carried off a large proportion of the inhabitants of Iceland, the King of Denmark fell on a device to repeople the country, which succeeded to a wish. A law was made, authorising young women in that island to have bastards, even to the number of six, without wounding their reputation.* The young women were so zealous to repeople their <25> country, that after a few years it was found proper to abrogate the law.

Modesty is by nature intended to guard chastity, as chastity is to guard matrimony. And modesty, like chastity, is one of those delicate principles that make no great figure among savages. In the land of Jesso, young women sometimes go naked in summer: if however they meet a stranger, they hang the head, and turn away through shame. Nature here is their only instructor.[†] Some savage tribes have so little notion of modesty, as to go naked, without even covering their privy parts. Regnard reports, upon his own knowledge, that in Lapland, man, woman, and child, take the hot bath promiscuously, and are not ashamed to be seen in that condition, even by a stranger. As this appeared singular, I took an opportunity to mention it to Dr. Solander, who had made more than one visit to that country. He said, that Regnard's report might be true; but without any imputation on the modesty of <26> the Laplanders, for that their place of bathing is always so dark that nothing can be seen. He added, that the females in Lapland, both married and unmarried, are extremely chaste. The inhabitants of Otaheite, if Bougainville can be trusted, seem to have as little notion of

* Don Juan de Ulloa, in his voyage to Peru, mentions a very singular taste prevalent in that country, that a man never takes a virgin to wife; and thinks himself dishonoured if his wife have not, before marriage, enjoyed many lovers. If we can trust Paulus Venetus, a young woman of Thibet, in Asia, is not reckoned fit to be married till she be defloured.

† Doth not modesty prevail among many animals? Elephants are never seen in copulation, nor cats, nor beasts of prey.

3. The 1st edition adds: "Bougainville reports, that in the island of Otaheite, or King George's island, a young woman is free to follow her inclinations; and that her having had many lovers gives her not the less chance for a husband" [1:180].

modesty as of chastity. But many of that author's facts stand contradicted by later voyagers. The women of New Zealand are both chaste and modest. Captain Cook, in his voyage round the world, stumbled upon some of them naked, diving for lobsters; and they were in great confusion for being seen in that condition by strangers.

But now, if pairing in the strictest sense be a law of nature among men, as among some other animals, how is polygamy to be accounted for, which formerly was universal, and to this day obtains among many nations? Polygamy, I answer, is derived from two sources; first, from savage manners, once universal; and next, from voluptuousness in warm climates, which instigates men of wealth to transgress every rule of temperance. These two sources I propose to handle with care, <27> because they make a large branch in the history of the female sex.

With respect to the first, sweetness of temper, a capital article in the female character, displays itself externally by mild looks and gentle manners. But such graces are scarce discernible in a female savage; and even in the most polished women, would not be perceived by a male savage. Among savages, strength and boldness are the only valued qualities: in these females are miserably deficient; and for that reason, are contemned by the males, as beings of an inferior order. The North-American tribes glory in idleness: the drudgery of labour degrades a man in their opinion, and is proper for women only. To join young persons in marriage is accordingly the business of parents; and it would be unpardonable meanness in the bridegroom, to shew any fondness for the bride. Young men among the Hottentots, are admitted into society with their seniors at the age of eighteen; after which it is disgraceful to keep company with women. In Guiana, a woman never eats with her husband; but after every meal attends him with water for washing. In <28> the Carribbee islands, she is not permitted to eat even in presence of her husband; and yet we are assured (a), that women there obey with such sweetness and respect, as never to give their husbands occasion to remind them of their duty; "an example," adds our sage author, "worthy the imitation of Christian wives, who are daily instructed from the pulpit in the duties of obedience and conjugal fidelity, *but to very little purpose.*"

(a) Labat's voyages to the American islands.

Dampier observes in general, that, among all the wild nations he was acquainted with, the women carry the burdens, while the men walk before, and carry nothing but their arms. Women even of the highest rank are not better treated. The sovereign of Giaga, in Africa, has many wives, who are literally his slaves: one carries his bow, one his arrows, and one gives him drink; and while he is drinking, they all fall on their knees, clap their hands, and sing. Not many centuries ago, a law was made in England, prohibiting the New Testament in English to be read by women, 'prentices, journeymen, <29> or serving men (*a*). What a pitiful figure must the poor females have made in that age! In Siberia, and even in Russia, the capital excepted, men treat their wives in every respect as slaves. The regulations of Peter I. put marriage upon a more respectable footing among people of rank; and yet such are the brutal manners of the Russians, that tyrannical treatment of wives is far from being eradicated.

The low condition of the female sex among savages and barbarians, paved the way to polygamy. Savages, excited by a taste for variety, and still more by pride, which is gratified by many servants, delight in a multiplicity of wives. The pairing principle, though rooted in human nature, makes little figure among savages, yielding to every irregular appetite; and this fairly accounts why polygamy was once universal. It might indeed be thought, that animal love, were there nothing else, should have raised women to some degree of estimation among the men. But male savages, utter strangers to decency or refinement, gratify animal love <30> with as little ceremony as they do hunger or thirst.

Hence appears the reason of a practice that will surprise those who are unacquainted with ancient customs; which is, that a man purchased a woman to be his wife, as one purchases an ox or a sheep to be food. Women by marriage became slaves; and no man will give his daughter to be a slave, but for a valuable consideration. The practice was universal. I begin with the Jews. Abraham bought Rebekah, and gave her to his son Isaac for a wife (*b*). Jacob, having nothing else to give, served Laban fourteen years for two

(*a*) 34th and 35th Henry VIII. cap. 1.
(*b*) Genesis, xxiv. 53.

wives (*a*). Sechem demanding in marriage Dinah, Jacob's daughter, said, "Ask me never so much dowry and gift, and I will give according as ye shall say unto me: but give me the damsel to wife" (*b*). To David demanding Saul's daughter in marriage, Saul said, "The king desireth not any dowry, but an hundred foreskins of the Philistines" (*c*). In the Iliad, Agamemnon offers his daugh-<31>ter to Achilles for a wife; and says, that he would not demand for her any price. Pausanias reports of Danaus, that no suitors appearing to demand any of his daughters, he published, that he would give them without dowry. In Homer, there is frequent mention of nuptial gifts from a bridegroom to his bride's father. From terming them gifts, it is probable that the former method of purchase was beginning to wear out. It wore out before the time of Aristotle; who infers, that their forefathers must have been a very rude people. The ancient Spaniards purchased their wives. We have the authority of Herodotus and of Heraclides Ponticus, that the Thracians followed the same practice. The latter adds, that if a wife was ill treated, her relations could demand her back, upon repaying the price they got for her. In the Roman law mention is made of matrimony *per aes et libram,* which was solemnized by laying down a quantity of brass with a balance for weighing it, understood to be the price paid for the bride. This must have been once a reality; though it sunk down to be a mere ceremony, after it became custo-<32>mary for a Roman bride to bring a dowry with her. The Babylonians and the Assyrians, at stated times, collected all the marriageable young women, and disposed of them by auction. Rubruquis, in his voyage to Tartary *anno* 1253, reports, that there every man bought his wife. "They believe," he adds, "that their wives serve them in another world as they do in this; for which reason, a widow has no chance for a second husband, whom she cannot serve in the other world." Olaus Magnus, remarking that among the ancient Goths no dower was provided on the bride's part, gives a reason, better suited perhaps to the time he lived in, than to what he describes. "Apud Gothos, non mulier viro sed vir mulieri dotem assignat; ne conjux, ob magnitudinem dotis insolescens, aliquando

(*a*) Genesis, chap. xxix.
(*b*) Genesis, xxxiv. 12.
(*c*) 1 Samuel, xviii. 25.

ex placida consorte proterva evadet, atque in maritum dominari conten-
dat";* as if the hazard of petulance in a wife would hinder a man to accept
a dower with her:—<33>a sad doctrine for an heiress. There is preserved
in the abbey of St. Peter a charter, judged to be 700 years old, in which the
Countess of Amiens gifts to the said abbey land she received from her husband at their marriage, "according to the Salic law," says she, "obliging the
husband to give a dowry to his wife." By the laws of King Ethelbert, sect.
32. a man who committed adultery with his neighbour's wife, was obliged
to pay him a fine, and to buy him another wife. Giraldus Cambrensis, in
his description of Wales, says, that formerly they hardly ever married without a prior cohabitation; it having been customary for parents to let out
their daughters to young men upon trial, for a sum of money told down,
and under a penalty if the girls were returned. This I believe to be a mistake.
It is more probable, that in Wales men purchased their wives, as was done
all the world over, with liberty to return them if they proved not agreeable.
The bride's parents retained the dowry, and her chance for a husband was
as good as ever.

The same custom continues among barbarous nations. It continues
among the <34> Tartars, among the Mingrelians, among the Samoides,
among the Ostiacs, among the people of Pegu, and of the Molucca islands.
In the island of Sumatra a man purchases his wives. He may return a wife
to her relations; but they keep the purchase-money. If a woman dislike her
husband, she or her relations must pay to him double the purchase-money.
In Timor, an East-Indian island, men sell even their children to purchase
more wives. The Prince of Circassia demanded from the Prince of Min-
grelia, who was in suit of his daughter, a hundred slaves loaded with tapestry
and other household furniture, a hundred cows, as many oxen, and as many
horses. We have evidence of the same custom in Africa, particularly in Biledulgerid, among the negroes on the sea-coast, and in Monomotapa.
Among the Caribbees there is one instance where a man gets a wife without
paying for her. After a successful war, the victors are entertained at a feast,

---

* "Among the Goths, a man gave a dowry for his bride, instead of receiving one with
her; to prevent pride and insolence, that commonly accompany riches on the woman's
part."

where the General harangues on the valour of the young men who made
the best figure. Every man who has marriageable daughters, is fond to offer
them to such young men without any price. The <35> purchasing of wives
is universal among the wild Arabs. When the bargain is concluded, the
bridegroom is permitted to visit the bride: if she answer not his expectations, he may turn her off; but has no claim for the price he paid. In Arabia,
says Niebuhr, a young married woman suspected of not being a virgin, is
sent back to her father, who must restore the price that was paid for her.[4]
The inland negroes are more polished than those on the coast; and there is
scarce any remains among them of purchasing wives: the bridegroom
makes presents to his bride, and her father makes presents to him. There
are remaining traces in Russia of purchasing wives. Even so late as the time
of Peter I. Russians married without seeing each other; and before solemnization, the bride received from the bridegroom a present of sweet-
meats, soap, and other little things.

The purchasing of wives made it a lawful practice, to lend a wife as one
does a slave. The Spartans lent their wives to their friends; and Cato the
elder is said to have done the same. The Indians of Calicut frequently exchange wives. <36>

If brutish manners alone be sufficient to degrade the female sex, they
may reckon upon harsh treatment when purchased to be slaves. The Giagas,
a fierce and wandering nation in the central parts of Africa, being supinely
idle at home, subject their wives and their slaves to every sort of drudgery,
such as digging, sowing, reaping, cutting wood, grinding corn, fetching
water, &c. These poor creatures are suffered to toil in the fields and woods,
ready to faint with excessive labour; while the monsters of men will not
give themselves the trouble even of training animals for work, though they
have the example of the Portuguese before their eyes. It is the business of
the women among the wandering Arabs of Africa, to card, spin, and weave,
and to manage other household affairs. They milk the cattle, grind, bake,
brew, dress the victuals, and bring home wood and water. They even take
care of their husband's horses, feed, curry, comb, bridle, and saddle them.
They would also be obliged, like Moorish wives, to dig, sow, and reap their

4. "In Arabia, says . . . paid for her": added in 2nd edition.

corn; but luckily for them the Arabs live entirely upon plunder. Father Joseph Gumilla, in his ac-<37>count of a country in South America, bordering upon the great river Oroonoko, describes pathetically the miserable slavery of married women there; and mentions a practice, that would appear incredible to one unacquainted with that country, which is, that married women frequently destroy their female infants. A married woman, of a virtuous character and good understanding, having been guilty of that crime, was reproached by our author in bitter terms. She heard him patiently with eyes fixed on the ground; and answered as follows:

> I wish to God, Father, I wish to God, that my mother had by my death prevented the manifold distresses I have endured, and have yet to endure as long as I live. Had she kindly stifled me at birth, I had not felt the pain of death, nor numberless other pains that life hath subjected me to. Consider, Father, our deplorable condition. Our husbands go to hunt with their bows and arrows, and trouble themselves no farther. We are dragged along, with one infant at the breast, and another in a basket. They return in the evening without any burden: we return with <38> the burden of our children; and, tho' tired with a long march, are not permitted to sleep, but must labour the whole night, in grinding maize to make chica for them. They get drunk, and in their drunkenness beat us, draw us by the hair of the head, and tread us under foot. And what have we to comfort us for slavery that has no end? A young wife is brought in upon us, who is permitted to abuse us and our children, because we are no longer regarded. Can human nature endure such tyranny! What kindness can we show to our female children equal to that of relieving them from such oppression, more bitter a thousand times than death? I say again, would to God that my mother had put me under ground the moment I was born.

One would readily imagine, that the women of that country should have the greatest abhorrence at matrimony: but all-prevailing nature determines the contrary; and the appetite for matrimony overbalances every rational consideration.

Nations polish by degrees; and, from the lowest state to which a human crea-<39>ture can be reduced, women were restored to their native dignity. Attention to dress is the first symptom of the progress. Male savages, even of the grossest kind, are fond of dress. Charlevoix mentions a young American hired as a rower, who adjusted his dress with care before he entered the boat; and at intervals inspected his looking-glass, to see whether violence of motion had not discomposed the red upon his cheeks. We read not of passion for dress in females of such savage nations: they are too much dispirited to think of being agreeable. Among nations in any degree humanized, a different scene opens. In the isthmus of Darien government has made some progress, and a chieftain is elected for life: a glimmering of civility appears among the inhabitants; and as some regard is paid to women, they rival the men in dress. Both sexes wear rings in their ears and noses; and are adorned with many rows of shells hanging from the neck. A female in a sultry climate submits to fry all day long, under a load of twenty or thirty pounds of shells; and a male under double that load. Well may they exclaim with Alexander, "Oh Athe-<40>nians! what do I not endure to gain your approbation!" The female Caribbeans and Brasilians, are no less fond of ornament than the males. Hottentot ladies strive to outdo each other in adorning their crosses, and the bag that holds their pipe and tobacco: European ladies are not more vain of their silks and embroideries. Women in Lapland are much addicted to finery. They wear broad girdles, upon which hang chains and rings without end, commonly made of tin, sometimes of silver, weighing perhaps twenty pounds. The Greenlanders are nasty and slovenly, eat with their dogs, make food of the vermin that make food of them, seldom or never wash themselves; and yet the women, who make some figure among the men, are gaudy in their dress. Their chief ornaments are pendants at their ears, with glass beads of various colours; and they draw lines with a needle and black thread between their eyes, cross the forehead, upon the chin, hands, and legs. The negroes of the kingdom of Ardrah in Guinea have made a considerable progress in police, and in the art of living. Their women carry dress and finery to an extrava-<41>gance. They are cloathed with loads of the finest satins and chintzes, and are adorned with a profusion of gold. In a sultry climate, they gratify vanity at the expence of ease. Among the inland negroes, who are more polished than those on the sea-coast, the women, beside domestic concerns, sow, plant, and reap. A man however suffers in the esteem of his neighbours, if he permit his wives to toil like slaves, while he is indulging in ease.

From that auspicious commencement, the female sex have risen, in a slow but steady progress, to higher and higher degrees of estimation. Conversation is their talent, and a display of delicate sentiments: the gentleness of their manners and winning behaviour, captivate every sensible heart. Of such refinements, savages have little conception: but, when the more delicate senses are unfolded, the peculiar beauties of the female sex, internal as well as external, are brought into full light; and women, formerly considered as objects of animal love merely, are now valued as faithful friends and agreeable companions. Matrimony assumes a more decent form, being the union, not of a master and slave, <42> but of two persons equal in rank uniting to form a family. And it contributed greatly to this delicious refinement, that in temperate climes animal love is moderate, and women long retain good looks, and power of procreation. Thus marriage became honourable among polished nations: which banished the barbarous custom of purchasing wives; for a man who wishes to have his daughter advantageously matched, will gladly give a dowry with her.[5]

Polygamy is intimately connected with the custom of purchasing wives. There is no limitation in purchasing slaves: nor has a woman purchased as a wife or a slave, any just cause for complaining that others are purchased as she was: on the contrary, addition of hands for performing the servile offices of the family, is some relief to her. Polygamy accordingly has always been permitted, where men pay for their wives. The Jews purchased their wives, and were indulged in polygamy (a). Diodorus Siculus says, that polygamy was permitted in Egypt, except to priests (b). This probably was the case originally; <43> but when the Egyptian manners came to be polished, a man gave a dowry with his daughter, instead of receiving a price for her; witness Solomon, who got the city of Gazer in dowry with the King of Egypt's daughter. When that custom became universal, we may be certain that it put an end to polygamy. And accordingly Herodotus affirms, that polygamy was prohibited in Egypt (c). Polygamy undoubtedly pre-

(a) Leviticus, xviii. 18.
(b) Lib. 1.
(c) Lib. 2 § 92.
5. The 1st edition adds: "instead of selling her as a slave" [1:190].

vailed in Greece and Rome, while it was customary to purchase wives; but improved manners put an end to the latter, and consequently to the former. Polygamy to this day obtains in the cold country of Kamskatka; and in the still colder country round Hudson's bay. In the land of Jesso, near Japan, a man may have two wives, who perform every sort of domestic drudgery. The negroes in general purchase their wives, and indulge in polygamy: and this is also law in Monomotapa. Polygamy and the purchasing wives were customary among the original inhabitants of the Canary islands, and among the people of Chili. <44>

The low condition of women among barbarians introduced the purchasing them for wives, and consequently polygamy. The just respect paid to them among civilized nations, restored the law of nature, and confined a man to one wife. Their equality as to rank and dignity, bars the man from taking another wife, as it bars the woman from taking another husband. We find traces in ancient history of polygamy wearing out gradually. It wore out in Greece, as manners refined; but such was the influence of long habit, that though a man was confined to one wife, he was indulged in concubines without limitation. In Germany, when Tacitus wrote, very few traces remained of polygamy. "Severa illic matrimonia, nec ullam morum partem magis laudaveris: nam prope soli barbarorum singulis uxoribus contenti sunt, exceptis admodum paucis, qui non libidine, sed ob nobilitatem, plurimis nuptiis ambiuntur."* <45> As polygamy was in that country little practised, we may be certain the purchasing wives did not remain in vigour. And Tacitus accordingly, mentioning the general rule, "dotem non uxor marito, sed uxori maritus offert,"† explains it away by observing, that the only *dos* given by the bridegroom were marriage-presents, and that he at the same time received marriage-presents on the bride's part (*a*). The equality of the matrimonial engagement for the mutual benefit of husband and

---

* "Marriage is there rigidly respected; nor is there any part of their morality more laudable: for they are almost the only race of barbarians who are contented with a single wife; a very few excepted, who, not from incontinency, but from an ambition of nobility, take more wives than one."

† "The husband gives a dowry to the wife, but the wife brings none to the husband."

(*a*) De moribus Germanorum, cap. 18.

wife, was well understood among the Gauls. Caesar (*a*) says, "Viri quantas pecunias ab uxoribus dotis nomine acceperunt, tantas ex suis bonis, aesti-matione facta, cum dotibus communicant. Hujus omnis pecuniae con-junctim ratio habetur, fructusque servantur. Uter eorum vita superarit, ad eum pars utriusque cum fructibus superiorum temporum pervenit."* In Japan, and in Nicara-<46>gua, a man can have but one wife; but he may have many concubines. In Siam, polygamy is still permitted, though the bride brings a dowry with her: but that absurdity is corrected by refined manners; it being held improper, and even disgraceful, to have more than one wife. The purchasing wives wore out of fashion among the ancient Tuscans; for it was held infamous, that marriage should be the result of any motive but mutual love. This at the same time put an end to polygamy. Polygamy was probably early eradicated among the ancient Persians; for the bride's dowry was settled in marriage-articles, as among us. And there is the same reason for presuming, that it was not long permitted in Mexico; marriage there being solemnized by the priest, and the bride's dower spec-ified, which was restored in case of separation. In the countries where the Christian religion was first propagated, women were fast advancing to an equa-<47>lity with the men, and polygamy was wearing out of fashion. The pure spirit of the gospel hastened its extinction; and though not pro-hibited expressly, it was however held, that Christianity is a religion too pure for polygamy.

But, as hinted above, it was by slow degrees that the female sex emerged out of slavery, to possess the elevated station they are entitled to by nature. The practice of exposing infants among the Greeks and many other na-tions, is an invincible proof of their depression, even after the custom ceased of purchasing them. It is wisely ordered by Providence, that the affection of a woman to her children commences with their birth; because during infancy all depends on her care. As during that period, the father is

---

* "Whatever sum the husband has received as his wife's portion, he joins as much of his own effects. An account is kept of this joint stock, and the fruits of it are preserved. Upon the death of either, the surviving spouse has the property of both the shares, with the fruits or profits."

(*a*) Lib. 6. cap. 19. De bello Gallico.

of little use to his child, his affection is but slight, till the child begin to
prattle and shew some fondness for him. The exposing an infant therefore
shows, that the mother was little regarded: if she had been allowed a vote,
the practice never would have obtained in any country. In the first book of
the Iliad, Achilles says to Agamemnon, who threatened to force from him
his mistress <48> Briseis, "Another thing I will tell thee: record it in thy
soul. For a woman these hands shall never fight, with thee nor with thy
foes. Come, seize Briseis: ye Argives, take the prize ye gave. But beware of
other spoil, which lies stowed in my ships on the shore. I will not be plundered farther. If other be thy thoughts, Atrides, come in arms, a trial make:
these very slaves of thine shall behold thy blood pouring around my spear."*
The comedies of <49> Menander, Philemon, and Diphilus, are lost; but
manners must have been little polished in their time, as far as can be conjectured from their translators or imitators, Plautus and Terence. Married
women in their comedies are sometimes introduced and treated with very
little respect. A man commonly vents his wrath on his wife, and scolds her
as the cause of the misconduct of their children. A lady, perhaps too in-
quisitive about her husband's amours, is addressed by him in the following
words.

> Ni mala, ni stulta sis, ni indomita imposque animi,
> Quod viro esse odio videas, tute tibi odia habeas.

---

* Pope disguises that sentiment as follows:

> Seize on Briseis, whom the Grecians doom'd
> My prize of war, yet tamely see resumed;
> And seize secure; no more Achilles draws
> His conqu'ring sword in any woman's cause.
> The gods command me to forgive the past;
> But let this first invasion be the last:
> For know, thy blood, when next thou dar'st invade,
> Shall stream in vengeance on my reeking blade.

Such contempt of the female sex as expressed by Achilles was perhaps thought too gross
for a modern ear. But did not Pope discover, that one capital beauty in Homer, is the
delineation of ancient manners? At that rate, had it fallen to his share to describe Julius
Caesar, he would have dressed him like a modern beau. And why not? for in a genteel
assembly, what a savage would he appear, without breeches, and without linen!

Praeter hac si mihi tale post hunc diem
Faxis, faxo foris vidua visas patrem.*

So little formerly were women regarded in England, that the benefit of clergy was not extended to them, till the days of William and Mary, when an act of parliament was made, bestowing that privilege on them. <50>

One will not be surprised that women in Greece were treated with no great respect by their husbands. A woman cannot have much attraction who passes all her time in solitude: to be admired, she must receive the polish of society. At the same time, men of fashion were so much improved in manners, as to relish society with agreeable women, where such could be found. And hence the figure that courtezans made at that period, especially in Athens. They studied the temper and taste of the men, and endeavoured to gain their affection, by every winning art. The daily conversations they listened to, on philosophy, politics, poetry, enlightened their understand-ing, and improved their taste. Their houses became agreeable schools, where every one might be instructed in his own art. Socrates and Pericles met frequently at the house of Aspasia: from her they acquired delicacy of taste, and, in return, procured to her public respect and reputation. Greece at that time was governed by orators, over whom some celebrated courte-zans had great influence; and by that means entered deep into the govern-ment. It was said of the famous Demosthenes, "The mea-<51>sure he hath meditated on for a year, will be overturned in a day by a woman." It appears accordingly from Plautus and Terence, that Athenian courtezans lived in great splendor. See in particular Heautontimoroumenos, Act 3. Scene 2.

I proceed to the other cause of polygamy, viz. opulence in a hot climate. Men there have a burning appetite for animal enjoyment; and women be-come old, and lose the prolific quality, at an age which carries them little beyond the prime of life in a temperate climate. These circumstances dis-

---

* Would you be held a wise and virtuous spouse,
   And of discretion due, observe this counsel:
   Whatever I, your lord, blame or approve,
   Still let your praise or censure be the same.
   But hearkee,—be this reprimand the last:
   If you again offend, no more a wife
   Within these walls;—your father has you back.

pose men of opulence to purchase their wives, that they may not be confined to one; and purchase they must; for no man, without a valuable consideration, will surrender his daughter, to be one of many who are destined
to gratify the carnal appetite of a single man. The numerous wives and
concubines in Asiatic harems, are all of them purchased with money. In
the hot climate of Hindostan polygamy is universal, and men buy their
wives. The same obtains in China: After the price is adjusted and paid, the
bride is conducted to the bridegroom's house, locked in a sedan, and the
<52> key delivered to him: If he be not satisfied with his bargain, he sends
her back, at the expence of losing the sum he paid for her: If satisfied, he
feasts his male friends in one room, and she her female friends in another.
A man who has little substance takes a wife for his son from an hospital,
which saves him a dowry.

It has been pleaded for polygamy in warm climates, that women are fit
for being married at or before the age of ten; that they are past child-bearing
at twenty-five, while men are yet in the prime of life; and therefore that a
second wife ought to be permitted who can bear children. Are women then
created for no other purpose but procreation merely, to be laid aside as
useless animals when they cease to bear children? In the hottest climates, a
woman may be the mother of ten or twelve children; and are not both
parents usefully employed, in rearing such a number, and fitting them to
do for themselves? After this important task is performed, is not the woman
well entitled, for the remainder of life, to enjoy the conjugal society of a
man, to whom she dedicated the flower of her youth? But, even <53> attending to the male sex only, without paying any regard to the other sex, it
ought to be considered, that a man, by taking a second wife, prevents some
other man from having any. The argument for polygamy would indeed be
conclusive, were ten females born for one male, as is erroneously said to be
the case in Bantam: But, as an equality of males and females is the invariable
rule of Nature, the argument has no force. All men are born equal by Nature; and to permit polygamy in any degree, is to authorise some to usurp
the privilege of others.

Thus, in hot climates, women remain in the same humble and depen-
dent state, in which all women were originally, when all men were savages.
As polygamy is a forced state, contradictory to nature, locks and bars are

the only sure means for restraining a number of women confined to one husband. When the King of Persia, with his wives, removes from Ispachan to any of his villas, the hour of his departure, and the street through which he is to pass, are proclaimed three days before, in order that every man may keep out of the way.[6] Women, by the law <54> of Hindostan, are not admitted to be witnesses, even in a civil cause; and I blush to acknowledge that, in Scotland, the same law has not been long in disuse.

In contradiction to the climate, Christianity has banished polygamy from Ethiopia, though the judges are far from being severe upon that crime. The heat of the climate makes them wish to indulge in a plurality of wives, even at the expense of purchasing each of them. Among the Christians of Congo polygamy is in use, as formerly when they were Pagans. To be confined to one wife during life, is held by the most zealous Christians there, to be altogether irrational: Rather than be so confined, they would renounce Christianity.

Beside polygamy, many other customs depend on the nature of the matrimonial engagement, and vary according to its different kinds. Marriage-ceremonies, for that reason, vary in different countries, and at different times. Where the practice is to purchase a wife, whether among savages or among pampered people in hot climates, payment of the price completes the marriage without any other ceremony. Other ceremonies, however, are sometimes <55> practised. In old Rome, the bride was attended to the bridegroom's house with a female slave carrying a distaff and a spindle, importing that she ought to spin for the family. Among the savages of Canada, and of the neighbouring countries, a strap, a kettle, and a faggot, are put in the bride's cabin, as symbols of her duty, viz. to carry burdens, to dress victuals, and to provide wood. On the other hand, the bride, in token of her slavery, takes her axe, cuts wood, bundles it up, and lays it before the door of the bridegroom's hut. All the salutation she receives is, "It is time to go to rest." The inhabitants of Sierra Leona, a negro country, have in all their towns a boarding-school, where young ladies are educated for a year, under the care of a venerable old gentleman. When their education is completed, they are carried in their best attire to a public assembly; which

6. "As polygamy is . . . of the way": added in 3rd edition.

may be termed a matrimonial market, because there young men convene to make a choice. Those who fit themselves to their fancy, pay the dowry; and, over and above, gratify the old superintendant for his extraordinary care in educating the bride. In the island of Java, the bride, in token of <56> subjection, washes the bridegroom's feet; and this is a capital ceremony. In Russia, the bride presents to the bridegroom a bundle of rods, to be used against her when she deserves to be chastised; and at the same time she pulls off his boots. The present Empress, intent upon reforming the rude manners of her subjects, has discountenanced that ceremony among people of fashion. Very different were the manners of Peru, before the Spanish conquest. The bridegroom carried shoes to the bride, and put them on with his own hands. But there, purchasing of wives was unknown. Marriage-ceremonies in Lapland are directed by the same principle. It is the custom there for a man to make presents to his children of rain-deer; and young women, such as have a large stock of these animals, have lovers in plenty. A young man looks for such a wife, at a fair, or at a meeting for paying taxes. He carries to the house of the young woman's parents, some of his relations; being solicitous in particular to have an eloquent speaker. They are all admitted except the lover, who must wait till he be called in. After drinking some spirits, brought along for <57> the purpose, the spokesman addresses the father in humble terms, bowing the knee, as if he were introduced to a prince. He styles him, the worshipful father, the high and mighty father, the best and most illustrious father, &c. &c.

In viewing the chain of causes and effects, instances sometimes occur of bizarre facts, starting from the chain without any cause that can be discovered. The marriage-ceremonies among the Hottentots are of that nature. After all matters are adjusted among the old people, the young couple are shut up by themselves; and pass the night in struggling for superiority, which proves a very serious work where the bride is reluctant. If she persevere to the last without yielding, the young man is discarded; but, if he prevail, which commonly happens, the marriage is completed by another ceremony, no less singular. The men and women squat on the ground in different circles, the bridegroom in the centre of one, and the bride in the centre of another. The Suri, or master of religious ceremonies, pisses on the bridegroom; who receives the stream with eagerness, and rubs it into

the furrows of the fat with which he is <58> covered. He performs the same
ceremony on the bride, who is equally respectful. The ceremonies of marriage among the present Greeks are no less bizarre. Among other particulars,
the bridegroom and bride walk three rounds; during which they are kicked
and cuffed heartily. Our author Tournefort adds, that he only and his companions forbore to join in the ceremony; which was ascribed to their rusticity and ignorance of polite manners.[7] Marriage-ceremonies among the
Kamskatkans are extremely whimsical. A young man, after making his pro-
posals, enters into the service of his intended father-in-law. If he prove
agreeable, he is admitted to the trial of the *touch*. The young woman is
swaddled up in leathern thongs; and in that condition is put under the
guard of some old women. Watching every opportunity of a slack guard,
he endeavours to uncase her, in order to touch what is always the most
concealed. The bride must resist, in appearance at least; and therefore cries
out for her guards; who fall with fury on the bridegroom, tear his hair,
scratch his face, and act in violent opposition. The attempts of the lover
prove <59> sometimes unsuccessful for months; but the moment the *touch*
is atchieved, the bride testifies her satisfaction, by pronouncing the words
Ni, Ni, with a soft and loving voice. The next night they bed together without any opposition. One marriage-ceremony among the inland negroes, is
singular. As soon as preliminaries are adjusted, the bridegroom, with a number of his companions, set out at night, and surround the house of the
bride, as if intending to carry her off by force. She and her female attendants, pretending to make all possible resistance, cry aloud for help, but no
person appears. This resembles strongly a marriage-ceremony that is or was
customary in Wales. On the morning of the wedding-day, the bridegroom,
accompanied with his friends on horseback, demands the bride. Her
friends, who are likewise on horseback, give a positive refusal, upon which
a mock scuffle ensues. The bride, mounted behind her nearest kinsman, is
carried off, and is pursued by the bridegroom and his friends, with loud
shouts. It is not uncommon on such an occasion to see two or three hundred
sturdy Cambro-Britons riding at full speed, cross-<60>ing and jostling, to
the no small amusement of the spectators. When they have fatigued them-

7. "The ceremonies of . . . of polite manners": added in 2nd edition.

selves and their horses, the bridegroom is suffered to overtake his bride. He leads her away in triumph, and the scene is concluded with feasting and festivity. The same marriage-ceremony was usual in Muscovy, Lithuania, and Livonia, as reported by Olaus Magnus (*a*).

Divorce also depends on the nature of the matrimonial engagement. Where the law is, that a man must purchase his wife as one does a slave, it follows naturally, that he may purchase as many as he can pay for, and that he may turn them off at his pleasure. This law is universal, without a single exception. The Jews, who purchased their wives, were privileged to divorce them, without being obliged to assign a cause (*b*). The negroes purchase their wives, and turn them off when they think proper. The same law obtains in China, in Monomotapa, in the isthmus of Darien, in Caribeana, and even in the cold country round Hudson's bay. All the savages of South America who live <61> near the Oroonoko, purchase as many wives as they can maintain; and divorce them without ceremony.

Very different is a matrimonial engagement between equals, where a dowry is contracted with the bride. The nature of the engagement implies, that neither of them should dismiss the other, without a just cause. In Mexico, where the bride brought a dowry, there could be no divorce but by mutual consent. In Lapland, the women who have a stock of rain-deer, as above mentioned, make a considerable figure. This lays a foundation for a matrimonial covenant as among us, which bars polygamy, and consequently divorce, without a just cause. And, when these are barred in several instances, the prohibition in time becomes general.

I proceed to adultery, the criminality of which depends also in some measure on the nature of the matrimonial engagement. Where wives are purchased, and polygamy is indulged, adultery can scarce be reckoned a crime in the husband; and, where there are a plurality of wives, sound sense makes it but a venial crime in any of them. But, as men are the lawgivers, the <62> punishment of female adultery, where polygamy takes place, is generally too severe. It is, however, more or less severe in different countries, in proportion as the men are more or less prone to revenge. The Chinese

(*a*) Lib. 14. cap. 9.
(*b*) Deuteronomy, chap. 24.

are a mild people, and depend more on locks and bars for preventing adultery, than on severity; the punishment being only to sell an adulteress for a slave. The same law obtains in the kingdom of Laos, bordering upon China. An adulteress among the ancient Egyptians was punished with the loss of her nose. In ancient Greece, a pecuniary penalty was inflicted on an adulterer (*a*). An adulteress was probably punished more severely. Among the negroes, who have very little delicacy, adultery is but slightly punished; except in the kingdom of Benin. There, an adulteress, after a severe whipping, is banished; and the adulterer forfeits his goods, which are bestowed on the injured husband. Among the ancient Germans, a grave and virtuous people, adultery was rare. An adulteress was deprived of her hair, expelled from her husband's house, and whipped through the <63> village (*b*). In Japan, where the people are remarkably fierce, female adultery is always punished with death. In Tonquin, a woman guilty of adultery is thrown to an elephant to be destroyed. By the law of Moses, an adulteress is punished with death, as also the adulterer (*c*). Margaret of Burgundy, Queen to Lewis Hutin King of France, was hanged for adultery; and her lovers were fleaed alive. Such were the savage manners of those times. There is an old law in Wales, that, for defiling the Prince's bed, the offender must pay a rod of pure gold, of the thickness of the finger of a ploughman who has ploughed nine years, and in length from the ground to the Prince's mouth when sitting.

Matrimony between a single pair, for mutual comfort, and for procreating children, implies the strictest mutual fidelity. Adultery, however, is a deeper crime in the wife than in the husband: in him it may happen occasionally, with little or no alienation of affection; but the superior modesty of the female sex is such, that a <64> wife does not yield, till unlawful love prevails, not only over modesty, but over duty to her husband. Adultery, therefore, in the wife, is a breach of the matrimonial engagement in a double respect: it is an alienation of affection from the husband, which unqualifies her to be his friend and companion; and it tends to bring a spurious

(*a*) Odyssey, b. 8. l. 384.
(*b*) Tacitus, De moribus Germanorum, Cap. 19.
(*c*) Leviticus, xx. 10.

issue into the family, betraying the husband to maintain and educate children who are not his own.

The gradual advance of the female sex to an equality with the male sex, is visible in the laws of female succession that have been established at different times, and in different countries. It is not probable that, in any country, women were early admitted to inherit land: they are too much despised among savages, for so valuable a privilege. The fierceness and brutality of the ancient Romans in particular unqualified the women to be their companions: it never entered their thoughts that women should inherit land, which they cannot defend by the sword. But women came to be regarded in proportion as the national manners refined. The law prohibiting female succession in land, esta-<65>blished in days of rusticity, was held to be rigorous and unjust when the Romans were more polished. Proprietors of land, such of them as had no sons, were disposed to evade the law, by ample provisions to their daughters, which rendered the land of little value to the collateral heir-male. To reform that abuse, as termed by those who adhered to ancient customs, the *lex Voconia* was made, confining such provisions within moderate bounds: and this regulation continued in force, till regard for the female sex broke through every legal restraint, and established female succession in land, as formerly in moveables.* The barbarous nations who crush-<66>ed the Roman power, were not late in adopting the mild manners of the conquered: they admitted women to inherit land, and they exacted a double composition for injuries done to them. By the Salic law among the Franks, women were expressly prohibited to inherit land: but we learn from the forms of Marculfus, that this prohibition was in time

---

* Justinian, or more properly the lawyers employed by him upon that absurd compilation the Pandects, is guilty of a gross error, in teaching that, by the Twelve Tables, males and females of the same degree succeeded equally to land. The *lex Voconia* (explained in *Alexandri ab Alexandro geniales dies, lib. 6. cap.* 15.) vouches the contrary. And one cannot see, without pain, Justinian's error, not only adopted by an illustrious modern, but a cause assigned for it so refined and subtile, as to go quite out of sight, [[Montesquieu]] *L'esprit des loix, liv.* 27. *chap.* 1. I venture to affirm, that subtile reasoning never had any influence upon a rough and illiterate people; and therefore, at the time of the Decemvirs, who composed the Twelve Tables of law, the subtile cause assigned by our author could not have been the motive, had the Decemvirs introduced female succession in land, which they certainly did not.

eluded by the following solemnity. The man who wanted to put his daughter upon a footing with his sons, carried her before the commissary, saying, "My dear child, an ancient and impious custom bars a young woman from succeeding to her father: but, as all my children are equally given me by God, I ought to love them equally; therefore, my dear child, my will is, that my effects shall divide equally between you and your brethren." In polished states, women are not excluded from succeeding even to the crown. Russia and Britain afford examples of wo-<67>men capable to govern, in an absolute as well as in a limited monarchy.*

What I have said regards those nations only where polygamy is prohibited. I take it for granted, that women are not admitted to inherit land where polygamy is lawful: they are not in such estimation as to be entitled to a privilege so illustrious. <68>

Among the Hurons in North America, where the regal dignity is hereditary, and great regard paid to the royal family, the succession is continued through females, in order to preserve the royal blood untainted. When the chief dies, his son succeeds not, but his sister's son; who certainly is of the royal blood, whoever be the father: and, when the royal family is at an end, a chief is elected by the noblest matron of the tribe. The same rule of succession obtains among the Natches, a people bordering on the Mississippi; it being an article in their creed, That their royal family are children of the sun. On the same belief was founded a law in Peru, appointing the heir of the crown to marry his sister; which, equally with the law men-

---

* The kingdom of Gurrah in Hindostan was governed by Queen Dargoutté, eminent for spirit and beauty. Small as that kingdom is, it contained about 70,000 towns and villages, the effect of long peace and prosperity. Being invaded by Asaph Can, not many years ago, the Queen, mounted on an elephant, led her troops to battle. Her son, Rajah Bier Shaw, being wounded in the heat of action, was by her orders carried from the field. That accident having occasioned a general panic, the Queen was left with but 300 horsemen. Adhar, who conducted her elephant, exhorted her to retire while it could be done with safety. The heroine rejected the advice. "It is true," said she, "we are overcome in battle; but not in honour. Shall I, for a lingering ignominious life, lose a reputation that has been my chief study! Let your gratitude repay now the obligations you owe me: pull out your dagger, and save me from slavery, by putting an end to my life." The kingdom of Agonna in Guinea was governed by a Queen when Bosman wrote.

tioned, preserved the blood of the sun in the royal family, and did not incroach so much upon the natural order of succession.

Female succession depends in some degree on the nature of the government. In Holland, all the children, male and female, succeed equally. The Hollanders live by commerce, which women are capable of as well as men. Land at the <69> same time is so scanty in that country, as to render it impracticable to raise a family by engrossing a great estate in land; and there is nothing but the ambition of raising a family, that can move a man to prefer one of his children before the rest. The same law obtains in Hamburgh, for the same reasons. Extensive estates in land support great families in Britain, a circumstance unfavourable to younger children. But probably in London, and in other great trading towns, mercantile men provide against the law, by making a more equal distribution of their effects among their children.

After transversing a great part of the globe with painful industry, would not one be apt to conclude, that originally females were every where despised, as they are at present among the savages of America; that wives, like slaves, were procured by barter; that polygamy was universal; and that divorce depended on the whim of the husband? But no sort of reasoning is more fallible, than the drawing general conclusions from particular facts. The northern nations of Europe, as appears from the foregoing sketch, must be excepted <70> from these conclusions. Among them, women were from the beginning courted and honoured, nor was polygamy ever known among them.[8]

We proceed now to a capital article in the progress of the female sex; which is, to trace the different degrees of restraint imposed upon married women in different countries, and at different times in the same country;

---

8. "But no sort . . . known among them": added in 2nd edition. In 1st edition: "Such a conclusion however would be rash; for upon a more accurate scrutiny, an extensive country is discovered, where polygamy never was in fashion, and where women were from the beginning courted and honoured as among the most polished nations. But the reader is humbly requested to suspend his curiosity, till he peruse the following sketch, concerning the progress of manners, which appears to be the proper place for that curious and interesting subject" [1:206]. In the 1st edition the order of the present sketch and the sketch concerning the progress of manners is reversed.

and to assign the causes of these differences. Where luxury is unknown, and where people have no wants but what are suggested by uncorrupted nature; men and women live together with great freedom, and with great innocence. In Greece anciently, even young women of rank ministered to men in bathing.

> While these officious tend the rites divine,
> The last fair branch of the Nestorian line,
> Sweet Polycasté, took the pleasant toil
> To bathe the Prince, and pour the fragrant oil (*a*).

Men and women among the Spartans bathed promiscuously, and wrestled together stark naked. Tacitus reports, that the Germans had not even separate beds, but lay promiscuously upon reeds or heath a-<71>long the walls of the house. The same custom prevails even at present among the temperate Highlanders of Scotland; and is not quite worn out in New England. A married woman is under no confinement, because no man thinks of an act so irregular as to attempt her chastity. In the Caribbee islands, adultery was unknown, till European Christians made settlements there. At the same time, there scarce can be any fewel for jealousy, where men purchase their wives, put them away at pleasure, and even lend them to a friend. But when, by ripening sensibility, a man feels pleasure in his wife's attachment to him, jealousy commences; jealousy of a rival in her affections. Jealousy accordingly is a symptom of increasing esteem for the female sex; and that passion is visibly creeping in among the natives of Virginia. It begins to have a real foundation, when inequality of rank and of riches takes place. Men of opulence study pleasure: married women become objects of a corrupted taste; and often fall a sacrifice, where morals are imperfect, and the climate an incentive to animal love. Greece is a delicious country, the people handsome; and when the <72> ancient Greeks made the greatest figure, they were miserably defective in morals. They became jealous of rivals; which prompted them, according to the rough manners of those times, to exclude women from society with men. Their women accordingly were never seen in public; and, if my memory serve me, an accidental interview of a man

(*a*) Odyssey, book 3. See also book 8. line 491.

and a woman on the public street brings on the catastrophe in a Greek tragedy. In Hecuba, a tragedy of Euripides, the Queen excuses herself for declining to visit Polymestor, saying, "that it is indecent for a woman to look a man in the face." In the Electra of Sophocles, Antigoné is permitted by her mother Jocasta to take a view of the Argian army from a high tower: an old man who accompanies her, being alarmed at seeing some females pass that way, and afraid of censure, prays Antigoné to retire; "for," says he, "women are prone to detraction; and to them the merest trifle is a fruitful subject of conversation."* Spain is a country that scarce <73> yields to Greece in fineness of climate; and the morals of its people in the dark ages of Christianity, were not more pure than those of Greece. By a law of the Visigoths in Spain, a surgeon was prohibited to take blood from a free woman, except in presence of her husband, or nearest relations. By the Salic law (a), he who squeezes the hand of a free woman shall pay a fine of fifteen golden shillings. In the fourteenth century, it was a rule in France, that no married woman ought to admit a man to visit her in absence of her husband. Female chastity must at that time have been extremely feeble, when so little trust was reposed in the fair sex.

To treat women in that manner, may possibly be necessary, where they are in request for no end but to gratify animal love. But, where they are intended for the more elevated purposes of being friends and companions, as well as affec-<74>tionate mothers, a very different treatment is proper. Locks and spies will never answer; for these tend to debase their minds, to corrupt their morals, and to render them contemptible. By gradual openings in the more delicate senses, particularly in all the branches of the moral sense, chastity, one of these branches, acquires a commanding influence over females; and becomes their ruling principle. In that refined state, women are trusted with their own conduct, and may safely be trusted: they make delicious companions, and uncorruptible friends; and that such at

---

* Women are not prone to detraction, unless when denied the comforts of Society. The censure of Sophocles is probably just with respect to his countrywomen, because they were locked up. Old maids have the character with us of being prone to detraction; but that holds not, unless they retire from society.

(a) Tit. 22.

present is generally their case in Britain, I am bold to affirm. Anne of Britanny, wife to Charles VIII. and to Lewis XII. Kings of France, introduced the fashion of ladies appearing publicly at court. This fashion was introduced much later in England: even down to the Revolution, women of rank never appeared in the streets without a mask. In Scotland, the veil, or plaid, continued long in fashion, with which every woman of rank was covered when she went abroad. That fashion has not been laid aside above forty years. In I-<75>taly, women were much longer confined than in France; and in Spain the indulging them with some liberty is but creeping into fashion. In Abyssinia, polygamy is prohibited; and married women of fashion have by custom obtained the privilege of visiting their friends, though not much with the good-will of many husbands.

It were to be wished, that a veil could be drawn over the following part of their history. The growth of luxury and sensuality, undermining every moral principle, renders both sexes equally dissolute: wives in that case deserve to be again locked up; but the time of such severity is past. In that case, indeed, it becomes indecent for the two sexes to bathe promiscuously. Men in Rome, copying the Greeks, plunged together in the same bath; and in time men and women did the same (*a*). Hadrian prohibited that indecent custom. Marcus Antoninus renewed the prohibition; and Alexander Severus, a second time: but to so little purpose, that even the primitive Christians <76> made no difficulty to follow the custom: such appetite there is for being *nudus cum nuda,* when justified by fashion. This custom withstood even the thunder of general councils; and was not dropt till people became more decent.

In days of innocence, when chastity is the ruling passion of the female sex, we find great frankness in external behaviour; for women above suspicion are little solicitous about appearances. At the same period, and for the same reason, we find great looseness in writing; witness the Queen of Navarre's tales. In the capital of France, at present, chastity, far from being practised, is scarce admitted to be a female virtue. But people who take much freedom in private, are extremely circumspect in public: no indecent expression nor insinuation is admitted, even into their plays or other writ-

(*a*) Plutarch, Life of Cato.

ings. In England, the women are less corrupted than in France; and for that reason are not so scrupulous with respect to decency in writing.

Hitherto of the female sex in temperate climes, where polygamy is prohibited. Very different is their condition in hot <77> climes, which inflame animal love in both sexes equally. In the hot regions of Asia, where polygamy is indulged, and wives are purchased for gratifying the carnal appetite merely, it is vain to think of restraining them otherwise than by locks and bars, after having once tasted enjoyment. Where polygamy is indulged, the body is the only object of jealousy, not the mind, as there can be no mutual affection between a man and his instruments of sensual pleasure. And, if women be so little virtuous as not to be safely trusted with their own conduct, they ought to be locked up; for there is no just medium between absolute confinement and absolute freedom. The Chinese are so jealous of their wives, as even to lock them up from their relations; and, so great is their diffidence of the female sex in general, that brothers and sisters are not permitted to converse together. When women go abroad, they are shut up in a close sedan, into which no eye can penetrate. The intrigues carried on by the wives of the Chinese Emperor, and the jealousy that reigns among them, render them unhappy. But luckily, as women are little regarded <78> where polygamy is indulged, their ambition and intrigues give less disturbance to the government, than in the courts of European princes. The ladies of Hindostan cover their heads with a gauze veil, even at home, which they lay not aside except in company of their nearest relations. A Hindoo buys his wife; and the first time he is permitted to see her without a veil is after marriage, in his own house. In several hot countries, women are put under the guard of eunuchs, as an additional security; and black eunuchs are commonly preferred for their ugliness. But, as a woman, deprived of the society of men, is apt to be inflamed even with the *appearance* of a man, some jealous nations, refining upon that circumstance, employ old maids, termed *duennas,* for guarding their women. In the city of Moka, in Arabia Felix, women of fashion never appear on the streets in day-light; but it is a proof of manners refined above those in neighbouring countries, that they are permitted to visit one another in the evening. If they find men in their way, they draw aside to let them pass. A French surgeon being called by one of the King of Ye-<79>man's chief officers, to cure a rheumatism

which had seized two of his wives, was permitted to handle the parts affected; but he could not get a sight of their faces.

I proceed to examine more minutely the manners of women, as resulting
from the degree of restraint they are under in different countries. In the
warm regions of Asia, where polygamy is indulged, the education of young
women is extremely loose, being intended solely for animal pleasure. They
are accomplished in such graces and allurements as tend to inflame the
sensual appetite: they are taught vocal and instrumental music, with various
dances that cannot stand the test of decency: but no culture is bestowed
on the mind, no moral instruction, no improvement of the rational faculties; because such education, which qualifies them for being virtuous
companions to men of sense, would inspire them with abhorrence at the
being made prostitutes. In a word, so corrupted are they by vicious education, as to be unfit objects of any desire but what is merely sensual. Asiatic
wives are not trusted even with the management of household affairs, which
would afford <80> opportunities for infidelity. In Persia, says Chardin, the
ladies are not permitted, more than children, to choose a gown for themselves: no lady knows in the morning what she is to wear that day. The
education of young women in Hindostan is less indecent. They are not
taught music nor dancing, which are reckoned fit only for ladies of pleasure:
they are taught all the graces of external behaviour, particularly to converse
with spirit and elegance: they are taught also to sew, to embroider, and to
dress with taste. Writing is neglected; but they are taught to read, that they
may have the consolation of studying the Alcoran; which they never open,
nor could understand if they did. Notwithstanding such care in educating
Hindostan females, their confinement in a seraglio renders their manners
extremely loose: the most refined luxury of sense, with idleness, or with
reading love-tales still worse than idleness, cannot fail to vitiate the minds
of persons deprived of liberty, and to prepare them for every sort of intemperance. The wives and concubines of grandees in Constantinople are
permitted sometimes to walk <81> abroad for air and exercise. A foreigner
stumbling accidentally on a knot of them, about forty in number, attended
with black eunuchs, was in the twinkling of an eye seized by a brisk girl,
with the rest at her heels: she accosted him with loose amorous expressions,
attempting at the same time to expose his nakedness. Neither threats nor

intreaties availed him against such vigorous assailants; nor could the vehemence of their curiosity be moderated, by representing the shame of a
behaviour so grossly immodest. An old Janizary, standing at a little distance,
was amazed: his Mahometan bashfulness would not suffer him to lay hands
upon women; but, with a Stentorian voice, he roared to the black eunuchs,
that they were guardians of prostitutes, not of modest women; urging them
to free the man from such harpies:—All in vain (*a*).

Very different are female manners in temperate climes, where polygamy
is prohibited, and women are treated as rational beings. These manners,
however, depend < 82 > in some measure on the nature of the government.
As many hands are at once employed in the different branches of republican
government, and a still greater number by rotation; the males, who have little
time to spare from public business, feel nothing of that languor and weariness
which to the idle make the most frivolous amusements welcome. Married
women live retired at home, managing family-affairs, as their husbands do
those of the state: whence it is, that simplicity of manners is more the tone
of a republic, than of any other government. Such were the manners of the
female sex during the flourishing periods of the Greek and Roman com-
monwealths; and such are their manners in Switzerland and in Holland.

There will be occasion afterward, to display an important revolution in
manners, resulting from chivalry (*b*). One branch of it must be handled
at present, that which concerns the intercourse between the sexes. The Cru-
sades were what first gave a turn to the fierce manners of our ancestors.
The combatants, fighting more for glory than for revenge or interest, be-
<83>came eminent for magnanimity and heroism. After so active a life
abroad, they could not bear idleness at home, especially when there was
such a demand for their prowess. Europe had never been worse governed
than at that period: dissension and discord were universal; and every chieftain bore deadly feud against his neighbours. Revenge was the ruling passion, which was licentiously indulged, without the least regard to justice.
The heroes who had signalized themselves abroad, endeavoured to acquire
fame at home: they entered into bonds of chivalry, for redressing wrongs,

(*a*) [[Sir James Porter,]] Observations on the religion, laws, &c. of the Turks.
(*b*) Book 2. Sketch 6.

and protecting widows and orphans. An object so noble and humane, tempered courage with mildness, and magnanimity with courtesy. The protection given to widows and orphans improved benevolence; and female beauty, which makes the deepest impression on the benevolent, came to be the capital object of protection. Each knight took under his peculiar care the beauty that inflamed him the most; and each knight was disposed to elevate the goddess of his heart above all rival beauties. In his heated imagination, she was perfection <84> without frailty, a paragon of nature. Emulation for the fame of a beloved object has no bounds, because there is nothing selfish in it: she is exalted into a sort of divinity: the lover descends to be a humble votary. And mark, that devotion to a visible deity always flames the highest. This connection, which reverses the order of nature, by elevating women far above men, produced an artificial sort of gallantry, that was carried to extravagance: the language of devotion became that of love, and all was bombast and unnatural. Chastity, however, was a gainer by this mode of love: it became necessarily the ruling principle, to be preserved in purity without spot or blemish; possession dissolves the charm; for, after surrendering all to a lover, a female cannot hope to maintain her angelic character a moment.[9] Duke John de Bourbonnois, anno 1414, caused it to be proclaimed, that he intended an expedition to England with sixteen knights, in order to combat the like number of English knights, for glorifying the beautiful angel he worshipped. Instances of this kind, without number, stand upon record. René, styled *King of* <85> *Sicily and Jerusalem,* observes, in writing upon tournaments, that they are highly useful in furnishing opportunities to young knights and esquires to display their

---

9. "There will be . . . character a moment": added in 2nd edition. In the 1st edition: "In a monarchy, government employs but few hands; and those who are not occupied with public business, give reins to gallantry, and to other desires that are easily gratified. Women of figure, on the other hand, corrupted by opulence and superficial education, are more ambitious to captivate the eye than the judgement; and are fonder of lovers than of friends. Where a man and a woman thus disciplined meet together, they soon grow particular: the man is idle, the woman frank; and both equally addicted to pleasure. Such commerce must in its infancy be disguised under the appearance of virtue and religion: the mistress is exalted into a deity, the lover sinks into a humble votary; and this artificial relation produces a bombast sort of love, with sentiments that soar high above nature" [1:213–14].

prowess before their mistresses. He adds, "that every ceremony regarding tournaments is contrived to honour the ladies. It belongs to them to inspect the arms of the combatants, and to distribute the rewards. A knight or esquire who defames any one of them, is beat and bruised till the injured lady condescend to intercede for him." Remove a female out of her proper sphere, and it is easy to convert her into a male. James IV. of Scotland, in all tournaments, professed himself knight to Anne Queen of France. She summoned him to prove himself her true and valorous champion, by taking the field in her defence against Henry VIII. of England. And, according to the romantic gallantry of that age, the Queen's summons was thought to have been James's chief motive for declaring war against his brother-in-law. The famous Gaston de Foix, general of the French at the battle of Ravenna, rode from rank to rank, calling by name several officers, and even private <86> men, recommending to them their country and their honour; adding, "that he would see what they would perform for love of their mistresses." During the civil wars in France, when love and gallantry were carried to a high pitch, Monsieur de Chatillon, ready to engage in a battle, tied round his arm a garter of Mademoiselle de Guerchi his mistress. De Liques and d'Etrees were both suitors to Mademoiselle de Fouquerolles for marriage. De Liques prevailed, and the marriage-day was fixed. But that very day, he was taken prisoner by his rival in a battle anno 1525. The lady wrote a letter to d'Etrees, demanding her husband; and d'Etrees instantly sent him to her without even demanding a ransom.*[10]

In peaceable times, the sovereign power having acquired more authority, the ne-<87>cessity of private protection ceased. But the accustomed spirit of gallantry did not cease. It could not, however, subsist forever against nature and common sense: it subsided by degrees into mutual affability and politeness, such as ought always to obtain between the sexes. But observe, that, after a most intimate connection, matters could not fall back to the

---

* We are indebted to Brantom for what follows. In the time of Francis I. of France, a young woman, having a talkative lover, ordered him to be dumb. His obedience for two long years made all the world believe that he was sunk in melancholy. One day, in a numerous assembly, the young woman, who was not known to be his mistress, undertook to cure him, and did it with a single word, *Speak*.

10. "De Liques prevailed . . . demanding a ransom": added in 2nd edition.

former decency and reserve. The intimate connection remained; and a more substantial gallantry took place, not always innocent. This change of manners was first visible in monarchy. Monarchy employs but a few hands; and those who are not occupied in public affairs, find leisure for gallantry and for desires that are easily gratified. Women of rank, on the other hand, laid open to corruption by opulence and superficial education, are more ambitious to captivate the eye than the judgment; and are fonder of lovers than of friends. Where a man and a woman thus prepared meet together, they soon grow particular: the man is idle, the woman frank; and both equally addicted to pleasure.[11] Unlawful commerce between the sexes becoming thus common, high gallantry vanishes of <88> course: the bombast style appears ridiculous, and the sensual appetite is gratified with very little ceremony. Nothing of love remains but the name; and, as animal enjoyment without love is a very low pleasure, it soon sinks into disgust when confined to one object. What is not found in one, is fondly expected in another; and the imagination, roving from object to object, finds no gratification but in variety. An attachment to a woman of virtue or of talents, appears absurd: true love is laughed out of countenance; and men degenerate into brutes. Women, on the other hand, regarding nothing but sensual enjoyment, become so careless of their infants, as even, without blushing, to employ mercenary nurses.* In Persia, <89> it is a common practice

* Les femmes d'un certain état en France trouvent qu'elles perdent trop à faire des enfans, et à cause de cela même, la plupart vivent celibataires, dans le sein même du marriage. Mais si l'envie de se voir perpetuer dans une branche de descendans, les porte à se conformer aux voeux de l'hymen; la population, dans cette classe, n'en est pas plus avancée, pars que leur delicatesse rend inutile leur propagation; car, parmi les femmes du premier et second rang en France, combien y en a-t-il qui nourissent leurs enfans? Il seroit facile de les compter. Ce devoir indispensable de mere, a cessé chez nous d'en être un. [[Goudar,]] *Les Interests de la France, vol.* 1. *p.* 234.—[*In English thus:* "The women of a certain rank in France find that they lose too much by child-bearing; and for that reason, even though married, live in a state of celibacy. But population is not advanced, even by those who, from a desire of seeing themselves perpetuated in their descendents, conform to the purpose of marriage; for their delicacy counterbalances their fertility. How few of the first and second rank of women in France suckle their children? It would be easy to count the number. This indispensable duty of a mother has now ceased to be one with us."]—As such woful neglect of education is the fruit of voluptuousness, we may take it for granted, that the same obtains in every opulent and luxurious capital.
    11. "In peaceable times . . . addicted to pleasure": added in 2nd edition.

among women of fashion to use drugs that cause abortion; because after
pregnancy is advanced, the husband attaches himself to other women, it
being held indecent to touch a woman who is pregnant.[12] Such a course of
life cannot fail to sink them into contempt: marriages are dissolved as soon
as contracted; and the state is frustrated of that improvement in morals and
manners, which is the never-failing product of virtuous love. A state enriched by conquest or <90> commerce, declines gradually into luxury and
sensual pleasure: manners are corrupted, decency banished, and chastity
becomes a mere name. What a scene of rank and dissolute pleasure is exhibited in the courts of Alexander's successors, and in those of the Roman
emperors!

Gratitude to my female readers, if I shall be honoured with any, prompts
me to conclude this sketch with a scene, that may afford them instruction,
and cannot fail of being agreeable; which is, the figure a woman is fitted
for making in the matrimonial state, where polygamy is excluded. Matrimony among savages, having no object but propagation and slavery, is a
very humbling state for the female sex: but delicate organization, great sensibility, lively imagination, with sweetness of temper above all, qualify
women for a more dignified society with men; which is, to be their companions and bosom-friends. In the common course of European education,
young women are trained to make an agreeable figure, and to behave with
decency and propriety: very little culture is bestowed on the head; and still
less on the heart, if it be not the <91> art of hiding passion. Such education
is far from seconding the purpose of nature, that of making women fit
companions for men of sense. Due cultivation of the female mind would
add greatly to the happiness of the males, and still more to that of the
females. Time runs on; and when youth and beauty vanish, a fine lady, who
never entertained a thought into which an admirer did not enter, surrenders
herself now to discontent and peevishness. A woman, on the contrary, who
has merit, improved by virtuous and refined education, retains in her decline an influence over the men, more flattering than even that of beauty:
she is the delight of her friends, as formerly of her admirers.

Admirable would be the effects of such refined education, contributing

12. "In Persia, it . . . who is pregnant": added in 2nd edition.

no less to public good than to private happiness. A man, who at present must degrade himself into a fop or a coxcomb in order to please the women, would soon discover, that their favour is not to be gained but by exerting every manly talent in public and in private life; and the two sexes, instead of corrupting each other, would be rivals in the race of virtue. Mutual esteem <92> would be to each a school of urbanity; and mutual desire of pleasing, would give smoothness to their behaviour, delicacy to their sentiments, and tenderness to their passions.

Married women in particular, destined by nature to take the lead in educating children, would no longer be the greatest obstruction to good education, by their ignorance, frivolity, and disorderly manners. Even upon the breast, infants are susceptible of impressions;* and the mother hath opportunities without end of instilling into them good principles, before they are fit for a male tutor. Coriolanus, who made a capital figure in the Roman <93> republic, never returned from war without meriting marks of distinction. Others behaved valiantly, in order to acquire glory: he behaved valiantly, in order to give pleasure to his mother. The delight she took in hearing him praised, and her weeping for joy in his embraces, made him in his own opinion the happiest person in the universe. Epaminondas accounted it his greatest felicity, that his father and mother were still alive to behold his conduct, and enjoy his victory at Leuctra. In a Latin dialogue about the causes that corrupted the Roman eloquence, injudiciously ascribed to Tacitus, because obviously it is not his style, the method of education in Rome, while it flourished as a commonwealth, is described in a lively manner. I shall endeavour to give the sense in English, because it chiefly concerns the fair sex. "In that age, children were suckled, not in the hut of a mercenary nurse, but by the chaste mother who bore them. Their

---

* May not a habit of chearfulness be produced in an infant, by being trained up among chearful people? An agreeable temper is held to be a prime qualification in a nurse. Such is the connection between the mind and body, as that the features of the face are commonly moulded into an expression of the internal disposition; and is it not natural to think, that an infant in the womb may be affected by the temper of its mother? Its tender parts make it susceptible of the slightest impressions. When a woman is breeding, she ought to be doubly careful of her temper; and in particular to indulge no ideas but what are chearful, and no sentiments but what are kindly.

education during nonage was in her hands; and it was her chief care to instil into them every virtuous principle. In her presence, a loose word or an improper <94> action, were strictly prohibited. She superintended, not only their serious studies, but even their amusements; which were conducted with decency and moderation. In that manner the Gracchi, educated by Cornelia their mother, and Augustus, by Attia his mother, appeared in public with untainted minds; fond of glory, and prepared to make a figure in the world." In the expedition of the illustrious Bertrand du Guesclin against Peter the Cruel, King of Castile, the governor of a town, summoned to give it up, made the following answer, "That they might be conquered, but would never tamely yield; that their fathers had taught them to prefer a glorious death before a dishonourable life; and that their mothers had not only educated them in these sentiments, but were ready to put in practice the lessons they had inculcated." During the civil wars in France between the Catholics and Protestants, Bari, governor of Leucate, having fallen by surprise into the hands of the Catholics, wrote from prison to his spouse Constance Cezelli not to surrender even though they should threaten to put <95> him to death. The besiegers brought him within her sight; and threatened to massacre him if she did not instantly open the gates. She offered for his ransom her children and all she had in the world—but that the town belonged to the King, and was not at her disposal. Would one think it possible, that any man ever did exist so brutal as to put her husband to death? Yet this was done in cold blood.[13] Let the most profound politician say, what more efficacious incentive there can be to virtue and manhood, than the behaviour of the Spartan matrons, flocking to the temples, and thanking the gods that their husbands and sons had died gloriously, fighting for their country. In the war between Lacedemon and Thebes, the Lacedemonians having behaved ill, the married men, as Plutarch reports, were so ashamed of themselves, that they durst not look their wives in the face. What a glorious prize is here exhibited, to be contended for by the female sex!

By such refined education, love would take on a new form, that which

---

13. "During the civil . . . in cold blood": added in 2nd edition.

nature inspires, for making us happy, and for softening the distresses of chance: it would <96> fill deliciously the whole soul with tender amity, and mutual confidence. The union of a worthy man with a frivolous woman, can never, with all the advantages of fortune, be made comfortable: how different the union of a virtuous pair, who have no aim but to make each other happy! Between such a pair emulation is reversed, by an ardent desire in each to be surpassed by the other.

Rousseau, in his treatise of Education, affirms, that convents are no better than schools of coquettery; and that among Protestants, women make better wives and more tender mothers than among Roman Catholics; for which, says he, no reason can be given but convent-education, which is universal among the latter. He then goes on in the following words: "Pour aimer la vie paisible et domestique il faut la connoître; il faut en avoir senti les douceurs des l'enfance. Ce n'est que dans la maison paternelle qu'on prend du goût pour sa propre maison, et toute femme que sa mere n'a point elevée n'aimera point elever ses enfans. Malheureusement il n'y a plus d'education privée dans les grandes <97> villes. La societé y est si generale et si melée qu'il ne reste plus d'asile pour la retraite, et qu'on est en public jusques chez soi. A force de vivre avec tout le monde en n'a plus de famille, à peine connoît-on ses parens; on les voit en etrangers, et la simplicité des moeurs domestiques s'eteint avec la douce familiarité qui en faisoit le charme. C'est ainsi qu'on suce avec le lait le gout des plaisirs du siècle et des maximes qu'on y voit regner." *Rousseau, Emile.* [14]

Cultivation of the female mind, is not of great importance in a republic, where men pass little of their time with women. Such cultivation, where

---

14. "The charms of a peaceful family life must be known to be enjoyed; their delights should be tasted in childhood. It is only in our father's home that we learn to love our own, and a woman whose mother did not educate her herself will not be willing to educate her own children. Unfortunately, there is no such thing as home education in our large towns. Society is so general and so mixed there is no place left for retirement, and even in the home we live in public. We live in company till we have no family, and scarcely know our own relations: we see them as strangers, and the simplicity of home life disappears together with the sweet familiarity which was its charm. In this wise do we draw with our mother's milk a taste for the pleasures of the age and the maxims by which it is controlled" (bk. V, p. 421). Paragraph added in 2nd edition.

polygamy is indulged, would to them be a deep misfortune, by opening their eyes to their miserable condition. But in an opulent monarchy, where polygamy is prohibited, female education is of high importance; not singly with respect to private happiness, but with respect to the society in general. <98>

APPENDIX

Concerning Propagation of Animals, and
Care of Progeny

The natural history of animals, with respect to pairing and care of progeny, is susceptible of more elucidation, than could regularly be introduced into the sketch itself, where it makes but a single argument. Loth to quit a subject that eminently displays the wisdom and benevolence of Providence, I embrace the present opportunity, however slight, to add what further occurs upon it. M. Buffon, in many large volumes, bestows scarce a thought on that favourite subject; and the neglect of our countrymen Ray and Derham is still less excusable, considering that to display the conduct of Providence was their sole purpose in writing natural history.

The instinct of pairing is bestowed on every species of animals to which it is necessary for rearing their young; and on no other species. All wild birds pair: but with a remarkable difference between <99> such as place their nests on trees, and such as place them on the ground. The young of the former, being hatched blind and without feathers, require the nursing care of both parents till they be able to fly. The male feeds his mate on the nest, and cheers her with a song. As soon as the young are hatched, singing yields to a more necessary occupation, that of providing food for a numerous issue, a task that requires both parents.

Eagles and other birds of prey build on trees, or on other places difficult of access. They not only pair, but continue in pairs all the year; and the same pair procreate together, year after year. This at least is the case of eagles: the male and female hunt together; and during incubation the female is fed by the male. A greater number than a single pair never are seen in company.

Gregarious birds pair, in order probably to prevent discord, in a society confined to a narrow space. This is the case particularly of pigeons and rooks. The male and female sit on the eggs alternately, and divide the care

306

of feeding their young. During incubation, the male raven <100> is always at hand to defend the female against birds of prey. No sooner does a kite appear than he gets above it, and strikes it down with his bill.

Partridges, plovers, pheasants, seafowl, grouse, and other kinds that place their nests on the ground, have the instinct of pairing; but differ from such as build on trees in the following particular, that after the female is impregnated, she completes her task without needing any help from the male. Retiring from him, she chuses a safe place for her nest, where she can find plenty of worms and grass-seed at hand. And her young, as soon as hatched, take foot and seek food for themselves. The only remaining duty incumbent on the dam is, to lead them to proper places for food, and to call them together when danger impends. Some males, provoked at the desertion of their mates, break the eggs if they happen to find them. If a Turkey hen die during hatching, the cock takes her place in the nest; and after the young are hatched, he tends them as a hen does. Not only so, but when the female is engaged with a new brood, the cock takes care of the for-<101>mer brood, leads them about for food, and acts in every respect as the female did before.[15] Eider ducks pair like other birds that place their nests on the ground; and the female finishes her nest with down plucked from her own breast. If the nest be destroyed for the down, which is re-markably warm and elastic, she makes another nest as before. If she be robbed a second time, she makes a third nest; but the male furnishes the down. A lady of spirit observed, that the Eider duck may give a lesson to many a married woman, who is more disposed to pluck her husband than herself. The black game never pair: in spring the cock on an eminence crows, and claps his wings; and all the females within hearing instantly resort to him.*

Pairing birds, excepting those of prey, flock together in February, in or-der to chuse their mates. They soon disperse; and are not seen afterwards but in pairs.

Pairing is unknown to quadrupeds that feed on grass. To such it would

* A hen that had hatched several broods of ducklings, carried her own chickens to the water, thrust them in by force, and rested not till they were all drowned. Such is the force of custom, even against nature. [[Note added in 2nd edition.]]

15. "If a Turkey . . . female did before": added in 2nd edition.

be use-<102>less; as the female gives suck to her young while she herself is feeding. If M. Buffon deserve credit, the roe-deer are an exception. They pair, though they feed on grass, and have but one litter in a year.

Beasts of prey, such as lions, tigers, wolves, pair not. The female is left to shift for herself and for her young; which is a laborious task, and frequently so unsuccessful as to shorten life. Pairing is essential to birds of prey, because incubation leaves the female no sufficient time to search for food. Pairing is not necessary to beasts of prey, because their young can bear a long fast. Add another reason, that they would multiply so fast by pairing, as to prove troublesome neighbours to the human race.

Among animals that pair not, males fight desperately about a female. Such a battle among horned cattle is finely described by Lucretius. Nor is it unusual, that seven or eight lions wage bloody war for a single female.

The same reason that makes pairing necessary for gregarious birds, obtains with respect to gregarious quadrupeds; those especially who store up food for winter, <103> and during that season live in common. Discord among such, would be attended with worse consequences than even among lions or bulls, who are not confined to one place. The beavers, with respect to pairing, resemble birds that place their nests on the ground. As soon as the young are produced, the males abandon their stock of food to their mates, and live at large; but return frequently to visit them, while they are suckling their young.

Hedge-hogs pair, and several of the monkey kind. We are not well acquainted with the natural history of these animals; but it may be presumed that the young require the nursing care of both parents.

Seals have a singular oeconomy. Polygamy seems to be a law of nature among them, as a male associates with several females. The sea-turtle has no occasion to pair, as the female concludes her task with laying her eggs in the sand. The young are hatched by the sun; and immediately crawl to the sea.

In every other branch of animal oeconomy concerning the continuance of the species, the hand of Providence is equally <104> conspicuous. The young of pairing birds are produced in the spring, when the weather begins to be comfortable; and their early production makes them firm and vigorous before winter, to endure the hardships of that rigorous season. Such early production is in particular favourable to eagles, and other birds of prey; for in the spring they have plenty of food, by the return of birds of passage.

Though the time of gestation varies considerably in the different quadrupeds that feed on grass, yet the female is regularly delivered early in summer, when grass is in plenty. The mare admits the stallion in summer, carries eleven months, and is delivered the beginning of May. The cow differs little. A sheep and a goat take the male in November, carry five months, and produce when grass begins to spring. These animals love short grass, upon which a mare or a cow would starve. The observation holds in climates so temperate as to encourage grass in the spring, and to preserve it in verdure all the summer. I am informed that in Italy, sheep copulate from June to July: the female goes twenty weeks, and is delivered in November <105> or December, precisely at the time when grass there is in the greatest plenty. In April the grass is burnt up; and sheep have nothing but shrubs to browse on. This appears to me a signal instance of providential care.*[16] The rutting-season of the red deer is the end of September, and beginning of October: it continues for three weeks; during which time, the male runs from female to female without intermission. The female brings forth in May, or beginning of June; and the female of the fallow-deer brings forth at the same time. The she-ass takes the male the beginning of summer; but she bears twelve months, which fixes her delivery to summer. Wolves and foxes copulate in December: the female carries five months, and brings forth in April, when animal food is as plentiful as at any other season; and the she-lion brings forth about the same time. Of this early birth there is <106> one evident advantage, hinted above: the young have time to grow so firm as easily to bear the inclemencies of winter.

Were one to guess what probably would be the time of rutting, summer would be named, especially in a cold climate. And yet to quadrupeds who

---

* I have it upon good authority, that ewes pasturing in a hilly country choose early some snug spot, where they may drop their young with safety. And hence the risk of removing a flock to a new field immediately before delivery: many lambs perish by being dropped in improper places.

16. "The observation holds . . . of providential care" (but not the appended note): added in 2nd edition.

carry but four or five months, that oeconomy would throw the time of delivery to an improper season, for warmth, as well as for food. Wisely is it ordered, that the delivery should constantly be at the best season for both.

Gregarious quadrupeds that store up food for winter, differ from all other quadrupeds with respect to the time of delivery. Beavers copulate about the end of autumn, and bring forth in January, when their granary is full. The same oeconomy probably obtains among all other quadrupeds of the same kind.

One rule takes place among all brute-animals, without a single exception, That the female never is burdened with two litters at the same time. The time of gestation is so unerringly calculated by nature, that the young brood can provide for themselves before another brood comes on. Even a hare is not an exception, tho' many <107> litters are produced in a year. The female carries thirty or thirty-one days; but she suckles her young only twenty days, after which they provide for themselves, and leave her free to a new litter.

The care of animals to preserve their young from harm is a beautiful instance of Providence. When a hind hears the hounds, she puts herself in the way of being hunted, and leads them from her fawn. The lapwing is no less ingenious: if a person approach, she flies about, retiring always from her nest. A partridge is extremely artful: she hops away, hanging a wing as if broken: lingers till the person approach, and hops again.* A hen, timid by nature, is bold as a lion in defence of her young: she darts upon every creature that threatens danger. The roebuck defends its young with resolution <108> and courage. So doth a ram; and so do many other quadrupeds.

Let me add a few words about the nature of instinct in animals. Instinct is an impulse of nature to perform necessary acts where reason is deficient. The actions of brute animals are generally directed by instinct; but, as in man, the rational principle is more vigorous, he is trusted to the conduct

---

* The following incident hardly deserves to be mentioned, it is so common, but that the tear is scarce dry which the sight wrung from me. A man mowing a field for hay, passed over a partridge sitting on her eggs. Turning about to cut down a tuft that had been left, he unhappily brought up the partridge on the point of his scythe. Such affection there is even for a brood not yet brought to light. [[Note added in 2nd edition.]]

of that principle, and is not left to be directed by instinct, except in singular cases where reason cannot be of use. The instincts of animals are finely adjusted to the other branches of their constitution. An ox, which chews the cud, swallows greedily, and grinds after at leisure. A horse, which does not chew the cud, grinds carefully in eating. Monsieur Buffon admits, that, by instinct, birds of passage change their habitation; and yet, so crude are his notions of instinct, as to assign causes for the change, which require both reflection and foresight far above the glimmering reason they are endued with. Quails, says he, during summer, are always travelling north, because they are afraid of heat; or, perhaps, to leave a country where the harvest is over, for ano-<109>ther where it is later. This would be a degree of knowledge denied even to man, unless from experience. Aristotle, with as little accuracy, maintains, that it is from a thorough knowledge of the seasons that birds of passage change their habitation twice a year. It is, I admit, the final cause of their migration; but undoubtedly blind instinct is the efficient cause. The magpy, he observes, covers its nest, leaving only a hole in the side to get in and out at; well knowing that many birds of prey are fond of its eggs. Yet the same Buffon observing, that, when a sparrow builds under a roof, it gives no cover to its nest, covering it only when it builds on a tree; and that a beaver, which erects a strong dam-dike to keep a running water always at the same height, never thinks of such an operation when it settles on the brink of a lake which varies little in height; maintains these variations to be the perfection of instinct. Is it not apparent that reason is necessary to make a being to vary its conduct according to circumstances; and that what is observed of the sparrow and beaver is evidence of no slight degree of reflection? Instinct, on the contrary, is <110> a blind impulse of nature, which prompts always the same uniform course, without regard to variation of circumstances.[17]

It is observed by an ingenious writer (*a*), that nature sports in the colour of domestic animals, in order that men may the more readily distinguish their own. It is not easy to say why colour is more varied in such animals, than in those which remain in the state of nature: I can only say, that the

(*a*) Pennant.
17. Paragraph added in 3rd edition.

cause assigned is not satisfactory. One is seldom at a loss to distinguish one animal from another; and Providence never interposes to vary the ordinary course of nature, for an end so little necessary as to make the distinction still more obvious. I add, that it does not appear, in any instance, the intention of Providence, to encourage inattention and indolence.

The foregoing particulars are offered to the public as hints merely: may it not be hoped, that they will excite curiosity in those who relish natural history? The field is rich, though little cultivated; and I know no other branch of natural history that opens finer views into the conduct of Providence. <111>

Progress and Effects of Luxury

The wisdom of Providence is in no instance more conspicuous than in adjusting the constitution of man to his external circumstances. Food is extremely precarious in the hunter-state; sometimes superabounding with little fatigue, sometimes failing after great fatigue. A savage, like other animals of prey, has a stomach adjusted to that variety: he can bear a long fast; and gorges voraciously when he has plenty, without being the worse for it. Whence it is, that barbarians, who have scarce any sense of decency, are great and gross feeders.* The <112> Kamskatkans love fat; and a man entertains his guests by cramming into their mouths fat slices of a seal, or a whale, cutting off with his knife what hangs out.[1] Barbarians are equally addicted to drunkenness; and peculiarly fond of spiritous liquors. Drinking was a fashionable vice in Greece, when Menander, Philemon, and Diphilus, wrote, if we can rely on the translations or imitations of their plays by Plautus and Terence. Cyrus preparing to attack his brother Artaxerxes, King of Persia, published a manifesto, that he was more worthy of the throne than his brother, because he could swallow more wine.[2] Diodorus Siculus reports, that, in his time, the Gauls, like other Barbarians, were much addicted to drinking. The ancient Scandinavians, who, like other savages,

---

* In the Iliad of Homer, book 9. Agamemnon calls a council at night in his tent. Before entering on business, they go to supper, (line 122). An embassy to Achilles is resolved on. The ambassadors again sup with Achilles on pork griskins, (line 271). Achilles rejects Agamemnon's offer; and the same night Ulysses and Diomed set out on their expedition to the Trojan camp: returning before day, they had a third supper.

1. "The Kamskatkans love . . . what hangs out": added in 2nd edition.
2. "Cyrus preparing to . . . swallow more wine": added in 2nd edition.

were intemperate in eating and drinking, swallowed large cups to their gods, and to such of their countrymen as had fallen bravely in battle. We learn from the 25th fable of the Edda, which was their sacred book, that to hold much liquor was reputed a heroic virtue. Contarini the Venetian ambassador, who wrote anno 1473, says, that the Russians were abandoned to <113> drunkenness; and that the whole race would have been extirpated, had not strong liquors been discharged by the sovereign.

A habit of fasting long, acquired as above in the hunter-state, made meals in the shepherd state less frequent than at present, though food was at hand. Anciently people fed but once a-day, a fashion that continued even after luxury was indulged in other respects. In the war of Xerxes against Greece, it was pleasantly said of the Abderites, who were burdened with providing for the King's table, that they ought to thank the gods for not inclining Xerxes to eat twice a-day. Plato held the Sicilians to be gluttons, for having two meals every day. Arrian (*a*) observes, that the Tyrrhenians had the same bad habit. In the reign of Henry VI. the people of England fed but twice a-day. Hector Boyes, in his history of Scotland, exclaiming against the growing luxury of his contemporaries, says, that some persons were so gluttonous, as to have three meals every day.

Luxury, undoubtedly, and love of so-<114>ciety, tended to increase the number of meals beyond what nature requires. On the other hand, there is a cause that kept down the number for some time, which is, the introduction of machines. Bodily strength is essential to a savage, being his only instrument; and with it he performs wonders. Machines have rendered bodily strength of little importance; and, as men labour less than originally, they eat less in proportion.* Listen to Hollinshed, the English historian, upon that article: "Heretofore, there hath been much more time spent in eating and drinking, than commonly is in these days; for whereas, of old, we had breakfasts in the forenoon, beverages or nuntions after dinner, and thereto rear suppers when it was time to go to rest; now these odd repasts, thanked be God, are very well left, and each one contenteth himself with

---

* Before fire-arms were known, people gloried in address and bodily strength, and commonly fought hand to hand. But violent exercises, becoming less and less necessary, went insensibly out of fashion.

(*a*) Lib. 4. cap. 16.

dinner and supper only." Thus, before cookery and luxury crept in, a mo-<115>derate stomach, occasioned by the abridging bodily labour, made eating less frequent than formerly. But the motion did not long continue retrograde: good cookery, and the pleasure of eating in company, turned the tide; and people now eat less at a time, but more frequently.

Feasts in former times were carried beyond all bounds. William of Malmsbury, who wrote in the days of Henry II. says, "That the English were universally addicted to Drunkenness, continuing over their cups day and night, keeping open house, and spending the income of their estates in riotous feasts, where eating and drinking were carried to excess, without any elegance." People who live in a corner imagine that every thing is peculiar to themselves: what Malmsbury says of the English is common to all nations, in advancing from the selfishness of savages to a relish for society, but who have not yet learned to bridle their appetites. Giraldus Cambrensis, speaking of the Monks of Saint Swithin, says, that they threw themselves prostrate at the feet of King Henry II. and with many tears complained, that the Bishop, who <116> was their abbot, had withdrawn from them three of their usual number of dishes. Henry, having made them acknowledge that there still remained ten dishes, said, that he himself was contented with three, and recommended to the Bishop to reduce them to that number.[3] Leland (*a*) mentions a feast given by the Archbishop of York, at his installation, in the reign of Edward IV. The following is a specimen: 300 quarters of wheat, 300 tons of ale, 100 tons of wine, 1000 sheep, 104 oxen, 304 calves, 304 swine, 2000 geese, 1000 capons, 2000 pigs, 400 swans, 104 peacocks, 1500 hot venison pasties, 4000 cold, 5000 custards, hot and cold. Such entertainments are a picture of manners. At that early period, there was not discovered in society any pleasure but that of crowding together in hunting and feasting. The delicate pleasures of conversation, in communicating opinions, sentiments, and desires, were to them unknown. There appeared, however, even at that early period, a faint dawn of the fine arts. In such feasts as are mentioned above, a curious desert was sometimes exhibited, term-<117>ed *sutteltie,* viz. paste moulded into the shape of ani-

---

(*a*) Collectanea.

3. "Giraldus Cambrensis, speaking . . . to that number": added in 2nd edition.

mals. On a saint's day, angels, prophets, and patriarchs, were set upon the table in plenty. A feast given by Trivultius to Lewis XII. of France, in the city of Milan, makes a figure in Italian history. No fewer than 1200 ladies were invited; and the Cardinals of Narbon and St. Severin, with many other prelates, were among the dancers. After dancing, followed the feast, to regulate which there were no fewer employed than 160 master-households. Twelve hundred officers, in an uniform of velvet, or satin, carried the victuals, and served at the side-board. Every table, without distinction, was served with silver-plate, engraved with the arms of the landlord; and beside a prodigious number of Italian lords, the whole court, and all the household of the King, were feasted. The bill of fare of an entertainment given by Sir Watkin Williams Wynn to a company of 1500 persons, on his coming of age, is a sample of ancient English hospitality, which appears to have nothing in view but crowding and cramming merely. The following passage is from Hollinshed: "That <118> the length and sumptuousness of feasts formerly in use, are not totally left off in England, notwithstanding that it proveth very beneficial to the physicians, who most abound where most excess and misgovernment of our bodies do appear." He adds, that claret, and other French wines, were despised, and strong wines only in request. The best, he says, were to be found in monasteries: for "that the merchant would have thought his soul would go straightway to the devil, if he should serve monks with other than the best." Our forefathers relished strong wine, for the same reason that their forefathers relished brandy. In Scotland, sumptuous entertainments were common at marriages, baptisms, and burials. In the reign of Charles II. a statute was thought necessary to confine them within moderate bounds.

Of old, there was much eating, with little variety: at present, there is great variety, with more moderation. From a household-book of the Earl of Northumberland, in the reign of Henry VIII. it appears that his family, during winter, fed mostly on salt meat, and salt fish; and <119> with that view there was an appointment of 160 gallons of mustard. On flesh-days, through the year, breakfast for my Lord and Lady was a loaf of bread, two manchets, a quart of beer, a quart of wine, half a chine of mutton, or a chine of beef boiled, on meagre days, a loaf of bread, two manchets, a quart of beer, a quart of wine, a dish of butter, a piece of salt fish, or a dish of buttered eggs. During lent, a loaf of bread, two manchets, a quart of beer, a quart of wine, two pieces of salt fish, six baconed herring, four white herring, or a dish of sproits. There was as little variety in the other meals, except on festival days. That way of living was at the time high luxury: a lady's waiting-woman, at present, would never have done with grumbling at such a table. We learn from the same book, that the Earl had but two cooks for dressing victuals to more than two hundred domestics. In those days, hen, chicken, capon, pigeon, plover, partridge, were reckoned such delicacies, as to be prohibited, except at my Lord's table (a).

But luxury is always creeping on, and <120> delicacies become more familiar. Hollinshed observes, that white meats, milk, butter, and cheese, formerly the chief food of his countrymen, were in his time degraded to be the food of the lower sort; and that the wealthy fed upon flesh and fish. By a roll of the King of Scotland's household expence, anno 1378, we find, that the art of gelding cattle was known. The roll is in Latin, and the gelt hogs are termed *porcelli eunuchi.* Mention is also made of chickens, which were not common on English tables at that time. Olive oil is also mentioned.

In this progress, cooks, we may believe, came to make a figure. Hollinshed observes, that the nobility, rejecting their own cookery, employed as cooks musical-headed Frenchmen and strangers, as he terms them. He says, that even merchants, when they gave a feast, rejected butcher's meat as unworthy of their tables; having jellies of all colours, and in all figures, representing flowers, trees, beasts, fish, fowl, and fruit. Henry Wardlaw, Archbishop of St. Andrews, observing the refinements in cookery introduced by James First of Scotland, who had <121> been eighteen years a prisoner in England, exclaimed against the abuse in a parliament held at Perth 1433: he obtained a law, restraining superfluous diet; and prohibiting the use of baked meat to any under the degree of gentlemen, and permitting it to gentlemen on festival-days only; which baked meat, says the bishop, was never before seen in Scotland. The peasants in Sicily regale themselves with ice during summer. They say, that scarcity of snow would be more grievous to them than scarcity of corn or of wine. Such progress has luxury made,

(a) Household book above mentioned.

even among the populace. People of fashion in London and in Paris, who employ their whole thoughts on luxurious living, would be surprised to be told, that they are still deficient in that art. In order to advance luxury of the table to the *acme* of perfection, there ought to be a cook for every dish, as in ancient Egypt there was a physician for every disease.

Barbarous nations, being great eaters, are fond of large joints of meats; and love of show retains great joints in fashion, even after meals become more moderate: a wild boar was roasted whole for a sup-<122>per-dish to Anthony and Cleopatra; and stuffed with poultry and wild-foul, it was a favourite dish at Rome, termed the *Trojan boar*, in allusion to the Trojan horse. The hospitality of the Anglo-Saxons was sometimes exerted in roasting an ox whole. Great joints are left off gradually, as people become more and more delicate in eating. In France, great joints are less in use than formerly; and in England, the enormous surloin, formerly the pride of the nation, is now in polite families banished to the side-board. In China, where manners are carried to a high degree of refinement, dishes are composed entirely of minced meat.*

In early times, people were no less plain <123> in their houses than in their food. Toward the end of the sixteenth century, when Hollinshed wrote, the people of England were beginning to build with brick and stone. Formerly houses were made of timber posts, wattled together and plastered with clay to keep out the cold: the roof was straw, sedge, or reed. It was an observation of a Spaniard in Queen Mary's days, "These English have their houses of sticks and dirt, but they fare as well as the King." Hollinshed mentioning multitudes of chimneys lately erected, observes, upon the authority of some old men, that in their younger days there were not above two or three, if so many, in most uplandish towns of the realm, religious houses and manor places of their lords excepted; but that each made his

* The size of an animal may be abridged by spare diet; but its strength and vigour are not abridged in proportion. Our highlanders live very poorly; and yet are a hardy race. The horses bred in that mountainous country are of a diminutive size; but no other horses can bear so much fatigue. Camels in the desarts of Arabia are trained to long abstinence. They are loaded more and more as they grow up; and their food is diminished in proportion. Plenty of succulent food raises an animal to its greatest size; but its solids are soft and flexible in proportion to its size. [[Note added in 2nd edition.]]

fire against a rere-dosse in the hall, where he dined, and dressed his meat. From Lord Northumberland's household-book, it would seem, that grates were unknown at that time, and that they burnt their coal upon the hearth: a certain sum is allotted for purchasing wood; because, says the book, coals will not burn without it. There is also a certain sum <124> allotted for purchasing charcoal, that the smoke of the sea-coal might not hurt the arras. In the fourteenth century, the houses of private persons in Paris, as well as in London, were of wood. Morrison, who wrote in the beginning of the last century, says, that at London the houses of the citizens were very narrow in the street-front, five or six stories high, commonly of wood and clay with plaster.[4] The streets of Paris, not being paved, were covered with mud; and yet for a woman to travel these streets in a cart, was held an article of luxury, and as such prohibited by Philip the Fair. Paris is enlarged two thirds since the death of Henry IV. though at that time it was perhaps no less populous than at present.

People were equally plain in their household-furniture. While money was scarce, servants got land instead of wages. An old tenure in England, binds the vassal to find straw for the King's bed, and hay for his horse. From Lord Northumberland's household-book, mentioned above, it appears, that the linen allowed for a whole year amounted to no more but seventy ells; of which there were to be eight table-<125>cloths (no napkins) for his Lordship's table, and two towels for washing his face and hands. Pewter vessels were prohibited to be hired, except on Christmas, Easter, St. George's day, and Whitsunday. Hollinshed mentions his conversing with old men who remarked many alterations in England within their remembrance; that their fathers, and they themselves formerly, had nothing to sleep on but a straw pallat, with a log of wood for a pillow; a pillow, said they, being thought meet only for a woman in childbed; and that if a man in seven years after marriage could purchase a flock-bed, and a sack of chaff to rest his head upon, he thought himself as well lodged as the lord of the town; who peradventure lay seldom on a bed entirely of feathers. Another thing they remarked, was change of household-vessels from timber plates into pewter, and from wooden spoons into tin or silver.

4. "Morrison, who wrote . . . clay with plaster": added in 2nd edition.

Nor were they less plain in their dress. By an act of parliament in Scotland, *anno* 1429, none were permitted to wear silk or costly furs, but knights and lords of 200 merks yearly rent. But luxury in dress advanced so fast, that by another <126> act, *anno* 1457, the same dress was permitted to aldermen, bailies, and other good worthy men within burgh. And by a third act, *anno* 1471, it was permitted to gentlemen of L. 100 yearly rent. By a sumptuary law in Scotland, *anno* 1621, cloth of gold and silver, gold and silver lace, velvet, satin, and other silk stuffs, were prohibited except to noblemen, their wives and children, to lords of parliament, prelates, privy counsellors, lords of manors, judges, magistrates of towns, and to those who have 6000 merks of yearly rent. Such distinctions, with respect to land especially, are invidious; nor can they ever be kept up. James, the first British monarch, was, during infancy, committed to the care of the Dowager-Countess of Mar, who had been educated in France. The King being seized with a cholic in the night-time, his household servants flew to his bedchamber, men and women, naked as they were born; the Countess only had a smock.

During the reign of Edward III. the imports into England were not the seventh part of the exports. Our exports at that time were not the seventh part of our pre-<127>sent exports; and yet our luxury is such, that with all our political regulations, it is with difficulty that the balance of trade is preserved in our favour.

Men in different ages differ widely in their notions of luxury: every new object of sensual gratification, and every indulgence beyond what is usual, are commonly termed *luxury;* and cease to be luxury when they turn habitual. Thus, every historian, ancient and modern, while he inveighs against the luxury of his own times, wonders at former historians for characterising as luxury what he considers as conveniencies merely, or rational improvements. Here the Roman historian, talking of the war that his countrymen carried on successfully against Antiochus King of Syria: "Luxuriae enim peregrinae origo ab exercitu Asiatico invecta urbem est. Ii primum lectos aeratos, vestem stragulam pretiosam, plagulas et alia textilia, et quae tum magnificae supellectilis habebantur, monopodia et abacos Romam advexerunt. Tunc psaltriae, sambusistriaeque, et convivalia ludionum oblectamenta addita epulis: epulae quoque ipsae et cura et sumptu majore ad-

<128>parari coeptae: tum coquus, vilissimum antiquis mancipium aestimatione et usu, in pretio esse; et, quod ministerium fuerat, ars haberi coepta. Vix tamen illa, quae tum conspiciebantur, semina erant futurae luxuriae" (*a*).* Household-furniture at Rome must at that period have been wonderfully plain, when a carpet and a one-footed table were reckoned articles of luxury. When the gelding of bulls and rams was first practised, it was probably considered as abominable luxury. Galvanus Fiamma, who in the fourteenth century wrote a history of Milan, his na-<129>tive country, complains, that in his time plain living had given way to luxury and extravagance. He regrets the times of Frederic Barbarossa and Frederic II. when the inhabitants of Milan, a great capital, had but three flesh meals in a week, when wine was a rarity, when the better sort made use of dried wood for candles, and when their shirts were of serge, linen being confined to persons of the highest rank. "Matters," says he, "are wonderfully changed: linen is a common wear: the women dress in silk, ornamented frequently with gold and silver; and they wear gold pendants at their ears." A historian of the present times would laugh at Fiamma, for stating as articles of luxury what are no more but decent for a tradesman and his wife. John Musso, a native of Lombardy, who also wrote in the fourteenth century, declaims against the luxury of his contemporaries, particularly against that of the citizens of Placentia, his countrymen. "Luxury of the table," says he, "of dress, of houses and household furniture, in Placentia, began to creep in after the year 1300. Houses have at present halls, rooms with chim-<130>neys, portico's, wells, gardens, and many other conveniencies, unknown to our ancestors. A house that has now many chimneys, had none in the last age. The fire was placed in the middle of the house, without any

---

* "For the Asiatic soldiers first introduced into Rome the foreign luxury. They first brought with them beds ornamented with brazen sculptures, painted coverings, curtains and tapestry, and what were then esteemed magnificent furniture, side-boards, and tables with one foot. Then to the luxury of our feasts were added singing girls, female players on the lute, and morris-dancers: greater care and expence were bestowed upon our entertainments: the cook, whom our forefathers reckoned the meanest slave, became now in high esteem and request; and what was formerly a servile employment, was now exalted into a science. All these however scarcely deserve to be reckoned the seeds or buds of the luxury of after times."

(*a*) Tit. Liv. lib. 39. cap. 6.

vent for the smoke but the tiles: all the family sat round it, and the victuals
were dressed there. The expence of household-furniture is ten times greater
than it was sixty years ago. The taste for such expence comes to us from
France, from Flanders, and from Spain. Eating-tables, formerly but twelve
inches long, are now grown to eighteen. They have table-cloths, with cups,
spoons, and forks, of silver, and large knives. Beds have silk coverings and
curtains. They have got candles of tallow or wax in candlesticks of iron or
copper. Almost every where there are two fires, one for the chamber, and
one for the kitchen. Confections have come greatly in use, and sensuality
regards no expence." Hollinshed exclaims against the luxury and effeminacy that prevailed in his time. "In times past," says he, "men were contented to dwell in houses builded of sallow, <131> willow, plumtree, or elm;
so that the use of oak was dedicated to churches, religious houses, princes
palaces, noblemens lodgings, and navigation. But now, these are rejected,
and nothing but oak any whit regarded. And yet see the change; for when
our houses were builded of willow, then had we oaken men; but now that
our houses are made of oak, our men are not only become willow, but many,
through Persian delicacy crept in among us, altogether of straw, which is
a sore alteration. In those days, the courage of the owner was a sufficient
defence to keep the house in safety; but now, the assurance of the timber,
double doors, locks and bolts, must defend the man from robbing. Now,
have we many chimneys, and our tenderlings complain of rheums, catarrhs,
and poses. Then, had we none but rere-dosses, and our heads did never ake.
For as the smoke in those days was supposed to be a sufficient hardening
for the timber of the house; so it was reputed a far better medicine to keep
the goodman and his family from the quack or pose, where-<132>with very
few were then acquainted." Not many more than fifty years ago, French
wine, in Edinburgh taverns, was presented to the guests in a small tin vessel,
measuring about an English pint. A single drinking-glass served a company
the whole evening; and the first persons who insisted for a clean glass with
every new pint, were accused of luxury. A knot of highlanders benighted,
wrapped themselves up in their plaids, and lay down in the snow to sleep.
A young gentleman making up a ball of snow, used it for a pillow. His father
(a), striking away the ball with his foot, "What, Sir," says he, "are you turn-

(a) Sir Evan Cameron.

ing effeminate?" Crantz, describing the kingdom of Norway and the manners of the people, has the following reflection. "Robustissimos educat viros, qui, nulla frugum luxuria moliti, saepius impugnant alios quam impugnantur."* In the mountainous island <133> of Rum, one of the western islands of Scotland, the corn produced serves the inhabitants but a few months in winter. The rest of the year they live on flesh, fish, and milk; and yet are healthy and long-lived. In the year 1768, a man died there aged 103, who was 50 years old before he ever tasted bread. This old man frequently harangued upon the plain fare of former times; finding fault with his neighbours for indulging in bread, and upbraiding them for toiling like slaves to produce such an unnecessary article of luxury. The inhabitants of Canada, before they were known to Europeans, were but thinly cloathed in a bitter cold climate. They had no covering but a single skin, girded about them with a belt of leather. The coarse woollen cloath which they were taught to wear by the French, raised bitter lamentations in their old men for increase of luxury and decline of manners.[5]

Thus, every one exclaims against the luxury of the present times, judging more favourably of the past; as if what is luxury at present, would cease to be luxury when it becomes customary. What is the foundation of a sentiment so universal? <134> In point of dignity, corporeal pleasures are the lowest of all that belong to our nature; and for that reason persons of delicacy dissemble the pleasure they have in eating and drinking (a). When corporeal pleasure is indulged to excess, it is not only low, but mean. But as, in judging of things that admit of degrees, comparison is the ordinary standard; every refinement in corporeal pleasure beyond what is customary, is held to be a blameable excess, below the dignity of human nature. For that reason, every improvement in living is pronounced to be luxury while recent, and drops that character when it comes into common use. For the same reason, what is moderation in the capital, is esteemed luxury in a country-town. Doth luxury then depend entirely on comparison? is there

* "It produces a most robust race of men, who are enervated by no luxury of food, and are more prone to attack and harrass their neighbours than subjected to their attacks."

(a) Elements of Criticism, vol. 1. p. 356. edit. 5.

5. "The inhabitants of . . . decline of manners": added in 2nd edition.

no other foundation for distinguishing moderation from excess? This will hardly be maintained.

This subject is rendered obscure by giving different meanings to the term *luxury*. A French writer holds every sort of food to be luxury but raw flesh and acorns, which were the original food of savages; <135> and every sort of covering to be luxury but skins, which were their original cloathing. According to that definition, the plough, the spade, the loom, are all of them instruments of luxury; in which view, he justly extols luxury to the skies. We are born naked, because we can clothe ourselves; and artificial cloathing is to man as much in the order of nature, as hair or feathers are to other animals. But whatever accords to the common nature of man, is right; and for that reason cannot in a proper sense be termed *luxury*. Shoes are a refinement from walking barefoot; and Voltaire, taking this refinement to be luxury, laughs at those who declaim against luxury. Let every man enjoy the privilege of giving his own meaning to words: but when a man deviates so far from their usual meaning, the neglect to define them is inexcusable. In common language and in common apprehension, luxury always implies a faulty excess; and upon that account, is condemned by all writers, such only excepted as affect to be singular.

Faulty excess is clearly one branch of the definition of luxury. Another is, that <136> the excess must be habitual: a single act of intemperance, however faulty, is not denominated luxury: reiteration must be so frequent, as to become a confirmed habit.

Nor are these particulars all that enter into the definition of luxury. There are many pleasures, however intemperate or habitual, that are not branded with that odious name. Mental pleasure, such as arises from sentiment or reasoning, falls not within the verge of luxury, to whatever excess indulged. If to relieve merit in distress be luxury, it is only so in a metaphorical sense: nor is it deemed luxury in a damsel of fifteen to peruse love-novels from morning till evening. Luxury is confined to the external senses: nor does it belong to every one of these: the fine arts have no relation to luxury. A man is not even said to be luxurious, merely for indulging in dress, or in fine furniture. Hollinshed inveighs against drinking-glasses as an article of luxury. At that rate, a house adorned with fine pictures or statues, would be an imputation on the proprietor. Thus, passing in review every pleasure of external sense, we find, <137> that in proper language the term luxury is not applicable to any pleasure of the eye or ear. That term is confined to the pleasures of taste, touch, and smell, which appear as existing at the organ of sense, and upon that account are held to be merely corporeal (*a*).

Having thus circumscribed our subject within its proper bounds, the important point that remains to be ascertained is, Whether we have any rule for determining what excess in corporeal pleasure may justly be denominated faulty. About that point we are at no loss. Though our present life be a state of trial, yet our Maker has kindly indulged us in every pleasure that is not hurtful to the mind nor to the body; and therefore no excess but what is hurtful falls under the censure of being luxurious: it is faulty, as a transgression of self-duty; and, as such, is condemned by the moral sense. The most violent declaimer against luxury will not affirm, that bread is luxury, or a snow-ball used for a pillow: these are innocent, because they do no harm. As little will it be affirmed, that dwelling-houses, more capacious than <138> those originally built, ought to be condemned as luxury; seeing they contribute to cheerfulness as well as to health. The plague, some centuries ago, made frequent visits to London, promoted by air stagnating in narrow streets and small houses. From the great fire *anno* 1666, when the houses and streets were enlarged, the plague has not once been in London.

Man consists of soul and body, so intimately connected, that the one cannot be at ease while the other suffers. In order to have *mens sana in corpore sano,* it is necessary to study the health of both: bodily health supports the mind; and nothing tends more than cheerfulness to support the body, even under a disease. To preserve this complicated machine in order, certain exercises are proper for the body, and certain for the mind; which ought never to incroach the one on the other. Much motion and bodily exercise tend to make us robust; but, in the mean time, the mind is starved: much reading and reflection fortify the mind, but, in the mean time, the body is starved. Nor is this all: excess in either is destructive to both; for exercise too violent, whether of <139> mind or body, wears the machine. Indolence, on the other hand, relaxes the machine, and renders it weak or

(*a*) See Elements of Criticism, Introduction.

useless. Bodily indolence breeds the gout, the gravel, and many other diseases: nor is mental indolence less pernicious, for it breeds peevishness and
pusillanimity. Thus health, both of mind and body, is best preserved by
moderate exercise. And hence a general proposition, That every indulgence
in corporeal pleasure, which favours either too violent or too languid exercise, whether of mind or body, is hurtful, and consequently is luxury in
its proper sense. It is scarce necessary to be added, that every such indulgence is condemned by the moral sense; of which every man can bear testimony from what he himself feels.

Too great indulgence in corporeal pleasure seldom prompts violent exercise; but instances are without number, of its relaxing even that moderate
degree of exercise which is healthful both to mind and body. This, in particular, is the case of too great indulgence in eating or drinking: such indulgence, creating a habitual appetite for more than nature requires, <140>
loads the stomach, depresses the spirits; and brings on a habit of listlessness
and inactivity, which renders men cowardly and effeminate.* And what
does the epicure gain by such excess? In a grand palace, the master occupies
not a greater space than his meanest domestic; and brings to his most sumptuous feast perhaps less appetite than any of his guests. Satiety withal makes
him lose the relish even of rarities, which afford to others a poignant pleasure. Listen to a sprightly writer handling this subject. "Le peuple ne
s'ennuie guerre, sa vie est active; si ses amusemens ne sont pas variés, ils
sont rares; beaucoup de jours de fatigue lui font gouter avec délices quelques
jours de fêtes. Une alternative de longs travaux et de courts loisirs tient
lieu d'assaisonement aux plaisirs de son etat. Pour les riches, leur grand
fleau <141> c'est l'ennui: au sein de tant d'amusemens rassemblés à grands
fraix, au milieu de tant de gens concourans à leur plaire, l'ennui les consume
et les tue; ils passent leur vie à le fuir et à en être atteints; ils sont accablés
de son poids insupportable: les femmes, sur-tout, qui ne savent plus
s'occuper, ni s'a-muser, en sont dévorées sous le nom de vapeurs." *Rousseau,*

---

* Luxury and selfishness render men cowards. People who are attached to riches or
to sensual pleasure, cannot think, without horror, of abandoning them. A virtuous man
considers himself as placed here in order to obey the will of his Maker: he performs his
duty, and is ready to quit his post upon the first summons.

*Emile.*⁶ What enjoyment, then, have the opulent above others? Let them bestow their riches in making others happy: benevolence will double their own happiness; first, in the direct act of doing good; and next, in reflecting upon the good they have done, the most delicate of all feasts.

Had the English continued Pagans, they would have invented a new deity to preside over cookery. I say it with regret, but must say it, that a luxurious table, covered with every dainty, seems to be their favourite idol. A minister of state never withstands a feast; and the link that unites those in opposition, is the cramming one another.* I shall not be surprised to <142> hear, that the cramming a mistress has become the most fashionable mode of courtship. Luxury in eating is not unknown in their universities; the only branch of education that seldom proves abortive. It has not escaped observation, that between 1740 and 1770, no fewer than six Mayors of London died in office, a greater number than in the preceding 500 years: such havock doth luxury in eating make among the sons of Albion.† How different the manners of their forefathers! Bonduca their Queen, ready to engage the Romans in a pitched battle, encouraged her army with a pathetic speech, urging in particular the following consideration: "The great advantage we have over them is, that they cannot, like us, bear hunger, thirst, heat, nor cold. They must have fine bread, wine, and warm houses:

---

* This was composed in the year 1770. [[That is, presumably, before the fall of Grafton, and the start of the North ministry.]]

† Suicide is not influenced by foggy air; for it is not more frequent in the fens of Lincoln or Essex, than in other parts of England. A habit of daily excess in eating and drinking, with intervals of downy ease, relax every mental spring. The man flags in his spirits, becomes languid and low: nothing moves him: every connection with the world is dissolved: a *tedium vitae* ensues; and then—[[Note added in 2nd edition.]]

6. "The lower classes are seldom dull, their life is full of activity. If there is little variety in their amusements they do not recur frequently; many days of labour teach them to enjoy their rare holidays. Short intervals of leisure between long periods of labour give a spice to the pleasures of their station. The chief curse of the rich is dullness; in the midst of costly amusements, among so many men striving to give them pleasure, they are devoured and slain by dullness; their life is spent in fleeing from it and in being overtaken by it; they are overwhelmed by the intolerable burden; women more especially, who do not know how to work or play, are a prey to tedium under the name of the vapours" (bk. IV, p. 378). "Listen to a . . . *Emile*": added in 2nd edition.

every herb and root <143> satisfies our hunger; water supplies the want of wine; and every tree is to us a warm house" (a).*

If it should be asserted, that no excess in eating or drinking is better entitled to be termed luxury, than the universal use of fermented liquors, rejecting water entirely; the proposition would be ridiculed, as proceeding from some low-spirited ascetic. Water, it will be said, is indeed the original drink of animals, and a wholesome drink it is. But why deny to the ingenuity of man improvements in nourishment, as well as in habitation and cloathing? I grant there can be no reasonable objection to fermented liquors, used as a delicacy, by people of easy fortune. But what I condemn, is there being the sole drink of all ranks, not even excepting those who live on charity. Consider the quality of ani-<144>mal and vegetable food that can be produced on land employed entirely in raising vines, barley, and other materials of fermented liquors. The existence of many thousands is annually prevented by that species of luxury.[7]

The indulging in down-beds, soft pillows, and easy seats, is a species of luxury; because it tends to enervate the body, and to render it unfit for fatigue. Some London Ladies employ an operator for pairing their nails. Two young women of high quality, who were sisters, employed a servant with soft hands to raise them gently out of bed in a morning. Nothing less than all-powerful vanity can make such persons submit to the fatigues of a toilet: how can they ever think of submitting to the horrid pangs of childbearing! In the hot-climates of Asia, people of rank are rubbed and chaffed twice a-day; which, beside being pleasant, is necessary for health, by moving the blood in a hot country, where sloth and indolence prevail. The Greeks and Romans were curried, bathed, and oiled, daily; though they had not the same excuse for <145> that practice: it was luxury in them, though not in the Asiatics.

Nations, where luxury is unknown, are troubled with few diseases, and

---

* Providence has provided the gout as a beacon on the rock of luxury to warn against it. But in vain: during distress, vows of temperance are made: during the intervals, these vows are forgot. Luxury has gained too much ground in this island, to be restrained by admonition.

(a) Dion Cassius.

7. Paragraph added in 3rd edition.

have few physicians by profession. In the early ages of Rome, women and slaves were the only physicians, because vegetables were the chief food of the people; who beside were constantly employed in war or in husbandry. When luxury prevailed among the Romans, their diseases multiplied, and physic became a liberal profession.[8]

With respect to exercise, the various machines that have been invented for executing every sort of work, render bodily strength of less importance than formerly. This change is favourable to mental operations, without hurting bodily health. The travelling on horseback, though a less vigorous exertion of strength than walking, is not luxury, because it is a healthful exercise. I dare not say so much for wheel-carriages: a spring-coach, rolling along a smooth road, gives no exercise; or so little, as to be preventive of no disease: it <146> tends to enervate the body, and, in some measure, also the mind. The increase of wheel-carriages within a century is a pregnant proof of the growth of luxurious indolence. During the reign of James I. the English judges rode to Westminster on horseback, and probably did so for many years after his death. Charles I. issued a proclamation, prohibiting hackney-coaches to be used in London, except by those who travel at least three miles out of town. At the Restoration, Charles II. made his public entry into London on horseback, between his two brothers, Dukes of York and Gloucester. We have Rushworth for our voucher, that in London, not above a hundred years ago, there were but twenty hackney-coaches; which did not ply on the streets, but were kept at home till called for. He adds, that the King and council published a proclamation against them, because they raised the price of provender upon the King, nobility, and gentry. At present, 1000 hackney-coaches ply on the streets of London; beside a great number of stage-coaches for travelling from London to all parts of the kingdom. The <147> first coach with glasses in France was brought from Brussels to Paris, anno 1660, by the Prince of Condé. Sedan-chairs were not known in England before the year 1634. Cookery and coaches have reduced the military spirit of the English nobility and gentry to a languid state: the former, by overloading the body, has infected them with dispiriting ailments; the latter, by fostering ease and indolence, have banished labour, the

---

8. Paragraph added in 2nd edition.

only antidote to such ailments.* Too great indulgence in the fine arts consumes part of the time that ought to be employed on the important duties of life: but the fine arts, even when too much indulged, produce one good effect, which is, to soften and humanize our manners: nor do they harm the body, if they relax not that degree of exercise which is necessary for supporting it in health and vigour. <148>

The enervating effects of luxury upon the body, are, above all, remarkable in war. The officers of Alexander's army were soon tainted with Asiatic manners. Most of them, after bathing, had servants for rubbing them, and, instead of plain oil, used precious ointments. Leonatus, in particular, commissioned from Egypt the powder he used when he wrestled, which loaded several camels. Alexander reproved them mildly: "I wonder that men who have undergone such fatigues in war, are not taught by experience, that labour produces sweeter and sounder sleep than indolence. To be voluptuous, is an abject and slavish state. How can a man take care of his horse, or keep his armour bright, who disdains to employ his own hands upon what is dearest to him, his own body?" (*a*)

With respect to the mind in particular, manifold are the pernicious effects of luxury. Corporeal pleasures are all of them selfish; and, when much indulged, tend to make selfishness the leading principle. Voluptuousness accordingly, relaxing every <149> sympathetic affection, brings on a beastly selfishness, which leaves nothing of man but the external figure. Luxury beside renders the mind so effeminate, as to be subdued by every distress: the slightest pain, whether of mind or body, is a real evil: and any higher degree becomes a torture. The French are far gone in that disease. Pictures

---

* J'ai toujours vu ceux qui voyageoient dans de bonnes voitures bien douces, rêveurs, tristes, grondans ou souffrans; et les piétons toujours gais, legers, et contens de tout. Combien le coeur rit quand on approche du gîte! Combien un repas grossier parôit favoureux! avec quel plaisir on se repose à table! Quel bon sommeil on fait dans un mauvais lit! *Rousseau, Emile.* [["I notice that those who ride in nice, well-padded carriages are always wrapped in thought, gloomy, fault-finding, or sick; while those who go on foot are always merry, light-hearted, and delighted with everything. How cheerful we are when we get near our lodging for the night! How savoury is the coarse food! How we linger at table enjoying our rest! How soundly we sleep on a hard bed!" (bk. V, trans. Foxley, p. 449). Note added in 2nd edition.]]

(*a*) Plutarch.

of deep distress, which attract English spectators, are to the French unsupportable: their aversion to pain overcomes the attractive power of sympathy, and debars from the stage every distress that makes a deep impression. The British are gradually sinking into the same weakness: *Venice Preserved*[9] collects not such numbers as it did originally; and would scarce be endured, were not our sympathy blunted by familiarity: a new play in a similar tone would not take. The gradual decay of manhood in Britain, appears from their funeral rites. Formerly the deceased were attended to the grave by relations and friends of both sexes; and the day of their death was preserved in remembrance, with solemn lamentation, as the day of their birth was with exhilarating cups. In England, a man was first <150> relieved from attending his deceased wife to the grave; and afterward from attending his deceased children; and now such effeminancy of mind prevails there, that, upon the last groan, the deceased, abandoned by every relation, is delivered to an undertaker by profession, who is left at leisure to mimic the funeral rites. In Scotland, such refinement has not yet taken place: a man is indeed excused from attending his wife to the grave; but he performs that duty in person to every other relation, his children not excepted. I am told, that people of high fashion in England begin to leave the care of their sick relations to hired nurses; and think they do their duty in making short visits from time to time.

Hitherto I have considered luxury with respect to those only who are infected with it; and, did its poison spread no wider, the case perhaps would be the less deplorable. But unhappily, where luxury prevails, the innocent suffer with the guilty. A man of oeconomy, whether a merchant, or a manufacturer, lays up a stock for his children, and adds useful members to the state. A man, on the contrary, who lives <151> above his fortune, or his profits, accustoms his children to luxury, and abandons them to poverty when he dies. Luxury, at the same time, is a great enemy to population: it enhances the expence of living, and confines many to the batchelor-state. Luxury of the table, in particular, is remarkable for that effect: "L'homme riche met toute sa gloire à consommer, toute sa grandeur à perdre, en un jour à sa table, plus de biens qu'il n'en faudroit pour faire subsister plusieurs

---

9. By Thomas Otway.

familles. Il abuse également et des animaux et des hommes: dont le reste demeure affamé, languit dans la misère, et ne travaille que pour satisfaire à l'appétit immodéré, et à la vanité encore plus insatiable, de cet homme; qui detruisant les autres par la disette, se detruit lui-même par les excés" (*a*).*
<152>

To consider luxury in a political view, no refinement of dress, of the table, of equipage, of habitation, is luxury in those who can afford the expence; and the public gains by the encouragement that is given to arts, manufactures, and commerce. But a mode of living above a man's annual income, weakens the state, by reducing to poverty, not only the squanderers themselves, but many innocent and industrious persons connected with them. Luxury is, above all, pernicious in a commercial state. A person of moderation is satisfied with small profits: not so the luxurious, who despise every branch of trade but what returns great profits: other branches are engrossed by foreigners who are more frugal. The merchants of Amsterdam, and even of London, within a century, lived with more oeconomy than their clerks do at present. Their country-houses and gardens make not the greatest articles of their expence. At first, a merchant retires to his country-house on Sundays only and holy-<153>days: but beginning to relish indolent retirement, business grows irksome, he trusts all to his clerks, loses the thread of his affairs, sees no longer with his own eyes, and is now in the high way to perdition. Every cross accident makes him totter; and in labouring circumstances, he is tempted to venture all in hopes of re-establishment. He falls at last to downright gaming; which, setting conscience aside, is a prudent measure: he risks only the money of his creditors, for he himself has nothing to lose: it is now with him, *Caesar aut nihil.*†
Such a man never falls without involving many in his ruin.

---

* "The sole glory of the rich man is, to consume and destroy; and his grandeur consists, in lavishing in one day upon the expence of his table what would procure subsistence for many families. He abuses equally animals and his fellow-creatures; a great part of whom, a prey to famine, and languishing in misery, labour and toil to satisfy his immoderate desires, and insatiable vanity; who, destroying others by want, destroys himself by excess."
† "Caesar or nothing."
(*a*) Buffon.

The bad effects of luxury above displayed, are not the whole, nor indeed the most destructive. In all times luxury has been the ruin of every state where it prevailed. Nations originally are poor and virtuous. They advance to industry, commerce, and perhaps to conquest and empire. But this state is never permanent: great opulence opens a wide door to indolence, sensuality, corruption, prostitution, <154> perdition.[10] But that more important branch of the subject is reserved to particular sketches, where it will make a better figure.

In the savage state, man is almost all body, with a very small proportion of mind. In the maturity of civil society, he is complete both in mind and body. In a state of degeneracy by luxury and voluptuousness, he has neither mind nor body.*

---

* In ancient Egypt, execution against the person of a debtor was prohibited. Such a law could not obtain but among a temperate people, where bankruptcy happens by misfortune, and seldom by luxury or extravagance. In Switzerland, not only a bankrupt but even his sons are excluded from public office till all the family debts be paid. [["In Switzerland, not . . . debts be paid": added in 3rd edition.]]

10. "Nations originally . . . prostitution, perdition": added in 3rd edition.